W9-AFH-963

Critical Essays on
Franz Kafka

Critical Essays on
World Literature

Robert Lecker, General Editor
McGill University

Critical Essays on
Franz Kafka

Ruth V. Gross

G. K. Hall & Co. • Boston, Massachusetts

First published 1990.
10 9 8 7 6 5 4 3 2 1

Library of Congress Cataloging-in-Publication Data

Critical essays on Franz Kafka / [edited by] Ruth V. Gross.
       p.   cm.—(Critical essays on world literature)
    Includes bibliographical references.
    ISBN 0-8161-8848-3 (alk. paper)
    1. Kafka, Franz, 1883-1924 — Criticism and interpreta-
tion.
    I. Gross, Ruth V.   II. Series.
    PT2621.A26Z6724   1990
    833'.912—dc20   90-4411
                                                      CIP

The paper used in this publication meets the minimum
requirements of American National Standard for Information
Sciences—Permanence of Paper for Printed Library Materials,
ANSI Z39.48-1984. ∞™

Printed and bound in the United States of America

CONTENTS

INTRODUCTION

In his last published story, "Josephine the Singer, or the Mouse People," Franz Kafka plays with his central narrative subject in such a way that everything that can possibly be said about her is said and at once contradicted.[1] The subject thus has every possible identity and yet no identity at all because the pure fullness of discourse envelops both its subject and its author. Kafka, the subject of a vast body of critical literature, is exactly like Josephine. He is precisely what can be said about him in critical discourse, and the six and one-half decades since his death have demonstrated that everything can be said about him and his writing.

Kafka himself seems to have predicted this situation in a letter he wrote to Felice Bauer, his more-than-one-time fiancée: "I have no literary interests, but am made of literature, I am nothing else. . . ."[2] Although Kafka meant something different and certainly wrote this statement in a different context, the reader of today is faced with a Kafka who is both literally and figuratively "nothing else" but literature. Even the so-called documents of his life, his letters and diaries, have become literary texts for interpretation. Perhaps the best book about Franz Kafka would not deal with him but would be a history of Kafka criticism through the decades, that is, an analysis of the changing and contradictory perspectives through which Kafka's work is read. Peter Beicken, in his thorough study, *Franz Kafka. Eine kritische Einführung*[3] approached Kafka in this way, illuminating the developments and problems in Kafka studies through the 1970s. But the present volume is not intended to be that kind of book; it is simply a collection of some of the best work written on Kafka. As such, it fits into a tradition of its own and, I hope, will add to it.

When Franz Kafka died in 1924, his reputation had already been firmly established, but only in a few circles of literary intellectuals. Translations, first of *The Metamorphosis* into Spanish, French, Italian, and English and later of his novels and other stories into English— *The Castle* (1930), *The Great Wall of China* (1933), and *The Trial*

(1933)—provided an international audience for the writer, whose works would serve as prescient evocations of the later twentieth-century experience. During the first decade after Kafka's death, writing on Kafka resembled commentary more than literary criticism. Many of the best-known writers of the day knew some of Kafka's work and circulated their ideas in various international periodicals. Rainer Maria Rilke, Hermann Hesse, Thomas Mann, Robert Musil, Kurt Tucholsky, Bertolt Brecht, Walter Benjamin, André Breton, Albert Camus, and André Gide, to name only a few, quickly recognized Kafka's originality, genius, and stylistic greatness and were instrumental in first spreading his fame. By 1934, on the occasion of the tenth anniversary of Kafka's death, literary commemorations were already in order, and Kafka had become a world author.

Kafka's reception, however, was soon to receive two major set-backs: the edition of Kafka's works compiled by Max Brod, Kafka's friend and advocate, failed to receive the attention and acclaim Brod had expected; and after 1935, the Nazis forbade publication of Kafka's works in Germany, where Kafka's major German-speaking audience resided. During the next ten years, Kafka "went abroad."

The year 1946 marks a real awakening for academic Kafka studies and scholarship. In that year Angel Flores, a long-time reader, admirer, and bibliographer of Kafka's works, edited the first anthology of Kafka criticism. *The Kafka Problem* included commentary by an impressive list of writers and scholars on all aspects of Kafka: biography, exegesis, theory, and criticism. As a work it was meant to serve as a general introduction to Kafka and his works as well as to present analyses of the various "literary, philosophical and social factors" important in his work and central to his (what was in 1946) growing influence on literature and thought.[4]

Flores's anthology became the first of a new genre—the anthology of Kafka criticism—that continues to flourish today. In the more than forty years since *The Kafka Problem* first appeared, there have been no fewer than *fifty* published collections of critical essays on this provocative author. This number includes the many published symposia and special issues of journals on Kafka. We know that it is not the quantity of an author's work that makes him a subject for innovative scholarly research. For an author whose oeuvre consists of three novels (all remained incomplete), various collections of short and very short stories, diaries, and letters, the amount of critical attention paid to Kafka has been enormous. With his clear prose style and his talent for creating the feelings of anxiety and terror at life's machinations, Kafka stands alone as a progenitor of both the modern and the postmodern (depending on the reading), a precursor of the existential, and a prophet of an age he did not live to see. Yet he remains impossible to categorize (thus thoroughly categorized). Therein lies his inexhaustibility as a source of continuing critical dialogue.

To characterize the mood of Kafka's narratives as applied to other literature and daily situations, the word *Kafkaesque* was invented. It was apparently first used by C. D. Lewis in 1938 in a discussion of a now forgotten novel by Edward Upward.[5] When first used, the term referred to a confrontation with the impersonalized bureaucratic state, the situation Joseph K. encounters in *The Trial*. The word did not attain wider usage until after World War II, when Kafka and the idea of the Kafkaesque became powerful ideological tools for the West with regard to its current situation and recent past. The depersonalized, deindividualized bureaucratic state took on a new meaning in the postwar era. Gone were the examples of such a state and condition from the right (the Nazis and Fascists); suddenly, it appeared in all-too-familiar form on the left in the Soviet Union. The world was being ideologically redefined, and Kafka and his works proved useful in making sense of the world in which people were living. If at first the world that Kafka allegedly forecast consisted of identifiably extremist political systems, as time went on the Kafkaesque totalitarian seemed applicable as well to the large-scale impersonal organizational systems of the modern communications universe.

Because Kafka was discovered through translation amid the catastrophically disrupted world of the 1930s and 1940s, he became in some strange way a posthumous emigré, not to say a postwar writer. It is really after World War II that Kafka returned to his homeland and to his original language. The Flores anthology of 1946 is the first of its kind and is a critical summary of Kafka's "life" abroad. To be sure, Flores included recollections by Kafka's contemporaries and compatriots like Franz Werfel, Johannes Urzidil, Oskar Baum, and Ludwig Hardt; for the most part, though, the contributions were by American, British, French, Italian, Argentinian, Czech, and Polish readers. The Kafka that emerges from this first major collection of criticism devoted to him is the universal genius whose works reveal a deep faith and religiosity. What was clear to Flores in 1946 and remains true to this day is that every critic "who writes on Kafka somehow immediately becomes an individual."[6] Many of the contributions to *The Kafka Problem* seem dated by the standards of today's approaches to criticism, but Flores's own assessment of Kafka, as summarized in his title for the collection, remains key, perhaps because Kafka will always be a problem without a definitive solution.

After 1946 Kafka criticism progressed through a number of stages. Through the influence of Max Brod, a major trend of writing on Kafka began to emphasize the religious aspects of his work and understood Kafka's Jewishness to be the motivation for his creativity. Brod's kind of religious-allegorical interpretation soon raised controversy because many critics could not accept his unequivocally theological reading of Kafka. Perhaps because of Brod's drive to explain Kafka's work from a narrowly theological perspective, Brod strenuously objected to the term Kafkaesque as applied to the man himself, stating that "Kafkaesque was what Kafka was not."[7] In his monograph *Franz Kafkas Glauben und Lehre*[8] Brod refuted the growing critical direction that placed Kafka in an existentialist context; indeed, he considered existentialism, with its nihilistic focus, to be antithetical to Kafka's profound metaphysicality.

Nonetheless, the existentialist Kafka grew in importance. In 1951 a monograph appeared that was to have profound influence on future scholarship. Günther Anders's *Franz Kafka, pro und contra*[9] was the first study to focus on Kafka's use of common everyday language. Although it was only one part of Anders's controversial monograph, the chapter "The Literal Metaphor" generated an entire direction of Kafka criticism that has centered on language and writing as the essence of the Kafkan text. Other often disputed elements of Anders's study, however, portrayed Kafka as a dangerous writer. Anders understood Kafka's world with its absence of nature and its concentration on the material to resemble Heidegger's existentialism with its attack on naturalism. Unlike Brod, Anders considered Kafka's works devoid of theology. For Anders, Kafka's literature posed a threat. It provided a "meaningful vision of the meaningless world"[10] and as such was considered harmful; if translated into action, it would lead to fascism. By emphasizing Kafka's pessimism, Anders was not debunking him but rather was creating a naive tribute that was often misunderstood by later critics.

During the following decade, Kafka studies continued to prosper. In 1958 Angel Flores, together with Homer Swander, edited yet another collection of critical essays on Kafka, but this anthology looked quite different from the first. The essays in *Franz Kafka Today*[11] unlike those of the 1930s and early 1940s, did not try to fit Kafka into a category imposed onto the text but used an approach advocated by Friedrich Beißner in his book *Der Erzähler Franz Kafka*,[12] by which the text itself was addressed. In this *text-immanent method*, as it was called, structure, style, narrative perspective, and meaning of the work became central; the life of the author and the context of his world, although generally discussed and reported, were not applied to the interpretation of the various texts. In their introduction, Flores and Swander even went so far as to state "with certainty: those who were closest to him (Kafka) knew him least, misunderstood him most."[13] Obviously directed at Brod, this remark declared independence from his view of the Jewish Kafka. To be sure, Brod was included as a contributor in this second anthology of Kafka criticism but almost solely as a reminder of the kind of criticism that had been.

There has been some discussion about the development of text-immanent criticism of the type that became especially popular in the 1950s and 1960s and was applied to Kafka. A raised consciousness about the atrocities of World War II created an inhospitable climate in German scholarship for the discussion of the particularly Jewish characteristics in Kafka's literature. To that end, the text-immanent approach created the illusion of a nonideological literary discourse. But consciously isolating Kafka from a cultural tradition is naturally to place him in another tradition. All readings take place within and create their own contexts. The text-immanent Kafka finds himself, then, not immanent within the boundaries of his own text at all but rather existing within the tradition of literary production that claims to put at the forefront its own formal concerns. That is to say, Kafka becomes the descendant of Flaubert and of Proust and emerges a classic writer of literary modernism. This is the new tradition, the new context.

By the middle of the sixties, if Kafka scholars read nothing else, they had to be familiar with three major books that would inform Kafka criticism for years to come: Wilhelm Emrich's *Franz Kafka*, Heinz Politzer's *Franz Kafka: Parable and Paradox*, and Walter Sokel's *Franz Kafka—Tragik und Ironie. Zur Struktur seiner Kunst.*[14] These three scholars, almost as if in reaction to text-immanent criticism, pushed Kafka scholarship into other directions.

Emrich's study redefined Kafka's existentialism, seeing in Kafka's use of metaphor and language the expression of alienation of the modern human in the working world. Emrich interpreted the court in *The Trial* and the Castle authority in *The Castle* as images of a gigantic world-apparatus that records and controls all of life's processes.[15] For him Kafka's works exemplify human existence and symbolize the world of the twentieth century. Unlike other existential interpretations that highlight a nihilistic absurdity in Kafka, however, Emrich portrayed a positive struggle in which the writer's intention is the attainment of freedom through knowledge. In the end Emrich understood Kafka as a utopian moralist. After the appearance of Emrich's book, it was generally held that no one could write on Kafka without taking Emrich as a point of departure.[16]

In a sense, although Heinz Politzer's book on Kafka was begun as a dissertation in Prague during the 1930s and to a great extent predated Emrich's book, even Politzer did not ignore Emrich's findings. But Politzer's approach was far less ponderous and more concrete, and it was, from the very start, a prime example of practical criticism. Arguing for the parabolic nature of Kafka's works, even of the long fragmentary novels, Politzer made visible in all of Kafka's works the same structural elements he displayed in his reading of Kafka's short parable "Give It Up!" For Politzer the open-endedness or unanswered question or paradox or "incomprehensibility" of a Kafkan work points not to its absurdity but rather to a formal structure that Kafka's works obey. Perceiving the general movement of the narrative within Kafka's works as circular and without end, Politzer, who had worked with Max Brod on the first volumes of the *Complete Edition* in the 1930s, was concerned with Kafka's narrative style and was particularly interested in conveying Kafka's wordplay, irony, and sense of language in general. In his readings the Kafkan parable, his starting point, always has a paradoxical message.

Sokel's approach combined psychological and sociological aspects of criticism and steered away from the theories that proclaimed Kafka's works either as precise in allegorical meanings or as essentially ambiguous and open-ended. Using Kafka himself as the basis and applying psychogenetic data and Freudian psychoanalytical methods, Sokel sought the unity of Kafka's works in the central figures and their struggles. Sokel saw Kafka's world not as an absurdity or a paradox but rather as a projection of the protagonists' inner states. He elucidated each work by its relationship to the other works in Kafka's oeuvre and revealed not Kafka's psyche but the way Kafka represented the psyche in general. By stressing the father-son conflict as the link that joined Kafka to his expressionist contemporaries, Sokel also claimed Kafka for expressionism.

By 1970 most of Kafka scholarship fell into three basic categories: 1) interdisciplinary—the application of the extraliterary criteria of philosophical, psychological, and sociological natures to Kafka's works; 2) positivist—concern mostly with evidence from biographical or bibliographical sources and documents; and 3) textualist—understanding of Kafka as a literary phenomenon who could be interpreted only by literary methods.[17]

As the amount of published material on Kafka increased, so did the tempo of anthologies of Kafka criticism. For the most part these volumes gathered together conference and symposium papers, already published articles, and chapters from the major works on Kafka. This type of book proliferated in the 1960s, 1970s, and 1980s and provided readers with introductions to some of the crosscurrents of thought on Kafka in an easily accessible form. Ronald Gray's *Kafka. A Collection of Critical Essays*, Heinz Politzer's *Franz Kafka*, Angel Flores's *The Kafka Debate*, J. P. Stern's *The World of Franz Kafka*, Kenneth Hughes's *Kafka: An Anthology of Marxist Criticism*, and Alan Udoff's *Kafka and the Contemporary Critical Performance: Centenary Perspectives*, among others, exemplify this genre.[18] In addition there have been a number of critical collections dealing with specific works of Kafka; for example, Peter Neumeyer's *Twentieth Century Interpre-*

tations of "The Castle," James Rolleston's *Twentieth Century Inter-pretations of "The Trial"* and Angel Flores's *The Problem of "The Judgment."*[19]

By now it must be clear to the reader that Kafka, more than any other author, has become a prime subject for the critical anthology. Something about the style, length, quantity, and open-endedness of his work (and life) lends itself to this genre. It allows the reader to deal with the plurality that is Kafka's essence without imposing a definitive form. The anthology is always implicitly open, unfinished, and fragmentary; like all of Kafka's work, it stands either as a collection of disparate parts or as a massive, if rough, sketch. In a sense, then, we might wish to ask ourselves whether Kafka himself was not the great self-anthologizer. Like his character Josephine, the Kafkan text seems an anthology of what can be said, with all of its contradictions, disagreements, and internal conflicts that create the classic Kafkan locution "the commentators' despair."

Thus we come to the present collection of essays on Kafka. With the wealth of exciting, thoughtful, and innovative criticism written on Kafka, I began to feel curiously anxiety-ridden, paranoid, and guilty. These feelings are normal for the critic who chooses to write about Kafka, but they become compounded when the critic must select a finite number of articles to represent Kafka criticism over the decades. The critical corpus is "a remarkable apparatus" that can cause just as much fear, satisfaction, anger, disagreement, forbearance, and ecstasy as the famous machine in the penal colony. In putting together this volume, I tried to select articles that, while demonstrating the consistently high quality of Kafka scholarship, taken together would also present a compendium of critical approaches to Kafka. In choosing the material, I deliberately stayed away from articles that have already been anthologized in the major collections, although part of the selection by Heinz Politzer was in Flores's first anthology and a few of the others have been published as part of the proceedings of Kafka colloquiums. I did not want to anthologize the anthologies that I have mentioned in this introduction. The reader should not fail to notice that most of the essays in this volume were written during the last two decades; this is not coincidental. If this collection is to be representative of Kafka criticism, the explosion of written work on Kafka in the last twenty years has to be acknowledged in some way, and so I used a system of proportional representation as well. There is even one essay for the future insofar as it was commissioned specifically for this collection.

I have divided the contributions to this anthology into five basic groupings whose headings I chose with trepidation. Again I felt like the narrator trying to characterize Josephine and finding that each perfect category was also perfectly wrong. Kafka, if he teaches us anything, shows us that discourse will escape from any category we devise to master it. Since my overriding criteria for selection were excellence and applicability to literary discourse—in a sense all of these selections are examples of practical criticism—I decided on thematic rather than chronological classification, fully realizing that there are any number of ways to organize a collection such as this one. Although my categories may be somewhat arbitrary, they should give the reader of this volume useful contexts for reflection.

The articles grouped together in the section "Kafka the Writer from Prague" represent various generations of criticism. The opening selection, "Somewhere Behind," by the emigré Czech writer Milan Kundera, explores the nature of the Kafkan and the uses of Kafka in modern discourse, repositioning him in a central European perspective. Ironically, Kafka has become the sociopolitical prophet of our age, although among his friends in Prague (writers such as Franz Werfel, Max Brod, and Egon Erwin Kisch), he was the most politically *dis*interested, writing not about the future but about a personal, solitary, and introspective world. Kundera sees Kafka as having become a creation of the West. Because our society has lost touch with the real, we displace *our* Kafka onto psychoanalysis, pure literature, religious or political allegory, and the like. To Kundera, the central European, Kafka is simply a poet, a person capable not of inventing but of discovering reality. In so doing he can say much more than any social or political thinker because he uncovers "truth." Kafka could not have known how much the complications that are the essence of almost all his tales would resemble modern-day Prague. He only discovered "a human possibility." In his analysis Kundera reveals the Kafkan as a world in which the punishment is the given and so must always seek the crime; that is, the accused must go out in search of his offense.

Another earlier view of Kafka as a writer from Prague, as presented in Walter Benjamin's "Conversations with Brecht," is significant in what it reveals about Kafka and about the Germans Benjamin and Brecht as well. For Brecht, Kafka's Prague was a place where literature was the reality, but an unimportant reality. Above all Brecht, as might be expected, seeks functional value in Kafka's works but finds mostly "obscurantism" for its own sake. As a representative of the West that Kundera articulated in his article, Brecht calls Kafka's *The Trial* "a prophetic book" and proceeds to allegorize it politically. Then, turning to a short explanation of Kafka's "The Next Village," Benjamin shows where Brecht and he differ in their readings. For Benjamin the cause of Kafkan anxiety is essential; for Brecht it is contingent. Benjamin believes that it is part of the human condition; Brecht believes that it is historical and can be overcome.

Kafka's origins are crucial to the idea of a minor literature as formulated by Gilles Deleuze and Félix Guattari in their book *Kafka: Toward a Minor Literature.* In the chapter entitled "What is a Minor Literature?" they define *a minor literature* as one that "a minority constructs in a major language." Kafka, the Jew from Prague who writes in German, creates his minor literature, the characteristics of which are "the deterritorialization of language, the connection of the individual to a political immediacy, and the collective assemblage of enunciation." In effect, language and its artificiality become the subject of their focus. Pushing Prague German to its extremes, Kafka intensifies expression to the point that the language system becomes estranged from itself. Kafka uses a subversive intertextuality, always appealing to a minority side that is built into the most dominant forms of discourse. To that extent Kafka liberates what the language itself oppresses, that is to say, its own oppression. For Kundera, Brecht, and Deleuze and Guattari, Kafka is above all a middle-class Prague Jew writing in German; one or another of these attributes is seen as primary. For Benjamin, however, the key to Kafka is more intrinsic and less accidental. Most criticism has followed Benjamin.

The second section of essays, entitled "Methods and Other Paradoxes," includes articles that provide three very different approaches to Kafka's works yet constantly circle back to a strategy that subordinates the criticism to the text. In his essay " 'Give It Up!' A Discourse on Method," Heinz Politzer becomes the first critic to do a line-by-line close reading of one of Kafka's short pieces. He understands Kafka's message—"Give it up!" expressed by the policeman in the parable—to be addressed to interpreters of Kafka who look at a single way of reading him. To demonstrate the validity of a variety of approaches, Politzer then explicates the parable using historical, psychological, religious, and existential methods, concluding that the readings he has given the piece are by no means mutually exclusive interpretations and that even if taken all together they do not sufficiently explain "the meaning hidden in the anecdote." As one of the first major Kafka critics to understand the plurality of meaning in Kafka's world, Politzer's work on Kafka is invaluable. He understands that often the interpretations of Kafka's works reveal more about their interpreters than they do about Kafka. To Politzer, Kafka "was a writer in his own right, a *littérateur* . . . the creator of word images, interested in their relationships to one another (which, however, he never clearly defined) and to their background (which he was altogether incapable of exploring)." Despite their simplicity of style, Kafka's narratives never explain themselves, as we would hope. According to Politzer, the mystical ambiguity that is the essence of Kafka's language ultimately leads to the paradox that is the message of Kafka's works. "Franz Kafka's importance derives from the fact that he was probably the first and certainly the most radical writer to pronounce the insoluble paradox of human existence by using this paradox as the message of his parables."

Larysa Mykyta's "Woman as the Obstacle and the Way" examines the connection between Kafka's writing and his perception of women as characters in his texts. Kafka alternately viewed writing as his salvation and as his damnation. Perceiving human contact, especially contact with women, as the obstacle that kept him from writing, he often created female characters who through their sexuality constitute both hindrances and paths for the male protagonists. In her discussion of *The Castle* and *The Trial*, Mykyta shows how the elusive essence of these characters sheds light on the elusive structures of authority. They have no organizing principle because they lack written structure. Exploring the intertwined relationship between women and writing, Mykyta's discussion of this complex issue represents the power that feminist readings of Kafka's works can generate.

"Kafka's Time Machines" by James Rolleston suggests a philosophical approach to the Kafkan text. Written in the year of Kafka's centenary, this article, like the two others in this section, points to a basic paradox in Kafka's writing: "the way in which a narration exuding commonsense and rationality strongly implies that it is communicating the opposite of the truth, that it is moving towards a self-destruction which alone can communicate truth." Aligning Kafka with the German romantics, Rolleston sees the bridge to Kafka's narratives as romantic time-theory, in which time, although perceived as a unity, is basically a dynamic relationality between past, present, and future. Experiencing a moment of temporal disruption at the beginnings of these narratives, Kafka's protagonists try to reintegrate their world in the course of the stories by prioritizing one component of the time trinity over the other two. Rolleston discusses three pairs of stories ("The Judgment" and "Josephine the Singer, or The Mouse People," "The Great Wall of China" and "Investigations of a Dog," and "In the Penal Colony" and "The Burrow"), in which the central figure's project is to create an exclusionary consciousness of one time-dimension: prescriptive (governed by the future), encyclopedic (governed by the past), and ecstatic (governed by the present). In all cases the character's failure (and the story's self-destruction) is clear from the outset. Rolleston's vision of Kafka as a romantic coincides with our vision of him as a modernist. As Jean-François Lyotard notes, the core of modernism is to point to the unrepresentability of a certain reality that is sublime in the Kantian sense.[20] In such a view the modernist and the romantic—Kafka and, for example, Kleist—both aim at and miss the same target.

Any author whose style is meticulously precise and realistic but whose textual world is fantastic and disorienting will lead his readers inevitably to a figural mode of comprehension. That is, they will naturally see such an author as a creator of metaphors, a world of "as-ifs," in order to escape the obstacles and paradoxes inherent in the tension between form and content, however construed. It is a matter of contention whether or not Kafka should be seen as a metaphoric writer. To a Kundera or a Brecht, Kafka must be seen as a realistic writer or the power of his Kafkan vision will be lost in a merely aesthetic discourse. But it is this ability of readers to understand Kafka's clear, unmetaphoric words as a keenly metaphoric language that has created Kafka the great modernist writer, as opposed to Kafka the prophet, and has provided the basis for an efflorescence of scholarship that began with Günther Anders's book *Kafka: pro und contra*, excerpted here as "Not Symbols but Metaphors."

Anders details Kafka's art of turning whole situations rather than concepts into images. In this way Kafka differs from symbolist writers and becomes a unique phenomenon. Rather than comparing reality to an image, he takes the image and makes it reality; the metaphor is made literal. "He [Kafka] does not invent images. He accepts them. Whatever may be sensory about these images, he puts under the microscope. . . ." Explaining Kafka's art in this way focuses attention on his language and leads to a kind of criticism that began to flourish a generation after Anders's book appeared.

Charles Bernheimer's "Crossing over: Kafka's Metatextual Parable" argues that all language is a continual transition between words signifying things metaphorically and words signifying things metonymically. Using Nietzsche's definition of language as an allusive transfer *(andeutende Übertragung)*, Bernheimer shows, on the basis of Kafka's "On Parables," how Kafka believed in the impossibility of expressing reality in writing. Language is merely an allusion to the real or phenomenal world. Nonetheless "when writing attempts to liberate itself from the limitations of reference by adopting the overreaching structure of metaphor, it is inevitably brought back to the realization of its necessary reliance on the phenomenal world." This hearkens back to Anders's idea of Kafka's idiom developing from "common language" but takes it in yet another direction, elucidating the difference between allusion and comparison. In Bernheimer's view the battles and conflicts that inform so many of Kafka's texts have a goal that is entirely structural; the goal is simply whether these confrontations can be maintained. For Kafka, who knew that language could never really express truth, parables became a means of crossing over.

In his article, "Kafka's Writing Machine: Metamorphosis in the Penal Colony," Arnold Weinstein has shown that Kafka's "In the Penal Colony" is a story that centralizes communication and language. From our post-1914 perspective, we cannot fail to read this tale as one about torture and atrocity, but Weinstein, with his metaphorical method, leads us to see the story in terms of Kafka's longing for a unification of language and substance, a language that can truly be understood. Yet Kafka knew that language can never *be* what it *says*. True understanding, the goal of language, can occur only when one being becomes another. So the officer, by releasing the prisoner and taking his place, undergoes a metamorphosis and enacts a drama of understanding: "Knowledge comes only through personal transformation. . . ." In Weinstein's article the connections among the machine, language, metamorphosis, and understanding become clear, and the machine is viewed as a "producer of immediate language."

The idea of metaphor is taken to its ultimate application in Henry Sussman's "The All-Embracing Metaphor: Reflections on 'The Burrow.' " For Sussman the burrow is Kafka's metaphor for his literary work. The animal-narrator is both animal as anticipatory-human and metahuman and is a "rendition of humanity from which the self has been excluded." In this way Sussman sees "The Burrow" as the inevitable end to Kafka's writing, a story or construction in which the creator is bound by his own creation. The metaphor is all-embracing inasmuch as everything it includes is fictive; although there may be absolutes outside the construction, they are eventually absorbed into the realm of its fictionality.

Kafka's works have often been the subjects of psychological approaches of interpretation, and these are represented by the selections in the section "Kafka and the Psyche." His own interest in Freud's writings heralded a century in which almost no form of interpretation has escaped the Viennese touch. Manifest versus latent contents, repressions, transferences and projections, desire and fantasy, displacements and condensations—all are the standard repertoire of modern interpretive criticism of various stripes. Part of Kafkan commentary and its discontents (which always come from too much rather than too little to say) is, no doubt, that his work seems at times too much a dramatization of the psychoanalytic *agon* or of the metanarrative of almost any depth psychology. The crystalline yet baffling surface of the Kafkan text evokes a latent world that also links Kafka to the German romantics, where self and language would become one. Yet this sort of romantic immersion is dangerous to the self; something must be repressed, and the nature of this repression has concerned much psychological writing on Kafka.

The contribution that was written earliest is Kurt Tucholsky's "In the Penal Colony." As a writer himself, Tucholsky, writing under a pseudonym when this piece was first published in Berlin's *Die Weltbühne* in 1920, is very aware of Kafka's precursors. His review of the story anticipates Kafka scholarship of later decades in its comparison of Kafka to the German writer Heinrich von Kleist. I have included this review of "In the Penal Colony" as a curiosity because I think it an especially good example of an interpretation of a story that most postwar critics like to read with hindsight as a demonstration of things to come. Obviously, Tucholsky, like Kafka himself, could have no knowledge of the world's future and so considers Kafka to be not a prophet but a descendant, in this case, of Kleist. Unburdened by the body of criticism that grew after the time of this review, Tucholsky approaches Kafka's writing in a highly personal and direct tone—writer on writer. He rejects any allegorical interpretation and chooses to read the story as a re-creation of a dream-wish, giving a basically psychological explanation of the story. Tucholsky understands it as a pure work of art in the Flaubertian sense. It need not correspond to anything and need not advance humanity. Having argued this, he then turns to irony at the end of his review by displacing the question of the interpretation of Kafka's story, making a verdict on Kafka dependent upon a verdict on Kleist. This displacement takes back the whole premise of the argument to that point and gestures toward a thoroughly modern undecidability.

Walter H. Sokel's "Kafka's Poetics of the Inner Self" explores the psychology of Kafka's writing. Sokel finds Kafka's basic theory of writing revealed in quotations from the early diaries. Until he completed "The Judgment," Kafka expected "truth" in writing, a complete merging of himself and language. Because being exists before language, this kind of poetics makes the inner self dominant over language and enables writing to become "a taking possession of language." Sokel's article suggests that a change took place in Kafka's thinking about writing when he began *The Trial*; ultimately Kafka believed that duplicity was built into the act of writing fiction and thus founded his poetics on an inherent paradox. Although only a "joke" and a "frustration," writing was nevertheless the axe that could break through the "frozen sea within us."

In "Freud as Literature?" Stanley Corngold has written a piece that may at first blush seem to have little to do with Kafka, progressing as it does from German terrorism to French repression of Germany to the French reading of Freud. But the essence of the article is Kafka and the Kafkan text as model of consciousness. To the French, Freud cannot be a literary text because it represses repression. It is a text arising from repression and as such "produces only a repressive discourse." To get beyond this vicious circle, Corngold proposes positing an outside text that can operate within the dictates of recent French criticism and in Freud so as to become its repressed text. The text he suggests is Kafka. By displacing Kafka into the Freudian text and both into the current discourse of continental criticism, Corngold proposes quite a different way of approaching Kafka and Freud. Kafka's text serves as the unconscious that Freud himself, in this view, represses while claiming to reveal. Like Jacques Lacan's performative prose, but within a literary discourse common to the modernist canon, Kafka can serve as the Freudian text that might have been written if the master's repression had not forbidden it. Kafka is "Freud as literature."

Although most psychological approaches to Kafka have been through Freud, J. Brooks Bouson applies Heinz Kohut's metapsychology, which shifts away from Freudian drive psychology to a focus on the central role of empathy in forming and maintaining the self. Kohut's "Tragic Man and Woman" are narcissistically disturbed individuals prone to rage, loneliness, and despair. For these individuals the core anxiety, what Kohut calls "disintegration anxiety," is loss of the self. Bouson sees *The Metamorphosis* as a narrative in which a narcissistic drama is enacted. Gregor's transformation becomes a metaphor of narcissism. Central to the drama is "Gregor's desperate need for attention," which becomes key in the reader's transactions with the character. Bouson's study, with its focus on empathic reading, makes us aware of the exchange relationship that goes on between the reader and the character, and the reader and the text, and provides a different psychological context for the Kafkan narrative.

The section entitled "Kafka and the Reader" shows newer directions in Kafka criticism. In recent years the objectivity of the Kafkan text as an idea has been called into question with a shift of emphasis away from the author, the narrator, and the text onto the reader. Put another way, the reader herself has become textualized, fictionalized, part of the positive world of the Kafkan text. Seen from this point of view, the intertextuality invoked by Kafka's clear and repeated use of proverbial language, for example, interweaves with a personal (yet impersonal because proverbial) network of proverbial associations to produce one reading of Kafka's text, "A Common Confusion," that turns out to be an allegorical performance of intertextuality itself, the "common place" where all reading occurs. My own contribution, "Rich Text/Poor Text: A Kafkan Confusion," uses a method suggested by Roland Barthes's S/Z to examine closely the referentiality of Kafka's text. Kafka's piece is a skeletal, or "poor," text in that one code of reading—the referential—dominates it while other codes present in a classic, or "rich," text are almost absent. The article juxtaposes the proverbial (or common-language) response evoked by the text with the personal reactions of a single reader. Kafka's obsession, the inability of common, proverbial language to make real communication possible, is allegorized in the brief tale of A and B, whose comings and goings are mirrored, and at times interfered with, by the language in which these events occur.

The final two selections deal with important questions about the acts of interpreting and reading Kafka's texts. Jonathan Baldo, in "The

Reader on Trial: Or, Is Reading Necessarily an Injudicious Act?"
reads Kafka's *The Trial* as a kind of prescient sendup of reader-
response theory in which the reader's judgment is just as much on
trial as Joseph K., questioning whether it is possible to read other
than injudiciously. By calling his protagonist Joseph K. and one of
the warders in the opening chapter of the novel Franz, Kafka divided
his own name, suggesting that the author cast himself as both accused
and guard. Baldo sees this duality replicated both within and without
the text in the character of the priest who doubles as storyteller and
interpreter and in the author who is both warder of the reader and
a reader on trial. The reader, too, always has a double, if not triple,
role as critic and reserve reader, and the critic doubles as counsel
and judge. In all this doubling, there is no continuity, thus making
reading a completely schizophrenic activity, always turning on the
question of authority in all senses of the word. Baldo's essay reflects
the dual feeling of power and paranoia in Kafka criticism as it confronts
Kafka's second century.

The final article in this anthology provides us with some insight
into why a variety of critical responses to any Kafkan text is inevitable.
Dierdre Vincent's " 'I'm the King of the Castle': Franz Kafka and
the Well-Tempered Reader" demonstrates, on the basis of *The Castle*,
Kafka's control over the reader. As the act of reading Kafka progresses,
the reader's own system of values becomes short-circuited. When she
begins to waver, she tries to explain what often cannot be rationally
explained. Because of the enigmatic nature of Kafka's prose, in which
a gap exists between the narrative and the narratee, readers are
compelled to provide their own bridges to comprehensibility, thus
constantly creating other texts that have been rendered harmless
through explanation. Vincent sees Kafka's prose as indicting the rational thought process that usually goes on in the act of reading. Her
article allows us to see Kafka as the authority firmly in charge of his
text and places the reader/critic into a position fraught with anxiety,
without much choice but to read Kafka again, which is what we all
do.

When beginning this introduction, I felt a little like Rotpeter the
ape in Kafka's "A Report to an Academy." To recall the span of
Kafka criticism, "a short space of time, perhaps, according to the
calendar, but an infinitely long time to gallop through at full speed,"
is what I set out to do. Like Rotpeter, "I am not appealing for any
man's verdict, I am only imparting knowledge, I am only making a
report. To you also, honored Members of the Academy, I have only
made a report." As Rotpeter (and Kafka) knew, however, no report
is only a report. Each has its goals, strengths, and weaknesses. In
this respect mine is no different.

Editor's note: Many of the articles reprinted in this volume originally included quotations in German from Kafka's works and other sources. For the purpose of this collection, translations into English have been substituted for the original German.

RUTH V. GROSS
University of Rochester/Eastman School of Music

Notes

1. For a detailed discussion of this argument, see Ruth V. Gross, "Of Mice and Women: Reflections on a Discourse in Kafka's 'Josefine die Sängerin oder das Volk der Mäuse,' " *Germanic Review* 60 (1985): 59–68.

2. Franz Kafka, *Letters to Felice*, ed. Erich Heller and Jürgen Born, trans. James Stern and Elisabeth Duckworth (New York: Schocken Books, 1973), 304.

3. Peter Beicken, *Franz Kafka, Eine Kritische Einführung* (Frankfurt am Main: Athenäum Fischer Taschenbuch Verlag, 1974).

4. Angel Flores, ed., *The Kafka Problem* (New York: New Directions, 1946; rep. New York: Octagon Books, 1963).

5. Hartmut Müller, *Franz Kafka: Leben—Werk—Wirkung*, in the series Hermes Handlexikon (Düsseldorf: ECON Taschenbuch Verlag, 1985), 159.

6. Angel Flores, *The Kafka Problem* (New York: New Directions, 1946), x.

7. Müller, *Franz Kafka*, 159.

8. Max Brod, *Franz Kafkas Glauben und Lehre* (Winterthur: Mondial Verlag, 1948; rep. Frankfurt am Main und Hamburg: Fischer Bücherei, 1966).

9. Günther Anders, *Franz Kafka, pro und contra* (München: C. H. Beck Verlag, 1951).

10. Ibid., 99.

11. Angel Flores and Homer Swander, eds., *Franz Kafka Today* (Madison: University of Wisconsin Press, 1958).

12. Friedrich Beißner, *Der Erzähler Franz Kafka* (Stuttgart: Kohlhammer, 1952).

13. Flores and Swander, *Franz Kafka Today*, 1.

14. Wilhem Emrich, *Franz Kafka* (Bonn: Athenäum, 1958); Heinz Politzer, *Franz Kafka: Parable and Paradox* (Ithaca: Cornell University Press; London: Oxford University Press, 1962); Walter Sokel, *Franz Kafka—Tragik und Ironie: Zur Struktur seiner Kunst* (Munich and Vienna: Albert Langen Müller, 1964), trans. as *Franz Kafka* (New York and London: Columbia University Press, 1966).

15. Emrich, *Franz Kafka*, 230.

16. Claude David, *Études Germaniques* XVI (1961): 39.

17. Emrich and Sokel are good examples of interdisciplinary scholarship; the many biographers of Kafka, such as Klaus Wagenbach, Ronald Gray, and Ernst Pawel, represent the positivist group; Beißner and his followers comprise the textualists.

18. Ronald Gray, *Kafka: A Collection of Critical Essays* (Englewood Cliffs, N.J.: Prentice-Hall, 1962); Heinz Politzer, *Franz Kafka* (Darmstadt: Wissenschaftliche Buchgesellschaft, 1973); Angel Flores, *The Kafka Debate* (New York: Gordian Press, 1977); J. P. Stern, *The World of Franz Kafka* (New York: Holt, Rinehart, and Winston, 1980); Kenneth Hughes, *Kafka: An Anthology of Marxist Criticism* (Hanover and London: New

England University Press, 1982); Alan Udoff, *Kafka and the Contemporary Critical Performance: Centenary Perspectives* (Bloomington: Indiana University Press, 1988).

19. Peter Neumeyer, *Twentieth Century Interpretations of "The Castle"* (Englewood Cliffs, N.J.: Prentice-Hall, 1969); James Rolleston, *Twentieth Century Interpretations of "The Trial"* (Englewood Cliffs, N.J.: Prentice-Hall, 1976); and Angel Flores, *The Problem of "The Judgment"* (New York: Gordian Press, 1977).

20. Jean-François Lyotard, *The Postmodern Condition: A Report on Knowledge*, trans. Geoff Bennington and Brian Massumi (Minneapolis: University of Minnesota Press, 1984), 77–79.

KAFKA THE WRITER
FROM PRAGUE

"Somewhere Behind"   Milan Kundera*

> Poets don't invent poems
> The poem is somewhere behind
> It's been there for a long long time
> The poet merely discovers it.
> —*Jan Skacel*

1

In one of his books, my friend Josef Skvorecky tells this true story:

An engineer from Prague is invited to a professional conference in London. So he goes, takes part in the proceedings, and returns to Prague. Some hours after his return, sitting in his office, he picks up *Rude Pravo*—the official daily paper of the Party—and reads: A Czech engineer, attending a conference in London, has made a slanderous statement about his socialist homeland to the Western press and has decided to stay in the West.

Illegal emigration combined with a statement of that kind is no trifle. It would be worth twenty years in prison. Our engineer can't believe his eyes. But there's no doubt about it, the article refers to him. His secretary, coming into his office, is shocked to see him: My God, she says, you're back! I don't understand—did you see what they wrote about you?

The engineer sees fear in his secretary's eyes. What can he do? He rushes to the *Rude Pravo* office. He finds the editor responsible for the story. The editor apologizes; yes, it really is an awkward business, but he, the editor, has nothing to do with it, he got the text of the article direct from the Ministry of the Interior.

So the engineer goes off to the Ministry. There they say yes, of course, it's all a mistake, but they, the Ministry, have nothing to do with it, they got the report on the engineer from the intelligence

* Reprinted from *The Art of the Novel* (New York: Grove Press, 1988). © 1988 by Grove Press, Inc. Used by permission of Grove Press, a division of Wheatland Corporation, and Faber and Faber, Ltd.

people at the London embassy. The engineer asks for a retraction. No, he's told, they never retract, but nothing can happen to him, he has nothing to worry about.

But the engineer does worry. He soon realizes that all of a sudden he's being closely watched, that his telephone is tapped, and that he's being followed in the street. He sleeps poorly and has nightmares until, unable to bear the pressure any longer, he takes a lot of real risks to leave the country illegally. And so he actually becomes an émigré.

2

The story I've just told is one that we would immediately call *Kafkan*. This term, drawn from an artist's work, determined solely by a novelist's images, stands as the only common denominator in situations (literary or real) that no other word allows us to grasp and to which neither political nor social nor psychological theory gives us any key.

But what is the *Kafkan*?

Let's try to describe some of its aspects.

One:

The engineer is confronted by a power that has the character of a *boundless labyrinth*. He can never get to the end of its interminable corridors and will never succeed in finding out who issued the fateful verdict. He is therefore in the same situation as Joseph K. before the Court, or the Land-Surveyor K. before the Castle. All three are in a world that is nothing but a single, huge labyrinthine institution they cannot escape and cannot understand.

Novelists before Kafka often exposed institutions as arenas where conflicts between different personal and public interests were played out. In Kafka the institution is a mechanism that obeys its own laws; no one knows now who programmed those laws or when; they have nothing to do with human concerns and are thus unintelligible.

Two:

In Chapter Five of *The Castle*, the village Mayor explains in detail to K. the long history of his file. Briefly: Years earlier, a proposal to engage a land-surveyor came down to the village from the Castle. The Mayor wrote a negative response (there was no need for any land-surveyor), but his reply went astray to the wrong office, and so after an intricate series of bureaucratic misunderstandings, stretching over many years, the job offer was inadvertently sent to K., at the very moment when all the offices involved were in the process of canceling the old obsolete proposal. After a long journey, K. thus arrived in the village by mistake. Still more: Given that for him there is no possible world other than the Castle and its village, his *entire* existence is a mistake.

In the Kafkan world, the file takes on the role of a Platonic idea. It represents true reality, whereas man's physical existence is only a shadow cast on the screen of illusion. Indeed, both the Land-Surveyor K. and the Prague engineer are but the shadows of their file cards; and they are even much less than that: they are the shadows of a *mistake* in the file, shadows without even the right to exist as shadows.

But if man's life is only a shadow and true reality lies elsewhere, in the inaccessible, in the inhuman or the suprahuman, then we suddenly enter the domain of theology. Indeed, Kafka's first commentators explained his novels as religious parables.

Such an interpretation seems to me wrong (because it sees allegory where Kafka grasped concrete situations of human life) but also revealing: wherever power deifies itself, it automatically produces its own theology; wherever it behaves like God, it awakens religious feelings toward itself; such a world can be described in theological terms.

Kafka did not write religious allegories, but the *Kafkan* (both in reality and in fiction) is inseparable from its theological (or rather: *pseudotheological*) dimension.

Three:

Raskolnikov cannot bear the weight of his guilt, and to find peace he consents to his punishment of his own free will. It's the well-known situation where *the offense seeks the punishment.*

In Kafka the logic is reversed. The person punished does not know the reason for the punishment. The absurdity of the punishment is so unbearable that to find peace the accused needs to find a justification for his penalty: the *punishment seeks the offense.*

The Prague engineer is punished by intensive police surveillance. This punishment demands the crime that was not committed, and the engineer accused of emigrating ends up emigrating in fact. *The punishment has finally found the offense.*

Not knowing what the charges against him are, K. decides, in Chapter Seven of *The Trial*, to examine his whole life, his entire past "down to the smallest details." The "autoculpabilization" machine goes into motion. *The accused seeks his offense.*

One day, Amalia receives an obscene letter from a Castle official. Outraged, she tears it up. The Castle doesn't even need to criticize Amalia's rash behavior. Fear (the same fear our engineer saw in his secretary's eyes) acts all by itself. With no order, no perceptible sign from the Castle, everyone avoids Amalia's family like the plague.

Amalia's father tries to defend his family. But there is a problem: Not only is the source of the verdict impossible to find, but the verdict itself does not exist! To appeal, to request a pardon, you have to be convicted first! The father begs the Castle to proclaim the crime. So it's not enough to say that the punishment seeks the offense.

In this pseudotheological world, *the punished beg for recognition of their guilt!*

It often happens in Prague nowadays that someone fallen into disgrace cannot find even the most menial job. In vain he asks for certification of the fact that he has committed an offense and that his employment is forbidden. The verdict is nowhere to be found. And since in Prague work is a duty laid down by law, he ends up being charged with parasitism; that means he is guilty of avoiding work. *The punishment finds the offense.*

Four:

The tale of the Prague engineer is in the nature of a funny story, a joke: it provokes laughter.

Two gentlemen, perfectly ordinary fellows (not "inspectors," as in the French translation), surprise Joseph K. in bed one morning, tell him he is under arrest, and eat up his breakfast. K. is a well-disciplined civil servant: instead of throwing the men out of his flat, he stands in his nightshirt and gives a lengthy self-defense. When Kafka read the first chapter of *The Trial* to his friends, everyone laughed, including the author.

Philip Roth's imagined film version of *The Castle:* Groucho Marx plays the Land-Surveyor K., with Chico and Harpo as the two assistants. Yes, Roth is quite right: The comic is inseparable from the very essence of the *Kafkan.*

But it's small comfort to the engineer to know that his story is comic. He is trapped in the joke of his own life like a fish in a bowl; he doesn't find it funny. Indeed, a joke is a joke only if you're outside the bowl; by contrast, the *Kafkan* takes us inside, into the guts of a joke, into the *horror of the comic.*

In the world of the *Kafkan,* the comic is not a counterpoint to the tragic (the tragi-comic) as in Shakespeare; it's not there to make the tragic more bearable by lightening the tone; it doesn't *accompany* the tragic, not at all, it *destroys it in the egg* and thus deprives the victims of the only consolation they could hope for: the consolation to be found in the (real or supposed) grandeur of tragedy. The engineer loses his homeland, and everyone laughs.

3

There are periods of modern history when life resembles the novels of Kafka.

When I was still living in Prague, I would frequently hear people refer to the Party headquarters (an ugly, rather modern building) as "the Castle." Just as frequently, I would hear the Party's second-in-command (a certain Comrade Hendrych) called "Klamm" (which was all the more beautiful as *klam* in Czech means "mirage" or "fraud").

The poet A., a great Communist personage, was imprisoned after a Stalinist trial in the fifties. In his cell he wrote a collection of poems in which he declared himself faithful to Communism despite all the horrors he had experienced. That was not out of cowardice. The poet saw his faithfulness (faithfulness to his persecutors) as the mark of his virtue, of his rectitude. Those in Prague who came to know of this collection gave it, with fine irony, the title "The Gratitude of Joseph K."

The images, the situations, and even the individual sentences of Kafka's novels were part of life in Prague.

That said, one might be tempted to conclude: Kafka's images are alive in Prague because they anticipate totalitarian society.

This claim, however, needs to be corrected: the *Kafkan* is not a sociological or a political notion. Attempts have been made to explain Kafka's novels as a critique of industrial society, of exploitation, alienation, bourgeois morality—of capitalism, in a word. But there is almost nothing of the constituents of capitalism in Kafka's universe: not money or its power, not commerce, not property and owners or the class struggle.

Neither does the *Kafkan* correspond to a definition of totalitarianism. In Kafka's novels, there is neither the party nor ideology and its jargon nor politics, the police, or the army.

So we should rather say that the *Kafkan* represents one fundamental possibility of man and his world, a possibility that is not historically determined and that accompanies man more or less eternally.

But this correction does not dispose of the question: How is it possible that in Prague Kafka's novels merge with real life while in Paris the same novels are read as the hermetic expression of an author's entirely subjective world? Does this mean that the possibility of man and his world known as *Kafkan* becomes concrete personal destiny more readily in Prague than in Paris?

There are tendencies in modern history that produce the *Kafkan* in the broad social dimension: the progressive concentration of power, tending to deify itself; the bureaucratization of social activity that turns all institutions into *boundless labyrinths;* and the resulting depersonalization of the individual.

Totalitarian states, as extreme concentrations of these tendencies, have brought out the close relationship between Kafka's novels and real life. But if in the West people are unable to see this relationship, it is not only because the society we call democratic is less Kafkan than that of today's Prague. It is also, it seems to me, because over here, the sense of the real is inexorably being lost.

In fact, the society we call democratic is also familiar with the process that bureaucratizes and depersonalizes; the entire planet has become a theater of this process. Kafka's novels are an imaginary, oneiric hyperbole of it; a totalitarian state is a prosaic and material hyperbole of it.

But why was Kafka the first novelist to grasp these tendencies, which appeared on History's stage so clearly and brutally only after his death?

4

Mystifications and legends aside, there is no significant trace anywhere of Franz Kafka's political interests; in that sense, he is different from all his Prague friends, from Max Brod, Franz Werfel, Egon Erwin Kisch, and from all the avant-gardes that, claiming to know the direction of History, indulged in conjuring up the face of the future.

So how is it that not their works but those of their solitary, introverted companion, immersed in his own life and his art, are recognized today as a sociopolitical prophecy, and are for that very reason banned in a large part of the world?

I pondered this mystery one day after witnessing a little scene in the home of an old friend of mine. The woman in question had been arrested in 1951 during the Stalinist trials in Prague, and convicted of crimes she hadn't committed. Hundreds of Communists were in the same situation at the time. All their lives they had entirely identified themselves with their Party. When it suddenly became their prosecutor, they agreed, like Joseph K., "to examine their whole lives, their entire past, down to the smallest details" to find the hidden offense and, in the end, to confess to imaginary crimes. My friend managed to save her own life because she had the extraordinary courage to refuse to undertake—as her comrades did, as the poet A. did—the "search for her offense." Refusing to assist her persecutors, she became unusable for the final show trial. So instead of being hanged she got away with life imprisonment. After fourteen years, she was completely rehabilitated and released.

This woman had a one-year-old child when she was arrested. On release from prison, she thus rejoined her fifteen-year-old son and had the joy of sharing her humble solitude with him from then on. That she became passionately attached to the boy is entirely comprehensible. One day I went to see them—by then her son was twenty-five. The mother, hurt and angry, was crying. The cause was utterly trivial: the son had overslept or something like that. I asked the mother: "Why get so upset over such a trifle? Is it worth crying about? Aren't you overdoing it?"

It was the son who answered for his mother: "No, my mother's not overdoing it. My mother is a splendid, brave woman. She resisted when everyone else cracked. She wants me to become a real man.

It's true, all I did was oversleep, but what my mother reproached me for is something much deeper. It's my attitude. My selfish attitude. I want to become what my mother wants me to be. And with you as witness, I promise her I will."

What the Party never managed to do to the mother, the mother had managed to do to her son. She had forced him to identify with an absurd accusation, to "seek his offense," to make a public confession. I looked on, dumbfounded, at this Stalinist mini-trial, and I understood all at once that the psychological mechanisms that function in great (apparently incredible and inhuman) historical events are the same as those that regulate private (quite ordinary and very human) situations.

5

The famous letter Kafka wrote and never sent to his father demonstrates that it was from the family, from the relationship between the child and the deified power of the parents, that Kafka drew his knowledge of the *technique of culpabilization,* which became a major theme of his fiction. In "The Judgment," a short story intimately bound up with the author's family experience, the father accuses the son and commands him to drown himself. The son accepts his fictitious guilt and throws himself into the river as docilely as, in a later work, his successor Joseph K., indicted by a mysterious organization, goes to be slaughtered. The similarity between the two accusations, the two culpabilizations, and the two executions reveals the link, in Kafka's work, between the family's private "totalitarianism" and that in his great social visions.

Totalitarian society, especially in its more extreme versions, tends to abolish the boundary between the public and the private; power, as it grows ever more opaque, requires the lives of citizens to be entirely transparent. The ideal of *life without secrets* corresponds to the ideal of the exemplary family: a citizen does not have the right to hide anything at all from the Party or the State, just as a child has no right to keep a secret from his father or his mother. In their propaganda, totalitarian societies project an idyllic smile: they want to be seen as "one big family."

It's often said that Kafka's novels express a passionate desire for community and human contact, that the rootless being who is K. has only one goal: to overcome the curse of solitude. Now, this is not only a cliché, a reductive interpretation, it is a misinterpretation.

The Land-Surveyor K. is not in the least pursuing people and their warmth, he is not trying to become "a man among men" like Sartre's Orestes; he wants acceptance not from a community but from an institution. To have it, he must pay dearly: he must renounce his solitude. And this is his hell: he is never alone, the two assistants sent by the Castle follow him always. When he first makes love with Frieda, the two men are there, sitting on the café counter over the lovers, and from then on they are never absent from their bed.

Not the curse of solitude but the *violation of solitude* is Kafka's obsession!

Karl Rossmann is constantly being harassed by everybody: his clothes are sold; his only photo of his parents is taken away; in the dormitory, beside his bed, boys box and now and again fall on top of him; two roughnecks named Robinson and Delamarche force him to move in with them and fat Brunelda, whose moans resound through his sleep.

Joseph K.'s story also begins with the rape of privacy: two unknown men come to arrest him in bed. From that day on, he never feels alone: the Court follows him, watches him, talks to him; his private life disappears bit by bit, swallowed up by the mysterious organization on his heels.

Lyrical souls who like to preach the abolition of secrets and the transparency of private life do not realize the nature of the process they are unleashing. The starting point of totalitarianism resembles the beginning of *The Trial:* you'll be taken unawares in your bed. They'll come just as your father and mother used to.

People often wonder whether Kafka's novels are projections of the author's most personal and private conflicts, or descriptions of an objective "social machine."

The *Kafkan* is not restricted to either the private or the public domain; it encompasses both. The public is the mirror of the private, the private reflects the public.

6

In speaking of the microsocial practices that generate the *Kafkan*, I mean not only the family but also the organization in which Kafka spent all his adult life: the office.

Kafka's heroes are often seen as allegorical projections of the intellectual, but there's nothing intellectual about Gregor Samsa. When he wakes up metamorphosed into a beetle, he has only one concern: in this new state, how to get to the office on time. In his head he has nothing but the obedience and discipline to which his profession has accustomed him: he's an employee, a *functionary,* as are all Kafka's characters; a functionary not in the sense of a sociological type (as in Zola) but as one human possibility, as one of the elementary ways of being.

In the bureaucratic world of the functionary, first, there is no initiative, no invention, no freedom of action; there are only orders and rules: *it is the world of obedience.*

Second, the functionary performs a small part of a large administrative activity whose aim and horizons he cannot see: *it is the world where actions have become mechanical* and people do not know the meaning of what they do.

Third, the functionary deals only with unknown persons and with files: *it is the world of the abstract.*

To place a novel in this world of obedience, of the mechanical, and of the abstract, where the only human adventure is to move from one office to another, seems to run counter to the very essence of epic poetry. Thus the question: How has Kafka managed to transform such gray, antipoetical material into fascinating novels?

The answer can be found in a letter he wrote to Milena: "The office is not a stupid institution; it belongs more to the realm of the fantastic than of the stupid." The sentence contains one of Kafka's greatest secrets. He saw what no one else could see: not only the enormous importance of the bureaucratic phenomenon for man, for his condition and for his future, but also (even more surprisingly) the poetic potential contained in the phantasmic nature of offices.

But what does it mean to say the office belongs to the realm of the fantastic?

The Prague engineer would understand: a mistake in his file projected him to London; so he wandered around Prague, a veritable *phantom*, seeking his *lost body*, while the offices he visited seemed to him a *boundless labyrinth* from some unknown *mythology*.

The quality of the fantastic that he perceived in the bureaucratic world allowed Kafka to do what had seemed unimaginable before: he transformed the profoundly antipoetic material of a highly bureaucratized society into the great poetry of the novel; he transformed a very ordinary story of a man who cannot obtain a promised job (which is actually the story of *The Castle*) into myth, into epic, into a kind of beauty never before seen.

By expanding a bureaucratic setting to the gigantic dimensions of a universe, Kafka unwittingly succeeded in creating an image that fascinates us by its resemblance to a society he never knew, that of today's Prague.

A totalitarian state is in fact a single, immense administration: since all work in it is for the state, everyone of every occupation has become an *employee*. A worker is no longer a worker, a judge no longer a judge, a shopkeeper no longer a shopkeeper, a priest no longer a priest; they are all functionaries of the State. "I belong to the Court," the priest says to Joseph K. in the Cathedral. In Kafka, the lawyers, too, work for the Court. A citizen in today's Prague does not find that surprising. He would get no better legal defense than K. did. His lawyers don't work for the defendants either, but for the Court.

7

In a cycle of one hundred quatrains that sound the gravest and most complex depths with an almost childlike simplicity, the great Czech poet writes:

> Poets don't invent poems
> The poem is somewhere behind
> It's been there for a long long time
> The poet merely discovers it.

For the poet, then, writing means breaking through a wall behind which something immutable ("the poem") lies hidden in darkness. That's why (because of this surprising and sudden unveiling) "the poem" strikes us first as a *dazzlement*.

I read *The Castle* for the first time when I was fourteen, and the book will never enchant me so thoroughly again, even though all the vast understanding it contains (all the real import of the *Kafkan*) was incomprehensible to me then: I was dazzled.

Later on my eyes adjusted to the light of "the poem" and I began to see my own lived experience in what had dazzled me; yet the light was still there.

"The poem," says Jan Skacel, has been waiting for us, immutable, "for a long long time." However, in a world of perpetual change, is the immutable not a mere illusion?

No. Every situation is of man's making and can only contain what man contains; thus one can imagine that the situation (and all its metaphysical implications) has existed as a human possibility "for a long long time."

But in that case, what does History (the nonimmutable) represent for the poet?

In the eyes of the poet, strange as it may seem, History is in a position similar to the poet's own: History does not *invent*, it *discovers*. Through new situations, History reveals what man is, what has been in him "for a long long time," what his possibilities are.

If "the poem" is already there, then it would be illogical to impute to the poet the gift of *foresight*; no, he "only discovers" a human possibility ("the poem" that has been there "a long long time") that History will in its turn discover one day.

Kafka made no prophecies. All he did was see what was "behind." He did not know that his seeing was also a fore-seeing. He did not intend to unmask a social system. He shed light on the mechanisms he knew from private and microsocial human practice, not suspecting that later developments would put those mechanisms into action on the great stage of History.

The hypnotic eye of power, the desperate search for one's own offense, exclusion and the anguish of being excluded, the condemnation to conformism, the phantasmic nature of reality and the magical reality of the file, the perpetual rape of private life, etc.—all these experiments that History has performed on man in its immense test tubes, Kafka performed (some years earlier) in his novels.

The convergence of the real world of totalitarian states with Kafka's "poem" will always be somewhat uncanny, and it will always bear witness that the poet's act, in its very essence, is incalculable; and paradoxical: the enormous social, political, and "prophetic" import of Kafka's novels lies precisely in their "nonengagement," that is to say, in their total autonomy from all political programs, ideological concepts, and futurological prognoses.

Indeed, if instead of seeking "the poem" hidden "somewhere behind" the poet "engages" himself to the service of a truth known from the outset (which comes forward on its own and is "out in front"), he has renounced the mission of poetry. And it matters little whether the preconceived truth is called revolution or dissidence, Christian faith or atheism, whether it is more justified or less justified; a poet who serves any truth other than the truth *to be discovered* (which is *dazzlement*) is a false poet.

If I hold so ardently to the legacy of Kafka, if I defend it as my personal heritage, it is not because I think it worthwhile to imitate the inimitable (and rediscover the *Kafkan*) but because it is such a tremendous example of the *radical autonomy* of the novel (of the poetry that is the novel). This autonomy allowed Franz Kafka to say things about our human condition (as it reveals itself in our century) that no social or political thought could ever tell us.

Conversations with Brecht   Walter Benjamin[*]

July 6 [1934].   Brecht, in the course of yesterday's conversation: "I often think of a tribunal before which I am being questioned. 'What was that? Do you really mean that seriously?' I would then have to admit: Not quite seriously. After all I think too much about artistic matters, about what would go well on the stage, to be quite serious; but when I have answered this important question in the negative,

[*]Excerpts pp. 204–10 from *Reflections: Essays, Aphorisms, Autobiographical Writings* by Walter Benjamin, translated by Edmund Jephcott, English translation copyright 1978 by Harcourt Brace Jovanovich, reprinted by permission of the publisher.

I will add a still more important affirmation: that my conduct is *legitimate.*" This formulation, it is true, came later in the conversation. Brecht had begun with doubts not of the legitimacy but of the effectiveness of his procedure, with a sentence that arose from some remarks I had made on Gerhart Hauptmann: "I sometimes wonder whether they are not, after all, the only writers who really achieve anything: the *writers of substance,* I mean." By this Brecht means writers who are entirely serious. And to explain this idea he starts from the fiction that Confucius had written a tragedy or Lenin a novel. One would think this inadmissible, he declares, conduct unworthy of them. "Let us suppose that you read an excellent political novel and afterward find out it is by Lenin; your opinion of both would be changed, and to the disadvantage of both. Nor would Confucius be allowed to write a play by Euripides; it would be thought undignified. Yet his parables are not." In short, all this points to a distinction between two literary types: the visionary, who is serious, on the one hand, and the reflective man, who is not quite serious, on the other. Here I raise the question of Kafka. To which of the two groups does he belong? I know, the question cannot be decided. And this very thing is for Brecht a sign that Kafka, whom he considers a great writer, like Kleist, Grabbe, or Büchner, is a failure. His starting point is really the parable, which is responsible to reason and therefore, as far as its wording is concerned, cannot be entirely serious. But this parable is then subject to artistic elaboration. It grows into a novel. And, strictly speaking, it carried the germ of one from the start. It was never quite transparent. Moreover, Brecht is convinced that Kafka would not have found his own form without Dostoyevsky's Grand Inquisitor and the other parabolic passage in *The Brothers Karamazov,* where the corpse of the saintly Starets begins to stink. In Kafka, therefore, parable is in conflict with vision. But as a visionary, Brecht says, Kafka saw what was to come without seeing what is. He stresses—as he had done earlier in Le Lavandou, but, to me, more clearly—the prophetic side of his work. Kafka, he says, had only one problem, that of organization. What seized him was fear of the ant-colony state: how people become estranged from themselves by the forms of their communal life. And certain forms of this estrangement he foresaw—for example, the procedure of the G.P.U. He did not, however, find a solution, and did not wake from his nightmare. Of Kafka's precision, Brecht says it is that of someone vague, a dreamer.

August 5.   Three weeks ago I gave B. my essay on Kafka. He certainly read it, but never spoke about it of his own accord, and both times I brought the conversation around to it, he replied evasively. Finally I took back the manuscript without a word. Yesterday evening he suddenly came back to this essay. The transition to it, somewhat abrupt and breakneck, was effected by the comment that I, too, could not be entirely absolved from the reproach of a diarist's style of writing, in the manner of Nietzsche. My Kafka essay, for example— he was concerned with Kafka merely from the phenomenal point of view—took the work as something that had grown by itself—the man, too—severed all its connections, even that with its author. It was always the question of *essence* that finally interested me. Whereas such a matter ought to be approached by asking the question of Kafka: what does he do? how does he behave? And by looking in the first place more at the general than at the particular. It then emerges that he lived in Prague in a bad milieu of journalists and self-important literati; in this world literature was the main, if not the only, reality. With this attitude Kafka's strengths and weaknesses are connected; his artistic value, but also his manifold futility. He is a Jewboy—as one might also coin the term Aryanboy—a skinny, unlikable creature, a bubble on the iridescent morass of Prague culture, nothing more. Nevertheless, he also had certain very inter- esting sides. These could be brought out; one would have to imagine a conversation between Lao-tse and his disciple Kafka. Lao-tse says: "Well now, disciple Kafka, the organizations, the leaseholds and other economic forms in which you live make you uneasy?" "Yes." "You can't cope with them any more?" "No." "A stock certificate worries you?" "Yes." "And now you are looking for a leader to hold on to, disciple Kafka." That is of course despicable, says Brecht. I reject Kafka. And he goes on to talk about a parable of a Chinese philosopher on "the pains of usefulness." In the forest there are various kinds of tree trunks. From the thickest, beams for ships are cut; from less thick but still respectable trunks, box lids and coffin sides are made; the very thin ones are used for rods; but nothing comes of the stunted ones—they escape the pains of usefulness. "In what Kafka wrote you have to look around as in such a forest. You will then find a number of very useful things. The images are good. But the rest is obscur- antism. It is sheer mischief. You have to ignore it. Depth takes you no further. Depth is a dimension of its own, just depth—which is why nothing comes to light in it." I explain to B. in conclusion that plumbing the depths is my way of going to the antipodes. In my essay on Kraus I did indeed come out there. I know that the one on Kafka was not so successful: I could not rebut the charge that it consisted of diarylike notes. Discussion within the frontier zone des- ignated by Kraus, and in another way by Kafka, did indeed interest me. I had not yet, I said, explored this area in Kafka's case. That it contained a good deal of rubbish and detritus, much real obscurantism, I fully realized. Nevertheless, other aspects were more decisive, and I had touched on a number of them in my essay. B.'s critical approach must, after all, prove itself in the interpretation of the particular. I opened "The Next Village." At once I was able to observe the conflict produced in B. by this suggestion. Eisler's remark that this story was "worthless" he rejected emphatically. On the other hand, he was equally unable to explain its value. "It would need close study," he thought. Then the conversation broke off; it was ten o'clock, and the radio news was on the air from Vienna.

August 31. The day before yesterday we had a long and heated debate on my Kafka. Its basis: the charge that it advanced Jewish fascism. It increased and propagated the obscurity surrounding this author instead of dispersing it. Whereas it was of crucial importance to clarify Kafka, that is, to formulate practicable proposals that can be derived from his stories. That proposals were derivable from them could be supposed, if only from the serene calm of their viewpoint. However, these suggestions would have to be sought in the direction of the great general abuses afflicting present-day humanity. Brecht tries to show their imprint in Kafka's work. He confines himself chiefly to *The Trial.* There above all, he thinks, we find the fear of the unending and irresistible growth of cities. He claims to know from personal experience the crushing weight of this phenomenon on human beings. The inexplicable mediations, dependencies, entanglements besetting men as a result of their present form of existence, find expression in these cities. They find expression in another way in the desire for a "Leader," who for the petit bourgeois represents the man whom—in a world where blame can be passed from one person to the next so that everyone escapes it—he can hold accountable for all his misfortunes. Brecht calls *The Trial* a prophetic book. "What can become of the Cheka you can see from the Gestapo." Kafka's perspective: that of the man who has gone to the dogs. Odradek is characteristic of this: Brecht interprets the janitor as representing the cares of the father of a family. Things must go wrong for the petit bourgeois. His situation is Kafka's. But whereas the type of petit bourgeois current today—that is, the fascist—decides in face of this situation to exert his iron, indomitable will, Kafka hardly resists; he is wise. Where the fascist imposes heroism, he poses questions. He asks for guarantees of his situation. But the latter is so constituted that the guarantees would have to exceed all reasonable measure. It is a Kafkaesque irony that the man who seemed convinced of nothing more than the invalidity of all guarantees was an insurance official. Moreover, his unrestricted pessimism is free of any tragic sense of fate. For not only has his expectation of misfortune a solely empirical foundation—albeit a perfect one; he also places the criterion of final success with incorrigible naïveté in the most trivial and banal of enterprises: the visit of a commercial traveler or an application to an authority. The conversation concentrated at times on the story "The Next Village." Brecht declares it a counterpart to the story of Achilles and the tortoise. Someone who composes the ride from its smallest particles—leaving aside all incidents—will never reach the next village. Life itself is too short for such a ride. But the error lies in the "someone." For just as the ride is deceptive, so, too, is the rider. And just as the unity of life is now done away with, so, too, is its brevity. No matter how brief it may be. This makes no difference, because a different person from him who started the ride arrives at the village. For my part, I give the following interpretation: the true measure of life is remembrance. Retrospectively, it traverses life with the speed of lightning. As quickly as one turns back a few pages, it has gone back from the next village to the point where the rider decided to set off. He whose life has turned into writing, like old people's, likes to read this writing only backward. Only so does he meet himself, and only so—in flight from the present—can his life be understood.

What Is a Minor Literature?   Gilles Deleuze and Félix Guattari*

   The problem of expression is staked out by Kafka not in an abstract and universal fashion but in relation to those literatures that are considered minor, for example, the Jewish literature of Warsaw and Prague. A minor literature doesn't come from a minor language; it is rather that which a minority constructs within a major language. But the first characteristic of minor literature in any case is that in it language is affected with a high coefficient of deterritorialization. In this sense, Kafka marks the impasse that bars access to writing for the Jews of Prague and turns their literature into something impossible—the impossibility of not writing, the impossibility of writing in German, the impossibility of writing otherwise.[1] The impossibility of not writing because national consciousness, uncertain or oppressed, necessarily exists by means of literature ("The literary struggle has its real justification at the highest possible levels"). The impossibility of writing other than in German is for the Prague Jews the feeling of an irreducible distance from their primitive Czech territoriality. And the impossibility of writing in German is the deterritoralization of the German population itself, an oppressive minority that speaks a language cut off from the masses, like a "paper language" or an

*Reprinted from *Kafka: Toward a Minor Literature*, translated by Dana Polan (Minneapolis: University of Minnesota Press, 1986).

artificial language; this is all the more true for the Jews who are simultaneously a part of this minority and excluded from it, like "gypsies who have stolen a German child from its crib." In short, Prague German is a deterritorialized language, appropriate for strange and minor uses. (This can be compared in another context to what blacks in America today are able to do with the English language.)

The second characteristic of minor literatures is that everything in them is political. In major literatures, in contrast, the individual concern (familial, marital, and so on) joins with other no less individual concerns, the social milieu serving as a mere environment or a background; this is so much the case that none of these Oedipal intrigues are specifically indispensable or absolutely necessary but all become as one in a large space. Minor literature is completely different; its cramped space forces each individual intrigue to connect immediately to politics. The individual concern thus becomes all the more necessary, indispensable, magnified, because a whole other story is vibrating within it. In this way, the family triangle connects to other triangles—commercial, economic, bureaucratic, juridical—that determine its values. When Kafka indicates that one of the goals of a minor literature is the "purification of the conflict that opposes father and son and the possibility of discussing that conflict," it isn't a question of an Oedipal phantasm but of a political program. "Even though something is often thought through calmly, one still does not reach the boundary where it connects up with similar things, one reaches the boundary soonest in politics, indeed, one even strives to see it before it is there, and often sees this limiting boundary everywhere. . . . What in great literature goes on down below, constituting a not indispensable cellar of the structure, here takes place in the full light of day, what is there a matter of passing interest for a few, here absorbs everyone no less than as a matter of life and death."[2]

The third characteristic of minor literature is that in it everything takes on a collective value. Indeed, precisely because talent isn't abundant in a minor literature, there are no possibilities for an individuated enunciation that would belong to this or that "master" and that could be separated from a collective enunciation. Indeed, scarcity of talent is in fact beneficial and allows the conception of something other than a literature of masters; what each author says individually already constitutes a common action, and what he or she says or does is necessarily political, even if others aren't in agreement. The political domain has contaminated every statement (énoncé). But above all else, because collective or national consciousness is "often inactive in external life and always in the process of break-down," literature finds itself positively charged with the role and function of collective, and even revolutionary, enunciation. It is literature that produces an active solidarity in spite of skepticism; and if the writer is in the margins or completely outside his or her fragile community, this situation allows the writer all the more the possibility to express another possible community and to forge the means for another consciousness and another sensibility; just as the dog of "Investigations" calls out in his solitude to *another science*. The literary machine thus becomes the relay for a revolutionary machine-to-come, not at all for ideological reasons but because the literary machine alone is determined to fill the conditions of a collective enunciation that is lacking elsewhere in this milieu: *literature is the people's concern.*[3] It is certainly in these terms that Kafka sees the problem. The message doesn't refer back to an enunciating subject who would be its cause, no more than to a subject of the statement *(sujet d'énoncé)* who would be its effect. Undoubtedly, for a while, Kafka thought according to these traditional categories of the two subjects, the author and the hero, the narrator and the character, the dreamer and the one dreamed of.[4] But he will quickly reject the role of the narrator, just as he will refuse an author's or master's literature, despite his admiration for Goethe. Josephine the mouse renounces the individual act of singing in order to melt into the collective enunciation of "the immense crowd of the heros of [her] people." A movement from the individuated animal to the pack or to a collective multiplicity–seven canine musicians. In "The Investigations of a Dog," the expressions of the solitary researcher tend toward the assemblage *(agencement)* of a collective enunciation of the canine species even if this collectivity is no longer or not yet given. There isn't a subject; *there are only collective assemblages of enunciation*, and literature expresses these acts insofar as they're not imposed from without and insofar as they exist only as diabolical powers to come or revolutionary forces to be constructed. Kafka's solitude opens him up to everything going on in history today. The letter *K* no longer designates a narrator or a character but an assemblage that becomes all the more machine-like, an agent that becomes all the more collective because an individual is locked into it in his or her solitude (it is only in connection to a subject that something individual would be separable from the collective and would lead its own life).

The three characteristics of minor literature are the deterritorialization of language, the connection of the individual to a political immediacy, and the collective assemblage of enunciation. We might as well say that minor no longer designates specific literatures but the revolutionary conditions for every literature within the heart of what is called great (or established) literature. Even he who has the misfortune of being born in the country of a great literature must write in its language, just as a Czech Jew writes in German, or an Ouzbekian writes in Russian. Writing like a dog digging a hole, a rat digging its burrow. And to do that, finding his own point of under-development, his own *patois*, his own third world, his own desert. There has been much discussion of the questions "What is a marginal literature?" and "What is a popular literature, a proletarian litera-ture?" The criteria are obviously difficult to establish if one doesn't start with a more objective concept—that of minor literature. Only the possibility of setting up a minor practice of major language from within allows one to define popular literature, marginal literature, and so on.[5] Only in this way can literature really become a collective machine of expression and really be able to treat and develop its contents. Kafka emphatically declares that a minor literature is much more able to work over its material.[6] Why this machine of expression, and what is it? We know that it is in a relation of multiple deter-ritorializations with language; it is the situation of the Jews who have dropped the Czech language at the same time as the rural environ-ment, but it is also the situation of the German language as a "paper language." Well, one can go even farther; one can push this movement of deterritorialization of expression even farther. But there are only two ways to do this. One way is to artificially enrich this German, to swell it up through all the resources of symbolism, of oneirism, of esoteric sense, of a hidden signifier. This is the approach of the Prague school, Gustav Meyrink and many others, including Max Brod.[7] But this attempt implies a desperate attempt at symbolic reterrito-rialization, based in archetypes, Kabbala, and alchemy, that accen-tuates its break from the people and will find its political result only in Zionism and such things as the "dream of Zion." Kafka will quickly choose the other way, or, rather, he will invent another way. He will opt for the German language of Prague as it is and in its very poverty. Go always farther in the direction of deterritorialization, to the point of sobriety. Since the language is arid, make it vibrate with a new intensity. Oppose a purely intensive usage of language to all symbolic or even significant or simply signifying usages of it. Arrive at a perfect and unformed expression, a materially intense expression. (For these two possible paths, couldn't we find the same alternatives, under other conditions, in Joyce and Beckett? As Irishmen, both of them live within the genial conditions of a minor literature. That is the glory of this sort of minor literature—to be the revolutionary force for all literature. The utilization of English and of every language in Joyce. The utilization of English and French in Beckett. But the former never stops operating by exhilaration and overdetermination and brings about all sorts of worldwide reterritorializations. The other proceeds by dryness and sobriety, a willed poverty, pushing deter-ritorialization to such an extreme that nothing remains but intensities.) How many people today live in a language that is not their own? Or no longer, or not yet, even know their own and know poorly the

major language that they are forced to serve? This is the problem
of immigrants, and especially of their children, the problem of mi-
norities, the problem of a minor literature, but also a problem for
all of us: how to tear a minor literature away from its own language,
allowing it to challenge the language and making it follow a sober
revolutionary path? How to become a nomad and an immigrant and
a gypsy in relation to one's own language? Kafka answers: steal the
baby from its crib, walk the tightrope.

Rich or poor, each language always implies a deterritorialization
of the mouth, the tongue, and the teeth. The mouth, tongue, and
teeth find their primitive territoriality in food. In giving themselves
over to the articulation of sounds, the mouth, tongue, and teeth
deterritorialize. Thus, there is a certain disjunction between eating
and speaking, and even more, despite all appearances, between eating
and writing. Undoubtedly, one can write while eating more easily
than one can speak while eating, but writing goes further in transforming words into things capable of competing with food. Disjunction
between content and expression. To speak, and above all to write,
is to fast. Kafka manifests a permanent obsession with food, and with
that form of food *par excellence*, in other words, the animal or meat—
an obsession with the mouth and with teeth and with large, unhealthy,
or gold-capped teeth.[8] This is one of Kafka's main problems with
Felice. Fasting is also a constant theme in Kafka's writings. His writings
are a long history of fasts. The Hunger Artist, surveyed by butchers,
ends his career next to beasts who eat their meat raw, placing the
visitors before an irritating alternative. The dogs try to take over the
mouth of the investigating hound by filling it with food so that he'll
stop asking questions, and there too is an irritating alternative: "[T]hey
would have done better to drive me away and refuse to listen to my
questions. No, they did not want to do that; they did not indeed
want to listen to my questions, but it was because I asked these
questions that they did not want to drive me away." The investigating
hound oscillates between two sciences, that of food—a science of
the Earth and of the bent head ("Whence does the Earth procure
this food?")—and that of music which is a science of the air and of
the straightened head, as the seven musical dogs of the beginning
and the singing dog of the end well demonstrate. But between the
two there is something in common, since food can come from high
up and the science of food can only develop through fasting, just as
the music is strangely silent.

Ordinarily, in fact, language compensates for its deterritorialization by a reterritorialization in sense. Ceasing to be the organ of
one of the senses, it becomes an instrument of Sense. And it is sense,
as a correct sense, that presides over the designation of sounds (the
thing or the state of things that the word designates) and, as figurative

sense, over the affectation of images and metaphors (those other things that words designate under certain situations or conditions). Thus, there is not only a spiritual reterritorialization of sense, but also a physical one. Similarly, language exists only through the distinction and the complementarity of a subject of enunciation, which is in connection with sense, and a subject of the statement, which is in connection, directly or metaphorically, with the designated thing. This sort of ordinary use of language can be called extensive or representative—the reterritorializing function of language (thus, the singing dog at the end of the "Investigations" forces the hero to abandon his fast, a sort of re-Oedipalization).

Now something happens: the situation of the German language in Czechoslovakia, as a fluid language intermixed with Czech and Yiddish, will allow Kafka the possibility of invention. Since things are as they are ("it is as it is, it is as it is," a formula dear to Kafka, marker of a state of facts), he will abandon sense, render it no more than implicit; he will retain only the skeleton of sense, or a paper cutout.

Since articulated sound was a deterritorialized noise but one that will be reterritorialized in sense, it is now sound itself that will be deterritorialized irrevocably, absolutely. The sound or the word that traverses this new deterritorialization no longer belongs to a language of sense, even though it derives from it, nor is it an organized music or song, even though it might appear to be. We noted Gregor's warbling and the ways it blurred words, the whistling of the mouse, the cough of the ape, the pianist who doesn't play, the singer who doesn't sing and gives birth to her song out of her nonsinging, the musical dogs who are musicians in the very depths of their bodies since they don't emit any music. Everywhere, organized music is traversed by a line of abolition—just as a language of sense is traversed by a line of escape—in order to liberate a living and expressive material that speaks for itself and has no need of being put into a form.[9] This language torn from sense, conquering sense, bringing about an active neutralization of sense, no longer finds its value in anything but an accenting of the word, an inflection: "I live only here or there in a small word in whose vowel. . . . I lose my useless head for a moment. The first and last letters are the beginning and end of my fishlike emotion."[10] Children are well skilled in the exercise of repeating a word, the sense of which is only vaguely felt, in order to make it vibrate around itself (at the beginning of The Castle, the schoolchildren are speaking so fast that one cannot understand what they are saying). Kafka tells how, as a child, he repeated one of his father's expressions in order to make it take flight on a line of nonsense: "end of the month, end of the month."[11] The proper name, which has no sense in itself, is particularly propitious for this sort of exercise. *Milena*, with an accent on the *i*, begins by evoking "a Greek or a Roman gone astray in Bohemia, violated by Czech, cheated of its accent," and then, by a more delicate approximation, it evokes "a woman whom one carries in one's arms out of the world, out of the fire," the accent marking here an always possible fall or, on the contrary, "the lucky leap which you yourself make with your burden."[12]

It seems to us that there is a certain difference, even if relative and highly nuanced, between the two evocations of the name Milena: one still attaches itself to an extensive, figurative scene of the phantasmic sort; the second is already much more intensive, marking a fall or a leap as a threshold of intensity contained within the name itself. In fact, we have here what happens when sense is actively neutralized. As Wagenbach says, "The word is master; it directly gives birth to the image." But how can we define this procedure? Of sense there remains only enough to direct the lines of escape. There is no longer a designation of something by means of a proper name, nor an assignation of metaphors by means of a figurative sense. But *like* images, the thing no longer forms anything but a sequence of intensive states, a ladder or a circuit for intensities that one can make race around in one sense or another, from high to low, or from low to high. The image is this very race itself; it has become becoming—the becoming-dog of the man and the becoming-man of the dog, the becoming-ape or the becoming-beetle of the man and vice versa. We are no longer in the situation of an ordinary, rich language where the word *dog*, for example, would directly designate an animal and would apply metaphorically to other things (so that one could say "like a dog").[13] *Diaries*, 1921: "Metaphors are one of the things that makes me despair of literature." Kafka deliberately kills all metaphor, all symbolism, all signification, no less than all designation. Metamorphosis is the contrary of metaphor. There is no longer any proper sense or figurative sense, but only a distribution of states that is part of the range of the word. The thing and other things are no longer anything but intensities overrun by deterritorialized sound or words that are following their line of escape. It is no longer a question of a resemblance between the comportment of an animal and that of a man; it is even less a question of a simple wordplay. There is no longer man or animal, since each deterritorializes the other, in a conjunction of flux, in a continuum of reversible intensities. Instead, it is now a question of a becoming that includes the maximum of difference as a difference of intensity, the crossing of a barrier, a rising or a falling, a bending or an erecting, an accent on the word. The animal does not speak "like" a man but pulls from the language tonalities lacking in signification; the words themselves are not "like" the animals but in their own way climb about, bark and roam around, being properly linguistic dogs, insects, or mice.[14] To make the sequences vibrate, to open the word onto unexpected internal intensities–in short, an asignifying *intensive utilization* of language. Furthermore, there is no longer a subject of the enunciation, nor a subject of the statement. It is no longer the subject of the statement who is a dog, with the subject of the enunciation remaining "like" a man; it is no longer the subject of enunciation who is "like" a beetle, the subject of the statement remaining a man. Rather, there is a circuit of states that forms a mutual becoming, in the heart of a necessarily multiple or collective assemblage.

How does the situation of the German language in Prague—a withered vocabulary, an incorrect syntax—contribute to such a utilization? Generally, we might call the linguistic elements, however varied they may be, that express the "internal tensions of a language" *intensives* or *tensors*. It is in this sense that the linguist Vidal Sephiha terms intensive "any linguistic tool that allows a move toward the limit of a notion or a surpassing of it," marking a movement of language toward its extremes, toward a reversible beyond or before.[15] Sephiha shows well the variety of such elements which can be all sorts of master-words, verbs, or prepositions that assume all sorts of senses; pronominal or purely intensive verbs as in Hebrew; conjunctions, exclamations, adverbs; and *terms that connote pain.*[16] One could equally cite the accents that are interior to words, their discordant function. And it would seem that the language of a minor literature particularly develops these tensors or these intensives. In the lovely pages where he analyzes the Prague German that was influenced by Czech, Wagenbach cites as the characteristics of this form of German the incorrect use of prepositions; the abuse of the pronominal; the employment of malleable verbs (such as *geben,* which is used for the series "put, sit, place, take away" and which thereby becomes intensive); the multiplication and succession of adverbs; the use of pain-filled connotations; the importance of the accent as a tension internal to the word; and the distribution of consonants and vowels as part of an internal discordance. Wagenbach insists on this point: all these marks of the poverty of a language show up in Kafka but have been taken over by a creative utilization for the purposes of a new sobriety, a new expressivity, a new flexibility, a new intensity.[17] "Almost every word I write jars up against the next, I hear the consonants rub leadenly against each other and the vowels sing an accompaniment like Negroes in a minstrel show."[18] *Language stops being representative in order to now move toward its extremities or its limits.* The connotation of pain accompanies this metamorphosis, as in the words that become a painful warbling with Gregor, or in Franz's cry "single and irrevocable." Think about the utilization of French as a spoken language in the films of Godard. There too is an accumulation of stereotypical adverbs and conjunctions that form the base of all the phrases—a strange poverty that makes French a minor language within French; a creative process that directly links the word to the image; a technique that surges up at the end of sequences in connection with the intensity of the limit "that's enough, enough, he's had enough," and a generalized intensification, coinciding with a panning shot where the camera pivots and sweeps around without leaving the spot, making the image vibrate.

Perhaps the comparative study of images would be less interesting than the study of the functions of language that can work in the same group across different languages—bilingualism or even multilingualism. Because the study of the functions in distinct languages alone can account for social factors, relations of force, diverse centers of power, it escapes from the "informational" myth in order to evaluate the hierarchic and imperative system of language as a transmission of orders, an exercise of power or of resistance to this exercise. Using the research of Ferguson and Gumperz, Henri Gobard has proposed a tetralinguistic model: vernacular, maternal, or territorial language, used in rural communities or rural in its origins; a vehicular, urban, governmental, even worldwide language, a language of businesses, commercial exchange, bureaucratic transmission, and so on, a language of the first sort of deterritorialization; referential language, language of sense and of culture, entailing a cultural reterritorialization; mythic language, on the horizon of cultures, caught up a spiritual or religious reterritorialization. The spatiotemporal categories of these languages differ sharply: vernacular language is *here;* vehicular language is *everywhere;* referential language is *over there;* mythic language is *beyond.* But above all else, the distribution of these languages varies from one group to the next and, in a single group, from one epoch to the next (for a long time in Europe, Latin was a vehicular language before becoming referential, then mythic; English has become the worldwide vehicular language for today's world).[19] What can be said in one language cannot be said in another, and the totality of what can and can't be said varies necessarily with each language and with the connections between these languages.[20] Moreover, all these factors can have ambiguous edges, changing borders, that differ for this or that material. One language can fill a certain function for one material and another function for another material. Each function of a language divides up in turn and carries with it multiple centers of power. A blur of languages, and not at all a system of languages. We can understand the indignation of integrationists who cry when Mass is said in French, since Latin is being robbed of its mythic function. But the classicists are even more behind the times and cry because Latin has even been robbed of its referential cultural function. They express regret in this way for the religious or educational forms of powers that this language exercised and that have now been replaced by other forms. There are even more serious examples that cross over between groups. The revival of regionalisms, with a reterritorialization through dialect or *patois*, a vernacular language—how does that serve a worldwide or transnational technocracy? How can that contribute to revolutionary movements, since they are also filled with archaisms that they are trying to impart a contemporary sense to? From Servan-Schreiber to the Breton bard to the Canadian singer. And that's not really how the borders divide up, since the Canadian singer can also bring about the most reactionary, the most Oedipal of reterritorializations, oh mama, oh my native land, my cabin, olé, olé. We would call this a blur, a mixed-up history, a political situation, but linguists don't know about this, don't want to know about this, since, as linguists, they are "apolitical," pure scientists. Even Chomsky compensated for his scientific apoliticism only by his courageous struggle against the war in Vietnam.

Let's return to the situation in the Hapsburg empire. The breakdown and fall of the empire increase the crisis, accentuate everywhere movements of deterritorialization, and invite all sorts of complex reterritorializations—archaic, mythic, or symbolist. At random, we can cite the following among Kafka's contemporaries: Einstein and his deterritorialization of the representation of the universe (Einstein teaches in Prague, and the physicist Philipp Frank gives conferences there with Kafka in attendance); the Austrian dodecaphonists and their deterritorialization of musical representation (the cry that is Marie's death in *Wozzeck*, or Lulu's, or the echoed *si* that seems to us to follow a musical path similar in certain ways to what Kafka is doing); the expressionist cinema and its double movement of deterritorialization and reterritorialization of the image (Robert Wiene, who has Czech background; Fritz Lang, born in Vienna; Paul Wegener and his utilization of Prague themes). Of course, we should mention Viennese psychoanalysis and Prague school linguistics.[21] What is the specific situation of the Prague Jews in relation to the "four languages?" The vernacular language for these Jews who have come from a rural milieu is Czech, but the Czech language tends to be forgotten and repressed; as for Yiddish, it is often disdained or viewed with suspicion—it *frightens*, as Kafka tells us. German is the vehicular language of the towns, a bureaucratic language of the state, a commercial language of exchange (but English has already started to become indispensable for this purpose). The German language—but this time, Goethe's German—has a cultural and referential function (as does French to a lesser degree). As a mythic language, Hebrew is connected with the start of Zionism and still possesses the quality of an active dream. For each of these languages, we need to evaluate the degrees of territoriality, deterritorialization, and reterritorialization. Kafka's own situation: he is one of the few Jewish writers in Prague to understand and speak Czech (and this language will have a great importance in his relationship with Milena). German plays precisely the double role of vehicular and cultural language, with Goethe always on the horizon (Kafka also knows French, Italian, and probably a bit of English). He will not learn Hebrew until later. What is complicated is Kafka's relation to Yiddish; he sees it less as a sort of linguistic territoriality for the Jews than as a nomadic movement of deterritorialization that reworks German language. What fascinates him in Yiddish is less a language of a religious community than that of a popular theater (he will become patron and impresario for the travelling theater of Isak Lowy).²² The manner in which Kafka, in a public meeting, presented Yiddish to a rather hostile Jewish bourgeois audience is completely remarkable: Yiddish is a language that frightens more than it invites disdain, "dread mingled with a certain fundamental distaste"; it is a language that is lacking a grammar and that is filled with vocables that are fleeting, mobilized, emigrating, and turned into nomads that interiorize "relations of force." It is a language that is grafted onto Middle-High German and that so reworks the German language from within that one cannot translate it into German without destroying it; one can understand Yiddish only by "feeling it" in the heart. In short, it is a language where minor utilizations will carry you away: "Then you will come to feel the true unity of Yiddish and so strongly that it will frighten you, yet it will no longer be fear of Yiddish but of yourselves. Enjoy this self-confidence as much as you can!"²³

Kafka does not opt for a reterritorialization through the Czech language. Nor toward a hypercultural usage of German with all sorts of oneiric or symbolic or mythic flights (even Hebrew-ifying ones), as was the case with the Prague school. Nor toward an oral, popular Yiddish. Instead, using the path that Yiddish opens up to him, he takes it in such a way as to convert it into a unique and solitary form of writing. Since Prague German is deterritorialized to several degrees, he will always take it farther, to a greater degree of intensity, but in the direction of a new sobriety, a new and unexpected modification, a pitiless rectification, a straightening of the head. Schizo politeness, a drunkenness caused by water.²⁴ He will make the German language take flight on a line of escape. He will feed himself on abstinence; he will tear out of Prague German all the qualities of underdevelopment that it has tried to hide; he will make it cry with an extremely sober and rigorous cry. He will pull from it the barking of the dog, the cough of the ape, and the bustling of the beetle. He will turn syntax into a cry that will embrace the rigid syntax of this dried-up German. He will push it toward a deterritorialization that will no longer be saved by culture or by myth, that will be an absolute deterritorialization, even if it is slow, sticky, coagulated. To bring language slowly and progressively to the desert. To use syntax in order to cry, to give a syntax to the cry.

There is nothing that is major or revolutionary except the minor. To hate all languages of masters. Kafka's fascination for servants and employees (the same thing in Proust in relation to servants, to their language). What interests him even more is the possibility of making of his own language—assuming that it is unique, that it is a major language or has been—a minor utilization. To be a sort of stranger *within* his own language; this is the situation of Kafka's Great Swimmer.[25] Even when it is unique, a language remains a mixture, a schizophrenic mélange, a Harlequin costume in which very different functions of language and distinct centers of power are played out, blurring what can be said and what can't be said; one function will be played off against the other, all the degrees of territoriality and relative deterritorialization will be played out. Even when major, a language is open to an intensive utilization that makes it take flight along creative lines of escape which, no matter how slowly, no matter how cautiously, can now form an absolute deterritorialization. All this inventiveness, not only lexically, since the lexical matters little, but sober syntactical invention, simply to write like a dog (but a dog can't write—exactly, exactly). It's what Artaud did with French— cries, gasps; what Celine did with French, following another line, one that was exclamatory to the highest degree. Celine's syntactic evolution went from *Voyage* to *Death on the Credit Plan*, then from *Death on the Credit Plan* to *Guignol's Band*. (After that, Celine had nothing more to talk about except his own misfortunes; in other words, he had no longer any desire to write, only the need to make money. And it always ends like that, language's lines of escape: silence, the interrupted, the interminable, or even worse. But until that point, what a crazy creation, what a writing machine! Celine was so applauded for *Voyage* that he went even further in *Death on the Credit Plan* and then in the prodigious *Guignol's Band* where language is nothing more than intensities. He spoke with a kind of "minor music." Kafka, too, is a minor music, a different one, but always made up of deterritorialized sounds, a language that moves head over heels and away.) These are the true minor authors. An escape for language, for music, for writing. What we call pop—pop music, pop philosophy, pop writing—*Wörterflucht*. To make use of the polylingualism of one's own language, to make a minor or intensive use of it, to oppose the oppressed quality of this language to its oppressive quality, to find points of nonculture or underdevelopment, linguistic Third World zones by which a language can escape, an animal enters into things, an assemblage comes into play. How many styles or genres or literary movements, even very small ones, have only one single dream: to assume a major function in language, to offer themselves as a sort of state language, an official language (for example, psychoanalysis today, which would like to be a master of the signifier, of metaphor, of wordplay)? Create the opposite dream: know how to create a be-coming-minor. (Is there a hope for philosophy, which for a long time has been an official, referential genre? Let us profit from this moment in which antiphilosophy is trying to be a language of power.)

Notes

1. See letter to Brod, Kafka, *Letters to Friends, Family, and Editors,* trans. Richard and Clara Winston (New York: Schocken Books, 1977), 289, and commentaries in Wagenbach, *Franz Kafka,* (Bern: Francke Verlag, 1958), 84.

2. Kafka, *Diaries, 1910–1913,* ed. Max Brod, trans. Joseph Kresh (New York: Schocken Books, 1948), 25 December 1911, 194.

3. Ibid., 193: "[L]iterature is less a concern of literary history, than of the people."

4. See "Wedding Preparations in the Country", in Kafka, *Complete Stories:* "And so long as you say 'one' instead of 'I,' there's nothing in it" (p. 53). And the two subjects appear several pages later: "I don't even need to go to the country myself, it isn't necessary. I'll send my clothed body," while the narrator stays in bed like a bug or a beetle (p. 55). No doubt, this is one of the origins of Gregor's becoming-beetle in "The Metamorphosis" (in the same way, Kafka will give up going to meet Felice and will prefer to stay in bed). But in "The Metamorphosis," the animal takes on all the value of a true becoming and no longer has any of the stagnancy of a subject of enunciation.

5. See Michel Ragon, *Histoire de la littérature prolétarienne en France* (Paris: Albin Michel, 1974) on the difficulty of criteria and on the need to use a concept of a "secondary zone literature."

6. Kafka, *Diaries,* 25 December 1911, 193: "A small nation's memory is not smaller than the memory of a large one and so can digest the existing material more thoroughly."

7. See the excellent chapter "Prague at the Turn of the Century," in Wagenbach, *Franz Kafka,* on the situation of the German language in Czechoslovakia and on the Prague school.

8. Constancy of the theme of teeth in Kafka. A grandfather-butcher; a streetwise education at the butcher-shop; Felice's jaws; the refusal to eat meat except when he sleeps with Felice in Marienbad. See Michel Cournot's article, "Toi qui as de si grandes dents," *Nouvel Observateur,* April 17, 1972. This is one of the most beautiful texts on Kafka. One can find a similar opposition between eating and speaking in Lewis Carroll, and a comparable escape into non-sense.

9. Franz Kafka, *The Trial,* trans. Willa and Edwin Muir (New York: Schocken Books, 1956): "[H]e noticed that they were talking to him, but he could not make out what they were saying, he heard nothing but the din that filled the whole place, through which a shrill unchanging note like that of a siren seemed to sing."

10. Kafka, *Diaries,* 20 August 1911, 61–62.

11. Kafka, *Diaries,* "Without gaining a sense, the phrase 'end of the month' held a terrible secret for me" especially since it was repeated every month—Kafka himself suggests that if this expression remained shorn of sense, this was due to laziness and

"weakened curiosity." A negative explication invoking lack or powerlessness, as taken by Wagenbach. It is well-known that Kafka makes this sort of negative suggestion to present or to hide the objects of his passion.

12. Kafka, *Letters to Milena*, (New York: Schocken Books, 1953), 58. Kafka's fascination with proper names, beginning with those that he invented: see Kafka, *Diaries*, 11 February 1913 (à propos of the names in *The Judgment*).

13. Kafka commentators are at their worst in their interpretations in this respect when they regulate everything through metaphors: thus, Marthe Robert reminds us that the Jews are *like* dogs or, to take another example, that "since the artist is treated as someone starving to death Kafka makes him into a hunger artist; or since he is treated as a parasite, Kafka makes him into an enormous insect" (*Oeuvres complètes*, Cercle du livre precieux, 5:311). It seems to us that this is a simplistic conception of the literary machine—Robbe-Grillet has insisted on the destruction of all metaphors in Kafka.

14. See, for example, the letter to Pollak in Kafka, *Letters*, 4 February 1902, 1–2.

15. See H. Vidal Sephiha, "Introduction à l'étude de l'intensif," in *Langages* 18 (June 1970): 104–20. We take the term *tensor* from J. F. Lyotard who uses it to indicate the connection of intensity and libido.

16. Sephiha, "Introduction," 107 ("We can imagine that any phrase conveying a negative notion of pain, evil, fear, violence can cast off the notion in order to retain no more than its limit-value—that is, its intensive value": for example, the German word *sehr*, which comes from the Middle High German word, *Ser* meaning "painful").

17. Wagenbach, *Franz Kafka*, 78–88 (especially 78, 81, 88).

18. Kafka, *Diaries*, 15 December 1910, 33.

19. Henri Gobard, "De la vehicularité de la langue anglaise," *Langues modernes* (January 1972) (and *L'Alienation linguistique: analyse tetraglossique*, [Paris: Flammarion, 1976]).

20. Michel Foucault insists on the importance of the distribution between what can be said in a language at a certain moment and what cannot be said (even if it can be *done*). Georges Devereux (cited by H. Gobard) analyzes the case of the young Mohave Indians who speak about sexuality with great ease in their vernacular language but who are incapable of doing so in that vehicular language that English constitutes for them; and this is so not only because the English instructor exercises a repressive function, but also because there is a problem of languages (see *Essais d'ethnopsychiatrie générale* [Paris: Gallimard, 1970], 125–26.

21. On the Prague Circle and its role in linguistics, see *Change*, No. 3 (1969) and 10 (1972). (It is true that the Prague Circle was only formed in 1925. But in 1920, Jakobson came to Prague where there was already a Czech movement directed by Mathesius and connected with Anton Marty who had taught in the German university system. From 1902 to 1905, Kafka followed the courses given by Marty, a disciple of Brentano, and participated in Brentanoist meetings.)

22. On Kafka's connections to Lowy and Yiddish theater, see Brod, *Franz Kafka*, 110–16, and Wagenbach, *Franz Kafka*, 163–67. In this mime theater, there must have been many bent heads and straightened heads.

23. "An Introductory Talk on the Yiddish Language," trans. Ernst Kaiser and Eithne Wilkins in Franz Kafka, *Dearest Father*, (New York: Schocken Books, 1954), 381–86.

24. A magazine editor will declare that Kafka's prose has "the air of the cleanliness of a child who takes care of himself" (see Wagenbach, *Franz Kafka*, 82).

25. "The Great Swimmer" is undoubtedly one of the most Beckett-like of Kafka's texts: "I have to well admit that I am in my own country and that, in spite of all my efforts, I don't understand a word of the language that you are speaking."

Methods and
Other Paradoxes

"Give It Up!"
A Discourse on Method
Heinz Politzer°

"It was very early in the morning, the streets clean and deserted, I was on my way to the railroad station. As I compared the tower clock with my watch I realized it was already much later than I had thought, I had to hurry, the shock of this discovery made me feel uncertain of the way, I was not very well acquainted with the town as yet, fortunately there was a policeman nearby, I ran to him and breathlessly asked him the way. He smiled and said: 'From me you want to learn the way?' 'Yes,' I said, 'since I cannot find it myself.' 'Give it up, give it up,' said he, and turned away with a great sweep, like someone who wants to be alone with his laughter."[1]

This paragraph was discovered among the papers which Franz Kafka left at his death. On its upper left corner the manuscript page shows in faded ink, but unmistakably in Kafka's handwriting, the title "A Commentary." Max Brod published the piece in 1936 calling it: "Give It Up!" Presumably it was written during Kafka's last years.[2]

At first sight it is simple enough. It does not make any extravagant demands on the reader's sensitivity or imagination, nor does it lead to any staggering conclusions. It seems to be self-contained and to say neither more nor less than what it actually says. For this reason it may serve us as an example of Kafka's narrative style. We shall try to determine its form and meaning, then apply some current methods of interpretation to test their validity for this particular text, and finally draw a few conclusions of our own. In the chapters to come there will be ample opportunity to check these conclusions against the evidence offered by Kafka's work at large.

At the outset one must admit that the form of our literary document is somewhat puzzling. It is both a narrative and a statement of truth, although a negative one. Its few lines contain lyrical impressions as well as a dramatic dialogue which is resolved at the end into

°Reprinted from *Franz Kafka: Parable and Paradox*, revised, expanded edition (Ithaca: Cornell University Press). (c) 1962, (c) 1966 by Cornell University. Used by permission of the publisher.

one decisive silent gesture. For the moment one might call the piece an aphorism extended into an anecdote.

The hybrid form of the story is appropriately reflected by the variety of stylistic devices Kafka has brought into play. The first sentence is composed of three short and almost disconnected phrases; its character is determined by monosyllabic words, which occur much less frequently in German than they do in English. The statement it makes is realistic. The early hour of the day explains the clean and empty streets. Undoubtedly the city will be full of noise and dirt once dawn has turned into day, and people have appeared to fill the streets. Nor is there anything conspicuous about the man who is introduced in the first person as "I." One is tempted to feel that he represents the narrator. At the same time he seems to be shy, for it strikes us as a personal trait that he mentions himself only after having described the time and place of the sketch. The early hour provides a good setting for him; we imagine him to be as fresh and lonely as the streets through which he makes his way to the railroad station.

There is no one to accompany him, nor does he mention anyone whom he may leave behind. He does not say why he turns his back on the place, nor does he indicate where he wants to go. We see him before us, but his figure is determined by what we are not told about him rather than by a description dwelling upon his distinctive features. We are able to make a few assumptions about his person; yet they are not based on what he actually is or does but on what he fails to disclose about himself.

The basic structure of the second sentence resembles that of the first except that the number of individual phrases is now greater, which makes the tempo of the whole sequence seem faster. Here the many commas no longer separate the short statements: instead they have the effect of clamping the parts together. The musical cadence of this sentence has a staccato quality. The word "breathlessly" which falls toward its end expresses the character of the whole. Thus the story moves to its climax; we are astonished, however, to notice that even though this sentence marks a turning point in the narrative, it does not abandon reality anywhere. It reports nothing a realist could not have expressed in exactly the same terms. On the other hand, if we probe the sentence for its actual content, we shall see that the words have been chosen in such a way that the reader is forced to focus his attention on what remains hidden behind and below the realistic narrative.

Let us examine this second sentence more carefully. The man compares his watch with a clock in a tower and discovers that he is late. This is an everyday occurrence; yet we feel strangely compelled to ask for the motivation of the wanderer's trivial action. His watch was slow; he must have sensed that he was behind time, or he would have had no reason to check up on it. Here two time systems seem to diverge: the man's personal time which had determined his way, the time which he carries as a watch on his own body and which has become almost as much a part of himself as his own heart, dissociates itself from the impersonal time, which runs its way up on the tower, completely unconcerned with the wanderer and the watch that had been setting his pace. He "had" believed in it. Kafka deliberately chooses the plu-perfect tense to indicate a past now left behind by the man. He starts to run. Now he no longer believes in his personal time; without even the slightest hesitation he accepts the impersonal time as correct. And yet—is it not possible that his personal time was right and that the clock in the tower was too fast?

The fact that the wanderer's watch disagrees with the clock in the tower has led him to what he calls a "discovery": he realizes that it is later than he thought. Because of the urgency of this insight he fails to consult a third watch or to check the time on the clock before he completely surrenders to panicky haste. The reader will sympathize with the man in the anecdote, for he may remember having done the same thing himself. Thus an identification with the man is established which will prevail until the end of the story. It may have been that the wanderer was overcome by the height, the nearness to heaven, of the clock in the tower. More likely than not, however, he was swayed by the mere fact that this clock showed a time outside and beyond himself. Not only is he willing to give precedence to whatever is outside of himself—as the first sentence of the anecdote has already demonstrated—he feels compelled to trust the extrapersonal power of the clock without any further ado. Hence the word *shock*, which breaks through the hitherto smooth surface of the narration with primitive force. The panic causes a second awakening, but this time the man is intellectually awakened. He realizes that his walk is no longer in step with a higher order of things. This realization tempts him to run; yet by running, he loses his way. Or to say it in other words, the attempt to regain the right time by running deprives him of the right direction in space.

At this point of the story we meet the phrase, "I was not very well acquainted with the town." First and foremost it seems to suggest that the narrator is neither a native nor a casual visitor, for in neither case would the problem of familiarity with the town have arisen. The fact that the man was not quite familiar with the city could explain his insecurity. Then his fear of being late would be associated with his fear of being a stranger, and both fears could have been allayed if he had only stayed in the neighborhood long enough to become acquainted with it. "Why don't you know your way?" he seems to be asking himself. "You could have known it better if only you had stayed a little longer."

Again, and this time more urgently, we are asking for the reasons behind the man's departure. The haste to which he has succumbed suggests a possible solution to the puzzle: it was impatience which caused him to leave the city before he had become sufficiently familiar with it. Because of impatience the wanderer was likewise incapable of stopping to check the time again or to contemplate his condition. Instead he surrendered to a panic incommensurate with the simple discovery that his watch was slow. Here is another, deeper motivation for the man's following the clock in the tower instead of his own watch: the fact that the impersonal time of the clock was later than his own time met his innate impatience halfway.

Impatience brings a sigh of relief from the wanderer when he catches sight of the policeman. German uses the words *Polizist* and *Schutzmann* interchangeably; yet here Kafka introduces the policeman deliberately as *Schutzmann*. It is *Schutz* which the man now craves most—protection from the strange city, from the elapsed time, from his own insecurity. Moreover, the policeman has not appeared suddenly, nor did he catch the eye of the running man by mere chance. He was nearby, standing there as if he had been on that very spot since time immemorial and intended to remain there forever. Towering there, the policeman seems to be associated with the tower that holds the clock; like the clock tower he represents a system of order ruling the world outside. And just as the man previously had accepted the "outer" time of the tower, so now he surrenders to the extrapersonal authority of the policeman. He does not stop to think or ask himself what business the officer had in this place at so early an hour. Because the street itself is deserted and free from traffic, a policeman is not needed. Destiny itself has clearly ordered the *Schutzmann* to take up his position at this spot and to protect the man for whom he seems to have been waiting.

The word *fortunately* is intended to express the fact that the man believes he has found again a complete agreement between the reality outside and the sense of direction inside himself; he again sees the relationship between the time shown by the clock in the tower and the way he was afraid he had lost, between a well-ordered world and his position in it. His haste now proves to have been utterly unnecessary. The policeman is to show him the way to the railroad station, the lost time will be regained, and all will end well. Our wanderer now relaxes to the extent that, for the first and only time in the story, he is able to describe himself directly. By calling himself "breathless," he reflects the impression which he is bound to give the policeman. For one split second he sees himself as he must appear to the outside world. Yet in this moment of extraversion he accepts, ironically, the policeman's point of view; from now on he will doubt

the information given him by the official as little as the time revealed to him by the clock.

During this second, fate appears to be favorably inclined toward the hapless wanderer. The policeman smiles. However, the smile immediately assumes a second, ominous meaning by the words which the policeman adds to it. Kafka has formulated the sentence in which this change occurs in a peculiarly skillful way. Its meaning is at first hidden under the policeman's smile, which only later turns out to have been false or at least ambiguous. The discomfort that the change intends to convey arises in the reader only gradually. Some time is needed to realize the strangeness of this information giver who answers a question with a counterquestion: "From me you want to learn the way?" Signposts are meant to point the way, not to raise questions about themselves. Nor can we miss the undertone of arrogance and indignation in the words of the policeman, who puts himself first in his question (in contrast to the man who had hidden himself at the end of the introductory sentence). The "I" of the official towers so forcefully above the "Thou" of the man that we do not realize right away the presumption underlying his words. He actually addresses the man with a "Thou" (*du*), instead of the formal "you" (*Sie*). In German one says *du* to inferiors, to children, or to animals, not to a solid citizen, with whom one conducts an official exchange of words. Putting his Ego before the humiliating "Thou," the policeman downgrades the information seeker.

And yet, are we not falling prey to a deception when we accept the impression the policeman is giving the man? His counterquestion, which is bound to sound like the epitome of unreasonable pride to the ears of the disappointed questioner, may just as well have been prompted by diffidence or uncertainty. The policeman may have resorted to parrying question with question because the answer was not known to him either. He may not have been familiar with this part of the city, may himself have been ignorant of the right way. The ambiguity of his return question may have been a sign of his incompetence, the *du* of his address an attempt to ingratiate himself with the man, for the German *du* also implies human proximity and brotherliness. Again the wanderer is offered an opportunity to deliberate and evaluate the situation confronting him. Again he misses it. Meekly, like a horrified child, he admits his helplessness.

The exchange between man and policeman is restricted to the barest minimum of words. While it is taking place, however, a general change occurs, unnoticeably but undeniably. In the beginning an ordinary man was asking for an ordinary way, but by now it has become clear to us that it could not have been the everyday way to an everyday railroad station which was on the policeman's mind. Although his counterquestion is phrased in the simplest of words, it points to another, more complex meaning of the word "way." It hints at an infinite variety of ways, without pointing them out or making a binding statement about them. After all, what answer could be more noncommittal than a question? Although man and policeman are conversing in the same language, they do not agree on the exact meaning of this one syllable "way." They talk past one another. Nevertheless, it is not impossible that the man, out of submissiveness and self-denial, eventually will make the policeman's deeper and darker idea of the way his own—whatever this idea may be.

Simultaneously the background of the story has changed without, to be sure, resulting in a change of the external scene. Since the way with which the policeman is concerned, cannot possibly be identical with the one sought by the man in reality, the very reality of the street on which the encounter is taking place has begun to dissolve. The setting which we assumed at first to have the three-dimensional quality of a real town has become unreal and intangible. Even the clock tower has disappeared from the story. Thus the man is deprived of his last pointer, and nothing is left to give him direction.

We are now prepared for the words, "Give it up!" with which the information giver finally dismisses the man. The finality of these words is stressed by their being repeated. On the other hand, it could also be that this repetition is due to the policeman's realization of the man's limited understanding: he talks to him as one talks to an infant or a person who is hard of hearing. We remain in the dark about the precise meaning of these syllables, which descend upon the man like a sixfold thunderbolt. What is he being asked to give up? As little as Kafka allows himself to be pinned down with regard to the meaning of the word "way," so little does he enlighten the reader about the intention of the truly impersonal pronoun "it" in "Give it up!"[3] This "it" is so elastic that it can easily be extended to mean the man's unreasonable haste. If this were the case, the policeman would seem to intimate that the man should abandon his breathlessness and impatience, that is, that he should quiet down. Similarly, the "it" may be understood as a reference to the man's travels and wanderings, or his departure in particular. Then the grim warning would have changed its tone completely and have become a friendly invitation encouraging the man to stay in the city, to look around and linger a while until he would know his way better than before. And yet we are already so intensely identified with the man and his way of thinking that we, too, hasten to substitute an "everything" for this "it." "Give everything up!" the policeman seems to be saying, "let all hope go, abandon the way and the desire ever to find it, give up your quest, your drive and your yearning, your very existence—yourself!" He has pronounced this verdict without giving his reasons, without specifying how it should be carried out, without even pronouncing it. He has simply repeated a few syllables, which can mean anything from benevolent advice to the most sinister urge to self-destruction.

The man listens to the verdict in complete silence. He neither questions nor contradicts it and seems to accept it fully. He still notices the "great sweep," with which the official turns away: yet this baroque gesture of the policeman seems even to precipitate the man's disappearance from the scene. The information giver remains silent with a flourish, as it were; thus he avoids giving an answer and shuns, ultimately, his duty. He "turned away. . ., as people do who want to be left alone with their laughter." Kafka uses the present tense here: the policeman's preoccupation with himself is meant to continue as a *praesens infinitum* while the narrator narrates and the reader reads this story.

The policeman returns to his duty, which, whatever it may be, has nothing to do with the claims the man has made upon him. The man has disappeared like the town around him. This statement is, however, only a surmise, unsupported by any textual evidence. By interrupting his narrative at this point, Kafka saves himself the trouble of informing us about the eventual outcome of his story. We are never told whether the man really found his way in the end.

Nor do we find any indication of the outcome in the tone of the story. We cannot decide whether we have been reading a tragic or a grotesquely comic tale. Its scene is plunged in a twilight in which the horrible freely blends with the absurd, and if we are in the right mood, even with the funny. The policeman smiles when his eyes catch the man; the man sees in the information giver a figure of monumental seriousness. The wanderer appears ludicrous to the reader, the official petty, pompous, and awe-inspiring. Yet Kafka does not decide for any one of these conflicting points of view. Instead he forces the reader to change continuously from one to another. Moreover these shifts of perspective occur so quickly that the contrasts are blurred, the opposites merge, and the contradictions are shrouded by all-encompassing ambiguity.

Whoever intends to extract an unequivocal meaning from this story will, like the man who is its central figure, hear a question instead of an answer. The policeman's "Give it up!" is also spoken to those interpreters of Kafka who seem to assume that he believed in existence of only one way leading in one direction to one aim.

Kafka's ultimate evasiveness can be demonstrated by subjecting our anecdote to some of the interpretations which the different approaches of literary criticism would suggest.

Historically the man who wants to leave the city at any cost suffers from acute claustrophobia. "Out of here—this is my aim,"

Kafka exclaims in a story which is the companion piece of our anecdote. As a German Jew in Czech Prague, Kafka lived in a triple ghetto: the Jewish community was encircled by hostile Slavs, who in turn were hemmed in and held down by the Austrian bureaucracy that ruled the city in the name of the Habsburg empire until the revolution of 1918. Also Kafka "was not very well acquainted with the town," even though he was born there. The German language, in which his books are written, separated him from the Czechs. Yet the servants and employees of his father were self-conscious and aggressive Slavs. On the other hand, his Jewish origins kept him estranged from the Austrian upper class, which more often than not indulged in a covert and inconsistent anti-Semitism and administered the city according to the prejudices of the moribund monarchy.

Kafka was not unaware of his relation to history. On January 13, 1921, he wrote Max Brod about his "present inner condition": "It is somewhat reminiscent of Old Austria. To be sure, it went quite well at times, in the evening one would lie on the couch in the nicely heated room. . .and enjoy some measure of peace, but it was only a peace of sorts, and not one's own. Just a trifle, the question of the Trautenau district court, perhaps, was needed to start the throne in Vienna rocking. A dentist's assistant. . .studies in a whisper on the balcony above, and the whole empire—really, the empire in its entirety—suddenly goes up in flames."[4] With this statement in mind, one could interpret the policeman in our story as the representative of an administration that is feared as well as despised. The old order still survives, and although its offices are still functioning, its subjects are unable to obtain any pertinent information, let alone effective protection. The policeman's withdrawal from the man's question could then be understood as Old Austria's admission that she was helpless and incapable of assisting her citizens politically. His retort, "Give it up!" would be the expression of historical apathy, symbolizing he death wish of the Habsburg empire, whose subjects felt that it was doomed to decline. Yet Kafka leaves the relationship between an and policeman, central figure and official, individual and society, vle open. Is our narrator merely a passive victim of the law's delay,e insolence of office? Does not, rather, a hidden rebellion smoulden his insistence on finding the right way in a time out of joint? e fragmentary nature of the anecdote excludes any clear-cut ans. Yet the historical approach enabled one historically minded ir preter (E. B. Burgum) to ascribe pre-Fascist tendencies to Kas heroes,[5] while another, likewise guided by political consideras (Paul Reimann), claimed them as proto-Communists.[6] Posing questions than it is able to answer, the historical approach h tendency to lead interpreters to mutually exclusive extremes. central problem remains untouched by it.

A psychological approach might indicate that our anecdote is first and foremost a case study in neurasthenia. Three times the narrator's nerves fail him: when he discovers that he is late, when he is mystified by the policeman's return question, and when in the end he succumbs to total silence. Age-old anxieties expose him to situations which he does not even try to master—the fear of arriving too late, which, to be sure, is only a thinly veiled fear of death, of losing one's life before one has come to its end and reached his goal. This phobia is accentuated by the horror inflicted upon the man by the policeman's blocking the very way he was supposed to have shown him.

It is possible to see in this fright an allegory of Kafka's childhood experiences, particularly of the role his father played in his upbringing. The long letter he wrote to his father in 1919 offers an abundance of material supporting a psychological interpretation of the story before us. For example, in the letter Kafka wrote, "For me you took on the enigmatic quality that all tyrants have whose rights are based on their person and not on reason"; in the story the policeman rises to a grandeur which stifles all the independent thoughts necessary to solve the enigma. Similarly Kafka wrote to his father, "It sometimes happened that you had no opinion whatsoever about a matter and as a result all opinions that were at all possible with respect to the matter were necessarily wrong, without exception"; the policeman first answers the man with a counterquestion and crushes him finally with the weight of his verdict—which is based on no opinion whatsoever. And finally he wrote, "When I began to do something you did not like and you threatened me with the prospect of failure, my respect of your opinion was so great that the failure then became inevitable";[7] in the story the man yields silently to the inevitable, which Kafka had taken great pains to describe as quite avoidable.

Furthermore, as a dream symbol the policeman would turn into a phallic image, as does the clock tower to which the policeman's symbolic relationship is thus again revealed. Following these associations, the reader might perceive behind the figure of the policeman the immensely inflated dream image of Kafka's father. It would bar the son's way into a life of normalcy, which appears to Kafka more and more as the only possible, the true, way. In letting the father figure pronounce the verdict, "Give it up!" over the son, Kafka might have been expressing doubts regarding his own virility. To be sure, he could write to his father: "Marriage is certainly the guarantee of the most acute form of self-liberation and independence, I should have a family, the supreme thing that one can achieve and so too the supreme thing you have achieved, I should be your equal, all old and everlasting new shame and tyranny would then be a mere history of the past." But then he recoils before the father—just as the man shrinks back from the policeman—when he cries out to him,

"But we being what we are, marrying is barred to me through the fact that it is precisely and particularly your most intimate domain" (DF, 190, 191).

The obvious flaw in this psychological interpretation is the all-too-frequent use it makes of the extraliterary raw material of personal confessions. If the policeman in our anecdote really functions as a dream symbol, a father image expanded to the proportions of a veritable nightmare, why does he still strike the reader with an impersonal, almost universal terror? The psychological interpretation goes a long way in elucidating the origins from which Kafka's visions sprang, but fails to explain their horrible individuality and their equally terrible general appeal. Moreover, it does not clarify the relationship between day and dream, reality and unreality in Kafka's books—it simply reduces the latter to the former. But did our narrator not wake up shortly before setting out on his way through the city? Was this awakening part of his dream? Did it merely open a trap door through which he tumbled from one level of unreality to another, deeper one? On the other hand, does not reality betray its transient and transparent character, that is, its innate unreality, by being exposed to the inexorable dream logic of Kafka's nightmares? Does the abrupt ending of this anecdote, its *fragmentary* character, result from a shocklike transition from the unreality of a dream experience to the rational sphere of reality? Or does Kafka interrupt his narrative because he (and the reader with him) awakened from a bad dream? The text of our anecdote holds no answer to these questions.

If we choose to interpret our story in the light of religion, then the policeman would no longer be a substitute for Kafka's physical father, but a messenger from a spiritual realm. As such, however, he has nothing to communicate to the human sphere but the command to "give it up," whereupon he turns majestically away and minds his own business. His own concerns are so remote from human under-standing that they can only be expressed by the silence following the end of the story. Man's unfamiliarity with his familiar surroundings, his alienation on earth, now acquire a metaphysical meaning. Nameless and yet as clearly allegorical as the Everyman in the mediaeval morality play, the man in our anecdote faces eternity, comparing his watch, the symbol of temporal time, with the clock in the tower, the image of infinity. Kafka knew that the balance between the "inner" time of man and the "outer" time of the universe was seriously disturbed. "The clocks are not in unison," he jotted down in his diary on January 16, 1922; "the inner one runs crazily on at a devilish or demoniac or in any case inhuman pace, the outer one limps along at its usual speed. What else can happen but that the two worlds split apart, and they do split apart, or at least clash in a fearful manner."[8] The time symbolism in this diary entry contradicts the imagery of our anecdote in that there the narrator's "inner" time is slower than the "outer" time of the clock in the tower. And yet the diary version seems truer, at least as far as Kafka and his figures are concerned. For the unbalanced speed of human time stems from a restlessness which drives these figures mercilessly in a metaphysical direction.

We have seen that this restlessness prompted the narrator to depart from the city, caused him to lose his way and to entrust himself to the policeman. Impatience assumes in Kafka's mind an importance almost equal to the weight attributed to original sin in a Christian conscience. "All human errors are impatience," he says in one of his aphorisms, "a premature breaking off of what is methodical, an apparent fencing in of an apparent thing." And still more out-spoken: "There are two main human sins from which all the others derive: impatience and indolence. It was because of impatience that man was expelled from Paradise; it is because of indolence that he does not return. Yet perhaps there is only one major sin: impatience. Because of impatience man was expelled, because of impatience he does not return" (DF, 34). This impatience is of a mystical nature; it was the reason why man once forfeited the divine realm, the very sphere he is now assailing in order to force his reentry. Yet because of this impatience the realm beyond remains forever inaccessible to the human grasp, for the domain of God cannot be taken by storm. From his impatience grows the man's uneasiness in the city as well as his fear of being too late, or rather, that it is too late for him. Impatience causes his anxiety that he will never be on time, that the clock in the tower will never agree with his watch, that no policeman will ever be there to point out the way he is seeking. Thus the misunderstanding between man and policeman is no longer due to semantic differences; it is a last, painfully lingering reminiscence of Paradise Lost. The verdict "Give it up!" reverberates with the echoes of a divine judgment.

In view of such a total alienation of the physical from the meta-physical world, the word *fortunately,* with which the narrator hails the appearance of the policeman, acquires an air of religious irony. For the man, unsheltered and homeless as he finds himself on earth, must consider it an unprecedented stroke of luck to catch even a glimpse of the policeman. The *Schutzmann* is, after all, a security officer and establishes some kind of order in an otherwise disorderly universe. In the end, the policeman deprives him of the security which it should have been his official duty to provide. Bitter sarcasm lies in the fact that the man will never benefit from the fortune his "fortunately" had so boldly and blindly anticipated. But it is a me-taphysical sarcasm, and the whole anecdote represents a statement about a situation in human history in which there is no certainty left to the individual. It depends on the individual's religious orientation whether or not he interprets this uncertainty metaphysically and sees in it a sign of the world's apostasy from its creator. "Is there any connection left at all between a sense and order in the universe and this nonsense, the disorder of the human world?" Martin Buber has asked, with Kafka's stories in mind.[9] Our story does not answer this question.

It is possible to claim the man in our anecdote as an existential hero. Then the policeman would appear as the spokesman of a universe totally unconcerned with the information seeker's personal destiny and radically hostile to him. This universe answers man's claim for direction with an icy silence.

Yet this silence releases the man from any and all obligation. Committed to nobody and nothing, he can easily leave the town. He can turn wherever he pleases; he does not even indicate to which destination the railroad is going to carry him. This is his existential advantage. How does he use it? Shocked by the discrepancy between his existence and the world outside—the comparison of his watch with the clock in the tower—he plays into the hands of the absurd policeman. It is perhaps the gravest symptom of the disorder disrupting Kafka's world that he can no longer distinguish between the social and the metaphysical authorities who govern it. And how could he distinguish between them since they seem united in opposing him?

This central problem has been formulated by Wilhelm Emrich, who asks, "How is it possible to assert the free 'self' amidst all the moving forces of life which converge upon us, in the final analysis, collectively?"[10] Emrich's study is the most thorough analysis of Kafka's imagery that we possess to date. Yet he uses the writer's images as building stones in an elaborate philosophical structure which presupposes that Kafka's "self" is basically free. He sees Kafka's heroes involved in a struggle with life's antinomies which can eventually be overcome, if only by the hero's tragic end. "Only then," Emrich says, "when *everything* is negated, both life with its contradictions and limitations, and the claim for the absolute. . .only then can responsibility be conferred upon the man. . . . Beforehand. . .he submitted to the conditions of life or to an unconditional command. Now he stands above both. Only this is his genuine position."[11] To be sure, Emrich did not have our anecdote in mind when he arrived at this conclusion. But his study so thoroughly integrates all of Kafka's images and ideas into one philosophical pattern that we feel justified in applying it also to the text at hand. Our anecdote, however, knows of the existential freedom stipulated by Emrich only as an opportunity patently missed by the narrator. Perhaps he wanted to grasp it when he started out on his journey, yet he allows himself to be bound—

spell-bound—by any and all restrictions he encounters on his way. The responsibility which the policeman's catastrophic "Give it up!" confers upon him either throws him back and forces him to stay in the place he had wanted to leave, or it advises him to end his way voluntarily rather than be destroyed by fate. The existential freedom to which he is released in the end may very well be tantamount to a freedom *from* all existence, the freedom one finds in death. In no case can we discern the trace of a victory—however hypothetical this victory may be—in the text of our story.

The interpretations so far presented are not mutually exclusive. On the contrary, if they are added together they still do not suffice to exhaust the meaning hidden in the anecdote. For Franz Kafka was incomparably more than a neurotic God-seeker whose whims and quirks were historically conditioned by the intellectual climate of his native country and his era. He was a writer in his own right, a *littérateur* if ever there was one, the creator of word images, interested in their relationships to one another (which, however, he never clearly defined) and to their background (which he was altogether incapable of exploring).

Since he was a border case in the literal meaning of the word, given to analytical thinking as well as to vision, a psychologist as well as a mystic, ambiguity became the very essence of his language. With the help of his imagery he was able to straddle the two realms of his experience: the pseudomythical underworld of his childhood, where the father held sway, and the cryptoreligious universe of his poetic vision, where God reigned in perfect inaccessibility. As the result of an ingrained *double-entendre* Kafka's imagery stands widely exposed to a background spanning both the abysm below and the abysm above, which he sometimes, erroneously, called "heaven."

That his images are endowed with an uncanny persuasiveness and that his epical structures have proved durable beyond his and anybody else's expectation are due to their utter simplicity; like most great documents of literature they reflect the tension between the individual and the universe. To be sure, Kafka refrains from discharging this tension tragically; nor does he dissolve it in the happy ending of a comedy. Yet farcical elements, like the change from smile to sternness on the policeman's face, merge with the stark brutality of a tragic ritual, like the policeman's almost hieratic "great sweep." Nor is this basic tension channeled into the chronological sequences of a conventional tale. Caught in an impressive image, it suddenly bursts on the reader, who, with the shock of recognition, may perceive in it the very condition of man. Thus this tension betrays the inexpressible without expressing it. Ludwig Wittgenstein may have had similar experiences in mind when he remarked in his *Tractatus Logico-*

Philosophicus: "There is indeed the inexpressible. This *shows* itself, it is the mystical."[12] Wittgenstein italicized the word *shows* in order to impress upon the reader his conviction that the mystery of existence may appear but cannot be translated into the logic and grammar of coherent language.

The suddenness with which Kafka's images show themselves frees them from the restrictions and limitations of epical time. They may deal with time, or play with it, but they are not to be measured or judged by the usual processes of time. Our anecdote, too, is set outside the flux of time; being a fragment, it has neither a beginning nor an end. The background into which the fragment opens swallows the time on the man's watch, the time of the clock in the tower, and any time which may have passed between the hour of the wanderer's awakening and his encounter with the policeman.

While the content and the purpose of Kafka's narratives are both ultimately and uniquely ambiguous, their style and structure nonetheless permit some closer exploration. The word *background* has repeatedly emerged in our argument. It is meant to be understood in the sense given it by Erich Auerbach in his book entitled *Mimesis: The Representation of Reality in Western Literature.* In the first chapter Auerbach compares the extensive style employed by Homer in the nineteenth book of the *Odyssey* with the intensive style which distinguishes the account of Isaac's sacrifice, given by the so-called Elohist in the twenty-second chapter of Genesis. He makes the following observation:

> It would be difficult, then, to imagine styles more contrasted than those of these equally ancient and equally epic texts. On the one hand, externalized, uniformly illuminated phenomena, at a definite time and in a definite place, connected together without lacunae in a perpetual foreground; thoughts and feelings completely expressed; events taking place in leisurely fashion and with very little of suspense. On the other hand, the externalization of only so much of the phenomena as is necessary for the purpose of the narrative, all else left in obscurity; the decisive points of the narrative alone are emphasized, what lies between is nonexistent; time and place are undefined and call for interpretation; thoughts and feeling remain unexpressed, are only suggested by the silence and the fragmentary speeches; the whole, permeated with the most unrelieved suspense and directed toward a single goal (and to that extent far more of a unity), remains mysterious and "fraught with background."[13]

To enlarge upon this comparison between the Elohist and Homer, it would be attractive to extend it to a comparison between Franz Kafka and James Joyce, whose *Ulysses* belongs by orientation—and title—in the Homeric tradition. Kafka's monolithic laconism would thus appear as the perfect counterpart of Joyce's mania for rendering the total picture, even the unconscious of the persons depicted. As Joyce's ideal form we could imagine a catalogue so complete as to become unreadable and, by including even the inexpressible, dissolving reality into absurdity; as Kafka's ideal form, a paragraph bursting with the absurdity of existence.[14] Yet even if we concentrate on the interpretation of our anecdote, we cannot fail to observe that Auerbach's characterization of the Elohist contributes considerably to our understanding of Kafka's style. From its beginning the anecdote has been calling for interpretation. The man's awakening, his walk through the early morning, the comparison of his watch with the clock in the tower, are told in such a fashion that they seem to be the last visible signs of invisible chain reactions which originate in the unknown, the not-knowable.

There is not one self-explanatory word in a typical Kafka narrative. His mature prose shows nothing but a surface spread over happenings that remain profoundly impenetrable. Paradoxically this enables Kafka, the visionary, to furnish his stories amply with realistic detail. Since even the inanimate objects he describes point to an undefined and mysterious background, they no longer relate to one another according to the customs and conventions of reality. Clefts, cracks, and crevices open, revealing the depth behind the realistic detail. The same is true of the figures acting on a stage thus prepared. Ostensibly most of them are well grounded in reality, even in the reality of Kafka's own life. Sometimes he provided them with assonances of his own name and other hints of his own biography, even if he didn't wish to introduce them simply as "I," as he does in the anecdote before us. Consequently, we are tempted to interpret the wanderer as Kafka. Yet the opposite may be true. The man in our story may be an image rather than the more or less true likeness of the author. For throughout these stories we are not dealing with portrayals of actual beings but rather with code ciphers conveying indecipherable messages, pawns in a game of chess played by invisible hands and obeying a master mind totally incomprehensible to them as well as to us. By calling this man "I," Kafka committed consciously, purposefully, and, we dare say, mischievously an "intentional fallacy."[15]

It is more than probable that he even shaped the "I" which expresses itself in his letters and diaries after the model of the heroes in his books—one more reason to be careful in the use of this biographical material for the interpretation of his literary writings. Instead of lifting the material of his books out of the shapeless mass of his life experiences, he may very well have lived his life as if it were one of his writings. Stylizations of this kind are not infrequent in modern literature, which to such a large extent describes the decomposition of human identity and substitutes literary symbols for it. We need only remember Dostoyevsky's diaries and Rilke's letters to realize that this literary treatment of biographical data has become a major preoccupation of modern writers in general. By the same token we shall have to admit the general unreliability of these personal documents as far as the discovery of the man behind the mask, the writer behind the writing, is concerned. Although it is impossible to disregard them, Kafka's diaries, conversations, letters, and aphorisms have to be treated with extreme circumspection and tact. The information they contain is tenuous and, more often than not, misleading. We cannot identify a reflected image by reflecting it in a second mirror.

We shall not be able to say much more about Kafka's figures than that they too are congenitally and intimately connected with their background. The background penetrates their words, determines their attitudes, and fills up their silences. This again makes them late descendants of the figures in the text of the Elohist. Even they, Auerbach notes, "can be represented as possessing 'background,' " more background, in any case, than Homer's heroes, for they

> have greater depths of time, fate, and consciousness. . ., though they are nearly always caught up in an event engaging all their faculties, they are not so entirely immersed in its present that they do not remain continually conscious of what has happened to them earlier and elsewhere; their thoughts and feelings have more layers, are more entangled. Abraham's actions are explained not only by what is happening to him at the moment, nor yet only by his character. . ., but by his previous history; he remembers, he is constantly conscious of, what God has promised him and what God has already accomplished for him—his soul is torn between desperate rebellion and hopeful expectation, his silent obedience is multilayered, has background.[16]

The man in our story resembles the Abraham of the Elohist in that his person is likewise both impersonal and more than personal: he is nameless as well as representative. His face is a complete blank, and yet it reminded us of Everyman. Similarly his actions cannot be explained by the events that actually occur, but by reasons hidden both below the threshold of his consciousness and beyond the frame of reference of what is actually told in his story. He too is suspended between hope and despair, indignation and expectation; and the silence in the end is so multilayered that we are unable to state with any degree of assurance whether it indicates his end and not, perhaps, a new beginning. Completely absorbed in his meeting with the policeman, the man experiences at the same time a meeting with powers which seem to draw him back to his childhood and, further still, to the unfathomable recesses of the memories of his race. Since, however, time seems to be suspended with regard to everything Kafka wrote, his narratives also point forward, to the future.

Kafka died in 1924. The generations that followed have frequently recognized their own destiny in the seemingly unreal fate of his heroes. In his fantastic visions he anticipated the Waste Land as the landscape of modern man. There he lives unsheltered and totally exposed to a regimen fraught with horror and imbued with nonsense. The *Schutzmann* who substitutes condemnation for protection is as contemporary an image as the man who wanders without knowing his way.

But here the parallels with the Elohist end. Biblical Abraham is open to a background replete with the presence of his God. He remembers Him when he accepts the unintelligible command to slaughter his firstborn son. His promise fills Abraham's consciousness even when he prepares for the sacrifice. The certainty of this belief not only connects Abraham with his background, it is identical with it. The background of Kafka's man, on the other hand, consists of a darkness symbolizing the complete absence of any such certainty. It is an eclipse of God, a *Gottesfinsternis,* like the one conjured up in a poem (1935) by Kafka's sometimes admired, sometimes scorned, friend and fellow countryman, Franz Werfel:

> Even from the heaven of your day
> Hangs suddenly God's eclipse. . .
>
> From the horizon, icy-grained
> The charging storm engulfs your house.
> All trees have eery shadows
> The like were never seen before.
> The leaves hang flabby and swollen
> Like soggy fruit that grew too big.
> The waters in the reed beyond
> Gurgle out a gruesome dialect. . .
>
> But insectlike
> You quite forgot the former light
> And give not one astonished moment
> To the distorted picture of the world
> And to its frozen heartless waste.
>
> At least be shocked and startled
> When the bats aroused at day
> Dash against your window in despair!
>
> (Auch an dem Glaubenshimmel deines Tages
> Hängt plötzlich Gottesfinsternis. . .
>
> Von Horizonten hagelt Sturmangriff
> Eishältig dir ums Haus.
> Die Bäume alle werfen
> So fremde Schatten, wie man nie gesehn.
> Die Blätter hängen schlaff

Und aufgeschwemmt gleich überwachsnen Früchten.
Das Wasser selbst im Rohr
Vergurgelt schauerlichen Dialekt. . .

Du aber hast
Insektenhaft das einstige Licht vergessen
Und schenkst dem ganz zerzognen Bild der Welt
Und ihrer Herzerfrorenheit
Nicht einen Augenblick Verwunderung.

Erschrick doch wenigstens,
Daß die am Tag erwachten Fledermäuse
Verzweifelt sich an deine Fenster werfen![17]

A lyrical paraphrase may be called for where textual analysis has proved unsatisfactory. Werfel's "completely distorted image of the world" holds all the realism Kafka ever attained in the description of his world. In the poem this distorted image is linked to the frozen heart of creation. But neither Werfel nor Kafka establish the principle of cause and effect between the emptiness of the heart and the disfiguration of the world outside. They simply mention one symptom after the other *as if* they belonged together. There is no light in this world, and yet the shadows deepen. The sun, the central source of life, has disappeared; certain forms stand out in a twilight produced by other, unnamed sources. Inanimate objects change their shape and function: leaves turn into fruit as, conversely, fruit may turn into leaves, thus rendering nature fruitless. Water speaks a dialect, like man, but it is an idiom which spreads horror before the trickle dries up and ends in silence. Man is like an insect; yet he is not, like a moth, attracted by the light but forgetful of it. Nocturnal bats join forces with the elements of nature to attack the last stronghold of man, his house, which is as empty and as frail as his heart.

Again, the border line between the inner and the outer world is extinguished, as is the difference between day and night. The background advances to envelop and engulf it all. Werfel differs from Kafka merely in calling this background by its name, *Gottesfinsternis.* Kafka, however, kept silent. All that Kafka ever wrested from the silence surrounding him was the insight "that the incomprehensible is incomprehensible, and this we knew already." The phrase is taken from a longer aphorism with the revealing title, "On Parables."[18]

The anecdote about the man and the policeman is such a parable about the incomprehensibility of the incomprehensible. It culminates in the policeman's "Give it up!" in which the incomprehensible asserts its intention to remain obscure. The tradition of his family's religion, the Jewish belief, exerted on Kafka an aftereffect still strong enough to suggest to him hidden depths of existence and powers holding sway beyond man's life. The policeman is nearby. Yet these extra-human powers cannot be asked for information, let alone assistance. They vanish before man's grasp. The policeman turns away, as people do who want to be left alone. The parable merely leads in the direction of these powers like a bridge dissolving in mist before it has reached the bank on the other side.

The command "Give it up!" reveals to the man the dilemma of his existence. Yet Kafka did not try to solve this dilemma, nor to translate it into any doctrinal message. He simply stated it with all the strength he could muster from the weakness of a man born late in the development of his civilization. His parables are as multilayered as their Biblical models. But, unlike them, they are also multifaceted, ambiguous, and capable of so many interpretations that, in the final analysis, they defy any and all. Like literary Rorschach tests they reveal the characters of the interpreters rather than their own.

Yet, taken by itself, the "Give it up!" of the policeman is a paradox, since it represents the only information given by an official whose task consists in giving information. Such a paradox will be generated wherever the natural and the supernatural meet, that is, when a message which is inaccessible to ordinary verbalization is to be translated into the vernacular of reasonable and generally intelligible communication. Kierkegaard already had recognized this function of the paradox when in *Fear and Trembling* he expressed the remoteness of his God by retelling the sacrifice of Isaac in a set of highly paradoxical parables. But he was still commenting upon a text to which he was committed by his belief, whereas Kafka turned the paradoxical parable into an independent literary genre.

Generally speaking, Kafka's parables center on their paradox, just as our anecdote revolves around the policeman's verdict. Circling around this nucleus, they maintain a suspense originating in the never-defined relation their actual plots maintain with their backgrounds. Only when the narrative stops to reveal its essentially fragmentary character will this background be thrown into bold relief. Otherwise it is reflected and refracted by an abundance of ambiguous word images. Thus imagery as well as background appear as expressions of the narrator's incapability of saying what these parables have been meant to say in the beginning. Franz Kafka's importance derives from the fact that he was probably the first and certainly the most radical writer to pronounce the insoluble paradox of human existence by using this paradox as the message of his parables. Therefore, any interpretation of his work will have to return to the text itself:

"It was very early in the morning, the streets clean and deserted, I was on my way to the railroad station. As I compared the tower clock with my watch I realized that it was already much later than I had thought, I had to hurry, the shock of this discovery made me feel uncertain of the way, I was not very well acquainted with the town as yet, fortunately there was a policeman nearby, I ran to him and breathlessly asked him the way. He smiled and said: 'From me you want to learn the way?' 'Yes,' I said, 'since I cannot find it myself.' 'Give it up, give it up,' said he, and turned away with a great sweep, like someone who wants to be alone with his laughter."

Notes

1. Franz Kafka, *Description of a Struggle*, trans. Tania and James Stern (New York: Schocken Books, 1958) 201. All future references to this work will be cited in text as *DS*.

2. Klaus Wagenbach *(Franz Kafka, Die Erzählungen* [Frankfurt: Fischer, 1961], 417–19) dates the piece between November and December 1922. References to this chronology are hereafter cited as "Wagenbach."

3. In the German original this "it" is even more obscure: there the pronoun "*es*" has been reduced to the letter *s*, which is fused with the imperative *gib* to "*Gibs auf!*" where "it" becomes almost inaudible.

4. Franz Kafka, *Briefe 1902–1924* (Frankfurt: Fischer, 1958; New York; Schocken Books, 1958), 288–89.

5. "The Bankruptcy of Faith," *The Kafka Problem*, ed. Angel Flores (New York: New Directions, 1946), 298–318.

6. "Die gesellschaftliche Problematik in Kafkas Romanen," *Weimarer Beiträge IV (1957):* 598–618.

7. *Franz Kafka, Dearest Father*, trans. Ernst Kaiser and Eithne Wilkins (New York: Schocken Books, 1954), 145, 152. All future references to this work will be cited in text as *DF*.

8. Franz Kafka, *The Diaries of Franz Kafka 1914–1923*, ed. Max Brod, trans. Martin Greenberg and Hannah Arendt (New York: Schocken Books, 1949), 202. All future references to this work will be cited in text as *DII*.

9. "Schuld und Schuldgefühle," *Merkur*, XI (1957): 722.

10. *Franz Kafka* (Bonn: Athenäum, 1958), 308.

11. "Franz Kafkas Bruch mit der Tradition und sein neues Gesetz," in *Protest und Verheissung* (Bonn: Athenäum, 1960), 243–44.

12. *Tractatus Logico-Philosophicus* (New York: Harcourt, 1933), 6.522.

13. *Mimesis: The Representation of Reality in Western Literature* (Garden City: Doubleday Anchor, 1957), 9.

14. A further example may be helpful to clarify the difference between "foreground" and "background" in modern fiction. When Thomas Mann, in 1939, delivered an introductory speech to his *The Magic Mountain* before the students of Princeton University, he felt compelled to defend his book against the idea that it was a social novel. "The critique of the sanitarium and its therapeutical methods is foreground, one of the foregrounds in a book the very essence of which is fraught with background" *(Der Zauberberg* [Frankfurt: Fischer, 1958], p. xii). Thereupon he proceeded to acclaim some critics who had interpreted his novel as an "initiation story" and a "quester legend." Mann's self-interpretation cannot be discussed here any further. Suffice it to say that he too chose the term "background" when he wished to indicate that his work was constructed on a level higher than reality.

15. W. K. Wimsatt, *The Verbal Icon* (Lexington: University of Kentucky Press, 1954), especially 3–18.

16. *Mimesis*, 9–10.

17. Franz Werfel, *Schlaf und Erwachen* (Berlin: Zsolnay, 1935), 110. For the English version of the poem, I am indebted to Professor Peter Salm, of Wesleyan University, Middletown, Conn.

18. Franz Kafka, *The Great Wall of China*, trans. Willa and Edwin Muir (New York: Schocken Books), 258.

Woman as the Obstacle and the Way

Larysa Mykyta*

Trial and. . .*Castle*, works that were both written under the provocation of the strangeness of the feminine.

—Maurice Blanchot, *L'Amitié*

The Trial and The Castle are steeped in sexuality and eroticism. They literally proliferate with women. Very few events, in either text, proceed without some kind of female involvement—either marginal (in the shadows, in neighboring rooms, in antechambers, on stairs, behind doors in *The Trial*) or central (the case of Frieda, Olga and the landlady in *The Castle*). This seeming obsession with women is paralleled in Kafka's life, which is filled with many intense and troubled relationships with women: Felice Bauer, Julie Wohryzek, Milena, Dora Diamant as well as Miss Bloch, an unknown woman from Zuckmantel, and an adolescent from Riva. The close attachments Kafka forms to women sometimes lead to formal engagements, which are then invariably broken, whereupon Kafka makes efforts to renew the interrupted relations.

Numerous passages in Kafka's *Diaries* and in his correspondence support the conviction that these disruptive involvements are profoundly bound up with writing, with the conflict between life and writing that haunted Kafka's existence. For on the one hand Kafka was convinced that he existed and could continue to exist only as a writer, as writing itself.[1] Therefore he continually sought the solitude that would enable him to totally devote himself to that activity. In that situation contact with women, indeed any human contact, would trouble that solitude and would threaten Kafka's very existence. On the other hand, Kafka viewed writing as damnation because it placed him outside of life, outside the law of the Father (whether religious or familial) and so outside of salvation in this world, a salvation for which he also incessantly strove and that he could best attain through

*Reprinted by permission of The Johns Hopkins University Press from *MLN*, vol. 95, 1980.

marriage. Thus any human contact, but especially contact with women, simultaneously presented an obstacle to an activity that incarnated the very essence of Kafka's life yet, from a slightly different standpoint, constituted the way of his salvation.

It is tempting to regard the prevalence of women in Kafka's fiction as a simple reflexion, repetition, or representation of his relationships in life. His texts, however, do not permit such a reading. Instead they disclose a much more ambiguous and tangled relationship between women and writing. They do this by revealing a complex and enigmatic perception of women that has radical consequences for the concept of literature itself.

At the outset in Kafka's texts women seem to be treated as expendable sexual entities to be used, discarded and forgotten. This is particularly blatant in *The Trial* where women are exchanged with amazing ease. Joseph K. visits his sweetheart Elsa, then conducts short flirtations with Frau Bürstner and the usher's wife and finally has a longer, more passionate, but ultimately unsuccessful liaison with Leni, lawyer Huld's companion-mistress-nurse. All the women except Elsa offer Joseph K. both help with his case and sexual favors. The women in *The Castle* are no longer exchanged but their attractiveness seems for the most part to be created by their connections to the Castle. This impression is strengthened since even women value themselves largely in relation to that allegedly central structure of authority. In spite of the fact that officials treat them in a brutal preemptory manner[2] Olga claims that women cannot help loving the officials who pay attention to them (*Castle*, 256) cannot help feeling that this attention is an honor to be prized. Only Amalia outrightly rebels against being used, rejecting the rapacious demand Sortini makes on her and seemingly severing her possible ties with the Castle. If K. is nonetheless interested in her and Olga it is mainly because of what he perceives as their brother's importance as a messenger to and from the Castle, an importance that even he admits is only minimal.

K.'s reaction to Pepi when she becomes Frieda's replacement in the taproom demonstrates the nature of the attraction exerted by anything even remotely linked to the Castle:

> And yet, in spite of her childish mind, she too, apparently, had connections with the Castle; if she was not lying, she had been a chambermaid; without being aware of what she possessed she slept through the days here, and though if he took this tiny plump, slightly round-backed creature in his arms he could not extort from her what she possessed, yet that could bring him in contact with it and inspirit him for his difficult task. Then could her case now be much the same as Frieda's? Oh no, it was different. One had only to think of Frieda's look to know that. K. would never have

touched Pepi. All the same, he had to lower his eyes for a little
now, so greedily was he staring at her. (*Castle*, 131)

Clearly K. is strongly attracted to Pepi only because of her contact
with the Castle, however unconscious, indirect, or ephemeral it might
be. His attraction for Frieda, however, is fraught with ambiguity since
it is not clear why her case is different from Pepi's: she may be more
desirable because her connections with Klamm, the focal point of
K.'s interest, are stronger or because desire for her is no longer
dependent on or governed by considerations pertaining to the Castle.
This ambiguity is present from the first encounter with Frieda. She
is described by K. as an "unobtrusive little girl with fair hair, sad
eyes, and hollow cheeks, but with a striking look of conscious superiority" (*Castle*, 46–47). Later he adds that she has a scrawny body
covered with oddly fitting clothes (*Castle*, 48). Except for the "look
of conscious superiority" these descriptions contain nothing that would
render Frieda particularly seductive physically. Furthermore K. asks
her to be his sweetheart only after she has disclosed that she is
Klamm's mistress. Her fairly indifferent physical appearance, combined with the temporal sequence of K.'s declaration of love, seem
to indicate that Frieda's attractiveness lies in her relationship with a
Castle official. However, when Klamm calls Frieda, K. cannot force
himself to encourage her to respond positively for he feels that "in
letting Frieda go he would lose all he had" (*Castle*, 54–55). In this
case a reversal takes place whereby the woman seems highly valued
in spite of her rejection of a Castle contact.

The ambiguity with regard to the causes of Frieda's seductiveness
is only one of the many conditions that make it impossible to reduce
the total significance of the strange and all-pervasive sexual atmosphere found in *The Trial* and *The Castle* to the banal truth that women
function only as means for attaining the goals that the protagonists
are trying to reach. It begins to demonstrate that the feminine cannot
be so easily dismissed because both texts deny and contradict, even
as they seem to affirm, a simple conception of women.

The image of woman as a controllable and useful entity is considerably weakened when it is shown to be simply the product of a
desire—a wish. Joseph K.'s recurring fantasy is that every woman's
"supple, voluptuous warm body. . .belonged to K. and to K. alone."[3]
But that desire is never fulfilled. Joseph K. never possesses Frau
Bürstner as he is convinced he will. Leni and the usher's wife "betray"
him by letting themselves be "seduced" by other men. And K. loses
Frieda to one of the assistants although he desperately wants to keep
her.

The female's dependability as a useful connection to the Courts
or Castle is also undermined in Kafka's two major texts by putting

into question the possible power of a sexual connection to the centers of authority. Sexual connections to these centers are highly prized but the power that they provide again is only determined by K.'s interpretations of a specific situation. When K. asks the landlady how she came to own the inn, she tells him that her husband's family gave it to the couple at a very low price and demanded absolutely no security. K. claims that the family must have been very anxious to be connected with the landlady if they gave the inn to the couple knowing that the husband was not a good worker and not yet aware of the landlady's immense capacity for work. He immediately presumes that their attitude was due to Klamm's influence, which would have yielded even better results had Klamm been explicitly asked to wield it. The landlady denies the truth of these conjectures by adamantly maintaining that a liaison with Klamm can produce no positive results because "Anybody that he stops summoning he has forgotten completely, not only as far as the past is concerned, but literally for the future as well" (*Castle*, 108). Similarly in *The Trial* it is implied that Leni's influence could be of significant consequence in the outcome of K.'s case whereas in fact its effects are rather limited and perhaps even damaging—Leni insists that K.'s only chance lies in confessing to guilt (*Trial*, 135).

In Kafka's fiction women also resist being reduced to unofficial connective stepping-stones to the Castle or Courts, because female sexuality is something that can neither be avoided nor manipulated at will. Its frequent appearances are not accidental. Female sexuality is always already a part of the Courts or the Castle: " 'You see, everything belongs to the Court' " (*Trial*, 188), says Titorelli in reference to the depraved and prematurely debauched young girls hanging about his studio. That women belong to such centers of authority as the Castle or Courts serves precisely to display the continual subversion of their power as governing centers that guarantee hierarchical differences. As sexual beings women contain the impurity and aberrance that erupts in what is ultimately seen as purity and absolute truth.[4] Sexual contact takes place in dirt and darkness— under tables, on floors, in puddles of beer. Sexuality appears at unexpected and improper moments—Frau Bürstner suggestively caresses her hip when Joseph K. speaks to her about his case. It is lewd and irregular like the pornography that K. finds instead of law books in the Court Offices. The usher's wife and Leni resemble prostitutes in their indiscriminate availability, as do Olga and Pepi in relation to the servants of the Herrenhof. The very physical presence of the usher's wife at K.'s first interrogation provokes a disturbance in the proceedings. And it is a disturbance definitely sexual in nature—a man shrieks as he violently embraces a woman in the corner (*Trial*, 58). The presence of women also has a disruptive power that endangers the uniqueness of the power of central authority. Pepi implies that Frieda's influence, indeed her command, prevented Klamm from coming to the Herrenhof when she was no longer there (*Castle*, 395). Although K. rejects this interpretation, it is perfectly in accord with Frieda's exceptional status—she is not punished for her "crime" of refusing Klamm's summons, and when she leaves K. she is reinstated to her former position in the taproom.

At this point it becomes apparent that there is a great discrepancy between what the protagonists and women in Kafka's works want women to be and what they actually "are." What does constitute the identity of women, however, is more difficult to specify. Their relation to impurity gives a glimpse of the enigma that their nature simultaneously conceals and displays. For they are no more impure than they are outside the power structures of the Castle and Courts. In spite of the fact that Kafka's works present sexuality as a phenomenon that is always unfitting and unsuitable regardless of time and place, none of the women ever shows evidence of guilt or shame. Lack of guilt does not, however, necessarily presuppose innocence. For this want of guilt is the outcome of the inability to determine guilt or innocence. "Whether she was at fault now or not, one could not tell" (*Trial*, 58), K. says about the washerwoman who disturbs the Court proceedings. Thus, just as forming a part of the authority of the Courts and Castle puts into question the very possibility of their authority, so too women's non-culpability invalidates the opposition of the categories pure/impure in reference to them. The non-culpability of the female characters appears to position them in a space beyond those particular categories and perhaps beyond all oppositions. Women, in other words, escape the rigidity of fixed molds, of definite predications—they appear to be undefinable.[5]

A more profound examination of the question posed by the essence of women will reveal a complex play of attitudes toward authority, power, property, death and literature (writing). In disrupting K.'s perception of the Castle or Courts as governing centers (whether interpreted as literature or as death),[6] women betray and contradict the protagonists' expectations and thereby focus attention on the non-central and elusive nature of these structures. For the Castle and Courts are both presented as lacking a central ordering power and as lacking it precisely as written structures. Olga describes the activity in the Castle as being essentially textual. This textuality negates the existence of any governing Logos, of any original text or authority that would guarantee the truth of all subsequent texts and function as a universal ordering principle (*Castle*, 233).

The writing activity which goes on in the Castle has no logical order. The messages that occasionally leave the Castle do not seem to fulfill any "real" communicative functions and are not relevant to any "real" events in time and space. Thus, letters that are supposedly from Klamm to K. are left lying for indefinite periods of time in piles of other written material. The letters are ignored until a clerk, with no previous directions from Klamm, suddenly decides to give them to Barnabas who, after another time lag, during which his sister nags him to do his duty, finally delivers them to K (*Castle*, 234–35). The contents of the letters are at best enigmatic and at worst totally absurd—one of the letters that K. receives praises him for surveying work he has never done. The textual activity of the Courts also undermines the possibility of any ultimate and coherent ordering principle. Cases are composed of vast accumulations of written materials that circulate endlessly without any hope of obtaining a final decision about them. Only ostensible acquittal and indefinite postponement of a case exist. Definite acquittal is only a legend (*Trial*, 163, 164, 165); power to grant it is reserved "for the highest Court of all, which is quite inaccessible to you, to me, and to all of us. What the prospects are up there we do not know. . ." (*Trial*, 197–98). The only way the protagonists can maintain the illusion that their goals are attainable is to force women into subordinate positions in relation to the Courts or Castle, positions from where they can no longer exert a disruptive influence. Joseph K. implicitly admits the importance of dominating women when he recognizes, as the usher's wife is carried away from him, that "this was the first unequivocal defeat that he had received from these people" (*Trial*, 73). The defeat lies in his inability to control female sexuality, the inability to situate it outside the Court as a useful tool in the amelioration of his case. Similarly K. refuses to accept Pepi's description of Frieda's power or the landlady's description of the official's forgetfulness. His acceptance would necessitate admitting that women could not be reduced to influential connections, admitting that the truth of the protagonists' perceptions and interpretations of the Castle and Courts were open to question. Hence it is clear that in Kafka's texts women do not really present obstacles in the attainment of the goal of literature as they do in his life, but that by their very nature they demonstrate that unattainability is an essential attribute of the protagonists' goals, be they literature or death.

There is another aspect of the lack of control over female sexuality that does present a threat to the fulfillment of the protagonists' wishes in much the same way that women are seen to threaten Kafka's wishes regarding the pursuit of literary activity. Ultimately, however, this resemblance proves to be deceptive. Through their sexuality women not only taint the uncorruptibility of the Castle and Courts as origins of authority, but they also exert the powerful fascination of "temptations of the flesh." In Kafka's short parable "The Silence of the Sirens" the force of this female allurement is symbolized in almost

superhuman terms through the image of the Siren. The strength of
the fascination that women generate explains why the protagonists
always enlist the help of *women* in their struggles with Castle and
Courts. The temptations that women incite divert the protagonists
from their goals or they impede the procedures that would allegedly
result in the attainment of those goals. Thus, Leni diverts Joseph K.
from serious official efforts to win his case either by physically dis-
tracting him during his conversations with lawyer Huld or by making
him sacrifice these conversations altogether for a few hours of sensual
pleasure. And Frieda proposes that K. totally abandon his goals when
she suggests that if K. and she are to really belong to each other,
they must leave the village and the Castle and go to some other
country—France or Spain (*Castle*, 180).

   With this suggestion she exposes a vitally important new dimension inherent to the problem of the pleasures of the flesh. By intro-
ducing the only reference to an extratextual reality to be found in
The Castle she makes possible the equation of the sensual with the
worldly. This equation is echoed in the text on the Sirens. Siren-
women "seduce by their *presence*, which can be articulated either
by song or by silence; and they are like the material and sensual
world fiendishly attractive and attractively fiendish."[7] If women in
their sexuality represent the snares of the world, however, then this
implies that they are obstacles to ends that are "not of this world."
This is particularly evident if taken in conjunction with Kafka's parable
about the Sirens. In a sense the text on the Sirens perfectly displays,
in a very condensed form, the nature of the issues at stake at the
heart of the mysterious relation between the protagonists and women.
Within the context of the Homeric epic a confrontation with the
monster-women is inevitable. It is obvious, however, that Odysseus
could have neutralized the dangers of his encounter by filling his
ears with wax as did the sailors but that he wanted to experience
and vanquish this perilous yet fascinating attraction. In Kafka's parable
the danger that these strange women represent is completely overcome by incorporating them into an abstract and visionary sphere—
Odysseus fixes his gaze on the distant horizon and ceases to be
conscious of the Sirens.[8] It could be said that women represent the
real world that must be confronted and then dismissed in order to
produce literature, while literature itself becomes an ideal presence
or the presence of an ideal and transcendent reality. Thus, at first,
Odysseus seems to achieve what neither of the protagonists in *The
Trial* and *The Castle* will be able to attain—he manages to experience
but not fall victim to the snares of the world, to conquer the sensual
strangeness of women, making it disappear on the backdrop of an
other-worldly horizon. In Kafka's texts the goal as literature—as that

which is outside of life—becomes in its opposition to worldliness the other life, the life of salvation.

It soon becomes apparent, however, that Kafka's parable itself, written earlier than *The Trial* and *The Castle*, already indicates that Odysseus' victory over the Sirens is perhaps not possible, that the position of the protagonists in the two longer texts is, from the beginning, unavoidable. For the protection that wax provides against the song of the Sirens is presented as an illusory one: "Naturally any and every traveler before him could have done the same, except those whom the Sirens allured even from a great distance; but it was known to all the world that such things were of no help whatever. The song of the Sirens could pierce through everything, and the longing of those they seduced would have broken far stronger bonds than chains and masts. But Ulysses did not think of that, although he had probably heard of it. He trusted absolutely to his handful of wax and his fathom of chain. . . . ("Silence of the Sirens," 430–31). Odysseus succeeds only as a result of a blind faith in his own devices and in a beyond. Other solutions are judged to be beyond human comprehension—miracles ("Silence of the Sirens," 432). Odysseus' victory then becomes an unprobable exception in a world in which all men must suffer captivation by female sexuality but where all subjugation of it is deceptive. Hence the text on the Sirens also demonstrates, almost in spite of itself, that women as sexual entities can neither be reduced to objects nor controlled but that they must nonetheless be confronted. It becomes clear that salvation as a goal is no more reachable than were the goals in *The Trial* and *The Castle*.

The text on the Sirens also clarifies why the very presence/essence of woman is a threat, why women by definition must inevitably frustrate the protagonists' wishes and why the protagonists, who so insistently seek women out, nevertheless consistently reject them. For the figures of the Sirens emphasize that woman's song, the song of her body, her attraction and desirability is destructive and deadly: "The Seirenes will sing his mind away on their sweet meadow lolling. There are bones of dead men rotting in a pile beside them and flayed skins shrivel around the spot."[9] The seductive power of women lies, then, in the invitation to the ultimate serenity of death that is concealed within sensuality, within the material "unconscious" of the real world. The insidiousness of this menace surfaces most clearly in K.'s description of his first sexual encounter with Frieda: "There hours went past, hours in which they breathed as one, in which their hearts beat as one, hours in which K. was haunted by the feeling that he was losing himself or wandering into a strange country, farther than ever man had wandered before, a country so strange that not even the air had anything in common with his native air, where one might die of strangeness, and yet whose enchantment was such that one could only go on and lose oneself further" (*Castle*, 54). This passage is lyrical in quality and couched in terms of a traditionally romantic vision of union with the beloved that universalizes the experience so that its effects apply to all women. A closer examination, however, discloses that the serene romantic framework conceals a threat of death in much the same way as do the Sirens. One cannot after all lose oneself except by dying or going mad. Thus the serenity with which women seduce, and which is so attractive, hides the abyss, ultimately reveals the non-existence embodied in the "presence" of women. And in becoming the living embodiment of that which is outside of life, woman has become the very image of the goals the protagonists are seeking—literature and/or death. Coming full circle through a series of slippages and displacements, woman moves from being an obstacle to literature to being a way of salvation, albeit unattainable, as literature for she can no longer be differentiated from that which she seemed originally to stand in the way of.

K.'s struggle against the feeling of comfort that Olga gives him as he walks leaning his weight on her (*Castle*, 43) is a struggle against the intense danger posed by the tranquillity that a woman can provide. Whenever K. rejects a woman's pleas for a loving union or tries to give women a solely instrumental value, he is rejecting woman's presence as absence and is attempting to eliminate all traces of the knowledge that a woman is impossibility or perhaps literature itself. K. refuses to see woman as a disruptive element which incessantly disturbs any unity from within without destroying it. He chooses instead to see her only as a step on the road toward the absolute presence and possibility of his goal of writing and/or death.

"The Metamorphosis" develops more fully the woman's essential and dual role in the presentation of literature (writing) and death as unreachable abysmal goals for the questing subject. The complex entity that women in general represent in *The Trial* and *The Castle* is divided into the separate figures of the mother and the sister in Kafka's short story. The mother represents the possibility of salvation; in this case salvation from writing. She holds out the hope that Gregor as the monstrous bug, as the "distorted metaphor," the unrepresentable[10] can still exercise a useful and salutary activity within the realms of the family and language. She tries to treat Gregor the monster as if he were nothing but her son—opposes emptying his room of furniture for fear that he will miss it. However, she cannot bear to look at him, at his monstrosity, cannot bear to see him as he is. The sister, almost from the outset, ministers to the needs of her brother as vermin—brings him garbage to eat, clears his room of furniture so that he can move freely over the walls. She rejects any possibility that Gregor could still be accommodated within the family (or within discourse). Gregor's readiness to attack her in order to protect his picture of the fur-clad lady is the last energetic attempt on his part to remain within the confines of the ordinary world of power and language.[11]

The very possibility of integration with the family is destroyed when Gregor undergoes a gradual symbolic castration-feminization at the hands of his father. First his father threatens him, then makes him bleed by roughly pushing him through the narrow door to his room and finally permanently cripples him by embedding an apple in his back. The wound in his back prevents Gregor from ever cleaning himself and thus deprives him of the only means he had of being presentable to the household. Instead he demonstrates a desire for what is both outside language and outside the family law—he is attracted to music, the "unknown nourishment"[12] and a system of signs outside discourse; his fantasies of chaste kisses on the neck during their never-ending sojourn in his room thinly veil a desire for an incestuous union with his sister and feminine double.[13] (The desire for incest could also perhaps be seen as a desire for the womb since the qualities Gregor exhibits as a bug indicate regression to the infantile pre-genital sexual phase where there are no longer any feelings of inhibition or disgust.) Music and woman are as inseparably bound together in this case as they are in the text on the Sirens— Grete attracts her brother with her violin playing just as the Sirens attract sailors with their songs. And just as the Sirens destroy those sailors Gregor's sister rejects his advances and sentences him to death. Like the Sirens she is abysmal and unattainable. One has to die, lose one's self and one's life before reaching her.

But although Gregor no longer wishes to remain in the ordinary world, he continues, consciously or unconsciously, to articulate his desires for the Outside—for his sister—in terms of that world, in terms of power and utility: "He would never let her out of his room, at least, not so long as he lived; his frightful appearance would become, for the first time, useful to him; he would watch all the doors of his room at once and spit at intruders" ("Metamorphosis," 131). Gregor's desire to dominate the incestuous relationship that remains out of his reach parallels K.'s desire to reach the Castle and Joseph K.'s to win his case in the Courts. All three protagonists desire to possess as presence what can never be present, which disappears when it is articulated, translated into systems of power and discourse.

Because the women in Kafka's fiction are paradoxically both sensual-material distractions and incarnations of the abyss, they can function in a doubly disruptive fashion. On the one hand, they undermine the possibility of the purity, the permanence, and uni-versality of hierarchical governing structures. On the other, they indicate that a state beyond the metaphysics of Presence is possible only as a glimpse, a fragment, a tear in the fabric of the Universal—

Olga states that there is supposed to be no distinction between the Castle and the village but that when anything important happens everyone can see that distinctions do exist (*Castle*, 256). Hierarchical differences always reappear. The existence of an Outside of Presence is just as impossible as pure Presence—both are continually being subverted. By revealing the illusory quality of the Courts and Castle as universal principles of a differentiating order, women help reveal that they are seamless textual worlds composed of the undifferentiated murmur of the play of language. However, as soon as this murmur becomes meaningful and articulate in the world outside the Castle, hierarchical relationships immediately reassert themselves. When Castle officials leave their writing desks, as they must occasionally do, they are violently distracted from their business by women. The officials then summon the women in a brutally possessive and degrading manner, keep them for a brief period to satisfy sexual urges and subsequently forget them. Women seem to be only temporary accidental ruptures and interruptions in the smooth flow of undifferentiated textuality. As was already noted, however, woman, as a sensually physical presence, was always already a part of the Castle, disturbing its undifferentiated play of language. The officials form only short liaisons with women and immediately forget them in an attempt to avoid recognizing that the disruption women cause is inevitable and incessant. The possessive and humiliating quality of their language emphasizes the unavoidable fall into a hierarchical structure.

Amalia's story demonstrates that the abyss which a woman embodies cannot be visible, cannot *be* in the world, any more than the Castle or the Courts can survive in their undifferentiated states upon contact with the world. Amalia's refusal of Sortini is a refusal to treat the Castle as absolute presence, source of all authority; her retreat into "silence"—an effort to exist outside Discourse, to *exist* as the Outside, the abyss. Her refusal does not sever her connection with the Castle—she brings K.'s second letter from the Castle (*Castle*, 159). It merely negates the hierarchical nature of connections and indicates the fundamental similarities between her and the Castle, between the nature of woman and that of literature (writing). Her efforts to remain outside language are, however, doomed to fail; her "silence" is impossible—it is forcibly recuperated into Discourse by the interpretation it undergoes in the world. Amalia's "punishment" is this inevitable recuperation into the structures of power.

Kafka ultimately subordinates literature to a constant preoccupation with salvation. But by virtue of his equally constant absorption with women, his texts are able to demonstrate that neither art nor eroticism in the form of female sexuality can be completely reduced to the orders of utility and representation. Remaining within those orders to be able to exist, they nonetheless always indicate that the integrity of those orders is and always has been deceptive.

Notes

1. See the letters of August 14 and 24 in Franz Kafka, *Briefe an Felice* (Frankfurt am Main: S. Fischer, 1967), 444 and 451: "I am not interested in literature, but rather am made of literature. I am nothing else and cannot be anything else" and "I don't have an inclination to write. . .not an inclination, but am completely myself. An inclination can be eradicated or suppressed. But I am that thing myself."

2. Franz Kafka, *The Castle,* trans. Willa and Edwin Muir, Eithne Wilkins, and Ernst Kaiser. (New York: Alfred A. Knopf, 1956), 255. All future references in text.

3. Franz Kafka, *The Trial,* trans. Willa and Edwin Muir and E. M. Butler (New York: Alfred A. Knopf, 1957), 71. All future references in text.

4. The presence of purity is implicit since impurity is presented as out of place and shocking. However, both the purity and absolute truth of the Castle and Courts are *interpretations* of these structures given only at certain moments in the text.

5. It is true that most characters and situations escape this rigidity since they are always presented as part of K.'s enterprise of interpretation and reinterpretation. This thesis vaguely coincides with that of Marthe Robert in her *L'ancien et le nouveau* (Paris: Grasset, 1963), and could be extended to the works in their entirety making them texts governed by an interpretative system that has no stable final referent. The woman's role is isolated because the inability to determine female identity most clearly illuminates the radical consequences that unfixed identities have for literature.

6. For an exposition of the dynamics involved in the perception of the Castle (and the Courts) as texts and/or as centers of authority I am indebted to Charles Bernheimer's articles: "Symbolic Bond and Textual Play: The Structure of Kafka's *Castle,*" in *The Kafka Debate,* ed. Angel Flores (New York: The Gordian Press, 1977), and "Letters to an Absent Father: A Structural Reading of Kafka's 'The Judgment,'" in *The Problem of the Judgment,* ed. Angel Flores (New York: The Gordian Press, 1976).

For a discussion of *The Castle* as a representation of death, see Maurice Blanchot, "Le langage de la fiction," in *La Part du feu* (Paris: Gallimard, 1949).

At this point it should again be noted that women are not the only elements that disrupt K.'s perception, and thus upset his expectations. They are, however, the factors that are crucial for the exploration of the interrelations between the rest of the phenomena in question.

7. Walter A. Strauss, "Siren-Language: Kafka and Blanchot," *Substance* 14 (1976): 20.

8. Franz Kafka, "The Silence of the Sirens," in *Franz Kafka: The Complete Stories,* ed. Nahum N. Glatzer (New York: Schocken Books, 1983), 431.

9. Homer, *The Odyssey,* trans. Robert Fitzgerald (Garden City: Anchor, 1963), 210–11.

10. See Stanley Corngold, "Kafka's 'Die Verwandlung': Metamorphosis of the Metaphor," *Mosaic* 3, no. 4 (1970): 101, 103.

11. Stanley Corngold, *The Commentators' Despair* (Port Washington, N.Y.: Kennikat Press, 1973), 11.

12. "The Metamorphosis," in *Franz Kafka: The Complete Stories,* 131.

13. Ibid. The similarity between the names of brother and sister—Gregor and Grete—increases the viability of viewing them as doubles.

Kafka's Time Machines   James Rolleston*

Flaubert and Kafka. In one sense the comparison between these two masters is an obvious one, as Flaubert is the writer most consistently and admiringly mentioned by Kafka in his diaries. Yet, until Charles Bernheimer's recent book on the subject,[1] the critical literature did not probe this fact deeply, leaving Flaubert as a sort of linguistic master-craftsman whom Kafka revered for that reason alone. What Bernheimer has done by setting up innumerable continuities between the two men, both as complex neurotics and as dreamers of the dream of writing, is to set the critical juices flowing in this centenary year: the relationship of Kafka to Flaubert is possibly more suggestive even than the better known links to Kleist, Kierkegaard and Dostoevsky. As a starting-point for my own argument I want to demonstrate a radical difference between Kafka and Flaubert which is in evidence at the very outset of Kafka's writing career. In a sentence: Flaubert's prose is conditioned by the obvious, ubiquitous, automatic functioning of the nineteenth century realistic style, while Kafka's is conditioned by the absolute impossibility of that same style. I am not simply saying that realism has declined and fallen, that Kafka finds himself in a *Sprachkrise*, a language crisis, forced back into the perspective of our century. This familiar version of Kafka is fuelled not only by thematic elements, bureaucracy, killing machines, and the like, but also by arguments like that of Georg Lukács as to who is the better realist, Kafka or Thomas Mann.[2] What the comparison with Flaubert suggests is that Kafka isn't *any* kind of a realist, that there is no mimetic impulse whatever in his prose, that his texts are governed by entirely different imperatives.

Citing a passage from Nietzsche, Bernheimer depicts Flaubert as the chronicler of a dead world, simultaneously contemptuous of it and dependent on it: "Flaubert. . .is a guardian of funerary monuments. . . . He watches over the triumph of death and uses that triumph as the vehicle of his own will to power. Thus it is striking that although nothing disgusted Flaubert more than the pervasive equalization of classes and values in the society around him. . . , it

*This essay was originally published in Roman Struc and J. C. Yardley, editors, *Franz Kafka (1883–1983): His Craft and Thought* (Waterloo, Ontario: Wilfrid Laurier University Press, 1986, for the Calgary Institute for the Humanities). Reprinted by permission.

is precisely the mechanism of making-equal that he transforms into an artistic principle demonstrating the nullity of all cultural endeavor."³ In other words the symbiosis of Flaubert's aesthetics with the vulgar world he hated could not be more complete: he gives us a mimesis not just of the world's surface but of its inward drive towards dragging down the beautiful. Flaubert's criticism of the world is so total that it turns out to be not criticism at all, but hermetically sealed identification with it: rigorously deconstructing all metaphysical alternatives, Flaubert finds beauty in a strict mimesis of the process of its soiling and destruction, to the point where that process must be infinitely, open-endedly extended in the grotesquerie of *Bouvard et Pécuchet*. This singleness, this transparency of texture is what we never find in Kafka, and the missing element is precisely that mimetic drive, Flaubert's untiring delight in the self-perpetuating circularity of meaningless detail and meaningless metaphysics. For Flaubert two non-meanings add up to one positive meaning, the meaning of purified aesthetics liberated from time. But, Bernheimer says, "The ideal Kafka opposed to his writing did not attempt to deny time, as did Flaubert's stylistic imperative. On the contrary, Kafka's ideal involved a perfect wedding of being and time. . . ."⁴ Flaubert's ideal is synonymous with his writing, Kafka's is radically opposed to his; we have arrived at the familiar double texture of Kafka's prose, the way in which a narration exuding commonsense and rationality strongly implies that it is communicating the opposite of the truth, that it is moving towards a self-destruction which alone can communicate truth. The critical difficulty has always been to say what that truth is, the truth that permeates every word of a Kafka text without ever becoming directly expressible. Walter Sokel asserts that the truth is the continuity of life itself; Gerhard Kurz has argued more recently that the truth is identical with death, that Kafka's work is a thanatology;⁵ and much recent criticism identifies truth with the fate of writing, with the necessary obliqueness of writing's existence in a world always ready to crush it, either violently or through indifference.⁶ The fruitfulness of this latter approach is that it unites Kafka's quest for a Flaubertian purity with both his self-hatred and the ceaseless thematizing of writing in his texts, the letters, messages, legal briefs, parables.

   The difficulty with the truth of writing, as with the truth of life and the truth of death, is that such truths do not really open up the texts to the extent these texts seem so desperately and imperiously to require. The reader finds himself in the position of the dog in "Investigations of a Dog": sensing the explosive significance of a Kafka-text, somewhat as the dog experiences the power of the musical dogs' performance, we rush to the critics for answers to the riddle. They are certainly not silent, like the investigator's fellow dogs, but their answers often come dangerously close to tautology. Indeed the happiest period of Kafka-criticism, at least from the critic's point of view, was when tautology was an acceptable, even esteemed mode of writing. One could demonstrate, often in microscopic detail, the mastery with which Kafka undermined his characters' claims and plotted the necessary stages of their self-elimination. There is authentic intensity in Wilhelm Emrich's[7] demonstration of Kafka's thematic and existential negations: the meaninglessness of the modern world was not yet a cliché. But it is now. Kafka's texts will not let us turn away from the hermeneutic struggle to articulate their truth, even though we may be absolutely certain our articulation will be inadequate. Writers other than Kafka have, of course, launched the interpretive tradition of their works (one thinks of Goethe); Kafka's radical quality is that his writing points immediately and exclusively towards that tradition, renouncing all claims to an "outside," a locus of origination. Kafka's texts require us to situate them in the widest possible horizon and to ignore no ships that may be moving on that horizon. If I regard the links and rifts between Kafka and Flaubert as more fruitful, closer to the author's "intention" (treacherous yet indispensable word) than, say, current biographical work, then I must be prepared to justify that belief by touching down on as much Kafka-territory as the scope of a single lecture permits.

In any given Flaubert text there are passages, such as the description of Charles's hat near the beginning of *Madame Bovary*,[8] in which the writing comes to rest in the specific scene or object, detaching it from its surroundings and simply delighting in the process of verbal mimesis. Usually, of course, descriptive passages are correlated with and, indeed, often anthologize a character's perspective, as Erich Auerbach so brilliantly demonstrated in the case of Emma watching Charles eating.[9] But the "thing-ness" of this world, its ultimate alienness from all human occupants, is not in doubt. Similarly, in the works of Flaubert with a contemporary setting, historical dates can always be reliably intuited, even when they are not explicitly mentioned. And in, say, *A Simple Heart* or *A Sentimental Education*, dates are indeed mentioned. In other words, the rhythmic sequence of bourgeois history, of revolution and reaction, is as much a given of Flaubert's world as nature's regularity or the eloquent furnishing of a character's room. His language breathes and flourishes within the conventions of realism, circling around the continuous, cell-like self-patterning of time and space, ready to move in for the assault, the kill and the alchemical transformation of pettiness and illusion into the denatured beauty of the pinioned butterfly. None of this is even imaginable in a Kafka-story. Although his texts are of course marked by an identifiable social ambience, all reference to contemporary public events is by definition excluded, and the exclusion becomes the more rigorous, the more obviously eventful the world becomes during World War I. And from the very beginning of Kafka's first work, "Description of a Struggle," all objects exist only in relation to the central character; we see this very literally as the speaker organizes the pastry on his plate and then finds, after beginning a conversation, that it tastes bad in his mouth. Kafka's own later word for this is *Motivation;* everything in the physical world is reducible to human "motivation." But the fatal next step, interpretively speaking, is to argue that his stories show solipsistic modern man in action. For the textual richness of an individual past, an environment, even a specific set of psychological tensions—all this is what we do *not* find in a Kafka character. Rather, we hear a well-organized speaking voice, a well-defended rationality, a skill at excluding whole areas of human experience. The text is filled, not so much with a character (although of course we refer to Joseph K. and Georg Bendemann by name as a kind of shorthand, a shorthand implicit already in their cipher-like names) as with an elaborate sketch for a character, a situation and a world all in one. In this experiment, the more the rigidity and alienness of each element are invoked, the more indissoluble the mutual equation becomes. But it stays an equation, with tension, distance, and change; there is never a collapse into mere individual psychology. Sometimes we think we can distill a psychological essence: the characters spend so much time justifying themselves that they miss the crucial openings of their situation. But Kafka says explicitly, "No one can live an unjustified life";[10] and when we look at a situation a second time, not only does it begin to seem reductive to stress a particular moment of choice as decisive—the story is always living a second or third life apart from the character's decision-making. In Stanley Corngold's phrase, a "ghostly narrator" is present, orchestrating the elements of psychology, ethics, and epistemology but assigning priority to none of them.

I have described what a Kafka text is *not,* in comparison to one by Flaubert; and I have used the word *experiment.* It is time to propose what I discern as the hypothesis governing these fictional experiments, to say what Kafka *is* that Flaubert is not. Here Bernheimer's phrase for the ideal Kafka saw as opposed to literature is a good starting-point: "a perfect wedding of being and time." Kafka made no secret of this ideal, which he associated with marriage and began to elaborate quasi-theologically from 1917 onwards: "Theoretically there is a perfect possibility of happiness: to believe in what is indestructible in oneself and *not* to strive towards it."[11] The ideal is thus completely impractical, inaccessible to human beings just because they are human, irrevocably bound to time and striving. But what really estranges Kafka's theoretical idealism from us is that it seems to have no place at all in realistic fiction, which starts with ordinary human striving, and whose conventions are obviously utilized by Kafka. Thus his abstract reflections tend to get placed in their own compartment, sometimes labelled as "preoccupation with Kierkegaard." But what if, as I have argued, Kafka is not a realist in any sense of the word? This question provokes further questions: what is he if he is not a realist? and how does all this help us build a bridge from the openly metaphysical speculations back into the rigidly low-keyed texture of Kafka's fictions? I have unequivocal answers to both questions, which I hope to justify in my analysis. First: I see Kafka as a direct exponent of Romantic poetics in the largest sense, with its assumption that fantasy, continually modulated by ironic consciousness, invents the world and not vice versa. Friedrich Schlegel wrote prophetically: "Idealism must project beyond itself, and therefore it constantly seeks realism. . . .Realism ultimately flows back into idealism."[12] These sentences apply to Kafka both in terms of literary history and as descriptive of the moves which his fictions make. Nineteenth century realism emerges from the Romantic program, particularly from E. T. A. Hoffmann; and for Kafka it is a completed phenomenon, a compendium of stylistic possibilities demanding a new kind of originating imagination, much as the original Romantics re-forged elements from the eighteenth century repertoire into a new kind of novel. The extraordinary variety among Kafka's stories reflects the sovereign freedom with which he exercises the Romantic imperative of combinatory process, *Kombinatorik:* any narrative element, parable, anecdote, fairy-tale, fantasy, may be synthesized with any other; the only certainty is that the conventions of realism, while they may still be deployed, have no more priority than did the conventions of the letter-novel for the Romantics.

We have noted that Kafka is indisputably interested in the rhythm of ordinary human striving and self-justification which so absorbed a full-blooded realist like Balzac. But Kafka articulates these drives in an abstract, almost mechanistic way, bloodless rather than full-blooded. And once his idealist, non-realist perspective is conceded, it becomes possible to discern the hypothesis being tested in these narrative experiments. Here we reach the decisive link between Kafka and the Romantics, the dynamics which, in Schlegel's terms, originally impelled idealism to generate realism out of itself: namely, the Romantic theory of time as simultaneously the dimension of man's exile from the absolute and the primary element of human creativity. Time, in this perspective, necessarily generates space (hence the realist impulse), but is ontologically prior to it—in Novalis' pithy words: "space as a precipitate of time—as a necessary consequence of time."[13] If we assemble a group of fragments from Kafka's notebooks on the question of time, we can perceive not only the uncanny identity of his views with those of the original Romantics but also the intuitive skill with which he enriched this temporal metaphysics from a post-realist perspective. In one notation Kafka sketches the precise implications of the Romantic absolute, an absolute which is by definition inaccessible yet constituted entirely by the empirical; containing the entirety of history within itself, the absolute defines the human mission as to engage that history through consciousness, acting out repeatedly the dream of regenerating a lost wholeness without forsaking the empirical texture of the world. Kafka writes: "To every moment there corresponds something outside time. The empirical world cannot be followed by a transcendent world, for transcendence is eternal, and therefore cannot touch the temporality of the empirical directly."[14] The antithesis between empirical and transcendent is of course problematic for Kafka, as it was for the Romantics; the antithesis is structurally necessary, yet the static implications of the word *ewig* (eternal) are misleading in this context; the whole thrust of this metaphysics is to re-imagine the absolute as immanent, directly implicated in every move of the human fantasy, the fantasy that is perpetually crystallizing the natural and ethical dimensions in ever new, ever shifting historical syntheses.[15] There are several Kafka passages on the conception of paradise as immanent, as present yet unperceived, like the Romantic fairy-tale world. Here is one in which he moves in a counter-direction, opening the experience of the moment towards the multiplicity, the richness of historical presence which, in imagist terms, overcomes the conceptual gap between immanence and transcendence: "The multiple realities which multiply revolve within the multiplicities of the single moment in which we live. And look, the moment is even now not over!"[16] And yet this emphasis on the moment, the potentially mystical perspective, is counterbalanced in Kafka, as in the Romantics, by an insistence on the historical imperative, on the project of compressing the past into a teleological story to be justified by the dream of a future and by that alone: "The decisive moment of human development is perpetual. Therefore the revolutionary spiritual movements, which declare the entire past to be negligible, are correct, for nothing has yet happened."[17]

The polar vision of the moment as both empty and full, of history as both rich and impoverished, of the individual consciousness as embedded simultaneously in intimate detail, in *Zufall,* and in the endlessly echoing human mythologies—this vision is as indispensable to Kafka as it was to the Romantics. And it is a vision which transcends nineteenth-century realism, or any definition of realism, which must assign priority to materiality, to a governing and singular past and to a spatial continuum defining temporal consciousness, not defined by it. The idealist vision, by contrast, refuses all limitations on the scope of consciousness, relativizes the validity of all functioning laws that would deny the power of the revolutionary "now" to transform

the texture of history. The only significant continuum, in this perspective, binds the self-exploring, self-generating individual indissol-
ubly, if enigmatically, to the sum of all past self-creations. As Novalis
summarizes: "The most wondrous eternal phenomenon is one's own
existence. Man is the greatest of all secrets to himself—the solving
of this eternal problem, in fact, constitutes world-history."[18] And
Kafka seems to echo these very words: "Far, far away world-history
proceeds, the world-history of your soul."[19]

We seem to have moved far, with this rich metaphysics, from
the generally impoverished atmosphere, the repetitive failures of
Kafka's fictional world. But we have only followed in Kafka's own
footsteps. And the bridge to Kafka's narratives is implicit in the
original gesture of the Romantic time-theory. For although the world
is constituted by time, its materiality the residue of past striving, the
multiple presence of "things" is the very opposite of temporal continuity; their persistence is the persistence of death, and their power
to instigate new becoming, new projections of consciousness, is steeped
in irony.[20] Thus the initiating projection of time-consciousness is a
disruption, a tearing open of the empty, deathly present and an
immediate assertion that time is not one but three, not a faceless
continuum but a dynamic relationality between past, present, and
future. And as soon as this tearing apart of time is achieved, the
fundamental human longing is to reunite the three blocks into which
our consciousness has divided time in order to give it a shaped
existence. For in the dimension of the absolute, the dimension which
stamps all history as exile, time is a unity; history thus becomes the
continuous re-imagining of that unity, a record of failure yielding
ever new dreams of success.

What Kafka has done in his narratives is to imagine again and
again the initial temporal disruption, a moment constituted by the
beginnings of his stories, and to chart his heroes' failure to reintegrate
their world as an intelligible unity. But what makes his use of an
idealist perspective so rich and varied is that he casts his heroes as
epistemologists, as people with a clear definition of their temporal
goals. Their problem is that their clarity depends on the assumed
priority of one particular time-dimension, whether it be past, present,
or future, and their story is the struggle to subordinate the other
two dimensions through the sheer structuring energy of their consciousness. The end of a Kafka-story is the flooding of the text by
the excluded dimensions, a definitive silencing of the individual consciousness which renews the dream of unity in the very language,
the very process of the collapsing project. I shall be briefly discussing
three pairs of Kafka-stories, each pair governed by a central figure
committed to one of the three time-dimensions. Time governed strictly
by self-projection into the future I term prescriptive time, and my

texts are "The Judgment" and "Josephine the Singer, or the Mouse Folk." When time past is the exclusive concern of consciousness, the story is structured as encyclopedic time, and the illustrative stories are "The Great Wall of China" and "Investigations of a Dog." And when consciousness is obsessed by the dimension of the present, the privileged moment which renders all other time negligible, then the narrative's domain becomes ecstatic time, and this is the zone of "In the Penal Colony" and "The Burrow." In each case the hypothesis, which makes us focus on the central character not as a psychological entity but as the generator of a project, is that human time can be reconstituted within a single dimension of consciousness. What the experiment reveals is that the shape such exclusionary consciousness must impose on the world is ultimately the shape of a monster. The story's self-destruction is thus a given from the outset, becoming ever more vividly manifest until the final implosion. The interdependence of a story and hero is such that the reader's urge to find an Archimedean point from which to "judge" the hero is invariably frustrated. Although ethical terms like guilt are indeed deployed, they connote an impersonal force which the hero is struggling to control. In Kafka's fiction guilt means an unsuccessful effort to force a recalcitrant dimension of experience into a time-zone already prescribed for it. The ghostly narrator is neither identical with the hero nor detached: strictly a function of the hero's project, the narrator weaves indefatigably the web binding self and world, revealing, like a faceless servant in a comedy of manners, the gaps between the threads of the weave. And the questions which the self-destroying story throws up in its final moments have been accumulating in these narrative gaps, mini-failures in the project which amount to a nullification of the whole. And they are translatable into the simple yet tormenting questions which dominate Kafka's late speculations. Why does the necessary temporal disruption at the origin of human creativity turn so ineluctably into permanent exile and death? Why does the interpretation of human life as a coherent synthesis of past, present, and future seem so out of reach? Why must all human striving degenerate into manipulation, "motivation," given that images of peace are so strong within us? "The entire visible world is perhaps nothing but a motivation of man longing to rest for a single moment."[21] Kafka's fictions explore the multiple forms and singular logic of that "motivation," destroying themselves, as manifestations of the negative, *das Negative*, with absolute strictness in order to force human consciousness one millisecond closer to the "positive" time which they can never express.[22] Never? I think I may have found the one exception, but will discuss it only at the end.

All Kafka stories begin by taking us *in medias res*, at the moment of temporal disruption when the singular human consciousness reaches or is forced into the direction of total definition of self and world. The anti-realism of this procedure is suggested by the status of the hero's background; the *Bildungsroman* is inconceivable for Kafka. Background is not non-existent, but neither is it definitional; it is an element, namely the dimension of the past, which must be integrated, forcibly as it always turns out, into the temporality which the hero's thoughts and actions automatically begin to circumscribe. The hero's freedom is in a sense absolute, but immediately starts to diminish as his "motivation" acquires its own momentum. First sentences are perhaps even more important in Kafka than in other writers, as they suggest, in the very language of freedom, the obsessive quality of the story's time-zone as it begins to suck all freedom into itself. "It was on a Sunday morning in the very height of spring." "Our singer is called Josephine."[23] Everything seems different about these sentences, notably tense and narrative perspective. But what they both do is point decisively towards the future: we want to know what "it" was that happened in the spring, and what Josephine will sing. This, of course, is basic procedure in storytelling. These characters are prescribing the time of their lives as a story and the very normality, the intelligibility of their behaviour enables the reader to sense the strangeness of their move into an exclusively prescriptive time-zone. The strategy of both stories is to dwell at length in the realm of commonsense, to demonstrate the very security of the character's roots at the same time as the process of self-uprooting is gradually becoming definitive. In "The Judgment" a titanic family drama seems to unfold, whereas "Josephine" aspires almost to the status of minimal art in its plotlessness, its elimination of the familiar "motivations" which pervade the earlier work. But the one "motivation" that drives "Josephine," the heroine's imposition of her theatre on the populace, is the key element in "The Judgment" also. Just as Josephine imposes her space-time on the shapelessness of the mouse-universe, turning little alcoves into instant theatres, frenzied rushing into the ritual of performance, so Georg has organized both the landscape and the relationships of his life into a theatre with himself at the centre. This close juxtaposition of apparently dissimilar texts enables us to see the thematic priority of prescriptive theatre in "The Judgment." For the story has become, to borrow Stanley Corngold's phrase, a commentator's despair, in that its motivic richness simply resists clear decoding on its own terms: no explanation based on Georg's guilt or the father's primeval power really does justice to the shattering acceleration of the ending. Such interpretations presuppose that Georg is uprooted from a normal world which he has illegitimately manipulated to his own ends. But once it is conceded that in Kafka there is *no* normal world, that the opening of the fiction coincides with the challenge to the hero to reintegrate the time of the world, then the story's transitions become comprehensible in terms of failure rather than guilt. Georg fails because he cannot transfer the entire world into the controlled environment of his personal stage. He stumbles off-stage inadvertently, into the darkness of his father's room, and there he finds that the subversive insects of death's continuum, its spiders and termites, have coalesced into the single monstrous figure of his father.

The disquieting quality of Kafka's prescriptive theatre is that it is not a theatre in the familiar sense, a theatre in some kind of relationship to an outside world, some alternative reality. Rather, Kafka is invoking the old image of a world-theatre, an earthly totality opposed only by heaven. And Kafka's heaven, his laconic renewal of the Romantic absolute, is inseparable from the hero's project, indeed is definable only as what the project's impossibility renders imaginable. The crucial point is that absolutely *no* alternative wisdom emerges from these fictions which might be set against the undertakings of Georg and Josephine. What happens to both of them is that their deployment of the world's population as stage-characters ultimately generates a monster: they make a slip, a momentary loss of control in Georg's case, a miscalculation in Josephine's, and their theatre is destroyed. But the counter-force has no counter-wisdom. The father demolishes Georg, then collapses himself. The mouse-folk in essence do the same: the narrator's bland prose introduces the father-image and tells us that the people are in effect setting a trap for Josephine. But as soon as we ask what their counter-truth consists of, we find literally nothing. Music, history, time itself, all are given definition by Josephine and by Josephine alone: without her singing there would be no distinctions in the mouse-consciousness; the very existence of time-zones like childhood and old age is made possible by her. Hence the inexorable logic of the final "judgment" on her: she has entered the pantheon of history but, since there is no such thing as history without her, we have an image of extinction as precise as the disappearance of Georg into the river. Through their projection of a world-theatre centred on themselves, Georg and Josephine give shape to chaos; with their deaths chaos returns. Kafka's own reading of "The Judgment" makes it clear that the father is Georg's creation, first his puppet, then his monster: at first he is "in" Georg, then he "emerges" from the friend and only gains destructive power because Georg "has nothing left but to gaze at his father."[24] The father has nothing but anti-wisdom: his words never at any point transcend the framework of Georg's theatre; all they do is cover the script with a childish scrawl, rendering it illegible, hence destroying it. The father is indeed primeval, but as pure negation, chaos, not as wisdom. Much as the mouse-narrator draws the negativity of his distracted people into himself, as the "opposition, with which I too am half in sympathy,"[25] destroying Josephine's story in the act of telling it, so Georg's father uses the long brooding years to actualize the deathly aimlessness of bourgeois time as a single act of atavistic destruction.

Everyone has a candidate for the most important line in "The Judgment"; mine is the father's "So now you know what else there was in the world besides yourself,"[26] with its powerful double meaning. On the one hand it is as nonsensical as the mouse-narrator's invocation of history; the father has told us nothing of a world outside Georg, has only annotated and subverted Georg's projections from a monstrous but strictly internal perspective. But on the other hand he articulates the crucial flaw of a life governed by prescriptive time, the impossibility of otherness. In order to project his life as the only story in the world-theatre, Georg's narcissism must be total, and the disaster is not ethical but temporal: without the resistance of otherness, the interweaving of future with past and present, time must accelerate, the monologue become more hysterical, and the end of the story can only be a willed death. Georg cannot resist his father precisely because the father is not other than he is, but his chief puppet running away with the script, rushing the play through to its given ending. We see a similar acceleration in Josephine's case: unlike Georg's father, the avowedly fatherly mouse-folk resist passively; but they do not resist in the name of any other principle, they have no shape other than what Josephine gives them. Their meaningless resistance has the same effect on Josephine as the highly charged subversion of the father on Georg: acceleration of the story into death. But these endings are implicit in the character's prescriptive temporality, which renders the world's otherness, whether past or present, inaccessible. Kafka remarks: "Whoever cares only for the future is less prudent than he who lives only for the moment, since the former doesn't even care for the moment but only for its prolongation."[27] Simply by drawing Georg's entire theatre into himself ("towering up around the father" is Kafka's vivid phrase in his diary), the father does indeed give Georg a glimpse of excluded time: all pastness has been manipulated by Georg into a mere springboard for the future, and all presentness is lived without "care," to echo Kafka's almost Heideggerian usage. The glimpse enables Georg to utter words in death which tell only of what his prescriptive time has excluded: "Dear parents, I have always loved you, all the same."[28] The sudden apparition of the past as a stable family tableau is yoked to an equally sudden and total commitment to the only present moment left open by his story, the moment of death. The words speak only of exclusion, not of alternative perspectives; the collapse of prescriptive time opens only into the renewed chaos of anti-space, anti-wisdom, anti-history. But provided the chaos is reached with rigorous logic and temporal truth, it is as stimulating to Kafka as it was to the Romantics. It is where the human imagination starts again.

Encyclopedic time, the valorizing of the past, is a project at the opposite extreme from prescriptive time, and would seem to offer good hope of success. For this time-project includes rather than excludes. Present and future are very much on the minds of Kafka's intellectually energetic heroes, the investigators of the Chinese wall and of the laws of dogdom. For present and future are to be coded as the rational onflow of the past, once it has been encyclopedically interpreted. Here the world is not a theatre populated by puppets; it is an organism, with its population understood as molecules in that organism. The narrator does not manipulate his fellow-beings; he affirms their autonomy and strives to ground it in what he calls laws, guarantees of temporal coherence through the past. And where the prescriptive hero is driven, through denial of the world's otherness, to accelerate time, the encyclopedist embraces that very otherness and seeks to stabilize its temporality, to extend his gaze backwards into the past and re-imagine the given deadness of time passing as a process alive and organic. What could go wrong with so admirable a project?

The immediate problem is that investigation does not reveal coherence. The narrator of the Chinese wall begins with the wall's status as the greatest collective project of his people, the embodiment of its encyclopedic wisdom. Everything about the wall makes sense, particularly the organization of the building, except for the most central thing about it, its function. It does not fulfill its function. The investigator is driven towards paradoxes that undermine the very concept of his encyclopedia, towards irrational legend, towards the limiting of askable questions, towards the dream-totality of the tower. The investigative dog, in contrast, is confronted not by projects but by their absence. Dogdom has no projects. But this neutrality is as inimical to the encyclopedia as the Chinese extravaganzas. For the dogs' past resists categorization; it refuses to become the past; its unity does not divide into the minimum duality necessary for rational organization. And so the dog, one of Kafka's most eloquent and passionate characters, becomes obsessed by the shaping of time itself. Perhaps his structural duality can become past and present, present behaviour classifiable through laws past yet perpetual. But as soon as he makes this move, the primacy of the past, so essential to his stabilizing project, is nullified, and the dimensions of present and future become unmanageable, looming as topoi of decadence and apocalyptic transformation: "dogs—I cannot put it in any other way— had not yet become so doggish as today, the edifice of dogdom was still loosely put together, the true word could still have intervened, planning or replanning the structure, changing it at will, transforming it into its opposite; and the word was there, was very near at least, on the tip of everybody's tongue, anyone might have hit upon it."[29] The key threat to the encyclopedia is incoherence, and the more the dog insists on the possibility of coherence, the longer and more religiously tinged his sentences become, the more vivid the threat becomes. For when the past is defined by antithesis to the present, it appears precisely not as a closed system of laws but as the quivering possibility of revelation.

The second paradox that these fictions uncover is the paradox of language or, rather, of the impossibility of language. The language-system of a people is the self-evident key to an encyclopedic project, both the container of the past and the expression of coherence through mastery of the world, a dictionary and a grammar. And yet it is precisely language that fails when Kafka's investigators summon its aid. There is a relation of silence between the non-communication of the emperor's message and the inaccessibility, the silence of the dog's fellow-creatures. To be sure the silence is not complete in either story, but the words which offer themselves as the laws of these organisms lack precisely that linking of individual and collective which could make the encyclopedia a living force like language itself. The words of the Chinese authorities are opaque, shrouded in legend. Conversely the laws of dogdom are delightfully void of all binding significance, reducible always to "Thou shalt do what thou art doing anyway." The dog himself has two experiences, of opposite kinds, through which he struggles to break the silence, to establish the gaps and differences which could be the basis of a rational reweaving. First he tries to transform the musician dogs into a viable legend by becoming their interpreter, making them the focus of a before and after which could be organized as history. Then he endeavours, by fasting, to give definition to dogdom's central imperatives involving food. The analogies to early Christianity, to the supreme single event and the subsequent forging of a collective identity through asceticism, are clear enough. But the dog's religion doesn't catch on; the past refuses to come to life as the guarantor of doggy time. The molecules of the projected organism will not cohere.

As with prescriptive time, though less obviously, the project's failure is inherent in its premises. Where the prescriptive heroes concentrate all experience into themselves as its centre, the two investigators explicitly renounce a centre, don the mantle of modesty and anonymity—and fail because of it. Again a Kafka speculation is suggestive: "The observer is in a certain sense a parasite; he attaches himself to the living, tries to keep in step with the wind. That I do not wish to be."[30] As the Romantics insisted, only the self can be the centre; the more these characters struggle to locate a centre outside themselves, in laws, customs, in a postulated temporal continuity, the more the very basis of their project, their rational language, ceases to be usable. They become like their fellows, they fall silent. The nominally fragmentary nature of both texts seems to be their only possible completion, the impossibility of an ending counterpointing the teleological urgency of prescriptive time. In both stories the silence is associated with a logic of separation between the investigator and his people, a separation which is expressed as a dislocation of present from past. The narrator of the Chinese wall wants to endorse the livingness of a message from the next province; such livingness would constitute precisely the continuity between past and present, the linguistic coherence he seeks; and it is this livingness which his people deny. In withdrawing into the past, they cancel its function as the past. Everything is legend, nothing is lived, there is no organism. The narrator can find no new language to continue. The investigative dog begins to declare that he is governed wholly by instinct, that his instinct has destroyed his analytic abilities, and that he rejoices in it. In other words he is plunging into the present, declaring himself to be a dog like all others. But of course he has no language for this; his final sentence, "But nevertheless freedom, nevertheless a possession,"[31] is self-contradictory, a temporal collapse. Freedom seems to invoke presentness, possession a petty bourgeois future. The alienness of this sentence to the dog's project is as evident as the alienness of Georg Bendemann's last words to his. Having projected encyclopedic time, the refusal of the self as centre, the dog cannot now lay claim to a centre. He must fall silent.

The most radical, yet the most clearly doomed time-projection in Kafka is the drive towards the privileged, isolated moment, ecstatic time. This time-zone has the most illustrious antecedents in mystical thought; it is the point of intersection between the immanent and transcendent worlds. But for Kafka, as for the Romantics, the relocation of transcendence within immanence, the redefinition of the absolute as the temporal fullness both defining and challenging temporal exile, renders ecstatic time totally paradoxical. For there is no inherent dimension of a single moment which can distinguish it from any other. Before the disruptive act of the imagination, the present, as Schlegel insists, is epistemologically dead, empty continuity; and there is no way of preventing an ecstatic moment, a moment in pure isolation, from collapsing back onto the "metalled ways/Of time past and time future," to borrow Eliot's phrase. The only strategy, one to which Kafka is strongly drawn, is to seal the moment off, to imprison it as it were, and then to become its guardian. And in the texts focussing on ecstatic time, the central characters accept this role. The officer is the machine's caretaker. And in the burrow-animal's fantasy of an ideal, impossibly isolated Castle Keep (Burgplatz), he is not inside it but outside, perpetually on guard: "Then peace would be assured there and I would be its guardian."[32] This self-imposed life between worlds, this secondary ecstasy brings us closer to Kafka's version of his own life than do the other temporal projects:

> My longing was for ancient times
> My longing was for the present
> My longing was for the future
> and with all that I am dying
> in a watchman's hut by the roadside,
> in an upright coffin, which has
> always been state property.
> I have spent my life restraining
> myself from breaking it to pieces.[33]

For Kafka himself, as Malcolm Pasley's researches have shown, the guardian's role was functional; he watched over the closure of his own texts, as it were, testing their viability through an oblique process of commentary and self-denigration.

Kafka's heroes, however, are inevitably driven towards the direct experience of ecstasy and tirelessly develop schemes for being simultaneously inside and outside, living the moment while guaranteeing its validity against all encroachment. Whereas the logic of encyclopedic time is blurred, insecure, crumbling, the logic of ecstasy is inexorable and the characters follow it to the end. The world is neither a theatre nor an organism, but a machine, a unique machine with the sole function of producing ecstasy. Other people are neither manipulated nor anxiously embraced but rigorously excluded; by definition life outside the machine is valueless—"senseless freedom" as the animal terms it. And time is neither accelerated nor stabilized but ritualized, structured as an approach to and withdrawal from the peak moment. The ritual is rigidly self-contained, for the moment of truth, the assigned wisdom of the machine, allows for no return, no rooting in everyday life. This ritual time, with its culmination in aggressive banality, in radically useless fulfillment, is well conveyed by the animal: "Then I usually enjoy periods of particular tranquillity, in which I change my sleeping place by stages, always working in toward the center of the burrow, always steeping myself more profoundly in the mingled smells, until at last I can no longer restrain myself and one night rush into the Castle Keep, mightily fling myself upon my stores, and glut myself with the best that I can seize until I am completely gorged."[34] Ecstasy and sleep are interwoven throughout the story: the isolated moment remains privileged only through the enveloping oblivion.

The impossibility of imposing ecstatic time on the world is a given at the outset of both stories. In a sense the animal spends the whole text vainly fending off his initial insight: "Here it is of no avail to console yourself with the thought that you are in your own house; far rather are you in theirs."[35] The machinery of ritual defines itself by opposition to dailiness, and can never divorce itself from this oppositional posture; and since it lays claim, not to transcendence but to the world itself, it ultimately disintegrates in the face of the world's indifferent presence. Kafka allows full play to the situation's paradoxes, which precisely invert those of encyclopedic time. In vain, as we have seen, do the investigators strive to open the necessary gap in their universe, to be filled by their encyclopedic discourse; conversely the officer and the burrow-animal are unable to close the gap opened by their project, and cannot impose a hierarchical language, the old Commandant's secret codes, on the world. Instead, they become the most voluble of Kafka's heroes, unable to check the flow of language. They despise the world's customs and categories of knowledge, their project is wholly solipsistic; yet they exhaust themselves in endless self-justification, defining their life ever more narrowly until it becomes clear that what they are defending is death. For these two characters it can only be death that counts: in their death they plan to enact the dream of self-destruction which was also Kafka's dream. The animal relishes this dream of identity, which will liberate him from the unwanted dialogue with the world and move him from the margin to the centre of the machine, from guardian to high-priest-and-victim-in-one: "My castle which can never belong to anyone else, and is so essentially mine that I can calmly accept in it even my enemy's mortal stroke at the final hour, for my blood will ebb away here in my own soil and not be lost."[36] This dream is of course denied to both characters: the officer dies, but his face is as it was in life; his machine destroys itself while he fails to do so; and the burrow-animal finds his dream of presentness ruthlessly parodied. To articulate his machine-world he has resorted to an activation of words like peace and stillness—the "murmur of peace," "the source of peace," and so forth. The hissing simply situates the privileged moment, its non-silence, in an endless before and after, collapsing ecstatic time back into the deathly present. The animal is forced to reopen the past of his life and to make half-hearted plans for adapting the machine to an unpleasant future. But his whole project has been devoted to cancelling past and future: unable to maintain his priestly rituals, unable either to sleep or to die in his machine, he, like the investigative dog in this one respect, must fall silent.

Although the dream of self-destruction is Kafka's own dream, often re-imagined, the passage where he speaks of it as a logical necessity[37] is also the passage where he describes the "entire visible world" as constituted by human "motivations." As soon as the logic of self-destruction is given temporal, experiential shape, it becomes its opposite, an unlivable perversity. The officer and the burrow animal seek self-destruction as ecstasy, which means they do not seek authentic self-elimination at all. They are secretly prescriptive, projecting a future, however compressed. Their temporal project is corrupted, the end of their narratives flooded by the very time-zones of past and future, the continuum of history and change which they have so rigorously excluded.

I said earlier that I think there is one Kafka-character who carries his temporal project to a successful conclusion. I think it is the hunger-artist and I base my opinion entirely on the final words describing him: "The firm though no longer proud persuasion that he was still continuing to fast."[38] The hunger-artist's career is initially purely prescriptive, a compressing of the world into the accumulation of fasting days. The impresario forces him to re-state his art as an art of moments, moments in which the truth of his being is to be ritually communicated; he dislikes this, but accommodates. And then the end of the story imposes another dimension on his project, the frame of historical fashion, which situates his fasting within the whole encyclopedia of social behaviour. And to this unpleasant context the artist also adapts, both by reviewing his own life as a whole, as a past, and by recommitting himself to the project of an indefinite fast. In his past he discovers the flaw, the undermining of all his official achievement, which he communicates to an indifferent ear with his last breath. This communication frees his project, "no longer proud," to enter a prescriptive time-zone devoid of all manipulation; and he will reach the supreme moment, the purity of self-elimination, without having willed this death. What he wills is "continuing to fast" *(das Weiterhungern)*. What makes this ending a model of achieved time is that it is explicitly counterpointed with its own failure. The artist has been a fraud and is now replaced by the panther. Yet the language tells us that the panther is the artist's legitimate successor. His freedom is "somewhere in his jaws" *(irgendwo im Gebiß)*, his pure voracity complementing the artist's finally purified asceticism. The care with which Kafka treats the motif of freedom is prefigured by Friedrich Schlegel: "Very significant is the expression that freedom is not a thing; it is also the only non-thing, the only anti-thing."[39] Images of freedom erupt at the end of all the stories discussed, but always illegitimately, epitomized by the dog's labelling of freedom as "a possession." Freedom is not a state, not a release, not a possession; it is oppositional, oppositional towards one's own "motivations." Only in freedom can a genuine time machine be launched; and only the hunger-artist earns the right to the word, precisely by refusing that right. His final communicative moment is simultaneously a renewed project, a definitive summary of his past and a cancellation of all alternatives to the present moment, which becomes thereby a death essentially identical to the panther's life, a completion of history at its point of origin.

Notes

The translations of Kafka's speculative fragments are my own. References are given to the standard German editions, thus: *H* = *Hochzeitsvorbereitungen auf dem Lande* (Frankfurt a.M.: S. Fischer Verlag, 1966); *E* = *Sämtliche Erzählungen* ed. Paul Raabe (Frankfurt a.M.: Fischer Taschenbuch Verlag, 1970).

1. Charles Bernheimer, *Flaubert and Kafka: Studies in Psychopoetic Structure* (New Haven: Yale University Press, 1982).

2. Georg Lukács, "Franz Kafka or Thomas Mann?" in *Realism in our Time* trans. J. and N. Mander (New York: Harper and Row, 1964).

3. Bernheimer, *Flaubert and Kafka*, 239.

4. Ibid., 242.

5. Walter H. Sokel, *Franz Kafka* (New York: Columbia University Press, 1966); Gerhard Kurz, *Traum-Schrecken: Kafkas literarische Existenzanalyse* (Stuttgart: J. B. Metzler, 1980).

6. Although Kafka himself, in "The Letter to the Father," evoked his writing as a mode of escape, Stanley Corngold regards that autobiographical document as "deluded" and emphasizes the tenacity and self-generating momentum of Kafka's commitment to literature: "The hero of 'The Metamorphosis' is 'The Judgment,' the insight liberated in that story: that Kafka must not betray his writing either by marrying or by supposing that his father is the source and goal of his art. This judgment metamorphoses Kafka's existence into *Schriftstellersein* in the mode of allegory: the mode that definitively detaches the particular entity from the plenum of which it dreams, whether this plenitude be conceived as an expansive state of mind, interpersonal recognition, or metaphysical truth." (Stanley Corngold, *The Commentators' Despair: The Interpretation of Kafka's 'Metamorphosis'* [Port Washington, N.Y.: Kennikat Press, 1973], 36.).

7. Wilhelm Emrich, *Franz Kafka* (Frankfurt a.M.: Athenäum, 1958).

8. Or the evocation of the journey to Trouville in "A Simple Heart."

9. Erich Auerbach, *Mimesis* (Princeton, N.J.: Princeton University Press, 1953), 482ff.

10. "Kein Mensch kann ein ungerechtfertigtes Leben leben" *(H, 122)*.

11. "Theoretisch gibt es eine vollkommene Glücksmöglichkeit: An das Unzerstörbare in sich glauben und nicht zu ihm streben" *(H, 47)*.

12. "Idealismus muß aus sich herausgehn, daher sucht er stets den Realismus. . . Der Realismus fließt endlich wieder in den Idealismus zurück." *Kritische Friedrich-Schlegel-Ausgabe*, vol. XVIII, ed. Ernst Behler (Paderborn: Ferdinand Schöningh, 1963), 358 (no. 451); 359 (no. 462).

13. "Der Raum, als ein Niederschlag aus der Zeit—als nothwendige Folge der Zeit." Novalis, *Schriften*, vol. III, ed. Richard Samuel (Stuttgart: W. Kohlhammer, 1968), 564 (no. 67).

14. "Jedem Augenblick entspricht auch etwas Außerzeitliches. Dem Diesseits kann nicht ein Jenseits folgen, denn das Jenseits ist ewig, kann also mit dem Diesseits nicht in zeitlicher Berührung stehn" *(H, 94)*.

15. The linguistic difficulty of articulating structural duality within the framework

of continuous ontological unity is apparent in the following fragment of Novalis; since time is the primary element of unity, the language of temporal sequence persists in the very process of its being re-imagined: "Ultimately there will be no more nature. Nature's destiny is to be transformed gradually into a spiritual world. Does not this imply that nature's unchangeable laws are an illusion, are exceedingly un-natural? Everything is governed by laws and nothing is governed by laws" ("Einst soll keine Natur mehr seyn. In eine Geisterwelt soll sie allmählich übergehn. Sollten die unab-änderlichen Gesetze der Natur nicht Täuschung—nicht höchst unnatürlich seyn. Alles geht nach Gesetzen und nichts geht nach Gesetzen.") (Novalis, III, 601 [no. 291]). For Novalis as for Kafka the process by which the absolute becomes manifest in the empirical is best imagined as a kind of stripping down, a falling away of the empirical, an emergence into presence of the non-law that is always ready prior to the laws organizing consciousness.

16. "Die Mannigfaltigkeiten, die sich mannigfaltig drehen in den Mannigfaltig-keiten des einen Augenblicks, in dem wir leben. Und noch immer ist der Augenblick nicht zu Ende, sieh nur!" H, 273).

17. Der entscheidende Augenblick der menschlichen Entwicklung ist immer-während. Darum sind die revolutionären geistigen Bewegungen, welche alles Frühere für nichtig erklären, im Recht, denn es ist noch nichts geschehen" (H, 39–40).

18. "Das wunderbarste, das ewige Phaenomen, ist das eigene Daseyn. Das größeste Geheimniß ist der Mensch sich selbst—Die Auflösung dieser unendlichen Aufgabe, in der That, ist Die Weltgeschichte." (Novalis, Schriften, vol. II, ed. Richard Samuel [Stuttgart: W. Kohlhammer, 1960], 362 [no. 21]).

19. "Fern, fern geht die Weltgeschichte vor sich, die Weltgeschichte deiner Seele" (H, 273).

20. For Friedrich Schlegel things are "frozen projects, petrified actions, in which the earth could not force its way through to its purpose" ("starr gewordene Versuche, versteinerte Handlungen, in denen die Erde zu ihrem Zwecke nicht durchdringen konnte.") Kritische Friedrich-Schlegel-Ausgabe, vol. XIII, ed. Jean-Jacques Anstett (Pad-erborn: Ferdinand Schöningh, 1964), 468.

21. ". . . die ganze sichtbare Welt ist vielleicht nichts anderes als eine Motivation des einen Augenblick lang ruhenwollenden Menschen" (H, 103).

22. I am alluding to a well-known aphorism of Kafka's, one which gains a rather precise significance from the Romantic diagnosis of time as both compulsory exile from and modality of longing for the prior harmony of the absolute: "Das Negative zu tun, ist uns noch auferlegt; das Positive ist uns schon gegeben" (H, 42). The negativity of Kafka's story-machines has the hopeless purpose of annihilating humanity's temporal exile.

23. "Es war an einem Sonntagvormittag im schönsten Frühjahr" (E, 23). "Unsere Sängerin heißt Josefine" (E, 172).

24. "nichts mehr hat als den Blick auf den Vater." (Diary-entry for Feb. 11, 1913: Kafka, Tagebücher [Frankfurt a.M.: S. Fischer Verlag, 1967], 296.)

25. ". . . diese Opposition, zu der auch ich halb gehöre. . ." (E, 174).

26. "Jetzt weißt du also, was es noch außer dir gab. . ." (E, 32).

27. "Wer nur für die Zukunft sorgt, ist weniger vorsorglich, als wer nur für den Augenblick sorgt, denn er sorgt nicht einmal für den Augenblick, sondern nur für dessen Dauer" (H, 116–67).

28. "Liebe Eltern, ich habe euch doch immer geliebt" (E, 32).

29. "die Hunde waren, ich kann es nicht anders ausdrücken, noch nicht so hündisch wie heute, das Gefüge der Hundeschaft war noch locker, das wahre Wort hätte damals noch eingreifen, den Bau bestimmen, umstimmen, nach jedem Wunsche

ändern, in sein Gegenteil verkehren können und jenes Wort war da, war zumindest nahe, schwebte auf der Zungenspitze, jeder konnte es erfahren" (E, 341).

30. "Der Betrachtende ist in gewissem Sinne der Mitlebende, er hängt sich an das Lebende, er sucht mit dem Wind Schritt zu halten. Das will ich nicht sein" (H, 114).

31. "Aber immerhin Freiheit, immerhin ein Besitz" (E, 354).

32. ". . .dann wäre dort der Friede gewährleistet und ich wäre sein Wächter" (E, 377).

33. "Meine Sehnsucht waren die alten Zeiten,
Meine Sehnsucht war die Gegenwart,
Meine Sehnsucht war die Zukunft,
und mit alledem sterbe ich in einem Wächterhäuschen
am Straßenrand,
einem aufrechten Sarg, seit jeher
einem Besitzstück des Staates.
Mein Leben habe ich damit verbracht,
mich zurückzuhalten, es zu zerschlagen" (H, 388).

34. "Dann pflegen besonders friedliche Zeiten zu kommen, in denen ich meine Schlafplätze langsam, allmählich von den äußeren Kreisen nach innen verlege, immer tiefer in die Gerüche tauche, bis ich es nicht mehr ertrage und eines Nachts auf den Burgplatz stürze, mächtig unter den Vorräten aufräume und bis zur vollständigen Selbstbetäubung mit dem Besten, was ich liebe, mich fülle" (E, 364).

35. "Hier gilt auch nicht, daß man in seinem Haus ist, vielmehr ist man in ihrem Haus" (E, 372).

36. ". . .meine Burg, die auf keine Weise jemandem anderen angehören kann und die so sehr mein ist, daß ich hier letzten Endes ruhig von meinem Feind auch die tödliche Verwundung annehmen kann, denn mein Blut versickert hier in meinem Boden und geht nicht verloren" (E, 372).

37. "Niemand kann sich mit der Erkenntnis allein begnügen, sondern muß sich bestreben, ihr gemäß zu handeln. Dazu aber ist ihm die Kraft nicht mitgegeben, er muß daher sich zerstören. . . .Vor diesem Versuch nun fürchtet er sich. . . .aber das Geschehene kann nicht rückgängig gemacht, sondern nur getrübt werden. Zu diesem Zweck entstehen die Motivationen. Die ganze Welt ist ihrer voll. . . ." (H, 102–3).

38. ". . .die feste, wenn auch nicht mehr stolze Überzeugung, daß er weiter-hungere" (E, 171).

39. "Sehr bedeutend ist der Ausdruck die Freiheit sei ein Unding; sie ist auch das einzige Nicht und Gegending." Kritische Friedrich-Schlegel-Ausgabe, vol. XIX, ed. Ernst Behler (Paderborn: Ferdinand Schöningh, 1971), 115 (no. 301).

KAFKA AND HIS METAPHORS

Not Symbols but Metaphors   Günther Anders[*]

Kafka is neither an allegorical writer nor a symbolist.

In the first chapter [of *Kafka: Pro und Contra*] we dealt with a cluster of interwoven problems. Two of these problems must be isolated, as they merit special consideration: first, the problem of "time-paralysis," for on this the "beauty" of the Kafkan text depends; and second, the problem of "inversion of guilt and punishment," for this encompasses *in nuce* his theory and theology of morality. These could be conventionally titled "Kafka as artist" and "Kafka as *homo religiosus.*"

Before we attack these two tasks, however, we must first complete a preliminary one: the explanation of the symbolic or allegoric mechanism in Kafka's works. How does it work? What drives it? What kind of transmission is it that translates the objects of "this" world into the objects of "his" world? Or perhaps, is what Kafka does a process all its own that cannot at all be designated by the usual categories of "symbolism" and "allegory"?

We started with the thesis that the "distortions" in his works aim at and prompt understanding. This thesis alone is insufficient. Even if we know that nature is forced to reveal her secrets through experimental models, nature still remains a mystery to us as long as we do not see through the models themselves. We must therefore show how the crossover from the real world to the Kafkan world is accomplished. According to what principle does Kafka cross over?

The writer of allegory starts his conventional (theological, mythological, etc.) mechanism of crossing over by substituting *images for concepts.* The real *symbolist* takes *partem pro toto,* that is, he lets one object stand for another because the one is apparently *consubstantial* with the other. Kafka does neither of these things. He translates situations, not concepts, into images. But being the "isolationist" that he is, he cannot create "symbols" in the usual sense: for only

[*]Translated by the editor for this volume from *Kafka: Pro und Contra* (München: C. H. Beck'sche Verlagsbuchhandlung, 1951), 39–42. © C. H. Beck'sche Verlagsbuchhandlung (Oscar Beck), München 1951.

the writer for whom the "Sym" is self-evident, by being part of a (godly or world) principle, can use "symbols." Because of their aversion to the "cold rationalism" of allegory, most interpreters have decided that Kafka is a "symbolist"; this reveals their superficial preference for "profundity," but not any capacity for establishing a new key for a new phenomenon (and Kafka's prose *is* a new phenomenon).

Kafka's starting point is no longer a common belief that allows symbols to grow out of it, but simply *common language* which is available even to him, the outsider, in all its breadth and depth. He cannot be robbed of it. He shares it with his courted enemy—the world. More precisely, *he borrows from the stock at hand, the imagistic element of language.* He takes metaphoric words at their word, making them literal.
Examples:

1. Because Gregor Samsa wants to live like an artist (i.e., free as air), he is a "dirty beetle" in the eyes of the respectable, "efficient" world. So in *The Metamorphosis*, Samsa wakes up as a beetle who likes to stick to the ceiling.

2. "You are all the same to me," we say of people about whom we do not care. Thus Kafka introduces as inescapable escorts of his hero on his stay two "assistants" who look exactly alike, and whom he calls by the same name, despite their allegedly individual names.

3. "To experience something personally" is a saying used when the reality of an experience is given expression. This is the basis for Kafka's "In the Penal Colony," in which punishment is not communicated orally, but rather inscribed on one's person with a needle.

4. "Living in the public eye" is a saying used to describe lack of privacy. Thus in *The Castle*, K's private life is carried on in a room of a house belonging to other people that is not even a private home; and his lovemaking to Frieda is commented on by fellow-lodgers.

But even these examples are by no means sufficient, for Kafka's language is the perfectly everyday language that even in its microscopic and abstract particles consists of metaphors. All the prepositions like "under," "with," "between" have a literal spatial significance, and many of the strangest situations in Kafkan novels become immediately understandable if we realize that Kafka has restored some cast-off visual meaning to a word or phrase.

This idea of taking language "at its word" reveals once again a method of *empiricism*, even if in an unusual sense. Human life as we live it is certainly no prelinguistic *factum brutum*, but rather one that is already interpreted in language by us. If we say, we want to "die of shame" or we are "attached to someone," or we are "uplifted" by a song, then we have already expressed something essential about human reality. What Kafka does consists of nothing more than highlighting these true pictures of language in his own. Not one of his sometimes quite absurd images is totally arbitrary: each one is based on a figurative expression that, long before Kafka, has already been applied to the human condition.

And so we have the fundamental difference between symbolism and allegory on the one hand and the Kafkan method on the other. Kafka no longer lives—as Bunyan did—in a world with which he shares accepted symbols and allegories. But he guards against thinking up allegorical inventions *ad libitum*, like Nietzsche and Wagner, those desperate creators of private mythologies. He does not invent images. He appropriates them. He puts whatever may be sensory about these images under the microscope, and, lo and behold, the metaphor shows such monstrous details that simply their description takes on a gruesome reality. The image, for which language bore the initial responsibility, is proven truthful by the detail.

Crossing over: Kafka's Metatextual Parable

Charles Bernheimer*

What I propose here is a close reading of one very short text by Kafka. . . . The text I have chosen was written in 1922 or 1923 and entitled by Kafka's friend and literary executor, Max Brod, "Von den Gleichnissen" (On Parables).[1]

On Parables

Many complain that again and again the words of the wise are merely parables [*Gleichnisse*] but useless in daily life, and this alone is all we have. When the wise man says: "Go across" [*"Gehe hinüber"*] he does not mean that one should go across to the other side, which one could accomplish without further ado if the result were worth the journey; but he means some fabulous beyond [*sagenhaftes Drüben*], something unknown to us, something which even he cannot designate more precisely [*näher*], and which therefore cannot help us here at all. Actually, all these parables are merely saying that the incomprehensible is incomprehensible, and that we knew already. But what we have to struggle with every day, those are other things.

*Reprinted from *Flaubert and Kafka: Studies in Psychopoetic Structure* (New Haven and London: Yale University Press, 1982).

Thereupon someone said: Why do you resist? Should you follow the parables, then you would yourselves become parables and with that already free of your daily labors.
Another said: I bet that is also a parable.
The first said: You have won.
The second said: But unfortunately only in parable.
The first said: No, in reality; in parable you have lost.

The complaint of "the many" concerns the question of the right use of language. These pragmatists have a clear sense of how words should function. They should be transparent vehicles of designation, unproblematic tools helping man to act more efficiently in his daily struggle with things. Linguistic signs should dissolve in favor of the objects they signify, they should refer precisely and unambiguously to the world we "have," the world present to us through sensual apprehension. Taken to its logical conclusion, the demand of the many is for a language that would radicalize the "natural" connection inherent in symbolic structure by covering each separate, heterogeneous object in the world with a word signifying that object and it alone. Such a language would be almost entirely metonymic, dependent on the spatiotemporal continuum of the outside world.

The reason the many distrust the words of the wise is that these words do not convey an immediately identifiable referential meaning. They do not designate the familiar world where the self struggles to master things but suggest instead a movement toward a fabulous beyond, toward some unknown and unspecifiable absence. Not that the sage uses words which are in themselves fabulous and incomprehensible; his horatory enunciation is obscure not because of its exotic vocabulary but because it lacks an intentional object. The many are told neither *what* to cross over nor to *where;* nor is the outcome of the suggested crossing elucidated. Without such clear designations, the many cannot judge the value of displacing themselves into a sphere outside their own empirical acquaintance. For them, "the other side" presents no epistemological or ontological problems. It exists in proximity and could be gone over to without difficulty, if the result could be shown to be worth the effort. Otherness is defined in terms of empirical differences, differences measurable, for instance, in terms of distance to be traversed and time to be spent in transit.

Thus, instead of being a guide to action, the sage's words perform a certain unsettling deviation in the many's relation to reality and to truth. They begin with a postulate: the man who says "Go across" is recognized to be a sage who speaks the parabolic language of wisdom. Yet this language subverts the many's sense that truth is immanent in the things of this world and that words are true insofar as they function mimetically to make those things intelligible and subject to order. The words of the wise, paradoxically, are wise precisely insofar as they allude to a meaning irrecuperable within the many's predominantly metonymic framework, the framework of Eros. Otherness, in the discourse of the wise man, escapes designation, cannot be thought of as "near" or "close." It is always elsewhere, always beyond, in the realm of myth, legend, or fable. This realm acts as an unknowable supplement to the world the many assume as given. As the etymology of *sagenhaft* implies (related to saying, to story), the constitution of this fabulous excess derives from the freedom of language to posit any referent regardless of its presence or absence. The *sagenhaft* exploits the metaphoricity of language, its irresponsible fictionality; hence the many's irritation at its uselessness in their daily struggle with things.

The difference between the many and the wise may be elucidated in terms of Nietzsche's distinction, in "On Truth and Lie in an Extra-Moral Sense," between the reasonable man and the intuitive man. Both, says Nietzsche, desire to rule over life, "the first by knowing how to obviate the principal difficulties through foresight, cleverness and regularity, the second, as an 'overly joyful hero,' by not seeing those difficulties and taking as real only life dissimulated as illusion [*Schein*] and beauty."[2] Nietzsche differentiates these two classes of men primarily through their attitudes to the fundamentally metaphoric quality of language. For as Nietzsche describes its genesis, language is at least doubly metaphoric: first a nerve impulse is transferred into an image, then that image is transformed into a sound. Each "crossing-over" involves "a complete leaping over spheres right into a totally other and new one" (373). In fact, Nietzsche finds that images, which he calls perceptual metaphors, are most often themselves submitted to further metaphorization before their transformation into sound. This happens because social training teaches us to condense potentially artistic and individualized first impressions into preexistent conceptual molds that bear the stamp of recognized truths. These truths are then no longer apprehended as metaphors, for their generation through a process of multiple transfers and leaps over gaps has been forgotten.

The reasonable man collaborates in this strategy of forgetting. "Only by forgetting that primitive world of metaphor," Nietzsche writes, "only by the hardening and numbing of a mass of images that originally streamed forth in ardent fluidity from the primal capacity of human fantasy, only through the unconquerable belief that *this* sun, *this* window, *this* table, is a truth in itself, in short only insofar as man forgets himself as subject, and indeed as *artistically creating* subject, does he live with some peace, security and consequence" (377). The reasonable man, like the many in Kafka's parable, wishes to live according to these values, the values of Eros. He does not want to have to question the status of his language or of the world designated in that language. Language for him performs the role of what Winnicott calls a "transitional object."[3] It functions to link the inner and the outer, the created and the found, but only so long as its own position in relation to these oppositions is not challenged. The many's reasonable confidence that a language of truth could symbolically "cover" the world derives from their trust in the necessary and proper link between words and things and in the stable identities of both subject and object. Consequently they believe that there is such a thing as "correct perception, which would mean," says Nietzsche, "the adequate expression of the object in the subject" (378).

The intuitive man, on the other hand, not only does not forget the metaphorical derivation of language but exploits its independence from the bonds of reference to exuberantly create new forms and ideas in the realm of myth and art. This man considers language to be entirely rhetorical, entirely figural, and hence, from the viewpoint of the reasonable man's truth-expectations, entirely deceitful. Language does not provide a transitional bridge from a subjective inside to an objective outside. Rather it establishes a free aesthetic relation in which both subject and object are created as loci of metaphoric transfers: "For between two absolutely different spheres," comments Nietzsche, "as between subject and object, there is no causality, no correctness, no expression, but rather, at best, an *aesthetic* relation, I mean an allusive transfer [*andeutende Übertragung*], a translation which stammers after in a completely foreign language—for which it would, however, in any case need a freely composing and freely inventing middle-sphere and middle-force" (378). Language is a dissimulating in-between that makes any supposed "knowledge" of self or other purely allusive and alien. The "overly joyful hero" celebrates this liberating ignorance by tearing apart the spatiotemporal continuities and the stable identities dear to the man of Eros: "The liberated intellect destroys [the scaffold of concepts], throws it into confusion, ironically puts it together again, pairing that which is most foreign and separating that which is closest" (382). By making all signifiers into interchangeable pieces free from any constraining context of reference, the intuitive man metaphorizes metonymy. Nietzsche seems to recognize the relation of this process to the death instinct when he remarks that the intuitive man "suffers more intensely [than the stoic man who governs himself with concepts] *when* he suffers; and indeed he suffers more often, because he does not understand how to learn from experience and always falls again into the same trap [pit] he fell into before" (383–84). Whereas the reasonable man searches to attain "peace, security and consequence" by putting faith in the cognitive value of his own experience, the intuitive man has no such faith, experience for him being a constantly renewable play of aesthetic possibilities. Creative as this play may be, it is threatening to the life that sustains art.

Let us return now to Kafka's parable. It remains to be demonstrated that the wise man in the parable is homologous to the intuitive man in "On Truth and Lie." An analysis of the closing dialogical section of the parable will, I think, justify the homology. The first speaker in this section appears to have taken upon himself the task of explaining the meaning of the wise man's exhortation to "Go across." His explanation, however, is itself in parabolic form, and hence just as useless in the daily life of the many as was the statement it purports to elucidate. This, in effect, is what the second speaker, a representative of the many, maintains, even stating his conviction in the form of a bet. The first agrees—yes, my statement is parabolic, you win. But only in your terms, that is, from the point of view of reality, from the point of view that insists on the referential, anaclitic function of words and encourages one to forget the free-floating metaphoricity of language. From the point of view of parable, the substitution of one metaphoric discourse for another does no more than reveal the very principle of parabolic structure. So the individual who imagines he can deconstruct parable by pointing to its lack of grounding in reality is a loser ignorant of parable's irresponsible independence from the world of reference.

Not only does the one parable substitute for the other, it also repeats that other. The first speaker's advice to follow the parables repeats the wise man's advice to go across to what the many conceive as a "fabulous beyond." The exigency of parable seems to remain the same no matter the form of its expression. The speaker simply identifies what is *sagenhaft* as parable itself and interprets the result of crossing over into that undefinable realm "beyond" as actually becoming parable. Thus the goal of the *Gleichnis* is to promote *gleichwerden*, the dissolution of conscious difference into the self-expression of words. Such a dissolution would do away with language as a stammering translation, aesthetic transfer, or allusive crossing. The sign in this state would be entirely enclosed within its own self-reflective system, self and world assimilated into the abstract metaphoricity of language. Such an assimilation, as the dialogic structure opposing win and loss indicates, signifies pure loss in terms of reality, i.e., death. To follow the parable is to fuse into language is to die to the world and thus be free of one's daily labors.

Clearly, neither the wise man nor his avatar, the first speaker, has taken his own advice, for had he done so he would himself have become *sagenhaft* and hence no longer able to "say." Thereby he would have radicalized the aesthetic activity of Nietzsche's intuitive man to the point of assimilating life entirely into the realm of rhetorical illusion. And, as Kafka remarked, "one cannot express that which one is, since that is precisely what one is; one can only communicate that which is not, i.e., the lie."[4] In effect, it is only because the wise have refused their own exhortation to become parable that they can be represented in the textual world, where the only truth is that of the lie. Their textual existence belies their advice and signifies the successful resistance of Eros to the urges of Thanatos.

It should be clear now that the goals both of the many and of the wise lie outside the reach of language. The many want words to signify things purely metonymically, the wise want words to signify other words purely metaphorically. But language can only exist as a constant process of crossing between these two unattainable limits, to which it can at most allude in what Nietzsche calls an *andeutende Übertragung*.

Hence the wise man's saying "Go across" may be read reflexively as defining the very structure of the text that inscribes it. This text mediates between the "here" of metonymic dependence and the "there" of metaphoric independence. This allusive mediation undermines the apparently clear-cut opposition between reality and parable. For "reality," as the many wish it to be signified, is based on the same kind of setting-at-equality that characterizes the goal of parable. In the one case words are set as equal to things, in the other as equal to themselves. The first operation is described by Nietzsche as follows: "All thought, judgment, perception as comparison [*Vergleichen*] has as its precondition a *positing* of equality [*Gleich*-setzen] and earlier still a *making*-equal [*Gleich*-machen]."[5] The second operation absorbs whatever lies outside perception and judgment. Its effect is suggested by Zarathustra's parodic reversal of the famous closing lines of the mystical chorus in Faust: "Alles das 'Unvergängliche'—das ist auch nur ein Gleichnis"[6] ("All that is 'unchangeable,' that too is merely a parable"). So the text may be seen as mediating between two modes of *Gleichnis*, one directed toward a metonymic positing-of-equality with reality *(das Vergängliche)*, the other toward a metaphoric positing-of-equality with parable *(das Unvergängliche)*.

The positions adopted by the two speakers at the close of Kafka's text can be articulated within a structure of mutual contradiction only because each speaker ignores the impossibility of the *Gleich-machen* that defines his own claim to truth. Each asserts that he stands on a firm basis from the perspective of which the grounding of the other appears fictional, mystified, illusory. But actually the ground of each is fictional from the outset. It is subject only to *Andeutung*, to approximate approach, but never to the perfect capture of self-coincidence or of antithetical contradiction. "My repugnance for antitheses is certain," Kafka wrote in his diary. "It is true that they make for thoroughness, fullness, completeness [*Gründlichkeit, Fülle, Lückenlosigkeit*], but only like a figure on the wheel of life; we have chased our little idea around the circle. [Antitheses] are as lacking in nuances as they may be different, they grow under one's hand as though bloated by water, beginning with a prospect of the unlimited, they always end up in the same medium size."[7]

Lückenlosigkeit (literally, "being without gaps") is the goal of *Gleich-machen.* Hence it motivates both speakers in the text and determines the structure of their opposition. That opposition dramatizes the conflict between the two poles of textual structure, both of which may be thought of as belonging to a parabolic *sagenhaftes Drüben.* This conflict, however, is staged within a text that implicitly develops a quite different notion of parabolic structure. In effect, Kafka's text does not advocate a *Gleich-machen* either in the Erotic sense of the many, or in the Thanatotic sense of the wise. Kafka's text goes across without advancing any goal to the crossing and without choosing between the opposed modes of otherness proposed by the many and the wise. In this sense, his text never "arrives." It articulates, as he says about antitheses, a middle or medium sphere of suspended significance. Unable to attach itself either to a subject or an object, a presence or an absence, it composes an aesthetic structure by transferring and translating in-between. It is metatextual not in the sense that it comments on an earlier text or scriptive act that it inscribes. Rather the metatext is *meta* in that it is structured as a dramatization of the conflict between the psychopoetic orientations that constitute it. If pursued exclusively, either one of these orientations becomes parabolic. Hence Kafka's text can be termed a parable of metatextuality only if it is understood that metatextual structure undoes the concept of parable advanced within the text itself. Nevertheless, the suggested existence of both parabolic poles is necessary to ensure the metatextual suspension that excludes them.

Nietzsche is often presented as a thinker who denied this necessity for polarity and believed that man could live, and a text be structured, solely by the free play of metaphoricity. Thus Derrida, in a well-known passage, speaks of the Nietzschean affirmation "which is no longer turned toward the origin, affirms freeplay and tries to pass beyond man and humanism, the name man being the name of that being who, throughout the history of metaphysics or of ontotheology—in other words, through the history of all of his history—has dreamed of full presence, the reassuring foundation, the origin and the end of the game."[8] Derrida's Nietzsche appears to be a man who has taken the sage's advice, has actually managed to cross over and, most astonishing of all, has been able to communicate from that sphere "beyond man and humanism." In effect, this interpretation of Nietzsche as a jubilantly affirmative "overly joyous hero" plays a kind of parabolic role in much contemporary criticism. Nietzsche himself, however, was by no means as ready as are some of his putative disciples to dismiss the unifying and binding function of Eros. Thus he declares on numerous occasions that man *cannot live* without a belief in some essential ground for knowledge. For example, in *The Will to Power*, he writes: "To make even the tiniest degree of knowledge possible an unreal and erroneous world had to be born: beings who believed in the permanent, in individuals, etc. It was necessary first of all that an imaginary world be born that was the contrary of the eternal flux. Then, on this *foundation* some knowledge could be built. In short, one can well see the fundamental error on which all is based (because antinomies can be thought), but this error can only be destroyed with life itself; the final truth, which is the eternal flux of all things, does not allow itself to be incorporated into us; our organs (which serve life) are made for error."[9] Permanence, identity, "man," these are, says Nietzsche, erroneous illusions built on a purely invented structure of opposition. But since they are nevertheless necessary for the continuance of life, their illusory quality must be forgotten, at least a good part of the time. Life must be sustained, even at the expense of a loss of lucidity and the preservation of illusions that, because we forget their error, generate knowledge which appears as true.

This explains why, despite Kafka's distaste for antitheses, his texts are so often structured in terms of conflict, confrontation, battle. Critics have repeatedly misread these texts by trying to define the goal of the struggle. But the goal is entirely structural: what is at issue is whether the struggle can be maintained, whether a confrontation is at all possible, whether lucidity will not destroy the life-sustaining illusions that make for error. The struggles of Joseph K. in *The Trial* and K. in *The Castle* are not battles against overwhelming paternal authorities but rather futile efforts to construct such authorities so that confrontation and battle can take place. Antithesis is a structure of error, Kafka recognizes, but one closely related to the wheel of life. It is capable of generating a ground for being on the basis of the Erotically charged attributes of *Gründlichkeit, Fülle, Lückenlosigkeit*. Thus, although both the mutually exclusive oppositions of the many to the wise (in Kafka) and of the rational to the intuitive man (in Nietzsche) are deluded in their antithetical structure, this delusion reflects the texts' truth to life as error. Kafka would agree with Nietzsche's declaration, in *Beyond Good and Evil*, that "without accepting the fictions of logic, without measuring reality against the purely invented world of the unconditional and self-identical [the world of the *Gleichnis*], without a constant falsification of the world by means of numbers, man could not live."[10]

Thus Nietzsche denies the possibility, evoked by Derrida in his name, of a complete break with human history and a celebration of the free play of metaphoricity. This free play, which would do away with the erroneous logical and metaphysical structures of opposition, contradiction, and antithesis, constitutes an unreachable limit that Nietzsche, like the wise man in Kafka's text, can imagine, but that only a superman, a being somehow always awaited in the fictional future, could embody. So despite Nietzsche's statement, in *The Gay Science*, that "one could conceive of such a pleasure and power of self-determination, such a *freedom* of the will that the spirit would take leave of all faith and every wish for certainty, being practiced in maintaining himself on insubstantial ropes and possibilities and dancing even near abysses,"[11] this conception defines an "overly joyful" utopia which falsely pretends that the truth of flux can be incorporated into man.

"Truth is indivisible," declares Kafka in one of his aphorisms, "therefore cannot know itself. Anyone who desires to know it must be a lie."[12] At the one pole of textual structure is the indivisibility of flux, death-oriented truth of the wise, at the other the indivisibility of individual objects, life-oriented truth of the many. The metatext treats this polar opposition as a lie necessary to life and to knowledge, and hence to its own generation. Yet it does not allow this structural lie to appear as its own truth. It recuperates that [truth] allusively by collapsing the opposition between truth and lie that seemed to constitute its ground, leaving a middle sphere limited to the irresolvable process of *Andeutung*.

The notion of *Andeutung* is related to the etymological meaning of the English word *parable*. *Deuten* in German means to interpret, explain, signify, while an as prefix refers to a temporal future or spatial remove. *Parable* derives from the Greek *paraballein*, to compare. This word in turn is composed of the verb *ballein*, to throw, plus the prefix *para*, which has a variety of meanings when employed in compounds: beside, beyond, subsidiary to, faulty, harmful.[13] So parable is a throwing to the side of, or in front of, with the implication that this act, performed in order to compare, is somehow faulty or wrongful. Etymologically it is closely related to *diaballein*, literally to throw across but figuratively to slander, and hence to *diabolus*, slanderer, devil. Thus the parable, which presents itself as a story illustrating a truth, suggests through its etymology that no truth can be illustrated, that any comparison is a diabolic throwing-across whose very figuration is a slanderous distortion. "Writing," Kafka wrote to Brod in 1922, "is the reward for serving the devil."[14]

Andeutung, I want to stress, operates in both directions of semantic structure, the metonymic and the metaphoric. But I would not be true to Kafka's intense spiritual exigency if I did not grant that the crucial going-across, for him as for the wise man, is to the metaphoric pole. Thus in an aphorism he uses the word *andeuten* to describe the only possible mode of writing about what is subjective or transcendent: "For all things outside the phenomenal world," Kafka declares, "language can be employed only in the manner of an illusion [*andeutungsweise*] but never even approximately in the manner of a comparison [*vergleichsweise*] since in accordance with the phenomenal world it is concerned with property and its relations."[15] The *Vergleich*, like the *Gleichnis*, works to equalize, to make the same. Only whereas the *Gleichnis* attempts to do this by excluding the opposed pole of psychopoetic structure, the aim of the *Vergleich* is to appropriate the metaphorical in terms of the metonymic, that is, to end the play of crossings and translations by binding the polar modes into one stable semantic union. In contrast, *Andeutung* respects and encourages this play. Thus, for Kafka, both the inward, psychological realm and the metaphysical world beyond can only be intimated as an always-elsewhere to which one can never cross over and to which no comparative structure can be thrown across.

But language is just as ineffectual and deceitful when dealing with the property relations to which it is, nevertheless, restricted. This is brought out in Kafka's diary entry for December 6, 1921: "Metaphors are one among many things that make me despair of writing. Writing's lack of independence, its dependence on the maid who tends the fire, on the cat warming itself by the stove, even on the poor old human being warming himself. All these are independent activities ruled by their own laws; only writing is helpless, cannot live in itself, is a joke and a despair."[16] Here Kafka bemoans the inevitable contamination of metaphor by metonymy. Metonymic structure forces language to be dependent on the juxtapositions given in the world (maid tending the fire by which lies the cat and next to which sits the man). Yet this very dependence keeps language at a distance from the self-determining status of the givens themselves. On the other hand, when writing attempts to liberate itself from the limitations of reference by adopting the overreaching structure of metaphor, it is inevitably brought back to the realization of its necessary reliance on the phenomenal world.

It is this dependence on the context of daily life ("and this alone is all we have") that deconstructive criticism tends to dismiss as naive, nostalgic, and mystified. Derrida attacks the notion of a constraining context for meaning, whether real or linguistic, by asserting that all writing is subject to being lifted out of its intentional framework and grafted onto any number of different signifying chains.[17] In contrast to the sophisticated appeal of this graft onto some "fabulous beyond," the many's attachment to the immediate experiential context of their daily labors may well seem unimaginative and limiting, even regressive if it is linked to the infantile experience of identification with the mother. But Kafka, unlike the contemporary advocates of the abyss, admits his vulnerability to the exigencies of this limit and does not pretend that either life or a text is conceivable apart from the structuring function of Eros. The many are not hopelessly unliterary because of their trust in the referentiality of language and their dependence on a world rendered intelligible through perception and experience. Their naiveté is as much a part of textual structure as is the disseminating force that frustrates its demands. So, textually speaking, the opposition of naive and disillusioned readings may be yet another erroneous distortion produced by the devil within the parable.

Notes

1. The German text, with an inaccurate English translation, is readily available in Franz Kafka, Parables and Paradoxes (New York: Schocken, 1961), 10–11.

2. Friedrich Nietzsche, "Über Wahrheit und Lüge im aussermoralischen Sinne," in *Nachgelassene Schriften 1870–1873*; Vol. 3, part 2 of *Nietzsche Werke*, ed. Georgio Colli and Mazzino Montinari (Berlin: Walter de Gruyter, 1973), 383. [All future in-text references are to this work.]

3. For more on this concept, see Bernheimer, "Introduction," in *Flaubert and Kafka: Studies in Psychopoetic Structure* (New Haven and London: Yale University Press), 19.

4. Kafka, *Hochzeitsvorbereitungen auf dem Lande und andere Prosa aus dem Nachlaß* (Frankfurt: S. Fischer, 1953), 343.

5. Friedrich Nietzsche, *Gesammelte Werke*, vol. 19 (München: Musarion Verlag, 1926), 22; *The Will to Power*, trans. and ed. Walter Kaufmann (New York: Vintage, 1967), 273–74.

6. Nietzsche, *Gesammelte Werke*, vol. 13 (München: Musarion Verlag, 1925), 166; *Thus Spake Zarathustra* in *The Portable Nietzsche*, trans. and ed. Walter Kaufmann (New York: Viking, 1954), 238.

7. Kafka, *Tagebücher 1910–1923* (Frankfurt: S. Fischer, 1951), 168. English translation: *Diaries 1910–1913* (New York: Schocken, 1965), 157.

8. Jacques Derrida, "Structure, Sign, and Play in the Discourse of the Human Sciences" in *The Languages of Criticism and the Sciences of Man: The Structuralist Controversy*. ed. Richard Macksey and Eugenio Donato (Baltimore: The Johns Hopkins University Press, 1970), 264–65.

9. Text quoted by Sarah Kofman, *Nietzsche et la métaphore* (Payot, 1972) 189.

10. Nietzsche, *Beyond Good and Evil*, trans. and ed. Walter Kaufmann (New York: Vintage, 1966), 12.

11. Nietzsche, *The Gay Science*, trans. Walter Kaufmann (New York: Vintage, 1974), 289–90.

12. Kafka, *Hochzeitsvorbereitungen*, 48.

13. My observations here are indebted to J. Hillis Miller's remarks on the uncanny character of the prefix *para* in "The Critic as Host," *Critical Inquiry*, 3, no. 3 (Spring 1977):441.

14. Kafka, *Letters to Friends, Family, and Editors* (New York: Schocken, 1977), 333.

15. Kafka, *Hochzeitsvorbereitungen*, 45.

16. Kafka, *Tagebücher*, 396. English translation: *Diaries 1914–1923* (New York: Schocken, 1965), 200–1.

17. Jacques Derrida, "Signature Évenement Contexte," in *Marges de la philosophie* (Éditions de Minuit, 1972). Translated in *Glyph 1* (Baltimore: The Johns Hopkins Press, 1977); see particularly 181–86.

Kafka's Writing Machine: Metamorphosis in the Penal Colony

Arnold Weinstein°

1

Like all of Kafka's best stories, "In the Penal Colony" is maddeningly rife with multiple and contradictory interpretations. Some have made it announce Auschwitz and Dachau; others have seen in it a grim reminder of harsher Old Testament values, according to which our modern liberal world stands either condemned or threatened; the brief tale has been read psychologically, psychoanalytically, anthropologically, historically, paradoxically and parabolically.[1] No matter how one reads it, however, the story's resolution, i.e., the explorer's response to the penal colony, appears so ambivalent that it becomes effectively impossible to do the very thing that is central here and happening everywhere in Kafka: pronounce judgment. My purpose, in proposing a new look at the story, is to centralize the notion of communication and language; in so doing, we begin to perceive the awesome coherence of Kafka's materials: the disturbing, echoing analogies between the narrative frame, the nature of the Machine, and the purposes of art.

"It's a remarkable *[eigentümlich]* piece of apparatus,"[2] Kafka's genius in mixing understatement and prophecy—so often in evidence in the first lines of his stories[3]—is fully displayed here. Just how *"eigentümlich,"* just how special the machine is, is something the explorer and, indeed, the reader must gradually come to understand. The entire story may, in fact, be seen as a gloss on these lines: how can the officer make the explorer adequately comprehend the machine? The critical debate concerning the story suggests that its readers have been equally perplexed, equally stymied in their grasp of these strange events. There is nothing contrived or redundant about Kafka's insistence on the process of understanding. The desperation and passion of the story lie precisely in the officer's efforts to reach the explorer, to bring the outsider over to his own point of

° Reprinted from *Studies in Twentieth Century Literature*, vol. 7, no. 1 (Fall 1982).

view.[4] One might even go so far as to say that the officer's project is more profoundly rhetorical than it is judgmental: to persuade the explorer counts ultimately more than punishing the prisoner. One even has the sense that the justice of the entire System (that of the Old Commander, to be sure) is strangely dependent on the explorer's verdict: to understand the special nature of the machine would restore Truth and Clarity to a world riddled with doubt and equivocation. This mutual drama of understanding is, as it were, the hidden script of the story, and Kafka's shows, if I may extend his own metaphor, just how thick our skin is.

There was a time, we are told, when the validity of the machine did not require such special pleading. The spectacle of justice being done was an occasion of civic and spiritual celebration, a time of community. Crowds came from far and near, and children were given preferential treatment in seating arrangements. It is no wonder that children witnessed these events, since they seem to have possessed a rather extraordinary educational potential. There was not yet any uncertainty or confusion in matters of innocence and guilt: all parties—including the victim—experienced a collective revelation of truth. These were halcyon days, epistemologically as well as morally: " '. . . often enough I would be squatting there with a small child in either arm. How we all absorbed the look of transfiguration on the face of the sufferer, how we bathed our cheeks in the radiance of that justice, achieved at last and fading so quickly! What times these were, my comrade!' The officer had obviously forgotten whom he was addressing: he had embraced the explorer and laid his head on his shoulder. The explorer was deeply embarrassed, impatiently he stared over the officer's head" (154). Notice how the moment of transparency is an irresistible moment of sharing and bonding. Moreover, the community spirit embodied in these public executions is again activated, communalized through narration: the officer embraces the explorer, as a natural extension of those brother days, but finds coolness, objectivity and embarrassment instead. The officer seeks, throughout the entire story, to "touch" the explorer; the explorer, man from another realm, keeps his distance. I am less interested in assessing the explorer's character than in underscoring his detachment, his quasi-professional sense of noninvolvement. Yet, as we shall see, distanced judgment counts for naught in Kafka; "understanding" something comes, sooner or later, to mean "entering" into it, and in this story such an entry will be literally enacted at the close. In Kafka's work, filled as it is with endless corridors, closed doors, secret chambers and labyrinthine passages, contact with the Other, sought, feared or enacted at every level of the narrative, is both the ultimate hunger and the ultimate taboo.

2

From our vantage point in the latter part of the 20th century, "In the Penal Colony" can hardly be viewed as anything other than a horror story, a torture story. The grotesque disproportion between crime and punishment, the radical assumption of guilt, the heinous nature of the sentence, the powerfully symbolic dysfunction of the machine, all this seems to constitute an irreversible indictment of the officer and his penal system. Finally, the machine itself appears to be on trial: technical know-how, mechanical expertise and scientific engineering have, as we know today better than Kafka can have known in 1914, a will and impetus of their own, determining rather than serving the human uses to which they are put. The machine may then be *"eigentümlich,"* in that it is the most seductive and potent agent of the story, the ultimate winner in the modernist game of rhetorical persuasion, the forerunner not only of Dachau and Auschwitz, but of all the technological nightmare of our own nuclear age.

And yet . . . Kafka's story refuses to fit this scenario. There is something great as well as something disturbing in Kafka's machine. Technical craft, fine-tuning and scientific precision must have a special *(eigentümlich)* appeal to any artist. Given what we know of Kafka's self-discipline as a writer, his torturous sense that what he had written would not quite do, we are compelled to feel that this complex, harmonious (up-to-now) perfectly functioning machine—with its complete adequation of ends and means—cannot be simply dismissed as evil. Finally, our post-1914 history, with its well-known atrocities, has, it is true, enabled us to read Kafka's story in a grimly prescient manner; but it has also led us to *misread* Kafka's story, to see in it the precursor of concentration camps, but to miss the echoes of Flaubertian aesthetics, the Flaubertian mystique of a *mot juste* that would miraculously wed language to reality. The most painstaking and scrupulous of authors, Kafka knew all too well that words veil as well as disclose, that they can only name, never be; how can he not have yearned for that Edenic realm where language and substance are united, that *Heimat* whose uniform the officer still wears, in poignant contrast to the homelessness of the explorer who is afloat in the relativism of his age and is rooted nowhere. Finding a potent language is then, the unifying thread of Kafka's story: in this light, the machine's special power perfectly images the drama of understanding and contact at the heart of the tale.

Understanding is the cornerstone of all community, and language has, since the beginning of human society, played a crucial bridge-making role in the interactions between men and their gods, between men and themselves. Much of Kafka's work seems polarized by the

two dominant modes of such relationships, the Old Law and the New
Law, the injunctions of authority versus the openness of love. In this
story, Kafka has introduced still another basic antithesis: the memory
of a time when Truth was known and despotically enforced, versus
our modern period of liberal relativism with its bureaucratic procedures. The written word, as Kafka well knew, has long been central
to the transmission of Truth; the German word for "writing" is
"*Schrift*," and Kafka significantly noted that it also stands for "Scriptures," for holy books. A number of critics have been drawn to this
connection, and they have sketched elaborate parallels between the
religiously guarded, hieroglyphic instructions for the machine and
the sacred books of the past;[5] but, whether it be Old Testament or
New, Torah or Talmud, this written document now fails to create its
community of believers. The explorer cannot decipher it. But, let us
not reduce the role of "*Schrift*" to the page of instructions for the
machine; if we apply to it the more modern sense of "language,"
"discourse," or "*écriture*," then we see the larger spectrum of communicative acts which make up the form and meaning of the tale.
The old absolute code may be defunct, but the machine remains, and
so, too, does human language. In the secular present, literature itself
may be called on to regenerate the interactions between men and
their gods, men and themselves. Written and spoken language are
the last remaining agents of connection. They are civilization's vehicle
for understanding, and if they can no longer peremptorily command
assent, they can perhaps strive for a still nobler goal: to invite response,
to incite love. Understanding and love enable mutuality in a world
that contains only individuals. Understanding and love are modes of
entry, promises of reciprocity. The writer, more than most, plays a
role in this drama, because his is the medium that bonds and connects.
In the old days, the machine made truth visible, and all understood,
together. As a means of commonality, such understanding has nothing
to do with logic or system; it is knowledge, in the biblical sense of
experience, of entry into things. Without this kind of understanding,
human beings are either logical robots or animals of instinct, achieving
no knowledge worth having, whether of the self or of the other. "In
the Penal Colony" is about the inadequacy of these extremes, and
it is in the creation of his macabre but mesmerizing machine that
we may find Kafka's strange remedy.

The distance maintained by the explorer has already been mentioned. Vaguely an emissary of "our" humanist society, he is perplexed
by the conflict between judgment and action; he disapproves, but
does not want to meddle. He leaves the island apparently unchanged
in his views, preventing the soldier and the prisoner from following
him. He threatens them with a heavy, knotted rope, as if they were
subhuman. And they are. Kafka has decribed the prisoner as "a man

with crude features and thick lips," whose passivity is "doglike and submissive"; his crime is strictly one of instinct: when whipped in the face by his superior, "instead of getting up and begging pardon, the man caught hold of his master's legs, shook him and cried, 'Throw that whip away or I'll eat you alive' " (146). The soldier and the prisoner, squatting in dirt and vomit, listen uncomprehendingly as the officer explains—in French no less, so that the opaqueness of our language is even more blatantly illustrated—the machine to the explorer. All we see is "the movement of his blubber lips, closely pressed together, [which] showed clearly that he [the prisoner] could not understand a word" (144). Asking if the prisoner even knows what his crime is, the explorer dutifully demonstrates his allegiance to the humanist code; but that code, predicated on the possibility of self-knowledge and implemented through the use of spoken and written language, is shattered by the officer's answer, an answer that resonates throughout the story: "There would be no point in telling him. He'll learn it on his body" (145). Whereas most critics have focused on the glaring injustice of such a procedure, the calm as-suredness that guilt need hardly be "proven" since it is concomitant with existence, what has gone largely uncommented is Kafka's radical view of communication itself. For now we see the awesome mediation which the machine is to provide: spoken language, French in this case, but arguably all language, including potentially this story, the full exchange between the officer and the explorer, the reader and the text, fails to deliver its message, fails to penetrate one's being, to get through one's skin, to make an entry, to effect intercourse or discourse, to transform animals into men.

Kafka is dealing with the most elemental problem known to verbal creatures. Language cannot *be* what it says. And men's skins are thick. This story depicts a search for language that is immediate rather than mediated, and it comes up with a terrible solution: we must learn viscerally, not verbally; the script must be in us, not in front of us. As if he were a geneticist, aware that our very chemistry and molecules perform linguistic operations, Kafka seems to be saying that the verbal message can achieve a magic oneness with its referent, only if it is encoded in our flesh. Kafka's machine is a writing machine. It actualizes and vitalizes all our tired metaphors and proverbs for knowledge: "*tief*," "deep" awareness, to understand something "vis-cerally," to scratch the surface, to be penetrated by knowledge, to have an "inner" certainty.[6] Thick-skinned, "thick-lipped" humans need no less. The machine provides deep knowledge; its prisoners achieve a visceral understanding of their crimes; its needles constantly furnish "a new deepening of the script." At the sixth hour, meta-morphosis occurs, and the dual event happens: animals become men, and individuals become a community:

Only about the sixth hour does the man lose all desire to eat I usually kneel down here at that moment and observe what happens. The man rarely swallows his last mouthful, he only rolls it around his mouth and spits it out into the pit. . . . But how quiet he grows at just about the sixth hour! Enlightenment comes to the most dull-witted. It begins around the eyes. From there it radiates. A moment that might tempt one to get under the Harrow oneself. Nothing more happens than that the man begins to understand the inscription, he purses his mouth as if he were listening. You have seen how difficult it is to decipher the script with one's eyes: but our man deciphers it with his wounds. . . (150).

Let there be no mistake about the double miracle at work here. It is a miracle of truth, but it is no less a miracle of art: transparency is at hand, and language is one with experience and knowledge.

3

Such knowledge and such language are fatal. Biologically, the individual is a closed system, but orifices and apertures play their role in our life. The animal body takes in and puts out food; the species cannot continue if the male does not enter the female. Safety is provided by enclosure, but the entries and exits of the body must have daily commerce if the organism is to survive. In Kafka's work, food and sex—the most basic modes of entry into the closed body—are portrayed in starkly ambivalent ways: K. and Frieda lick and nuzzle each other like dogs; Gregor Samsa starves to death, while sensing in the music and love of his sister that impossibly refined nourishment which he seeks; the hunger artist's rarefied art—his professional refusal of the body—is replaced by solid appetites of the panther. The prisoner, at the sixth hour, spits out the food so that he can attend to the new body language he is receiving. Kafka seems to feel horror at the body, but he reveres the human longing for sustenance and contact.[7] This yearning is viscerally experienced by many of his characters, but gratification does not appear to be fully imaginable, much less achievable. His are the most searching, uncompleted characters in modern literature. Hence, he has bequeathed to us the most thorough embodiment of walled-in, bureaucratized, reified man that we have. Functionaries inhabit Kafka's world, because functions have replaced relationships: mutuality and reciprocity are cut off at every turn. Demarcation is everywhere, preserving distances, making character into cipher, defying intercourse. "The Burrow" is merely an extreme instance of the fear of contact and violation, of being broken and entered, which is everywhere operative in his work.

Art would seem, in Kafka's world, to promise a finer intercourse,

an unthreatening commerce between selves, a penetration that gra-
tifies but does not maim. If nourishment and love cannot come through
the flesh, than perhaps the mind and its agency of language can
provide them. Thus, we return to the notions of understanding and
knowledge as openness to the Other. Language is doubtless the most
privileged vehicle of figurative contact; it renders possible a very
special type of exchange, wherein the self remains physically intact
but nonetheless entered. The beauty and horror of Kafka's story lie
in the creation of physical language, a material linguistics with a
distinct cutting edge that guarantees immediacy and requires no
translation. The enclosed nature of the self and the thickness of its
heart, mind and skin can at last be cut through. "In the Penal Colony"
presents a nightmarish version of the *open* self as the *opened* self,
with the attendant horror of violation and mutilation fully enacted.
The flesh itself must be rent, before understanding is achieved.

"In the Penal Colony" is ultimately a strange love story. It
registers at all levels the failure of communication, the falling short
of language, the unrelated and uncomprehending selves. The prisoner's ignorance of his "crime" is only one phase of the breakdown;
the main thrust of the tale, informed by the narrative strategy and
endowing the material with a muted urgency, lies in the officer's
declaration; his efforts to "touch" the explorer, to explain what is
special about the machine, to bring the past to life, are essentially
an attempt at seduction. All fails. The prisoner is left untouched. The
skeptical explorer does not respond to the officer's passion, the only
real emotion in the story. The pleas are received but unmet. The
explorer leaves, perhaps to explore other places. Has he understood
the machine? Has the reader understood the story?

4

In the end, as we know, the machine acts. When the explorer
fatefully denies the officer his help, when the effort to explain the
machine has been seen to fail, the exemplary, illuminating reversal
finally takes place. The officer frees the prisoner and takes his place.
The machine butchers him and self-destructs. Here, I think, we are
at the heart of Kafka's world. Many critics have understandably
focused on the behavior of the machine, suggesting either that it is
a travesty of justice (the officer is not "saved"), or that it is proper
poetic justice (the officer gets his just deserts). But the most eloquent
act of the tale is not that of the machine; it is the *geste* of the officer.
For he enacts the major transformation of the work: *the officer becomes
the prisoner*. His mission is no longer to supervise or explain, he will
encounter the machine himself, but from the inside, this time.

No more lessons. Explanations and instruction—whether deriving from holy books or as the modus operandi of modern life—are no more than a futile kind of verbal ping-pong, a doomed mode of knowledge. There is only one way to understand the machine: that is to become the prisoner. In becoming the prisoner, the officer breaks out of his role in the hierarchy and achieves, briefly, the experience of the Other. The machine breaks down because, in some profound way, its work has already been done, achieved by the officer's *geste*. The potent language offered by the machine is only one element of communication; response is the other. The officer is butchered, I think, because he has never been concerned with what truth or justice look like—from the other side. He has courted and pleaded with the explorer; yet he has regarded the prisoner as subhuman. Even though there is no sign of redemption on his face, there is no sign of torture either; the officer's act has granted him a bodily—rather than verbal—experience of justice, the fateful "inside" view that is required if one is to understand or judge others.

We know that Kafka remained dissatisfied with the last pages of the story, those that depict the explorer's visit to the tea house and final departure. The fragments that he wrote in 1917 suggest that the explorer was ultimately more implicated, more drawn in, than appears at first glance. In particular, he feels bonded to the officer, even to the extent of seeing the dead man in his imagination, with a spike protruding from his forehead. Asked if his appearance is magic, the ghost officer replies, "A mistake on your part; I was executed on your command."[8] I think it is fair to say that this fragment of a finale completes the communicative act; moreover, it restates the story's central truth: to understand the other is to become the other, to be intimately involved with his life and death.

In becoming the prisoner, the officer undergoes the fundamental Kafkaesque metamorphosis, the one that haunts his best work. To become another is the recurring structural drama of Kafka's stories: its twin faces are love and metamorphosis, understanding and trauma, transcendence of the flesh and rending of the flesh. The officer becomes the prisoner no less than Gregor Samsa becomes a bug. Kafka's country doctor experiences the same elemental upheaval: he projects, easily enough, onto the boy's wound the sexual drama at home; but he is made to lie, naked, on the bed with the boy, thereby revealing his manifold impotence, showing his own malady, becomes the patient. The officer, placing himself within the machine, illuminates Kafka's classic procedure: rational discourse and logical explanation are doomed to futility. Knowledge comes only through personal transformation, and it must be *"am eigenen Leibe erfahren,"* experienced in the flesh.

Thick-skinned humans come to knowledge of Others by an act of violent metamorphosis. In Kafka's stories, this transformation is frequently literal and monstrous, for the language bridge does not hold, and discourse remains sterile, short of understanding. But, *through* Kafka's stories, even that metamorphosis may be a figurative one of great beauty; through art, and perhaps only through art, we are able, without being dismembered or metamorphoses, to become another, to extend our first person onto the lives and events we read about. Kafka's painstaking narrative art, perhaps more than that of any other twentieth century writer, demands that extension of us, requiring that we experience, vicariously, the limits and sensations of a bug, the yearning of the hunger artist, the powerlessness of the doctor, the maze-like quandaries of K. and Joseph K., the fascination of the machine. Kafka's very narrative techniques, his skillful control of point-of-view, his intensely myopic realism, his courage to be literal—all these are features of his craft, his own writing machine, which are intended to *open* us to the world of the Other.

Many find "In the Penal Colony" a grisly, brutal story. Like the story of the exodus from the Garden, it is about the cost of knowledge. We are so accustomed to defining knowledge as information, so habituated to language as explanatory, that the high stakes and cruel outcomes of Kafka's parable seem melodramatic or Gothic. But his story depicts, with rare power, the drama of human understanding. In Borges' fine essay, "Kafka and his Precursors," he suggests that great art creates new constellations, that we see, as critics, both backwards and forwards in our efforts to discern intellectual kinship between authors. Kafka's metamorphic view of relationship and knowledge may serve as a model for literature's claim to tell us about Others. Using Borges as precedent, I would like to suggest two particular texts which leave us with the same dark knowledge. Melville's tortured tale, "Benito Cereno," depends entirely on point-of-view narrative, thereby showing that the perfectly innocent mind cannot see evil. But the underside of Melville's story is the unwritten narrative, the experience of Cereno himself which the reader begins to understand only when the tale is over. Masquerading as a white man in control, Cereno has in fact been forced to obey his Black "slaves" at every turn; the reader has seen the innocent version of events, but Cereno has experienced *from the inside,* the collapse of his role, the reality of the Blacks. And he dies. In somewhat similar manner, Faulkner's *Absalom, Absalom!* dramatizes the cost of knowledge: in this case, the two college boys, Quentin and Shreve, must somehow go beyond the data of history if they are to understand the past; in extremely elaborate ways, they achieve what Faulkner calls an "overpass to love," as they "become" the protagonists of the Civil War and experience, again from the inside, the human feelings that make up history, in this case, a bloody history of fratricide, both personal and national. Yet, here too, Faulkner does not minimize the cost of such an "overpass," and the book closes on a note of futility and exhaustion, a keen sense that we can become the Other only momentarily, and even then at the cost of our own integrity. The Melville and Faulkner examples are not properly metamorphic, but they have the same cardinal truth at their heart: knowledge of the other entails eclipse of the self, and can lead to death as well as to love.

Beyond even the metamorphosis, however, there is the machine. Kafka's writing machine is a mad figure for the role of art and understanding in a world filled exclusively with signs and flesh. How can signs and flesh be connected, the thickness of matter be penetrated by the logos of spirit? The Word of the past, the Word that spoke Truth and commanded Assent, is gone. But the writer remains. Kafka's machine depicts the need that every writer has felt for a language so potent, that it would become the reality whereof it speaks. The writing machine bespeaks and, à sa façon, remedies the absence of understanding in a degraded world: the animal body has no access to its soul; the individuals attain no contact with each other. The machine is indeed intolerable in its flagrant violation of the body, but it functions as a sublime symbol of Kafka's—and all artists'—aspirations: to read his work is to be penetrated by it; his words are inscribed in our flesh; our understanding of the story, of the Other, is to be both visceral and transcendent. The text is the machine: the metamorphosis is in us.

Notes

1. Needless to say, most Kafka commentators have, at some time or another, had something to say about "In der Strafkolonie." I have profited from the general work of Sokel. Emrich and, in particular, Politzer (Franz Kafka: Parable and Paradox [Ithaca: Cornell University Press, 1966]) who first alerted me to the notion of Schrift and its possible ramifications. Although I do not agree with Helmut Kaiser's Freudian findings ("Franz Kafkas Inferno: eine psychologische Deutung seiner Strafphantasie," in Franz Kafka, ed. Politzer [Darmstadt: Wissenschaftliche Buchgesellschaft, 1973]), his early reading remains a powerful case for character relationships in Kafka, even if sublimated or symbolic. More recent readings of Ingeborg Henel and Kurt J. Fickert have been helpful, and my thoughts about the end of the story are somewhat indebted to Richard Thieberger, "The Botched Ending of 'In the Penal Colony,' " in The Kafka Debate, ed. Flores (New York: Gordian Press, 1977). In general my interpretation is meant to shed new light on the role of language and metamorphosis in Kafka, particularly as they relate to the machine and the notion of communication. It seems to me that there has been considerable historicist work along these lines, concerning the Scriptures. Old and New Testament and the like: more recently, there has been the post-Structuralist work of Deleuze and Guattari, with very subtle and complex views of discourse theory. No one, to my knowledge, has suggested the connections I make between the machine, language, metamorphosis and the drama of understanding. Nor has anyone commented on the larger ramification of the writing machine as a producer of immediate language.

2. "In the Penal Colony," trans. W. and E. Muir, in *Kafka: The Complete Stories*, ed. Glatzer (New York: Schocken, 1976), 140. For the convenience of readers, I have used the Muir translation in the available paperback edition: all future references are taken from this edition.

3. One need merely consider the opening sentence of "Die Verwandlung": "Als Gregor Samsa eines Morgens aus unruhigen Träumen erwachte, fand er sich in seinem Bett zu einem ungeheuren Ungeziefer verwandelt." The first line of *Der Prozess* could also be cited.

4. Although much Kafka criticism has been concerned with point-of-view narrative, one of the most interesting studies on this issue is James Rolleston's *Kafka's Narrative Theater* (University Park: Pennsylvania State University Press, 1974). Rolleston's discussion of "In the Penal Colony" is both subtle and provocative in its emphasis on the posture of the explorer, his growing fascination with the machine and his bad faith in responding to it.

5. As mentioned, Politzer discusses some general ramifications of the term *Schrift*. The most detailed case for holy books has been made by Erwin Steinberg, "Die zwei Kommandanten in Kafkas 'In der Strafkolonie,' " in *Franz Kafka*, ed. Caputo-Mayr (Berlin: Agora Verlag, 1978).

6. Malcolm Pasley has also commented specifically on Kafka's manner of literalizing metaphor in this story; see his "In the Penal Colony" . . . in *The Kafka Debate*, ed. Angel Flores, (New York, Gordian Press, 1977).

7. The large and thorny issue of Kafka's attitude toward women and intimacy is dealt with by Hildegard Platzer in "The Dilemma of Mating in Kafka," *Mosaic* . . . 3, no. 4 (1970): 119–30.

8. I am indebted to Politzer's treatment of this issue and to his reference to Kafka's *Diaries;* see Politzer, *Kafka*, 112.

The All-Embracing Metaphor: Reflections on "The Burrow"   Henry Sussman[*]

> And the smaller rooms, each familiar to me, so familiar that in spite of their complete similarity I can clearly distinguish one from the other with my eyes shut by the mere feel of the wall: they enclose me more peacefully and warmly than a bird is enclosed in its nest.
>
> —"The Burrow"

1. The Extent of a Construction

The extended narrative monologue, "The Burrow," represents an extreme for Kafka's fiction while at the same time functioning as a horizon toward which certain of its decisive tendencies gravitate. From the bureaucratic spaces[1] that both engulf and exclude K. in *The Trial* and *The Castle*, from the deceptively open expanses of Karl

[*] Reprinted from *Franz Kafka: Geometrician of Metaphor* (Madison: Coda Press, 1979), dist. Johns Hopkins University Press.

Rossmann's America, writing has now descended to a scene that is, in its every dimension, severe—a self-contained subterranean enclosure whose reference to the outside is as incidental and deceptive as it is inescapable. Darkness is the only raw material available for metonymic annexation. The earthen passageways and walls of the burrow describe a barren narcissism. The absence of things to which the narrative voice may refer is matched by a dearth of actions that the text may pretend to dramatize. Early generalizations as to the nature of the burrow and its hollowing (325–33) provide a scenario for the specific movements taking up the remainder of the text, where the voice presumably furnishes a direct transcription of the action.[2] Such events are, however, like their setting, limited. The still silence of the burrow is articulated only by a brief visit to the outside, by abortive attempts to revise the structure, noises construed as issuing from an invisible adversary also inhabiting the depths, and, repeatedly, by sleep.

Kafka's term for the burrow is "the construction," *der Bau*. This terminology is inherently ironic, as the construction consists in hollowing, not protrusion, in the addition of complication, not assertion, in the expansion of darkness, not illumination. The construction is already deconstruction to the same extent that it has been constructed. This concept of a deconstruction equiprimordial to a constructive assertion preempts the fictive temporalizing underlying the history that traces the breakdown of civilization into its animal components. Here, the classical hierarchies are viewed a priori in the condition of reversal. Deconstruction has, from the outset, demanded and received the same ontological priority reserved for *arché* and production. In its anticipatory imaging of hierarchical implosion the text preempts any orientation toward deconstruction as finality or end.

Kafka has placed the monologue in the mouth of an unidentified burrowing animal, perhaps a mole. This animal is itself absurd. Although its behavior corresponds to what we would roughly expect from a carnivorous burrowing rodent, at several points (Fischer, 416, 436) it describes itself as "galloping" (*gallopieren*) through the tunnels. The discourse uttered by its voice is human discourse. The humanity of the discourse is, however, stripped away as its concerns increasingly reveal it to be human. Animalism is thus not merely an anticipation of humanity, a precursor on an evolutionary ladder, but is reached only after humanity has been lived, penetrated, and disqualified.[3] The concept of the animal in this text is a rendition of humanity from which the self has been excluded, a humanity whose concerns have been allowed to rise to their highest and starkest abstraction. It is in this sense that the primitively deconstructive setting implies its own evolution toward a more abstract statement of the conditions of fiction.

Absurd as it may seem, given the compexity of the novels, to insist upon an evolution in Kafka's writing toward the circumscription in a here and now characteristic of the sense-certainty where the Hegelian *Phenomenology* takes off, not ends, the containment of "The Burrow" serves indeed as an end to Kafka's writing, an ending worthy of the body, a culmination of its exploration into the limit disclosed in the process of metaphor. Containment in the construction bespeaks the same duplicity reaching its most elaborate expression in *The Trial* and *The Castle*. Although the transposition of the limit to the stark setting of a hole may entail a certain simplification, this does not imply simple reduction. Kafka's fortitude, in this case, consists in the intricacy and ambiguity that he is willing to implant in a hole. The metaphor stands at the fissure where development and reversion take off from one another. Orientation loses the naiveté ascribable to a simple progression, a thrust toward a yet-unrealized telos, for it has been marked by the stigma of infantility, regression, unadulterated yearning for the Earth-womb.

"I have completed the construction of my burrow and it seems to be successful" (325). Stepping into a human guise, the animal author of the construction begins its monologue, retrospectively evaluating the product of a life's work, conceding its strengths and weaknesses. Unified by plazas and tunnels, the corpus attains the fictive totality implicit in considering the work as a whole. Whether we regard the voice of self-critique as emanating from the animal, Kafka, or from Kafka's works, we are apprised from the outset that the project under construction is a literary as well as an architectural object, bespeaking the same duplicity, illusoriness, impenetrability, and limit characteristic of the literary text. "All that can be seen from outside is a big hole; that, however, really leads nowhere; if you take a few steps you strike against natural firm rock" (325). The construction begins as a false start and a deception. It incorporates both a stratum of apparently solid and "natural" reality and the convolutions of its internal logic, calculated to befuddle possible intruders. The construction resists penetration. One of its doubled openings is self-evident. This is the one, however, leading nowhere. The only available access is by way of fiction, through the moss camouflage that is the entrance's only protection. And yet, from the beginning the voice demonstrates its awareness that the construction is not necessarily in control of its own ruses, that its built-in controls may be transformed at any moment into subjection. "True, some ruses are so subtle that they defeat themselves" (325).

In its very opening, then, the construction sets into play the uncontrollable oppositions between appearance and reality, transparency and obscurity, and mastery and subjection. To these must be added two other oppositions, joined by mutual implication, that are crucial for the text as a whole. In its deceptions and strategies, the construction is calculated, from the outset, to be contemplated and interpreted by an autonomous and possibly malevolent Other. This adversative relation is presupposed by an even more fundamental tension between the interior and the exterior of the construction. "I live in peace in the inmost chamber of my house, and meanwhile the enemy may be burrowing his way slowly and stealthily straight toward me" (326). This sentence is suspended between the interior tranquillity of the burrow and the immanent threat posed by the malevolent Other, contrary assertions that do, however, coexist. The certainty of the belief in the adversary does not disqualify the imputed tranquillity of the interior. The existence of the adversary is certain, only nothing about this entity, by definition, can be known. Such incongruities are characteristic of all of the oppositions woven into the opening both of the construction and the narrative. These oppositions account for an indeterminable opponent (an exterior element, whether regarded as a ruse or an adversary) and are themselves indeterminable, resist any terminal resolution.

It is, then, in the sense of the construction as a literary work, a cumulative corpus, that its flaws are, according to the animal, inevitable: "It is always a fault to have only one piece (*ein Exemplar*) of anything" (330). Such a life's work is, necessarily, a limited edition of one. Revising the construction likewise takes the form of proofreading. "I begin with the second passage and let it take me back again to the Castle Keep, and now of course I have to begin at the second passage once more. . ." (342). When the monologue turns to the noise metamorphosed by the creature into a verification of the existence of the malevolent Other—whose scheme is to bracket or circumscribe the burrow (354–55)—the noise is described as an entry in an etymological dictionary, whose derivation (*Herkunft*, Fischer, 429) must be determined. There is no more prevalent hint of the textuality of the construction than the repeated use of the verb *graben* and its substantive forms to predicate the activity of digging. As will be elaborated below, this verb, in evidence both in the English *grave* and *engrave*, marks the coincidence of the text and interment.[4] The opposition between life and death must be added to the other duplicities in the text, duplicities whose discomposing facets are rendered more, not less immanent by virtue of their indeterminacy.

The factor of uncertainty in the text's decisive oppositions does not, however, prevent the construction from functioning as an epistemological instrument, a scientific enterprise conducted on the basis of research and experimentation. "It is certainly a risk to draw attention by this hole to the fact that there may be something in the vicinity worth inquiring into (*etwas Nachforschungswertes*)" (325). "I dig an experimental burrow, naturally at a good distance from the real entrance, a burrow just as long as myself, and seal it also with a covering of moss" (336). Although the creature's attitude toward the efficacy of the science varies from confidence ("That truth will bring me. . .peace. . ." [358]) to skepticism ("This trench will bring me certainty, you say?" [358]), such a process of verification naturally carries with it a technology: "In such cases as the present it is usually the technical problem that attracts me. . ." (341). Such pretensions, however absurd, to scientific rigor, join the textual duplicities staged by the narrative, its retrospective (critical) stance toward a whole corpus, and its functioning as an engraving, to suggest the close affinities linking the passages of the narrative to the passageways of the labyrinth. The commentary generated by "The Burrow" applies synecdochically to the totality of Kafka's writing as much as to the strengths and weaknesses of the burrow.

If the passages of the construction are the passages of the text, the construction is no less identified with the voice uttering it, with the animal self of which the text is presumably a transcribed expression. In an apostrophe directed at the passageways and the widened alcoves occasionally interspersing their path, the creature exalts: "What do I care for danger now that I am with you? You belong to me, I to you, we are united; what can harm us?" (342). Animal and burrow not only belong together but have, given the setting's sparseness and its removal from the external world, only each other—are united in a symbiotic relation. Identified, through the voice, with the animal self, the construction has only itself to refer to. The voice of the animal is therefore also the voice of construction, the voice of the rhetorical constructs employed in this particular production. Since this construction is defined by physical as well as referential circumscription, the voice of the animal becomes, in terms of this text, the voice of language in general. This perhaps explains why the occasional "autobiographical" references to the animal's life are hastily shunted aside as the narrative reverts to the temporal present and the physical setting of the construction.[5] The single sustained recollection of the past revealing something of the animal subject occurs at the very end of the text and serves only as a retrospective confirmation of the inevitability of that life's movements, registered corporeally in the subterranean engraving.

It is, then, with some skepticism that we must observe the animal "embrace" its work. The creature issues a voice to publicize the construction and preserve it for posterity. But the voice is already the house organ of the construction. The animal "self" which is the master of the voice is likewise already in the employ of this work. The creator finds itself circumscribed by its own creation, by the reality for which the construction serves as limit. The author embraces its work, but the labor, as is evident in the epigraph of this essay, hugs back, its grasp not constrained and certainly not so loving. The author may suffocate, loved to death by its own work. It is perhaps for this reason that air was for Kafka a genuine literary problem.

2. The Literal within the Metaphoric

The literary potential of the cartoon has yet to be fully explored. Within the stark two-dimensional plane framed by the cartoon, writing represents itself to the fullest degree of literality. What is revealed in the play between this depthless space and the line is the law of the line. In a bizarre sense, then, a logos capable of representing nothing less grandiose than the universe reaches its highest distillation in the cartoon, where the line is suspended squarely between its representational function and absolute meaninglessness, line acting as line. The animated cartoon opens the dimension of time within the plane of the line, abolishing the need for the separate and successive panels that constitute, in the printed media, the fictive basis for the cartoon's temporalizing. We have already observed how "The Burrow" is, in more senses than one, animated. Like the cartoon, Kafka accommodates a certain level of blunt literality within the action of his (narrative) line. The preoccupation with Charlie Chaplin most evident in *Amerika* also attests to the fact that Kafka's interest extended form the most enigmatic cloudy spots of fiction to the most mechanistic of events.[6] The literality that we observe pervading the work of construction in "The Burrow" makes the story a cartoon (in the highest sense) of movements characteristic of Kafka's entire fictive corpus.

To the strategy, ruse, and dissimulation making the construction metaphoric for the calculated schemes of fiction, Kafka adds a dimension of explicitness exhibiting the head-work in its most concrete form:

> My labors on the Castle Keep were also made harder, and unnecessarily so (unnecessary in that the burrow derived no real benefit from those labors) (*Leerarbeit*) by the fact that just at the place where, according to my calculations, the Castle Keep should be, the soil was very loose and sandy and had literally to be pounded into a firm state to serve as a wall for the beautifully vaulted chamber. But for such tasks the only tool I possess is my forehead. So I had to run with my forehead thousands and thousands of times, for whole days and nights, against the ground, and I was glad when the blood came, for that was a proof that the walls were beginning to harden; and in that way, as everybody must admit, I richly paid for my Castle Keep. (328)

Here, images of construction as originality or inspiration are bypassed in favor of the most literal, animal representation. The construction is the product of a head-banging concretized most fully when the hardened walls draw blood. In view of the demystified picture of the head's creation of the burrow, the description of the work as *Leerarbeit*, emptying, is ironic. What the creature describes as "a beautifully vaulted chamber" cannot be visualized by the reader as anything other than a void. If the construction represents a life's work, a complete corpus, the *Leerarbeit* implemented by the head proceeds by an ongoing emptying of significance.

The element of literality in the description of the burrow's production extends to the implicit posture of the narrator, the animal, toward the narrative. The reader is asked to believe in the concurrence of the text with the actions that the animal claims it is performing at the moment. If for no other reason than because these actions are mediated by a written text subject to time in different ways than the unidirectional thrust of experience, this presumption is absurd. The narrative confines itself, nevertheless, on the basis of this fictive temporal immediacy, to a now that is remarkably resistant to reversions to the past or projections into the future. The animal thus becomes the agent of a temporal paradox, that the now, capable of feeding upon itself endlessly, is wider-reaching both than the past, which is ended, and the future, which may be projected only so far as its underpinnings in the present can sustain it. Enclosure in the construction is complete because its lateral expanse is potentially endless. The narrative's containment in the now is every bit as complete, and likewise derives from an inexhaustible potential, the limitless capacity of immediacy to generate itself. Spatial enclosure and temporal immediacy arise within a context where the literal is allowed the same full play as the figurative and therefore attains the same status.

As a figure, then, the construction widens to embrace a certain ground of literality, utter explicitness, within its perimeters. There are varying degrees of figurativeness and literality within the metaphor, yet the entire text remains within the metaphoric sphere.

It is as a result of the bifurcations already within the figurativeness of the metaphor that the creature has difficulty in resolving certain decisions. Although the construction is the product of hollowing, it does have some contents, rations (*Vorräte*), in the form of animal carcasses. There is an ample rhetoric of ownership in the text to suggest that the creature presides over the burrow like the petit-bourgeois shopkeeper over a small business, economy on a limited but controllable scale.[7] Even in the world delineated by the construction, a world entirely closed off, except to the "small fry" who are its only links to the outside and its food supply, there is enough disquietude to make frenetic the choice between a centralized and a divided economy:

> Then it sometimes seems risky to make the Castle Keep the basis of defense; the ramifications of the burrow present me with manifold possibilities, and it seems more in accordance with prudence to divide up my stores somewhat, and put part of them in certain of the smaller rooms; thereupon I mark off every third room, let us say, as a reserve storeroom, or every fourth room as a main (*Haupt-*) and every second as an auxiliary storeroom (*Nebenvor-ratsplatz*), and so forth. Or I ignore certain passages altogether and store no food in them, so as to throw my enemy off the scent, or I choose quite at random a very few rooms according to their distance from the main exit. Each of these new plans involves of course heavy work.. . .(329)

The vulnerability of the burrow's centralized economy is felt despite the separation from the outside world, despite the burrow's situation entirely within the sphere of the metaphoric. The disquieting element that has already penetrated the metaphor takes the form, in this particular case, of the multiplicity of plans presenting themselves as alternatives to the centralized economy. Satisfaction is limited by the agonizing indecision between unity and diversity in the burrow's economy. Already in the above passage it is evident that it is in the nature of the disquietude to extend, in the nature of the bifurcation to proliferate. The indecision between centralization and decentralization is indicative of related tensions between the head and the body and between the eye and the less critical senses. The substantive stem *Haupt* recurring in this passage derives from the Latin *caput*, head both as a bodily element and in a hierarchy, a derivation evident in the English *capital*.[8] The opposition in the passage between main and subsidiary repositories (*Haupt-* and *Nebenvorratsplatz*) extends to that between the head and the body, between the center of thought and the segmented body, articulated by organs limited in their specialization. In a similar fashion, the eye loses its position at the head of the senses. The creature's relating to its rations through its nose (328, 330), as well as its complete preoccupation, in the latter third of the text, with the unidentifiable noise seeming to emanate from everywhere, suggest that the faculty of seeing has lost out to the less critical senses of smell and hearing. Thus, the problem posed by distribution is indicative of a variety of splits and limits already operative within the figurativeness of the metaphor. With a remarkable range, this fissure extends itself to tangential problematics.

The fissure within the metaphoric sphere asserts itself in spite of the attempt to segment the construction from the external world. The split's relentless penetration of the barriers erected to contain it occasions hysteria or frenzy on the part of that staid *Hausherr*, the animal. Having relented to a compulsive desire to see the inside from the outside, and having earned, upon its return, the "sweet" sleep of exhaustion, the creature will be (figuratively and literally) driven up a wall by the recommencement of the unidentifiable, sourceless noise. Kafka has not forgotten to provide us with a glimpse of the frenzy periodically breaking out as the bifurcation serves notice that it is free to penetrate the innermost thresholds of the construction: ". . .then I rush, then I fly, then I have no time for calculation; and although I was about to execute a perfectly new, perfectly exact plan, I now seize whatever my teeth hit upon and drag it or carry it away, sighing, groaning, stumbling, and even the most haphazard change can satisfy me" (329). This explosive activity is in the implementation of plans that would not occur to the creature had not a fundamental disquietude already invaded the metaphoric sphere. But the plans for revision are forgotten as soon as they are taken up (352). The onset and subsiding of frenzy comprise the model for repetition in the text, a decisive movement. Again and again, the facets of the metaphor regarded as absolute and inviolable (sleep, silence, security) will be disturbed by a frenzy-producing articulation (consciousness, noise, anxiety). The absolute belongs as much to the construction as do the factors of discomposure. While the temporality of frenzy is repetition, the bifurcating factors also move progressively, penetrating each successive barrier thrown in their path. It is not by accident that the final plan entertained by the creature is the encapsulation of the repository that is already the innermost sanctum by a new trench (346). This plan calls for a partition to bracket the ultimate partition. This attempted blockage is, in conformity with the infinite regress at the heart of the logic of bifurcation, doomed like all of the other partitions.

By incorporating the literal within the metaphoric, the construction reveals the full range of fissures within its architecture. An a priori duplicity, whether between singleness and multiplicity, Self and Other, or the absolute and the articulated, proliferates itself algebraically within the enclosed domain of the metaphor. The repetitive cycle of disturbance and pacification merges with the progressive thrust by which bifurcation articulates each successive threshold, describing a movement akin to the Yeatsian gyre. Bound like a book, the construction opens itself at every stratum, inviting infinite penetration.

3. The Inner Threat

There is room for only one metaphor in the Kafkan text, yet this exclusiveness does not prevent the preeminent structure of the Kafkan metaphor from being duplicity. As "Description of a Struggle" attests, singleness and duplicity are interdependent, part and parcel of one another. Within the closed world of "The Burrow" the bifurcations proliferate uncontrollably, yet not even one bifurcation could be registered were it not for containment, the movement toward singleness. The singleness of the metaphor is the still plane where the unending outgrowth of bifurcations inscribes itself. The bifurcation extends, systematically, from one aspect of enclosure (silence, tranquillity, Self, security, sleep) to the next. In this sense the construction, in its limited set of conditions, is indeed a controlled environment, justifying the creature's pretensions to scientific rigor (although in no way nullifying their absurdity).

Throughout the text, the bifurcation, upon revealing itself to the creature, maintains the capacity to instigate a crisis, to create frenzy. Recurrence does not, however, disqualify the presence of a disquieting split *ab origine*, as is apparent in the very sentence underlined above: "I live in peace in the inmost chamber of my house, and meanwhile the enemy may be burrowing his way slowly and stealthily straight toward me" (326). If the threat is always already present, the fiction of reemergence requires a mechanism of temporalizing akin to repression. The recurrent oblivion of sleep is one factor allowing the discomposing threat both to be continuously present and to emerge periodically, as if from nowhere.

The duplicity staged by the text receives its highest expression in the creature's postulation that the noise which has shattered its tranquillity emanates from "two [noise] centers" (345). At this moment the infinite regress establishes itself ultimately, for the bifurcation has passed from the realm of the interior/personal/Self to the discomposing sign that has articulated that realm. Not only has the creature presupposed the existence of a possibly malevolent opponent, but it has doubled the fundamentally unsignifying sound through which the adversary had made itself known.

On one hand, the movement toward this ultimate bifurcation is progressive. Oppositions staged since the beginning are developed and interconnected until the noise becomes their ultimate expression. There is, however, a sense in which this development is also a regression. The noise, as it will turn out, is the *only* basis for the oppositions elaborated so systematically and disinterestedly in the beginning. As we begin to grasp how the animal has fabricated ontological and teleological orders solely on the basis of the noise, itself merely an element of articulation, the system of oppositions with which we are confronted from the start becomes increasingly questionable. The bifurcation consolidates its power as it moves on. Not only does it extend its range, but it takes on a life of its own, becomes animated, released from the system of oppositions upon which its initial comprehension depended.

The narrative divides itself into an introductory section (325–33), where the animal describes the construction from a detached point of view as a compendium of accomplished facts and predictable potentialities, an interlude (333–40) where, unable to contain itself, the animal ventures briefly outside, relenting to a desire to see the inside from the outside, and the final meditation upon the noise that interrupts the creature's sleep upon its return (340–59). As suggested above, the system of oppositions with which we are confronted in the beginning, and which therefore preconditions our understanding of the situation, will be undermined as the meditation upon the noise sheds new light upon the basis of the animal's knowledge. In the introductory segment of the narrative, an opposition between the tranquillity and silence considered to be the construction's natural state and the threats posed both by adversaries of the deep and congenital flaws in the architecture is systematically put into play. To that paragon of propriety, the creature, under optimal conditions the construction could (and hence should) sustain uninterrupted placidity, unarticulated silence, and oblivion:

> But the most beautiful thing about my burrow is the stillness. Of course, that is deceptive. At any moment it may be shattered and then all will be over.. . .
> Every hundred yards I have widened the passages into little round cells; there I can curl myself up in comfort and lie warm. There I sleep the sweet sleep of tranquillity, of satisfaction, of achieved ambition; for I possess a house. . .but invariably every now and then I start up out of profound sleep and listen, listen into the stillness which reigns here unchanged day and night, smile contentedly and then sink with loosened limbs into still profounder sleep.. . .I lie here in a room secured on every side–there are more than fifty such rooms in my burrow–and pass as much time as I choose between dozing and unconscious sleep. (327)

Here, silence and sleep join as figures for fragile non-articulation. As described by the creature, silence within the burrow occasionally reaches the plateau of the absolute, "reigns here unchanged, day and night." "The sweet sleep of tranquillity, of satisfaction," is the goal of housekeeping, the reward for attending to the variegated concerns of ownership. Sleep is tantamount to the absence of consciousness (*bewußtlosem Schlaf*), an oblivion enabling the hours to pass in pure continuity, with no breaks in inertia to draw their duration to attention. In its beneficent aspect, the construction is truly an Earth-womb. Though extreme, this romanticized image of tranquillity is regarded as normative and original by the animal.

One of the more bizarre aspects of this text is that expressed generally, the opposition mounted against the series: interior/Self/ tranquillity/sleep/oblivion/perfection takes the form of consciousness itself. Self, tranquillity, and sleep are disrupted, respectively, by adversaries (whether "real" or "imaginary" is not yet important), noise, and consciousness. Consciousness is, from the outset, tantamount to the articulation of hypothetically absolute conditions. It is both articulated and articulating, like the architecture of the burrow. Consciousness of a fundamental flaw in the architecture (332, again, the actuality of the flaw is irrelevant) is what prompts the frenetic attempts at revision, redistribution, and reinterpretation taking up so much of the creature's activity. Though apparently operating according to the simple dichotomies Self/Other and security/danger, the beginning segment thus already describes the work of construction as an attempted blocking of consciousness, despite the fact that the construction is already a most conscious strategy. From the beginning, an internally split construction is opposed to an articulating consciousness whose effect is the same splitting.[9]

In the third section of the narrative it will, of course, become clear that the only positive basis for the creature's belief in the existence of adversaries and other dangers is the unarticulated noise. As critical readers we know that even this might be imaginary. The creature might be "hearing something." Remarkably, even though we know from the outset that the text issues from the mouth of an absurd galloping rodent, it dawns on us rather slowly that the factors opposed to the interior/Self/tranquillity might be mere figments of the imagination, because in the gradualness of its unfolding, the narrative demands that we impute a greater literality to certain constructs of the construction than others. This distinction is necessitated despite the fact that, as I have tried to demonstrate, the construction stands entirely within the sphere of the metaphoric. It is in this sense that the metaphor is, for Kafka, all-embracing. All of what it embraces is fictive, yet the fiction must also designate absolutes for purposes of legibility. These, like the creature, may briefly stand outside the construction, but they find themselves, as the text moves on, recycled within its fictionality. Other unsettling implications arise from the third segment of the narrative, where it becomes clear that the only possible source of the discomposing threats is the construction itself. If the threatening articulation takes the form of consciousness, and the revision of the construction proceeds by erecting further barriers against this penetration, then the textuality of the construction is barricaded against itself. In opposition to itself, the textuality of the text seeks a liberation from its own functioning.

But I anticipate the ending of my own story. At the beginning of the text (and we still find ourselves at the beginning) the threats posed to the construction's romantic tranquillity take the form of unknown adversaries and architectural flaws. Yet the existence of the enemies is already as dubious as the absolute serenity is unlikely.

This dubiousness should be apparent from the outset, because the first ontological proof of the existence of the predators takes the form of a literary footnote: "I have never seen them, but legend tells of them and I firmly believe in them. They are creatures of the inner earth; not even legend can describe them" (326). The adversary, whose existence and evil intentions provide the rationale for so much of the creature's activity and determine such a large part of its world-order, finds its initial grounding in the para-literary corpus of legend, hardly a systematic product of the imagination. As the passage continues, there is even a foreshadowing of the realization that the ultimate origin of the adversaries is nothing more significative than plain noise. "Their very victims can scarcely have seen them; they come, you hear the scratching of their claws just under you in the ground, which is their element, and already you are lost" (326). From the beginning, then, the threat to the creature's existence and security is identified at least possibly as a figment of the imagination, that is, as consciousness itself, which announces itself in the noise effecting the literal termination of sleep and oblivion. It should not pass unnoticed that this noise is unarticulated sound, sign devoid of significance. The romanticized image of pure serenity, whole existence, has been discomposed by a sign as inarticulate and absolute as itself. The discomposing sound is not yet subject to the bifurcation of which it is both evidence and cause.

The fictive extreme of the construction's absolute tranquillity and inarticulateness is also spoiled by a congenital defect in the architecture, but this threat, like that of invaders, rests on dubious ground, in this case, the language of the narrative: "My main entrance, I said in those days, ironically addressing my invisible enemies and seeing them all already caught and stifled in the outer labyrinth—is in reality a flimsy piece of jugglery (*eine viel zu dünnwandige Spielerei*) that would hardly withstand a serious attack or the struggles of an enemy fighting for his life" (331). The ur-defect, here and in the two preceding pages regarded as the potentiality for immanent disaster, turns out to be nothing more menacing than a *"zu dünnwandige Spielerei."* No adversary has managed to penetrate the burrow in the course of a career which is now, as we are repeatedly told (331, 357), nearing its end. The primal vulnerability, then, is nothing more serious than a *jeu de mots*. The weakness of the defenses around the one entrance that is open (and given its openness, how impermeable could it be?) is transposed to the animal's characterization of the flaw, the *"zu dünnwandige Spielerei."* The thinness of the walls at the opening of the construction is transformed, by punning, into the transparency of the deceptions essential to the defense. The derivation of the flaw spoiling the construction's inner perfection is suspect for the same reasons that the proof of the existence of the adversaries is questionable. The flaw is, in the end, a linguistic construction, a pun, a textual game, just as the initial substantiation of the threat rests on myths.

The prevalence of the verb *beobachten,* to observe, in the second section of the text, treating the creature's brief exit from the construction, is indicative of its growing awareness that its consciousness is by nature bifurcated. At the same time, the creature's rehashing the concerns and themes introduced in the initial segment of the text undermines the distinction between the interior and the exterior of the construction, a fundament of the creature's ontology. As the old concerns redescend after a brief moment of ecstatic release, the distinction between the interior and the exterior is retracted, and it becomes evident that the two spheres are identical. As opposed to representing the possibility of escape from one another, then, the two spheres only serve to reinforce the inevitability of a bifurcated consciousness.

What the initial moment of joyous freedom offers is a perspectival supplement completing the only consciousness that can prevail within the construction, a necessarily divided and limited one. It is insufficient that, "Then I usually enjoy periods of particular tranquillity" (330), that brief interludes of tranquillity within the construction occasionally recur. The absolute serenity must not merely be experienced. It must be recorded by a second (double) consciousness in order to be confirmed: "I seek out a good hiding place and keep watch on the entrance of my house—this time from outside—for whole days and nights. Call it foolish if you like; it gives me infinite pleasure and reassures me. At such times it is as if I were no so much looking at my house as at myself sleeping, and had the joy of being in a profound slumber and simultaneously of keeping vigilant guard over myself" (334).[10] By realizing that the romanticized state of oblivion must be recorded by an active consciousness in order to be fully appreciated, the creature acknowledges the necessity of a fissure within consciousness itself. This realization supersedes the simple opposition between security and danger, oblivion and consciousness, established prior to it in the narrative. And yet, if the satisfaction of knowing that oblivion has been achieved is fuller than the unmediated experience of oblivion itself, the optimal happiness may consist in observation, not in protection. The creature has considered this possibility: "The burrow has probably protected me in more ways than I thought or dared think while I was inside it. This fancy used to have such a hold over me that sometimes I have been seized by a childish desire never to return to the burrow again, but to settle down somewhere close to the entrance, to pass my life watching the entrance, and gloat perpetually upon the reflection—and in that find my happiness—how steadfast a protection my burrow would be if I were inside it" (335). For an instant, the creature has considered redefining the optimal state from oblivion to residence at the entrance, that is, to placement at the foyer of exchange, at the point where the interior and the exterior, and hence the absolute and the articulated, merge. Consistent with its character, though, the animal has considered this shift from an ontology of containment to an ontology of duplicity and synchronic disjunction only for a moment. In the very next sentences of this passage, the animal compulsively retreats into a more substantial dichotomy, posing danger against the possibility of absolute security: "Well, one is soon roughly awakened from childish dreams. What does this protection which I am looking at here from the outside amount to after all? Dare I estimate the danger which I run inside the burrow from observations which I make when outside?" (335).

It cannot be insignificant that in a matter of sentences following these questions, and only half way through the passage describing this ad-venture, the creature already debates returning to the "security" of the construction. "And I. . .find I have had enough of this outside life. . ." (335). Ironically, the threat posed by an imaginary predator projected outside of the system of construction is preferable to the threat entailed by entertaining textual double-vision and synchrony. Aware of the threat implicit in the critical stance of observation, the creature steps back. Immediately, the image of the predator and the dangers of the master/slave dialectic assert themselves: "No, I do not watch over my own sleep, as I imagined; rather it is I who sleep, while the destroyer watches" (335). The possible felicity of interchange between the interior and the exterior, between the unconscious and observing facets of consciousness, has been remetamorphosed into the threat of subjection and violence.

At this moment, the exterior ceases to be a supplement of the interior and becomes identical to it, a setting in which the bifurcated consciousness and the anxiety prevailing within the construction may be exactly reproduced. The sudden shift from a relation of supplementarity to one of identity between inner and outer worlds is established when the creature returns to its experimental diggings (*Versuchsgraben*) on the outside of the construction, near the entrance (335; also see 353, 357). From this point until the end of the second section (340), the major concerns of the initial segment will re-occupy the text, and in such a way as to indicate that they have not been significantly altered or elaborated. As usual, there is evidence of the danger ("And the danger is by no means a fanciful one," [337]) posed by the predator, who represents, in its own mortality, the possibility of the burrow creature's death. There is a predictable regret at having no confidant, and the usual retrospection as to how the structure should have been laid out. The text, having only briefly allowed itself to register the results of displacement, now begins to repeat on itself compulsively like an obsessional neurosis.[11] In light of this textual cud-chewing, it is no accident that as the creature reverts to the "original" setting of the bifurcation, the burrow, it is taken with the image of its own warehouse, filled to overflowing with meat (*Fleisch-vorräte*) (340).

In the final section of the text, the creature's attempts to interpret the recurrent noise drive it to further thresholds of frenzy. Ironically, the interpretative act presupposes the bifurcated consciousness as much as it strives to contain it. The interpretative preoccupation in this segment of the text is prefigured by the animal's desire to ascertain, through observation, that it is experiencing oblivion. For all of its scientific aspirations, however, the interpretative act only succeeds in conjuring increasingly apocalyptic images of horror in explanation of the noise. As it builds upon itself, the interpretation merges into pure invention, into the arbitrary willfulness of the imagination. As interpretation reveals itself to be the activator of anarchy, not its container, the oppositions that have formed a rigorous system for reading and comprehending the construction find themselves threatened. The existence of the threat from outside and of the predator, as well as the architectural inadequacy of the construction, are subjects accounting for vast segments of the narrative. Yet these dangers have been defined by interpretative deliberations that are first disclosed only at the end of the text. The fate of these presuppositions, the fate of the way the text offers to read itself, is the shared fate of the interpretative act as it progresses at the end of the story. This fate is, quite simply, ongoing discomposure and apocalypse.

The progress toward arbitrary fabrication in the interpretative act found in this section of the text does not imply that the "classical" oppositions (in terms of "The Burrow") have disappeared. On the contrary, these oppositions endure as an archaeological substratum upon which the frenzy plays itself out. After once inspecting the central repository upon its return from the outside, the creature can still claim, "Now that I have seen the Castle Keep I have endless time—for everything I do there is good and important and satisfies me somehow" (342). Here, the unthreatened tranquillity is figured on the abstract level of the uninterrupted temporality prevailing within the construction. The unendingly accommodating time is a function of the full measure of the reward constituted by the labors of construction. After the threat in the form of noise has asserted itself, however, time is not so generous. There is a premium on it. "Slowly I come to realize. . .that I merely disfigure the walls of my burrow, without taking time to fill up the holes again. . ." (348). "I do not surrender to it, I hurry on, I do not know what I want, probably simply to put off the hour" (352). The original opposition between the unarticulated ideal and the threat of articulation now plays itself out squarely along the coordinates of time.

Within the "classical" context carried over from the story's introduction and body, the development of the interpretative process itself becomes as horrific as are the successively extreme images of danger conjured by the creature. As it begins, the noise is innocent, "an almost inaudible whistling noise" (343). "This noise, however, is a comparatively innocent one; I did not hear it at all when I first arrived, although it must certainly have been there; I must first feel quite at home before I could hear it; it is, so to speak, audible only to the ear of the householder" (343). Although the "certainty" of the noise's being "already present" is undermined by the admission that it is audible "only" to the homeowner, at this point the noise is indeed relatively innocent. The interpretation itself will deprive the noise of its benign aspect.

> And what was it? A faint whistling, audible only at long intervals, a mere nothing to which I don't say that one could actually get used, for no one could get used to it, but which one could, without actually doing something about it at once, observe for a while; that is, listen every few hours, let us say, and patiently register the results, instead of, as I had done, keeping one's ear fixed to the wall and at every hint of noise tearing out a lump of earth, not really hoping to find anything, but simply so as to do something to give expression to one's inward agitation. All that will be changed now, I hope. And then, with furious shut eyes, I have to admit to myself that I hope nothing of the kind, for I am still trembling with agitation just as I was hours ago.. . .(348–49)

The "faint whistling," hardly more, almost less than nothing is, by itself, innocuous. It is the compulsive nature of the interpretative process, the inability to let up, the drive to stay on top of the noise and to do, in the absence of deliberate plans, *something*, that brings on the "trembling with agitation." It is also consistent with the compulsion motivating the interpretative act that the introspection gravitates naturally toward the most horrific potentiality: "But what avail all exhortations to be calm; my imagination (*Einbildungskraft*) will not rest, and I have actually come to believe—it is useless to deny it to myself—that the whistling is made by some beast, and moreover not by a great many small ones, but by a single big one" (353).

This passage represents one of the creature's rare glimpses of insight, one of the few occasions when even a partial realization of the extent of the disquietude enters its discourse. In this passage, the gravitation toward progressively horrific images of the threat is linked to the unbreakable momentum of *Einbildungskraft*, imagining power. The momentum of the imagination is as relentless as the noise is penetrating and unsettling. In this moment, the reader is also afforded a glimpse of what is the narrative's only discovery, and is certainly an implication bearing heavily on the interpretation of the construction as a whole—the discovery that the animal is the source as well as the object of the threats from outside. If this is so, the animal has erected the construction against itself, its self the powerless pawn of its imagination's compulsion. A prisoner of the imagination, the animal is equally the prisoner of its own construction.

The ability of such suggestive moments of insight to subside into oblivion before reaching a logical conclusion is fundamental to the story's temporality of obsessive repetition, to its rhythm of consciousness and sleep, anxiety and oblivion, threat and tranquillity. One reason why the story fails to reach any culmination is precisely the mechanism of erasure built into the animal's consciousness and into the narrative structure as a whole, a mechanism of relapse preempting any overall thrust toward realization. The story is disconcerting in the absolute inconsequentiality of the incisive moments when the creature verges on realizing the full extent of the bifurcating threat. The creature returns to its former anxieties as if the insights had never taken place.

These mechanisms of erasure and the text's capacity to sustain repetition enable the creature to ignore that it endows the threatening noise with the same internal indifference and inarticulateness characteristic of the construction in its idyllic state. "I listen now at the walls of the Castle Keep, and wherever I listen, high or low, at the roof or the floor, at the entrance or the corners, I hear the same noise" (347). Owing to the perforations in the creature's own consciousness, the categories it has established undergo a reversal of which it is not even aware. The noise, the menacing sign of a predator imagined to be increasingly horrific, takes on the inarticulateness characteristic of the Edenic state of the construction. The interpretative act by which the creature hopes to localize and contain the threat becomes an attempt to discern articulations within the inarticulate. The delineation of articulation thus passes from the nature of the threat to the only means of coping with it. The creature's admission that it once entertained the possibility of the existence of a doubled sound source comprises yet another instance of unrealized insight. In postulating a double origin, the animal passes from being the victim of the articulation to its originator. And yet, the animal, even in articulating the noise, continues to believe in its exteriority and autonomy, in the absoluteness of the partition defining the oppositions according to which it has arranged its life.

With the creature trapped in the cycle of its unrealized insights and regressions into old fears, oblivious while the categories it has set into play in an effort to grasp the situation reverse upon themselves, the only progressive thrust staged by the text is toward distraction and unintelligibility. "But this time everything seems difficult, I am too distracted. . ." (350). "Suddenly I cannot comprehend my former plan. I can find no slightest trace of reason in what had seemed so reasonable; once more I lay aside my work and even my listening; I have no wish to discover any further signs that the noise is growing louder; I have had enough of discoveries; I let everything slide; I would be quite content if I could only still the conflict going on within me" (352). The rational plans to contain the bifurcation silence one another in a babble of unintelligibility. In the service of rationality, interpretation has succumbed to the cacophony engendered by its own schemes. The architecture of the construction, the consummate product of speculation, is itself now illegible. Numbed by the confusion unearthed in the rational effort to suppress the bifurcation, the consciousness seeks only a release from itself. Once and for all, the inner strife is identified with the animal consciousness.

It is fitting that the no longer comprehensible "plan" mentioned in the above passage was to contain the innermost repository in yet a further partition (346). The idea of the ultimate partition shares the fate of the plan to erect it. The uncontained bifurcation comes closest to home near the end of the text, when the reader is finally permitted a glimpse of the creature's visualization of its predator. As should be no longer surprising, the animal that the animal visualizes is a double of itself, the very image of the animal that we extrapolate from the creature's characterization of its own activity: "It probably bores its snout into the earth with one mighty push and tears out a great lump. . ." (354). In this passage the creature bases the alterity of the predator on the different sound its digging makes. Yet surely a consciousness oblivious to the near-identical relation between the nature of the hypothetical tranquillity and that of the direct threats it imagines can also be oblivious to the sound of its own digging. Here the text comes closest to the realization that the animal has been driven to distraction by the sound of its own digging, of its own functions, breathing, eating, and running, contained, as it is, within an echo-chamber of reflection. With this possibility, the text comes closest to admitting how far the bifurcation it stages extends: as far back as the animal, as far back as the narrative voice itself.

With the admission of the possibility that the cause of the animal's frenzy has been its own activity, that a schizoid break has occurred, the text adds complexity to passages seeming otherwise to lend a dignified air of resolution:

> Between that day and this lie my years of maturity, is it not as if there were no interval at all between them? I still take long rests

from my labors and listen at the wall, and the burrower (*Graber*) has changed his intention anew, he has turned back, he is returning from his journey, thinking he has given me ample time in the interval to prepare for his reception. But on my side everything is worse prepared for than it was then; the great burrow stands defenseless, and I am no longer a young apprentice, but an old architect. (357)

From the standpoint of the creature's naiveté, this passage recapitulates past achievements and the fundamental opposition that alone remains unresolved. But all is not so simple if the *Graber* is the animal itself. A *Graber,* as opposed to a *Gräber,* is not merely a simple digger, but a graver/engraver. The passage simply describing the animal's anticipation of the *Graber* also characterizes the not so simple relation joining the narrative voice, the construction, and the writing which is the construction to death. The above passage describes the animal's entire adult life as having gotten lost in the transition between the initiation of the construction and the present. The work of construction and attentiveness to the concerns of the deep have absorbed that life. If the anticipation of the *Graber* is the anticipation of writing, the life absorbed in the work of construction, in its blindness, its progressive self-disqualification, and its incoherence, has always been subsumed by the textual sphere. If the *Graber* brings death, that death has already transpired, for the above passage defines the work of construction as the erasure of life. It may well be that death enters the narrative in the hyphens immediately succeeding the final words: "But all remained unchanged" (359). Within the enclosure of the construction—death, writing, and alterity all step into the *ich* set into play by the narrative voice, their claims to that voice equally legitimate. In its final section, the text allows its movement of bifurcation to revert back to the beginning and to anticipate death, the ultimate end. The bifurcation has penetrated the system of oppositions improvised to contain it, arriving at its (equally) primal loci: Self, consciousness, the narrative voice.

In the conjunction of death, writing, and duplicity that it stages, the all-embracing metaphor, the construction, serves as a setting for the discovery of textual limit. Both representing consciousness and articulating it, the text finds itself barricaded against itself, deadlocked in its internal contortions. Strive as it may for a release from its own functions, the text finds no exit. Although constantly shifting, for the sake of legibility, certain fictive entities *outside* the metaphoric sphere to serve as "objective" indices for obscurer enigmas, these realities invariably find themselves once again contained within a realm of indifferent fictionality admitting no definitive arbitration. The construction thus records a bizarre cycle. Contained within its own limits, it nonetheless opens a panorama revealing the penetration of all barriers by a bifurcation unsettling the animal soul.

In tracing the Kafkan text to its (dead) end, this text has nonetheless left certain of its own questions open. The present essay views the selection of an animal narrator in the context of an overall challenge to the notion of subjectivity. By its conclusion, however, the essay describes Kafka's text as finding itself "barricaded against itself" (162) or coming close to "admitting" certain "realizations" (170). The subjectivity and self ostensibly abolished by Kafka find themselves relocated, by my text, back to Kafka's story, which evidently takes on a life of its own.

In light of the creature's obsessions and the repetitive patterns of frenzy and forgetting, the automatic mechanism of Kafka's writing can come as no surprise. The story's circumscription, the abstract simplicity of its setting, shift even the most basic conditions for its writing or enunciation back to within its texture. The self so easily dismissed on the first page of Kafka's story appears to return in a more resilient form when the story's textuality becomes the subject of an interpretation. But it is a far different self, one so charged, as I have attempted to demonstrate, with repetition and reversal as to disfigure the concept of selfhood beyond recognition.

To be self-contained is not to be complete. Various levels of knowledge are delineated by my reading. Successive stages to some extent culminate or complete prior ones. As much as this may imply an overall orientation, it also initiates the endless movement of supplanting so typical of Kafka. We begin with an animal who knows less than the text of the story and a story in need of some reader or beast to whom it may disclose the differentiated knowledge. An interpretation steps forth to make this ironic situation explicit, but in order to do so, deploys constructs already rendered obsolete by the text under discussion. Like a cornered animal, the present text awaits a reader to release it from its regressions.

Notes

1. Franz Kafka, "The Burrow," in *The Complete Stories*, ed. Nahum Glatzer (New York: Schocken Books, 1983), 325–59. In-text citations refer to this edition. In few cases it will be necessary to refer to the German edition. These will be designated "Fischer" and will refer to Franz Kafka, *Sämtliche Erzählungen*, ed. Paul Raabe (Frankfurt am Main and Hamburg: S. Fischer, 1972), pp. 412–44.

2. This device, known in German as the *"erlebte Rede,"* has received considerable critical attention. For an exhaustive treatment of this device in relation to Kafka, see Hartmut Binder, *Motiv und Gestaltung bei Franz Kafka* (Bonn: Bouvier, 1966), pp. 201–20, 244–54, 340–46.

3. See Gilles Deleuze and Félix Guattari, *Kafka: Pour une littérature mineure* (Paris: Ed. de Minuit, 1975), pp. 15, 23–28, 32–33, and 40–41. In their treatment

of Kafka as a writer of "minor literature," Deleuze and Guattari have given Kafka's animalism its widest range of implications thus far. "Devenir animal" is an instance of the deterritorialization or disenfranchisement that constitutes perhaps the key element of minor literature. By implication, animalism joins a complex including the literature of the politically oppressed, bureaucratic phantasm (Kafka as prophet of future totalitarian and technocratic repression), and, on a sexual level, sadism and masochism.

4. *Der Große Duden: Herkunftswörterbuch*, Volume 7 (Mannheim, Vienna, and Zurich: Bibliographisches Institut, 1963), p. 230.

5. Aborted autobiographical references are to be found on pp. 327–28, 330, 332, 346, and 347.

6. In slapstick comedy as in the cartoon, physical motion seizes control of the subjects of the narrative, shattering the illusion of their subjectivity. Before his identity is revealed, Uncle Jacob appears as a Chaplin figure in *Amerika*, and it cannot be purely coincidental that the Nature Theater of Oklahoma episode corresponds exactly, in its position and its scenario of an ironic afterlife in which the entire cast of characters appears in this world as angels, to a wishful dream of Charlie's at the end of "The Kid."

7. The creature describes itself as a "master" (*Herr* or *Hausherr*) on pp. 333 and 335. The most extended application of a rhetoric of ownership appears on pp. 354–55, where within eight lines, "own" and "possess" appear four times. In the German, this rhetoric is even more pronounced, all terms of ownership being based on the substantive *Besitz* and its forms.

8. *Der Große Duden: Herkunftswörterbuch*, Volume 7, pp. 252–53.

9. In a completely different context, Jacques Derrida describes the splitting of another construct initially representing itself as self-present. The construct is, of course, the voice. The disquieting notion of auto-affection indicates a division, a primordial opposition, within the self-presence accompanying the voice. See Jacques Derrida, *Speech and Phenomena*, tr. David B. Allison (Evanston, Ill.: Northwestern University Press, 1973), p. 82:

And here again we find all the incidences of primordial nonpresence whose emergence we have already noted on several occasions. Even while repressing difference by assigning it to the exteriority of the signifiers, Husserl could not fail to recognize its work at the origin of sense and presence. Taking auto-affection as the exercise of the voice, auto-affection supposed that a pure difference comes to divide self-presence. In this pure difference is rooted the possibility of everything we think we can exclude from auto-affection: space, the outside, the world, the body, etc. As soon as it is admitted that auto-affection is the condition for self-presence, no pure transcendental reduction is possible. But it was necessary to pass through the transcendental reduction in order to grasp this difference in what is closest to it. . . . We come closest to it in the movement of differance.

10. Here Kafka comes closest to the Hegelian dialectic in which consciousness of self may be realized only in opposition to an other. This dialectic attains particular importance in the struggle between Master and Slave and in the passage immediately preceding it. See. G. W. F. Hegel, *Phänomenologie des Geistes* (Hamburg: Meiner, 1952), pp. 133–152.

11. Although Klaus Wagenbach informs us of Kafka's "early" (c. 1912) awareness of psychoanalysis (*Eine Biographie seiner Jugend* [Bern: Franke, 1958], 199), certain similarities between the creature's behavior and Freud's characterization of obsessional neurosis are so striking as to be uncanny. To begin, there is the gross similarity between our rodent hero and the pivotal obsessional image in one of Freud's celebrated case histories, "The Rat Man" (1909), in Sigmund Freud, *Three Case Histories*, ed. Philip

Rieff (New York: Collier, 1973), pp. 15–102. In this case, as in the more speculative *Totem and Taboo* (1913), trans. James Strachey (New York: Norton, 1950), Freud views obsession primarily as a function of failed instinctual repression and ambivalence. Particularly relevant to my reading of Kafka's story are Freud's description of the displacement, transference, and substitution of obsessional prohibitions (*Totems and Taboo*, pp. 27–30), projection of hostility onto potentially malevolent spirits (ibid., 64), and a "scrupulous conscientiousness" (ibid., 68). I have demonstrated how the disconcerting threat displaces itself from the interior to the exterior of the burrow, and it is self-evident that the creature is overly "scrupulous." As will be hypothesized below, the fullest realization of the story's duplicity comes in the faint suggestion that the creature's lifelong threat may have been all along a projection.

KAFKA AND THE PSYCHE

In the Penal Colony
Kurt Tucholsky*

When people say dreams are hazy it is not true. "Everyone is a Shakespeare while dreaming," says the sage, and even the most senseless phantasms of the night have contours and colors that are immovably solid. Trees are palpable and juicy green; and in the faces of those dreamed about, you can touch the little wrinkles with your fingers. Everything in a dream is clear and sharp. This dream by Franz Kaffka [sic], "In the Penal Colony,"[1] (published in Munich by Kurt Wolff), is just as inexorably hard, cruelly objective and crystal clear. This thin book, in a wonderful Drugulin edition, is a masterwork.

Since [Heinrich von Kleist's] *Michael Kohlhaas* there has not been a German novella that seemingly suppresses all inner feeling with such conscious energy and yet is so thoroughly marked by the stamp of the author. The story is simply about a rebellious soldier in the penal colony who is strapped to a crazy machine and is tortured on it. There, his punishment is that the rule "Honor your superior" is written onto his naked body—with needles.

Since the days of the perfumed salon sadist Ewers, these things have fallen into bad repute. One must always add today that with a book such as this, there is no question of enriching the reference libraries of the bloated shopkeepers of ready-to-wear merchandise. (This book is not to be confiscated either, Mr. State attorney!) When I got to the part where the naked man is lying under the machine and a piece of felt is shoved into his mouth from below so that he cannot scream—a felt remnant that has not been changed for years— and then the complicated machinery sets in motion, the needles write, and out of little channels water sprays away the blood—when I had read this far, I gulped down a faint taste of blood, searched for an excuse, and thought: allegory . . . military jurisdiction. . . .

But this work of art is so great that it needs no excuse, and an allegorical explanation is certainly not necessary. There is something

* Translated by Ruth V. Gross from Kurt Tucholsky, *Gesammelte Werke*, vol.1/664 (Reinbek bei Hamburg: Rowohlt Verlag, 1960). © 1960 by Rowohlt Verlag GmbH, Reinbek bei Hamburg.

entirely different going on. The chief officer explains to the foreign traveller the precise construction of the machine and accompanies every twitch of the tortured man with expert commentary. But he is not vulgar or cruel, he is something much worse. He is amoral. The matter has nothing at all to do with Christianity. This officer is not a torturer, and by no means is he a sadist. Even if after the sixth hour of torture he laps up the suffering agonies of the increasingly weakening man, he is simply boundlessly and slavishly bowing before the machine which he calls justice—in truth, he is bowing before power. And this power knows no limits.

To be able for once to rule without limits . . . do you still remember when we were small boys and were caught up in some confused sexual needs, we dreamed up a city or country in which the people, both men and women, all went naked or had on glass clothing. And in this country people had coitus all the time and without limits and without the least bit of soulful feelings. Love had nothing at all to do with it. We were simply luxuriating in the possibility of purely manufactured happening without the disturbing presence of a teacher or father or mother. (This is a kind of sensuality that normal adults can never again feel.) What stimulated the imagination of the boy was not only the sexual motive, but above all the lack of limits. Playing Indians was the preliminary step to this. For once to be able to rule without limits. . . .

This boundlessness is dreamed and shaped here in Kaffka. And the obstacles that hinder the regimented torture are also dreamlike. The torture does not founder because a whole society, order, the state, indignantly rise up to prevent it—no, the replacement parts of the machine are not in order, and the new commander of the penal colony, in contrast to the old one, is a modernist and does not really support the machine officer and his torture device, yet he does tolerate it. . . . And all this is told with such extreme cool and distance. The poet still has time to color in quite small details, just as sometimes in life and in a dream when catastrophes occur, the main thing one remembers about the event is a torn fingernail or a flower petal on the carpet. And this is the way the machine works before the eyes of the excited traveller, and the needles write and write.

And then the picture changes, and in a causal nexus that becomes understandable only through the fact of the dream, the officer lets the condemned man go. Because his machine cannot stand empty, he places himself under it and allows himself to be quickly tortured to death. Only because the machine cannot stand empty. And confused and dreamlike are the wheels of this horrible instrument that a child of Peter Behrens and Lyonel Feininger might have constructed; the round wheels rise and fall, and then the harrow spears the body of the officer, and the jib of the machine lifts the cadaver terribly slowly to the outside and lets it smack down into that ditch. . . .

The traveller and the condemned man and the soldier on duty watch powerlessly. And then they still go around in the city and then the traveller gets on a boat and leaves. And suddenly the book is at an end. You need not ask what it is all for. It is not for anything. It means nothing at all. Perhaps this book does not even belong in this time and it surely does not advance us. It has no problems and is not aware of any doubting or questioning. It is completely harmless (*unbedenklich*). As harmless as Kleist.

Note

1. Franz Kafka, *In der Strafkolonie* (München: Kurt Wolff Verlag, 1919).

Kafka's Poetics of the Inner Self   Walter H. Sokel°

When Kafka began to write, scepticism toward the writer's medium—language—and despair over the limitations inherent in it, were widespread, and not only in German and Austrian letters, although with special acuteness in these. The earliest piece of writing by Kafka, which is preserved, an entry in a young girl's album, dating from the year 1900, is a striking document of this *Sprachkrise* or *Sprachskepsis*, the crisis of faith in language.[1] Kafka, age seventeen, declares his impatience with the inadequacy of words for the task of conveying the intimate and inward aspect of memory, an inwardness which the German word for memory, "Erinnerung," etymologically suggests: "As though words could carry memories. (Als ob Worte erinnern könnten!) For words are clumsy mountaineers and clumsy miners. Not for them to bring down treasures from the mountains' peaks or up from the mountains' bowels."[2]

Kafka's earliest letters to his friend Oskar Pollak are marked by a profound disillusionment with the possibilities of genuine communication through language. The nature of language as a tool of generalizing and conceptual communication endangers the task of expressing essentially personal and intimate truths. Kafka's analogy of words to "bad mountaineers" and "bad miners" of the soul closely resembles another document of the *Sprachkrise*, Maurice Maeterlinck's passage from *Le Trésor des humbles*, which Robert Musil chose as the motto for his novel *Törleß*, composed three years after Kafka's

° Reprinted with permission from *Modern Austrian Literature*, vol. 11 (1978).

album entry: "As soon as we express something, we devalue it strangely. We believe ourselves to have dived down into the depths of the abyss, and when we once again reach the surface, the drops of water on our pale fingertips no longer resemble the ocean from which they came. We imagine we have discovered a treasure trove of wonderful treasures, and when we get back into the daylight again, we see we have brought up only fake gems and pieces of glass. Nevertheless, the treasure shimmers in the darkness unchanged."[3] Here we find the same critical questioning of language, the same denunciation of its inadequacy as in Kafka's earliest extant written statement. Language, in the process of utterance, devaluates and falsifies its content. It cannot do justice to and fails to retain the essence of what we wish to say. In the most famous document of the *Sprachkrise*, Hugo von Hofmannsthal's "A Letter," Lord Chandos says that if we could "think with the heart" expression would present no problem;[4] but such a language of the heart is given to us, if at all, only in rare moments of mystical enchantment. To some extent, this "critique of language," to use the title of Fritz Mauthner's three-volume work of 1903, reveals discontent with the worn-out, cliché-ridden, and pretentious idiom of much of late nineteenth-century writing—a discontent of which Karl Kraus became the outstanding exponent. However, the critique of language also envisages an inherent incapacity of words, insofar as words derive their being from generalizing thought, to express a highly individualized sensibility and inwardness. The social-utilitarian realm which language serves is held to bear no relationship to that inwardness of the individual which Hofmannsthal calls "the heart," and which Maeterlinck and Kafka designate by analogies to the depths of the sea or the interior of the earth. If we were to compare the linguistic concerns of these writers to the problems of communication encountered by Kierkegaard's Abraham in *Fear and Trembling*, the close relationship of the *Sprachkrise* to proto-existential thought would become apparent. The *Sprachkrise* possibly contributed more heavily to the Central European reception of Kierkegaard in the first two decades of this century than might be suspected.

However, even more directly relevant to an understanding of the *Sprachkrise*, and particularly to the role it plays in shaping Kafka's poetics, is an approach that benefits from the intellectual categories of Jacques Derrida. For the *Sprachkrise* provides an excellent example of that "metaphysical nostalgia" which, according to Derrida, finds it difficult to accept "the impossibility that a sign . . . be produced within the plenitude of a present and an absolute presence," the impossibility of that "full speech which claims to be truth. . . ."[5] What Derrida diagnoses as metaphysical nostalgia is the desire to abolish "la brisure," the gap between the signifier and "the reality" which is posited behind and beyond the verbal sign. The assumptions underlying the phenomenon of the *Sprachkrise*, and particularly the poetics of Kafka, are understandable in terms of that "ineluctable nostalgia for presence that makes of this heterogeneity [of word and being] a unity by declaring that a sign brings forth the presence of the signified."[6] The *Sprachkrise* is a symptom of the loss of faith in the actuality of such a statement. Its preoccupation would best be described by changing the indicative, "a sign brings forth" into the hortatory subjunctive, "a sign should bring forth the presence of the signified."

In the period between the beginnings of his diary and the writing of *The Judgment*, Kafka evolved a rudimentary theory of writing which, in its most confident form, seems to embody the intellectual tradition that Derrida associates with metaphysical nostalgia for the "absolute presence" in writing of that reality to which writing refers, a presence which, in Derrida's words, "claims to be truth." Kafka's goal was "truth," i.e., the perfect *adequatio* between word and feeling, between linguistic sign and inner being.[7] This "truth," to be sure, had two aspects pointing in opposite directions. One of those was communal, collective, and universalist, the other deeply personal, individual, and subjective. It is this second aspect of Kafka's "truth" which I want to explore here in some detail. His ideal was "to fill each word entirely with [himself]."[8] He strove for the ability to write a tale which would be linked to his life "from word to word," a tale that he could draw to his breast (*T*,39) (*D*,1:43). He graphically described how the length of a word written by him would equal exactly the extent of his "feeling" (*T*,60) (*D*,1:61–62). He spoke of "dwelling" in each of his thoughts (*T*,57) (*D*,1:58). He wished to "pour himself" into his writing (*T*,230) (*D*,1:222). He exulted in the "miracle" that every thought, "even the weirdest," could find words able to express it (*T*,293) (*D*,1:276). The precise agreement between inner experience and linguistic formulation was his criterion for literary value (*T*,186f) (*D*,1:173–74), and he insisted that where "the right feeling vanishes, writing loses all value" (*T*,39f) (*D*,1:41).

This "poetics" presupposes two distinct entities—the inner self or inner world, which is to be expressed, and the medium of expression—language. If perfect correspondence between the two is achieved, writing becomes the true vehicle of being. The fundamental precondition for this harmony does not lie in language, but in the inner world. Being is prior to words. The inner self conquers the word by "filling it out." It stands in a position of dominance to language. It is to take possession of language and, through language, of the social collective world to which language belongs.

In his earliest statement about the nature of his writing, a letter to his friend Oskar Pollak, the twenty-year-old Kafka describes his intention as a writer. It is "to lift, with one single heave, that which I believe I have in me (I do not always believe it)" (*B*,17) (*L*,7). This kind of writing he called "magic." Ten years later, in a diary entry of 1913, he writes of "the enormous world which I have in my head" (*T*,306) (*D*,1:288) and considers it his special mission and destiny "to liberate (himself) and to liberate it," even at the cost of his life: "The tremendous world I have in my head. But how free myself and free it without being torn to pieces. And a thousand times rather be torn to pieces than retain it in me or bury it. That, indeed, is why I am here, that is quite clear to me" (*D*,1:288) (*T*,306).

One year after that, he speaks of his special talent of representing his "dreamlike inner life" (*T*,420) (*D*,2:77), to which all his other potentialities have had to be sacrificed. His diaries show abundantly that his "dreamlike inner life" consisted not only of the most vivid and powerful night dreams, which Kafka frequently wrote down, but also of hallucinatory visions that obsessed him, especially shortly before falling asleep or immediately after waking up, and which greatly contributed to the insomnia of which he bitterly complained all his life. A tumult of deeply troubling oneiric images obsessed, tormented, and exhilarated him. He called these visionary hosts his "devils," "ghosts," and "demons."[9] One example may stand here for many: "This noon, before falling asleep . . . the upper part of the body of a wax woman lay on top of me. Her face was bent back over mine, her left forearm pressed against my breast" (*D*,1:152) (*T*,162).

These visions, as noted in his diaries, sometimes formed the point of departure for narratives. In a diary entry of late May, 1914, for instance, Kafka begins a fragmentary narrative which tells of a white horse suddenly appearing in an avenue of a city (*T*,375) (*D*,2:34–35). Two pages later, while criticizing the fragment, he makes clear how the inspiration for the story had come to him. The white horse had appeared to him the night before in a vision, as he was about to fall asleep. It seemed to have literally stepped out of his head: "Yesterday the white horse appeared to me for the first time before I fell asleep; I have an impression of its first stepping out of my head, which was turned to the wall, jumping across me and down from the bed and then disappearing" (*D*,2:35) (*T*,377).

This close connection between hallucinatory vision and narrative beginning sheds an interesting light on Kafka's creative method or process, in general, even as the specific image of the white horse sheds light on such tales as "A Country Doctor," in which magic horses play a crucial role, or "The New Advocate," in which the protagonist is a horse metamorphosed into a lawyer.

When Dr. Rudolf Steiner, founder of the Anthroposophic branch of the Theosophic movement, visited Prague, Kafka mentioned his visionary states to him. In his writing, he confessed to Dr. Steiner, he had had experiences "close to the clairvoyant states, as described by you, Herr Doktor" (T,57) (D,1:58). Kafka's statement receives its full meaning, if we recall that Rudolf Steiner had described elaborate methods for attaining extrasensory perceptions and transcendental insights. Perhaps Kafka's visionary states, some of which are described with frightening vividness in his diaries, were similar to hallucinations induced by drugs. In any case, these states seemed to give him feelings of transcending the quotidian self and reaching the frontiers of human potentialities. He found in these states, as he told Dr. Steiner, the "enthusiasm that probably characterizes the clairvoyant," except his peace, and "even that," he adds, was "not entirely" lacking (T,57) (D,1:58).

Thus Kafka equates the call of literature with a hidden, powerful inner world which, as the early letter to Oskar Pollak already clearly shows, stands in complete opposition to ordinary life. Physical health and strength, social intercourse, conversations, particularly with women—these are all seen by him as "the alternative" to "the magic" with which writing beckoned. He compares the conjuring up of the buried treasures of the inner self to "a mole's existence"—anticipating by twenty years the key image of his last fragment, "The Burrow"— and concludes his letter with the question whether an active physical and social life might perhaps not have been the real "magic" of his summer. If so, he implies, he would have been wrong to look for it in "the mole and his kind." The conflicting demands of inner and social self dominated Kafka's entire life and work.[10] Kafka's letters to Felice Bauer definitively show that Kafka tended to view his existence in terms of a struggle between these two selves.[11]

The struggle between the "two selves" can also be seen in terms of two kinds of linguistic intent—expression and communication, or, in Kafka's case, literature and conversation. In his early letter to Oskar Pollak, Kafka viewed his newly found ability *to talk* (to women), in other words, the social art of conversation, an alternative to the inner-directed "magic" of his writing. We thus encounter the paradox that one form of linguistic utterance, writing, stands in radical opposition to the essential function of language as the privileged form of human communication. This paradox has of course been a familiar one since Romanticism, or at least since Mallarmé's distinction between the "parole immédiate" of ordinary, informative discourse, and the "parole essentielle" of purely evocative poetry.[12] In fact, it is already contained in Kant's concept of "aesthetic ideas." An "aesthetic idea" for Kant is one that no language can ever "completely attain and make comprehensible."[13] Insofar as the "aesthetic idea" is transrational, Kafka's visionary utterances, which withhold any aid to the understanding, might be said to conform to "aesthetic ideas"

Critical Essays on Franz Kafka

in the Kantian sense. The visionary statement offers no explanatory context. It cannot "make itself comprehensible." Kafka himself considered his art irrational when he insisted that *The Judgment,* a visionary work of which he was particularly fond, was utterly inexplicable. This, to be sure, did not prevent him from putting his astute analytic intelligence to work at interpreting the tale.[14]

The problem of communicating the "aesthetic idea" lay of course at the core of the phenomenon of *Sprachkrise.* For Kafka this problem became a particularly acute conflict between the demands of the visionary inner world, insisting on being expressed, and the equally strong moral duty to communicate with the human species. As we have seen, Kafka from the beginning viewed the task of communication as the alternative to the "magic" of writing. The relationship between them, and therewith the strategy of Kafka's writing, will become clearer if we examine the contrast between the poetics of the early diaries and the entirely different poetics outlined in Kafka's famous letter to his father, the only sustained attempt at an autobiography which he left us.

Kafka's letter to his father begins by calling attention to his difficulty in communicating. The fear which his father had always instilled in him, Kafka claims, had deprived him of the confidence and power necessary for oral communication. By the terror which he struck in his son, his father had condemned him to be a stutterer. In any conversation he found himself at a loss for words. Max Brod contradicts Kafka's self-portrait in this respect. He presents his friend as a very articulate, sociable, and witty companion. However, if we are to believe Kafka's own statements about himself, Brod's image of him must have been Kafka's skillfully maintained social facade. For in his life documents he, like Jean-Jacques Rousseau, constantly laments his inability to talk coherently and successfully. The archetype of all oral communication remained, for Kafka, communication within his family and, above all, with his father. In this he had miserably failed, in his own view.

Writing, on the other hand, was at the opposite pole. It was the region to which the son could flee and which he cultivated because it was the one area in the world where his father's powerful influence did not extend. Speech was linked to the father's forbidding and threatening presence, but writing dealt with his absence: "My writing was all about you; all I did there, after all, was to bemoan what I could not bemoan upon your breast."[15]

Thus writing memorialized a twofold absence for Kafka—first the absence of a loving trusted parent, which had caused his grief initially, and then, the absence of the longed-for audience for this grief. In his writing, Kafka, according to his "Letter," was always bitterly aware of the unbridgeable "difference" between the subject matter and the act of writing. The unreachable father functioned like that "trace," which recalls to us the eternal absence of that which writing is about, and spells out the inevitable heterogeneity which makes writing different from being and gives it its autonomy. What is un-Derridian in the poetics of the "Letter" is the writer's nostalgia for the presence that is withheld. Writing for Kafka is not the confident assertion and affirmation of the "difference," but the everlasting regret of an imposed autonomy.

What Kafka omits from his autobiography is the substitution which his early diaries triumphantly proclaim. The place of the absent father, as the source of inspiration, was taken by the "inner self." Kafka's poetics, at least up to the composition of *The Judgment*, was the attempt to find the way to transcend the need for oral communication which, he felt, his father had made impossible for him. As viewed from Kafka's poetics in the diaries, writing is not the lament over an absence, but the celebration of a presence. This presence, to be sure, is no longer the father, but the inner self and its visionary truth. Kafka's writing, so conceived, represents a victory over the father, and more than that—a victory of the self over the social world of which his father was the earliest representative.

Kafka saw writing, in its ideal form, as a passionate penetration, a taking possession of language, and through language of the social world, originally embodied in the family, that language represents and contains. Kafka's early diaries are filled with recordings of creative experiences in which self-transcendence unites with the sensation of omnipotence. It is this merging of selflessness with self-exaltation which suggests a parallelism between writing and sexuality in Kafka's poetics. Kafka frequently associates inspirational writing with images of flowing, streaming, opening out. He mentions his "pouring himself" into his work, and compares his "outpouring" in his writing to an erotic relationship to a girl of his acquaintance (*T*,76) (*D*,1:76). Recalling the experience of writing *The Judgment* in the trance-like state of a single night, Kafka writes of an ecstatic self-abandonment, a flowing away of all boundaries of the self, an "absolute opening of body and soul." "Only *in this way* can writing be done . . ." (*D*,1:276) (*T*,294), he proclaims apodictically.[16] While writing *The Judgment*, as Max Brod relates, Kafka had experienced an ejaculation.[17] This complete abolishment of the boundaries and limits of the ego, to which the interview with Dr. Steiner also alludes, connects self-transcendence with self-aggrandizement. The loosening of the self seems to bestow magic powers on it: "In the evening and the morning my consciousness of the creative abilities in me is more than I can encompass. I feel shaken to the core of my being and can get out of myself whatever I desire" (*D*,1:76) (*T*,76).

In such moments, Kafka felt, any random sentence written down by him, would be perfect (*T*,42) (*D*,1:45). It is this merging of selflessness with self-exaltation which suggests the sexual aspect of Kafka's poetics. In the early stages of his courtship of Felice Bauer, Kafka made this parallelism between writing and eros explicit. He saw then in his writing the justification for his hope of winning her. Both writing and eros are, in the framework of Kafka's life as presented in his letter to his father, triumphs over the parentally induced inhibition of communication.

However, the essential precondition for successful writing, in Kafka's sense, was the genuineness of "the presence" of the truth in the act of writing. The act would have to be the direct outflow, the "unmediated vision," of the inner self. The "draft" or current of inspiration must never be interrupted. If it were, the truth would be gone, and with it, all the value the work might have. The greatest peril for this writing was self-deception—the writer's delusion that he was still in touch with the truth, while it had left him. Kafka's inhibiting perfectionism derives from his insistence upon the presence of the original feeling that inspired the writing. Any work in excess of that feeling, any embellishment or "fill-in," would make the work not only aesthetically worthless, but morally, and one should say ontologically, wrong. This insistence goes beyond the romantic and existential cult of authenticity.[18] The anxiety it engenders can be compared to the worshipper's dread of defilement of the Eucharist.

The consequence of this insistence upon the unadulterated presence of the inner truth in the work is Kafka's conviction that a good work can only be written in a single sitting, unconsciously, without any deliberation and artifice. *The Judgment*, he felt, qualified for such standards, and it was the only work of his to which he accorded unmixed and even enthusiastic approval. Having written it in one single night, without interruption, so that his legs were stiff when he rose in the morning, he could exclaim: "Only *in this way* can writing be done, only with such coherence, with such a complete opening out of the body and the soul" (*D*,1:276) (*T*,294). From this height of a coherent unity—a "Zusammenhang"—achieved between inspiration and result, he could only look down upon the novel—the first version of *Amerika*—with which he had been struggling for a long time, as on "lowlands" where he had wasted his efforts.

Kafka's contemptuous dismissal of the novel, and his complete satisfaction with the short tale point to his essential difficulty when faced with narratives that could not possibly be written in one sitting. Inherent in Kafka's approach to writing, it explains the numerous false starts and alternate versions of beginnings of narratives that were never continued beyond a few sentences or paragraphs. Most of his long stories and all his novels remained fragments; and even *The Trial*, Kafka's only novel with an ending, remained fragmentary in the middle and exhibits a mosaic-like structure of episodic scenes. This poetics, which was of course not an arbitrary and controllable choice, but the way in which Kafka's literary imagination seemed to work, also helps to explain the peculiarly painful conflict Kafka experienced between the demands of literature and human life. All human relationships represented fatal distractions from a work that brooked no interruption. Nothing short of the life-long self-confinement in the innermost chamber of a deserted cellar, of which he speaks to Felice, would seem to satisfy such rigorous requirements for concentration.

This explains the paradox that an activity conceived of by Kafka as a flowing outward, an inundation of the world by the inner self, seemed at the same time to require an absolute withdrawal, an inhuman solitude. One of Kafka's earliest diary entries states that "loneliness is best" for him. It "metamorphoses" him—Gregor Samsa's fate is here seen as a most positive occurrence—and has "a power over [him] which never fails" (T,34) (D,1:39). For it opens up his "inner self" and allows its deeper layers to come forth. With a dread bordering on panic, he seeks to ward off any disturbance of his creative loneliness. In a letter to Felice, several years later, he describes the ideal way of life for him. It would be to live "with writing utensils and a lamp, in the innermost chamber of a locked spacious cellar." Someone would come to bring him his food, but place it rather far away from his room, "behind the outermost door of the cellar." This arrangement would protect him from contact with the person feeding him. He would return to his desk in the innermost hiding place and, after eating, "immediately commence to write again! And the things I would then be able to write! From what depths I would tear them out! Without effort! For utmost concentration knows no effort!" (BF,250) (LF,156). To be sure, he adds, at the slightest slackening of inspiration he would probably go mad. He tells her of "invisible chains" binding him "to an invisible literature" and warns her that he would scream "if anyone should come near to touch my chains" (BF,450) (LF,308). That such auspices would not be favorable for his engagement to Felice was not difficult to see.

In his first attempt at a novel, "Wedding Preparations in the Country," Kafka presented the paradigm for the contradictory structure underlying his poetics. The protagonist, Raban, having to visit his fiancée in the country, wishes he could evade this dreary task by repeating in actual life what he had been accustomed to do in a recurrent fantasy of his childhood years. Faced with disagreeable social obligations, Raban imagined that he would separate his real self from his body. The former would stay in bed, in "the shape of a great beetle," (H,12), while his body would be sent to carry out Raban's tasks in the world outside. Meanwhile, Raban's true self, reclining in inhuman and solitary serenity, would be the absolute master, not only of his human facade, but of the entire world. The traffic below Raban's window would be utterly dependent on his whims. By withdrawing from humanity and totally identifying with his true desire, by becoming his truth, Raban is able to dominate the world from which he has withdrawn. This wish dream describes the structure underlying Kafka's inspirational poetics. In Stanley Corngold's formulation, the "omnipotent bug . . . suggests the inwardness of the act of writing."[19] By reducing his empirical person to the zero degree, and uniting with his "dreamlike inner life," the writer by the same token takes possession of society, through its medium— language. His total concentration on his writing immerses him in the essence of his community, as embodied in its language, and enables him to appropriate it so absolutely that he becomes the power that moves it.[20]

That Kafka pursued messianic ambitions in his writing has often been observed. The passage is frequently quoted in which he writes that he would receive permanent satisfaction from his writing only if he could "raise the world into the pure, the true, and the unchangeable" (T,534) (D,2:187). Messianism is the logical consequence of his need "to liberate" "the enormous world in [his] head" into articulated existence. For this inner world would or should be the power that by confronting the empirical world would help it to achieve transfiguration. This messianic task requires the writer to be a Messiah figure. Indeed the state of union between inner self and word that Kafka invokes in his poetics alludes to the incarnation, but reverses its terms. Here it is not the Word become flesh, but the flesh—the living individual of flesh and blood—become Word. "Ich bin nichts als Literatur," Kafka declares. In place of an incarnation we could speak of an "inlogozation." The self achieves divine power through "pouring itself" into the waiting body of language. Kafka, whose writing took place mainly during the night, copies a passage from Roskoff's History of the Devil which states that among the Caribs "he who works in the night is believed to be the creator of the world" (T,314) (D,1:295). A fairly crass example of the desire for divine transfiguration by virtue of the creative act appears in a dream which Kafka jotted down in his diary. His "literary projects" come on "an enormous chariot" and naked girls, resembling the houris of Islamic paradise, lift the author upward from his earthly "wretchedness," while his hand commands peace. He feels "the frontiers of human efforts," "at the farthest verge of human endeavor" (D,2:41),[21] "and, high up where I am, with suddenly acquired skill spontaneously execute a trick . . . I bend slowly backward (at that very moment the heavens strain to open to disclose a vision to me, but then stop), draw my legs and gradually *stand erect again* (*auferstehe*). Was this *the ultimate given to mankind?* [italics mine] (*D*,2:41) (*T*,383f). His inspired art, his "Kunststück," literally leads to the artist's "resurrection" and, even though Heaven fails to give the promised special sign to him, and the self-ironic stance is unmistakable, the hybris in this dream clearly alludes to a Faustian striving for the "ultimate" possibilities of man. In a late diary entry, Kafka sees his literary mission, which is born from "loneliness," as "an assault upon the ultimate frontier of earthly life." "This entire literature," by which, as the context makes clear, Kafka understands his own writing, could have "easily developed into a secret doctrine, a new cabala" (*T*,553) (*D*,2:203). Indications for this he sees in his work. However, it is a superhuman task requiring an "unimaginable genius" with the ability to recreate the past and to create the future. We see here how the distant descendant of Kant's "aesthetic idea," which Kafka's visionary poetics represents, likewise entails the corollary to it—Kant's doctrine of trans-rational genius. In Kant's aesthetics the genius functions like another demiurge giving his own laws to the second nature he creates in his art. Similarly Kafka finds that literature, as he conceives it, demands the strength and power of a demiurge of history. After *The Judgment*—a success that in Kafka's own eyes was never repeated— Kafka increasingly felt that such strength was utterly wanting in himself. Far from imagining that he possessed the quasi-divine powers required for his mission, he considered himself in his diaries and letters the least adequate instrument for his task—sluggish, feeble, sickly, ill-equipped in body, in feeling and in mind. Yet the demand persisted.

However, the gravest threat to this demand came from the nature of writing itself. Kafka's ideal was to give the most faithful expression to the truth within himself, and he thought he had achieved that in writing *The Judgment*. Such a faith seemed to justify all sacrifices. This faith required as its formal correlative the restriction of the narrative point of view to a single consciousness and the absence of an omniscient narrator interjecting himself between work and reader. According to Friedrich Beissner, this "unitary perspective" is the chief characteristic of Kafka's art in which its singular truthfulness resides.[22] Despite the profound modifications which Beissner's theory needs to become truly valid for Kafka's actual practice,[23] Kafka's literary judgments, as Hartmut Binder has shown,[24] tend to support Beissner's view. Kafka valued above all else the greatest possible closeness between the feelings of the fictional characters in a scene and those of the author in writing it. The union between writer and text thus established constituted for Kafka the truthfulness of the work in which the reader would naturally share. Thus writing would bring about by a detour that communication which speech had difficulty in achieving, and without which the messianic ambitions of literature would have no basis.

However, after *The Judgment*, in the period of *The Trial*, Kafka began to realize that his writing was by no means a vehicle of the truth, but the opposite—an instrument of counterfeit. In looking back on "the best" he "had written" (*T*,448) (*D*,2:102), he found that it derived its strength from duplicity. His best passages—according to him, always scenes of dying—were perfectly designed to fool the reader. Kafka enjoyed the dying of his protagonists and luxuriated in death scenes. His writing, however, masked his joy so completely that to the reader these scenes appeared terribly sad and deeply moving. By staying within the point of view of his protagonist, who viewed his death as "an injustice" or at least a harsh fate, the reader, made to identify with the character, shared his grievance, while the author savored "such descriptions secretly as a game":

> Indeed, in the death enacted I rejoice in my own death, hence calculatingly exploit the attention that the reader concentrates on death, have a much clearer understanding of it than he, of whom I suppose that he will loudly lament on his deathbed, and for these reasons my lament is as perfect as it can be, nor does it suddenly break off, as is likely to be the case with a real lament, but dies beautifully and purely away. It is the same thing as my perpetual lamenting to my mother over pains that were not nearly so great as my laments would lead me to believe. With my mother, of course, I did not need to make so great a display of art as with the reader. (*D*,2:102) (*T*,448f).

Such artful deceit and clever contriving for aesthetic effect, while attesting to Kafka's subtle mastery of the art of fiction, glaringly contradict his ideal of the writer's absolute faithfulness to and unity with the feeling permeating his work and embodied in his character. The bifurcation of perspectives of author and character, and thus of author and reader, gives the lie to the presence of the writer's "truth" in his text. Thus Kafka failed to find in his own work that indivisible unity between conception and execution which he demanded of literature. The mere restriction of the point of view to the protagonist does not, contrary to Beissner's claim, guarantee the truthfulness of the work. On the contrary, the apparent absence of an omniscient narrator only helps to hoodwink the reader all the more effectively by suggesting an identity between author and protagonist that is not there. The author in his concealment manipulates and dupes the reader, who, one can easily imagine, might be horrified to learn that his "tears" were a calculated side effect of the author's sado-maso-chistic "play."

There is a striking parallelism between Kafka's literary strategy, as described in this diary entry, and the structure of Raban's dream. Both, first of all, are seen as infantile devices. Raban's split self was originally a child's fantasy, and Kafka compares his literary artifice to the child's device of exaggerating his ailments to get his mother's sympathy. The hidden author, in Kafka's diary entry, corresponds to Raban's inhuman truth. The dying fictional character parallels Raban's pretended human self, and the outside world that is taken in by Raban's human facade has its equivalent in Kafka's deceived reader. Ironically it is the very idea of a "true self" that spells out deception. Raban sends out his "stand-in" to fake his presence in human relationships from which he is "really" absent. Thus precisely by becoming his "truth," Raban cheats. His fantasy, if taken seriously and carried over into life, would entail emotional disaster for his dupes.

Duplicity, Kafka comes to recognize, is built into the very act of writing fiction, since in it the self inevitably splits into the writer and the character, or into the subject and the object of reflection. The "eigene Gestalt" is for Kafka the primary subject of literature, and remains for him the prototype of all fictional characters. But in this self-reflection the unity between the writer and the writing is ruptured. In fact, it can never truly come about, or at any rate, it cannot be sustained for any length of time. For from the moment the writing self reflects on the subject it writes about, the perfect congruence of writer and subject, which is truth, becomes impossible. In its place a playful and coquettish self-regard arises which for Kafka is the infernal opposite of truth: "And the diabolic element in it [writing] seems very clear to me. It is vanity and sensuality which continually buzz about one's own or even another's form—and feast on him. The movement multiplies itself—it is a regular solar system of vanity. Sometimes a naive person will wish, 'I would like to be dead and see how everyone mourns me.' Such a writer is continually staging a scene: He dies (or rather he does not live) and continually mourns himself'' (L,334) (B,384f). Narcissism for Kafka is only the extreme and logical consequence of reflection, since it is the ultimate result of the separation from being and thus from truth, which occurs in reflection. Multiplication of characters in the literary work does not change the self-reflection at its basis, but merely intensifies it. Since fictional characters are self-projections of the author in varying degrees, "vanity" simply becomes "a solar system" instead of being confined to a single star.

With other authors of the *Sprachkrise*, Kafka held to the superiority of being over thinking, immediacy over reflection. What he dreaded in writing was its mediate character, its referential nature, and separation from being. The inevitably metaphoric nature of writing, its inability to be what it speaks about, describes, or evokes, brought on his despair. Half a year before the letter to Max Brod, from which I just quoted, Kafka noted in his diary: "Writing's lack of independence of the world, its dependence on the maid who tends the fire, on the cat warming itself by the stove; it is even dependent on the poor old human being warming himself by the stove. All these are independent activities ruled by their own laws; only writing is helpless, cannot live in itself, is a job and a despair" (D,2:201) (T,551).

Kafka's view of writing as "a joke" makes the comparison of his work with a "game"—even a Wittgensteinian "language game"[25]—plausible as long as we realize that it applies to Kafka's "despair," not to his ideal. Writing seen as self-referential "play" of language signals the breakdown of his faith in his own work as the medium of the truth buried in him. Self-reflection capped that fraudulence which, as the diary entry about his death scenes shows, Kafka found inherent in the strategy of "fiction."

In the ideal of writing, as Kafka conceived it, the author should be nothing but the medium for what wants to be expressed; but self-reflection steps between the inspiration and the act, and dams up and pollutes the flow from within. The self made object shuts out the vision of that "enormous world inside the head," that writing was to bring into view. Literature stifles that which the writer's word is to liberate. A book "must be the axe for the frozen sea within us," Kafka wrote at age twenty-one (L,16) (B,28). Any other use of literature, so he felt all his life, was mere "decoration." To demand sacrifices for such a purpose was a sin against life. However, self-reflection, in which for Kafka the nature of fiction resides, separates the self from its inner world and prevents truth from appearing. It perpetuates "the frozen sea" within the self.

We return here to the paradox which underlies Kafka's "Raban-esque" poetics. This poetics attempts to unite two contradictory projects. While it aims for the dissolution of the self to "allow the deeper layers to come to the fore" (T,34) (D,1:39), it also directs the writer toward extreme self-absorption. Its fundamental quest—lifting the inner world into language, and thus into articulated consciousness—also has the dream of the ego's magic and messianic omnipotence built into it. The radiant glimpse of that immense inner world, like the light from inside the law, in the prison chaplain's legend in *The Trial*, can show itself only when the shadow of the self no longer impedes vision. Yet, and this is the paradox which denied to Kafka "permanent satisfaction" with his works, self-regard was inseparable from an art that conceived of itself as "a descent" (B,384) (L,334) into the interior of the self. In terms of his own poetics, then, Kafka had to be what Walter Benjamin called him— "one stranded in life."[26]

The poetics, which I have tried to investigate here, alone cannot illuminate the peculiar impact and power of Kafka's writing. Even the impasse to which this poetics led him cannot be fully understood without the communal, collective, and universalist aspect which, in addition to the inward and subjective side on which we have dwelt here, marked Kafka's idea of "truth" and language. Furthermore, a strong desire for clarification and understanding—in the broadest sense, for self-preservation—runs side by side with the visionary element in his art. Only when these other concerns are investigated, can we hope to do justice to Kafka's "poetics." The present essay must be considered merely a first step toward that objective.

Notes

1. Cf. Theodore Ziolkowski's "James Joyces Epiphanie und die Überwindung der empirischen Welt in der modernen deutschen Prosa," *Deutsche Vierteljahrsschrift für Literaturwissenschaft und Geistesgeschichte* 35 (1969):596.

2. Franz Kafka, *Briefe, 1902–1924*, ed. Max Brod, S. Fischer Verlag Lizenzausgabe (New York: Schocken Books, 1958). Referred to in all future references in the text as *B*. English translation taken from *Letters to Friends, Family, and Editors*, trans. Richard and Clara Winston (New York: Schocken Books, 1977). References to this work are in text as *L*.

3. Quoted from Robert Musil, *Prosa, Dramen, Späte Briefe*, ed. Adolf Frisé (Hamburg: Rowohlt, 1957), 15. (Translation by the editor of this volume.)

4. Hugo von Hofmannsthal, "Ein Brief" *Gesammelte Werke*, vol. 2 (Berlin: S. Fischer, 1924), 180.

5. Jacques Derrida, *Of Grammatology*, trans. Gayatri Chakravorty Spivak (Baltimore and London: The Johns Hopkins University Press, 1976), 69–70.

6. Ibid., xvi.

7. Anthony Thorlby, in his stimulating essay, "Anti-Mimesis: Kafka and Wittgenstein," crassly contradicts Kafka's own poetics when he writes: "Kafka's stories illustrate the dreadful problem that language *is* something altogether different from what it says . . ." (*On Kafka: Semi-Centenary Perspectives*, ed. Franz Kuna [London: Paul Elek, 1976], 74.) This is precisely what Kafka cannot accept. "Language games" in Wittgenstein's sense are radically inappropriate to the intensely "realistic" and literal-minded seriousness with which Kafka pursues "truth" by means of his writing.

8. Franz Kafka, *Tagebücher, 1910–1923*, ed. Max Brod (New York: Schocken Books, 1948 and 1949), 34. Referred to in text as *T*. English translations taken from *The Diaries of Franz Kafka*, vol. 1, 1910–1913, ed. Max Brod, trans. Joseph Kresh (New York: Schocken Books, 1948), 39. Referred to in text as *D*,1, and *The Diaries of Franz Kafka*, vol. 2, 1914–1923, ed. Max Brod, trans. Martin Greenberg and Hannah Arendt (New York: Schocken Books, 1949). Referred to in text as *D*,2. (When the translation is the essayist's directly from the German, *T* will precede *D*,1 or *D*,2. When the translation is from the English edition, *D*1 and *D*2 will precede *T*.)

9. The close relationship between Kafka's writing and his dream life has frequently been noted. Cf. particularly S. Fraiberg, "Kafka and the Dream," *Partisan Review* XXIII (1956): 47–69; Michel Dentan, *Humour et création littéraire dans l'oeuvre de Kafka* (Geneva/Paris: Librairie Droz/Librairie Minard, 1961), *passim*; Friedrich Altenhöner, *Der Traum und die Traumstruktur im Werk Franz Kafkas* (diss. Münster 1962). Hartmut Binder has also pointed to the flood of visions that "crowded in" on Kafka so that he could consider "die Ausstoßung ins Kunstwerk als grosses Glück." (*Motiv*

und Gestaltung bei Franz Kafka [Bonn: Bouvier 1966], 117). A systematic investigation and analysis of the visionary element in Kafka's work has not yet been undertaken.

10. Cf. Walter H. Sokel, *Franz Kafka: Tragik und Ironie. Zur Struktur seiner Kunst.* (Munich/Vienna: Albert Langen-Georg Müller, 1964). Paperback edition: (Frankfurt: Fischer Taschenbuch Verlag, 1976).

11. Cf. particularly the long explanatory letter, dated end of October/beginning of November 1914, and the very last letter to Felice, dated October 16, 1917 in *Letters to Felice*, ed. Erich Heller and Jürgen Born, trans. James Stern and Elizabeth Duckworth (New York: Schocken Books, 1973) 436–41, 546–47. Future references to this work will be cited in text as *LF.*

12. Cf. my *The Writer in Extremis: Expressionism in Twentieth-Century German Literature* (Stanford: Stanford University Press, 1959), 12.

13. ". . . by an aesthetical Idea I understand that representation of the Imagination which occasions much thought, without, however, any definite thought, i.e., any *concept,* being capable of being adequate to it; it consequently cannot be completely compassed and made intelligible by language." Immanuel Kant, *Critique of Judgment,* Par. 49, trans. J. H. Bernard (London: MacMillan and Co., 1931), 197.

14. Cf. Franz Kafka, *Briefe an Felice und andere Korrespondenz aus der Verlobungszeit,* ed. Erich Heller and Jürgen Born (Lizenzausgabe von Schocken Books, Frankfurt: S. Fischer Verlag, 1967), 394, 396. (This volume will hereinafter be referred to as *BF.*) Side by side with the oneiric and fantastic tendency of Kafka's art, a strong rational current also runs through his work and forms a powerful complement to the visionary strain in it. His writing can be divided into two distinct types: visions and illustrations. The latter are similes or metaphors, serving basically explanatory purposes, and frequently extended into parabolic narratives. (Cf. particularly Karl-Heinz Fingerhut, *Die Funktion der Tierfiguren im Werke Franz Kafkas: Offene Erzählgerüste und Figurenspiele* [Bonn: H. Bouvier & Co., 1969], 37–40, 45–59, and Hartmut Binder, *Kafka in neuer Sicht: Mimik, Gestik und Personengefüge als Darstellung des Autobiographischen* [Stuttgart: J. B. Metzler, 1976], 7–20.) For the distinction between the two types of Kafka's narratives, see Walter H. Sokel, "Das Verhältnis der Erzählperspektive zu Erzählgeschehen und Sinngehalt in 'Vor dem Gesetz,' 'Schakale und Araber,' und 'Der Prozeß,' " *Zeitschrift für deutsche Philologie* 86 (1967): 267–300. Stanley Corngold's trenchant essay—"The Structure of Kafka's Metamorphosis: Metamorphosis of the Metaphor"—denies the metaphoric nature of Kafka's art and claims that Kafka "is the writer par excellence who came to detect in metaphorical language a crucial obstacle to his own enterprise." (*The Commentators' Despair: The Interpretation of Kafka's 'Metamorphosis' "* [Port Washington, New York/London: National University Publications Kennikat Press, 1973], 5.) The present essay certainly agrees with Corngold's approach, and particularly with his assertion that "the desire to represent a state of mind directly in language, in a form consubstantial with that consciousness," (Ibid., 7) was Kafka's avowed goal. However, as I shall try to show in a subsequent publication, Corngold does justice to only one aspect of Kafka's poetics and ignores other very powerful and contradictory intentions of his work.

15. Franz Kafka, *Hochzeitsvorbereitungen auf dem Lande und andere Prosa aus dem Nachlaß,* ed. Max Brod (New York: Schocken Books, 1953), 203. This volume will hereinafter be referred to as *H.* English translation from *Dearest Father: Stories and Other Writings* (New York: Schocken Books, 1954), 177.

16. Binder points out that Kafka's last great fragment, "The Burrow," was, according to Dora Diamant, also written in one single night. (Cf. *Motiv* . . . 118, and J. P. Hodin, "Erinnerungen an Franz Kafka," *Der Monat* 9 [1949]: 8–9, 89–96.)

17. Max Brod, *Über Franz Kafka* (Frankfurt: Fischer Taschenbuch Verlag, 1974), 114.

18. Cf. Lionel Trilling, *Sincerity and Authenticity* (Cambridge, Massachusetts: Harvard University Press, 1971, 1972), *passim*.

19. Corngold, 21.

20. A crucial image corroborates the link of Raban's wish dream to Kafka's poetics. Kafka frequently uses the image of "draft" or "current" ("Zug") to denote inspiration. His work, he states, can succeed only "in ganzem Zug" (*T*,267), in a single complete uninterrupted "draft" or "breath." In the passage of his early letter to Oskar Pollak, which I quoted, he speaks of "lifting in one single draft (Zug) that which I think I have in me." (My translation of "Zug" by "heave" obscures the close relationship to Raban's fantasy.) In Raban's dream of omnipotence, a draft of air always blows through his room. This image associates Raban's dream with Kafka's precondition for successful writing.

21. *The Diaries of Franz Kafka*, 1914–1923, ed. Max Brod, trans. Martin Greenberg with the cooperation of Hannah Arendt. First Schocken paperback edition, 1965. (New York: Schocken Books, 1974), copyright 1949.

22. Cf. Friedrich Beissner, *Der Erzähler Franz Kafka: Ein Vortrag* (Stuttgart: W. Kohlhammer, 1952).

23. Cf. especially Klaus-Peter Philippi, *Reflexion und Wirklichkeit: Untersuchungen zu Kafkas Roman 'Das Schloß'* (Tübingen, Max Niemeyer Verlag, 1966), 14–32.

24. Hartmut Binder, "Kafkas literarische Urteile," *Zeitschrift für deutsche Philologie* 86, no. 2 (1967): 230.

25. Cf. Thorlby.

26. "To do justice to the figure of Kafka in its purity and in its characteristic beauty, one must never forget one thing: it is that of one stranded in life." Franz Kafka, *Briefe*, vol. 2, ed. Gershom Scholem and Theodor W. Adorno (Frankfurt: Suhrkamp, 1966), 764. (Translation by editor of this volume.)

Freud as Literature?   Stanley Corngold[*]

The thought of wanting to help
me is a sickness and must be
put to bed to get well.[1]

—KAFKA

You have to dive down, as it were,
and sink more rapidly than that
which sinks in advance of you.[2]

—KAFKA

Doch konnten wir nicht
hinüberdunkeln zu dir:
es herrschte
Lichtzwang.[3]

—CELAN

In the fall of 1977 a convulsive series of events shocked Germany: the industrialist leader Hanns-Martin Schleyer was abducted by "terrorists" and was afterward found dead, bundled in the trunk of an automobile "parked outside a dilapidated tenement in Mulhouse in the French border region of Alsace."[4] Shortly before his death, other terrorists hijacked a Lufthansa jet, which they meant to ransom for the freeing of terrorists imprisoned in the maximum-security prison of Stammheim near Stuttgart. When, a few days later, the jet was recaptured by German commandos in Somalia, the imprisoned terrorists Baader, Raspe, and Ensslin reportedly committed suicide. All this terror, so concentrated, struck France as a lightning flash which, for one moment, illuminated the real Germany as a formless mass, blighted and blasted, a desert, marsh, or lunar landscape—sinister, shadowed, yet lurking too. For the French it was not possible, it seemed, to see anything in Germany except as what the flash of light, the flash of truth, lit up. Germany was darkness, nonbeing—thus unlike the light—but like the light too as light visibly subdued. If the lightning flash was terrible, *terrorist,* so too (wrote Jean Genet) was the real Germany terrible, terribly *violent.* The light flashed and also illuminated the hidden, blind, repressed violence of German nonbeing—German "not becoming," "not wanting." These phrases are Nietzsche's, and with others like them they were much in use.[5]

This was the view from west of the Rhine. But Germany saw too in the French account the familiar French travesty of clarity—what Nietzsche once called the French art of "making thin, simplifying, logicizing" (*WP,* 438). German writers reacted, saying that all the darkness, repression, and indefinite nonbeing that France had seen *in* the German object had been only the effect of the French repression *of* Germany. France had been chiefly bent on denying the interest for France of the German case. Yet the bombs that had gone off had been European explosions, not illuminations of Germany. What they should properly have produced in anyone with eyes to see and senses to feel was not insight but anxiety—terror of violence and of darkness stirring, but of a darkness everywhere, an anxiety for the fate of the whole decent world. French thought had pretended to be not "of" German, of European anxiety, in the genitive sense but in the detached, dissevering ablative—meaning thereby to detach itself from its own anxiety. But by virtue of the circular structure of anxiety, whereby the repression of anxiety (ablative) is itself the effect of the repression of anxiety (genitive). French thought had been, finally, only the effect of French anxiety. An old story: Thought as part of the holding action of repression, revealing nothing of its object and everything of its source, so that what the German reader finally concluded was only a variant of the ready complaint that "the preferred form of French self-criticism is attacking Germany."

According to this German reading, the French had constructed a sign for German terrorism, S/s. For "S," the signifier, read, "the flare-up, the apparent illumination, terroristic clarity and the clarity of terrorism." For "s," the signified, read "the daily landscape of German violence practiced through its repression, of violence that returns to blind itself, of effaced blindness masquerading as order"— the whole of the signified rooted in the Germans' repression of their guilt for the violence of the war. The bar of S/s meanwhile designated, for the French, the trope of litotes: terror is not negated violence, i.e., is the truth of unrepressed violence, whereas the bar designated for Germany (according to the French reading) only a benighted metaphor, of terror as cognate with the violent aggression of a few anarchic individuals.

The Germans did not fail to take their turn at reading the *whole* of the French reading as the new signifier "S'". The French had asserted a litotes whose clever, aggressive, negating style was in reality only the metonymy of French hostility toward Germany. That the French imagined an obscure German repression of German violence was nothing more than an expression of surplus hostility accompanying France's incomplete repression of the German object.[6]

A third reading, neither French nor German, would perceive the abuse (catachresis) in this argument by litotes, the rhetorical figure which asserts sameness through doubled difference or negation. The French action of distinguishing the German crisis as a litotes is the displacement of yet a third trope: France's *identity* with Germany. The displacement aims to dislodge French consciousness of this identity. For France to perceive this sameness would be to recognize the shame of its own repressed daily violence.[7]

Thus French rhetoric designates its own crisis: as often is the case, Germany is involved. What divides these countries, the Rhine, is in times of crisis a mirror with two faces. If from the French side the Germans are *outre-rhin* and thus effectively beyond the pale or *limes*, the French for the Germans are *jenseits des R(h)ein-en:* unclean. This is one way of avoiding paranoia.[8]

But the effort to shun at all costs the horror of similitude, one's gaze fixed immovably on the "perceived" difference of the other, can mean and meant in the French case self-evasion. The French reader of Baader/Schleyer fully effaced the term of the self and was less a reader than a voyeur. The Germans said that the one genuine access to the German object which the French had gained by the crisis was the annexation to their language of a new signifier: *schadenfreude*. Which brings me by indirections to my subject.

How I understand the French reading of Freud (1856–1939), hence Freud as a literary text, might now be fairly obvious. The parallel between the French reading of Baader/Schleyer and the

French reading of Freud is there for the asking. What the French have discovered in the light of their own reading of Freud is Freud's repression of (the discovery of) repression.[9] Suppose we turn French Freud around as the object of an imaginable Freudian analysis. The outcome is the specular doubling of all such closed systems. The new criticism appears violent and aggressive and invites the charge that it is terroristic.[10] Its discovery (of Freud's repression) is not made in the light of truth; it is a glimpse obtained through violent swerving. What the French have uncovered is not Freud's aversion to repression but their having averted themselves from the *determinist* Freud.

The French mood, the "soldierly" one, of accepting, even welcoming, the small death of self-expropriation in a structure of impersonal exchange, finally embraces Freud the old determinist so as to read the determinist out of him in the name of his more real undecidability. In the margin of undecidability, there is still the small mercy of "negative liberty."[11] It never was really to be supposed that the French were contemplating self-immolation, for their glorification of Freud is too bizarre. The French display of interpretive energy looks like a snook cocked at the father in the guise of model obedience to the father—at Freud the old arbiter.

What, if anything, is truthful in these French and German readings? It would be impossible from *within* such a text, produced by specular relations, to decide this question. Every thesis having the form of litotes, in the sense of deconstruction, "derepression," asserts that some other term ostensibly simple and positive is actually the negation, the exclusion or denial, of what within that very term is contradictory. Every such litotic thesis can be immediately disqualified, however. From another perspective the litotes—the logical figure of deconstruction—is only the catachresis of a virtual identity, namely, the disfigured expression of a will to power bent on masking its own contradiction. In such a system of texts, as in a dream, the principle of *non*contradiction operates, vertiginously. Where from the start no term in a system is self-identical, where none is "demystified from the start" in the sense of assuring the *play* and not the chaotic proliferation of difference between other terms,[12] where all *seeming* identity to self is based only on denial of the actual convergence of, first, what is other with, second, what is always and originally other in the self-same; then questions and answers cannot be distinguished, each being only the "effect" of the other, arrested in a moment of oscillation. Elements of such a pseudostructure do not have enough stability to allow for the stipulation of distinctions or even of "nodal points," let alone of hierarchies; and "leaping from node to node," which Jeffrey Mehlman offers as Leiris' desirable wisdom, is an invitation to vertigo.[13]

Nothing, then, in the pseudostructure of the readings which Freud has generated is properly literary. Freud can be given the stability of a literary text as an organization of ironical practice only by acts of exegetical terrorism. These acts are invited perhaps by the heroic aura of Freud's enterprise but are otherwise sheerly reckless in an order where "mental events are determined . . . [where] there is nothing arbitrary about them."[14]

The French proposition that the Freudian text repressed its discovery of repression contradicts a "literary" reading of the text, because as a blind text arising from repression, it produces only a repressive discourse. Unlike a literary text, it cannot disabuse the interlocutor by being ahead of him in its understanding; instead it annihilates him every step of the way, declaring each of his questions to be already determined as the effect of repression.[15]

The strong interpretive strategy must aim to organize the current and countercurrent of these effects. If the reversibility of valence attaching to each moment of a specular rhetoric suggests the instability of a dream, then the reading must be waked from its nightmare, cured of its vertigo. Yet "the thought of wanting to help," as Kafka's Hunter Gracchus says, "is a sickness and must be put to bed to get well."[16]

There is no account given in Freud for the therapeutic wonder that pronouncing the name of the determination could break its iron law. It is as if, for Freud, the law of determination produced an endlessly tautological sentence in which the captured subject kept reappearing as the predicate symptom, but the *name* of the determination could then begin another sentence, produce a liberating anacoluthon and a new text in turn.[17] As if too the language with which a nightmare were deciphered, a language inconsistent with the text of the nightmare, could, on being inserted within that first, silent text, awaken the dreamer into a different dream. But if this account is right, and if the therapeutic word is construed on the model of a deciphering (interpreting) phrase, the question arises as how this phrase could be accommodated within the scene of the primary text, which has no place for it, which cannot accept it without being blasted apart, ceasing to contain the captured subject, text, and dream. There could be only languages in parallel, and freedom would indeed be only a leap.

There is moreover a theory of waking and curing already implied in the model of political terror which denies to psychoanalytic discourse any such healing or arresting effect. Reading Baader/Schleyer the French considered the illumination they provided as the bracing lucidity which could wake the Germans from their sleep of reason, cure them of their national melancholy.

By what means does the silent interlocutor (the analyst) produce in the patient the deviant sentence that frees him from the repetition

of his suffering, wakes him from the tautology that he lives as help-
lessly as the dreamer his dream? Where does the French reader find
his lights to cure Freud of his tautology, his repression of repression?
With what speculum?

Until the text of Freud supplies the instrument with which the
deconstructor can deconstruct Freud without in turn being annihilated
by it, there can be no good claim that in Freud we have a literary
text. Freud's vertiginous instability is not harmless for the interpreter-
subject, who must realize that the ensuing dissolution of the subject
is one in which he collaborates only because he does not *live* it.[18]
He cannot live this dissolution and also maintain that it is his light
in which Freud can be deciphered, let alone be cured of his repression.

Lacan's rereading of Freud—under the banner of a return to
Freud—is in fact a turn to, and within, a French intellectual tradition,
one characterized by Nietzsche as the "voluptas psychologica," artistic
passion, and a flair for mediation.[19] To this one could add the recent
acquisition assuring French superiority: intellectual terrorism. It is in
the light produced by a self-conscious production of the French spirit,
the commentator's own, that Freud is to be deciphered, and indeed
cured of his repression (of repression). This cure takes place through
the clarity of a psychoanalytical reading. But one worries with
Nietzsche: "How can man know himself? It is . . . a tormenting, a
dangerous enterprise to dig at oneself . . . and descend by force on
the first route into the shaft of one's being. How easily a man damages
himself this way. So [fatally] that no physician can heal him."[20]

Consider, however, the opening of Lacan's "Function of Language
in Psychoanalysis," whose confident lucidity—perhaps an intended
irony—means to produce a healing. Addressing Freud's "Promethean
discovery" (of repression), Lacan writes: "Such awe seizes man when
he unveils the lineaments of his power that he turns away from it
in the very action employed to lay its features bare."[21]

The word *awe* above conceals more than it reveals. This is the
language of "negative pleasure," of the Kantian sublime, but it exalts
too high the modality of intimidated blindness, smooths over what
Thomas Weiskel called "the logic of terror."[22] The image of the
Promethean act of a man laying bare the lineaments of his power is
in principle troubled. A Promethean act reveals art and design, illuminates with fire; a human act thus emulating Prometheus' could
indeed inspire awe. But it is also an act of defiance and impiety,
entailing horrible tortures; the mind that turns away from this implication is not sublime but defensive.[23] "Too concerned with guarding
the flame," declares Stuart Schneiderman, and "refusing to repeat
the act of theft that acquired fire in the first place, [analysts] let the
fire go out [and] . . . turn theory into dogma."[24] Lacan's account
represses this implication of defensiveness, but it, rather than the

language of sublimity, proves more faithful to the history of the dynamic of repression in Freud. For one can trace in Freud's work the only hesitant process by which the term repression (*Verdrängung*) achieves any sort of meaning independent of that of defense (*Abwehr*).[25]

Thus the picture which reveals Freud's repression of repression itself masks repression as defense. We are still inside the specular circle, where the point is not to stay inside it but to get out of it in the right way. We need a text which operates within the text of recent French criticism and in Freud as the repressed third term. Lacan's image suggests that this text may be Kafka, whom both Freud and the French rewriting of the human sciences in the last twenty years have left strikingly *hors compte*.[26]

What is the empirical case? Freud nowhere explicitly alludes to Kafka, although it is certain that he knew him, as a visit to his library on the Berggasse confirms. Freud would have been aware of Kafka also, because he read Stekel (who gets mixed reviews in the *Interpretation of Dreams*),[27] and Stekel devoted a couple of paragraphs in his *Pathological Disturbances of the Instinctual and Affective Life* of 1917 to *The Metamorphosis*, diagnosing it as a zooanthropic fantasy (wrong) of transformation into a louse (wrong) and hence as denoting the self-aimed sadistic component of unhappy homosexuality (probably wrong). Kafka wrote to Felix Weltsch on September 22, 1917, asking to read Stekel's comments. If these lines ever did come into his hands, he cannot have been very much instructed.

A more perceptive reader, Hellmuth Kaiser, published in *Imago* in 1931 an essay on Kafka's "phantasy of punishment" in which the metamorphosis, and in particular the "forcible impregnation" of Gregor's back by two small hard apples fired by his father, represents not the sadistic but the masochistic component: Gregor nearly dies of mingled pleasure and pain at the *coitus per anum*. The official position of the Freudian school on Kafka was to hammer "given existing pieces" into the machine.

What does it mean for the status of Freud as a literary text that Freud sanctioned so vacuous a reading of the very writer through whom he might have read, in an inspired way, the therapeutist in himself?[28] The image of Freud's fundamentalist corrector Lacan—of man turning in awe from his own Promethean fire—leads one to Kafka for further correction.

Kafka records in his *Diaries* a moment like that which Lacan describes. Lacan writes of dazzlement at the "unveiling" of man's work of knowledge. For Kafka: "Our art is a way of being dazzled by truth; the light on the flinching grimacing face is true, and nothing else."[29] The light for Kafka is inhuman; the genius provides a maximum of surface, he is the twisted foil for the light. Art includes the moment of being struck, of being wounded, of shrinking back, of being unequal: the wound, a moment between hesitation and flight, generates the productive disparity of the text.

The instant of the copresence of man and illumination in Kafka is negative. The dynamic of occlusion is more humbling than countertransference, as if in the fullest sense of the word an obscure mechanism had to compensate for the presence of a more than ordinary measure of illumination by producing a more than ordinary measure of opacity and disturbance in response to it. From out of the gates of the Law there streams an inextinguishable radiance, but of those who huddle near the light, the doorkeeper has turned his back to it, and the suppliant bribes him with words and implores the fleas on the doorkeeper's fur collar to help him. It is not awe that keeps him from advancing toward the Law. On the bed of the Castle functionary Bürgel, who is on the verge of revealing to the land surveyor K. how one might "enter" the Castle, K. grows drowsy, inattentive, falls asleep. In the early diary entry—" 'You,' I said"— the experience by the bachelor of his "depth" (Grund) forces him to freeze in forgetfulness of the moment.[30]

Kafka's text can be analyzed as a series of cognates of such moments of inequality and disparity *without ethical content*, suggesting that the moment is not one that can in principle ever be cleared-up, made right, enlightened, or controlled.

We have two accounts, then, of the dynamic of repression: on the one hand, that of the French and Freud, that moves between dazzled "awe" and prudent self-defense, both in principle intelligible, auspicious, and contributing to a cure; on the other, an implacable aversion and wounding, incorrigible except for the minimal hope that by a process which Kafka called *Tat-Beobachtung*—"the action of observation," the observation of the trauma of repression—there might be "a leap out of Murderer's Row."[31]

But the leap shown in the "Hunter Gracchus" is only the drifting of a lucid ruin. The wandering Hunter, who cannot die and who suffers from his solitude, says, "I do not shout to summon help, even though at moments—when I lose control over myself . . .—I think seriously of it. But to drive out such thoughts I need only look round me and verify where I am, and—I can safely assert—have been for hundreds of years."[32] What he describes at first is a derepression of desire (the loss of control) and next, a moment of observation, the effect of which is actually to strengthen the original repression. His glance discovers no new object of liberated desire; instead it wounds desire by driving out, as futile, thoughts of freedom. The Hunter continues: "I am here, more than that I do not know, further than that I cannot go." The moment of observation is thus a moment held together by style, and the experience is without practical salvational import: "My ship has no rudder, and it is driven by the wind that blows in the undermost regions of death."

Other features of Kafka's work suggest a model of a literary text with which the text of French Freud can be contrasted. Here are some salient features of the model.

Kafka is supposed to have said, "The dream reveals the reality, which conception lags behind. That is the horror of life—the terror of art."[33] The sentence distinguishes the terror of art from the banal violence (horror) which the French reading of Baader/Schleyer attached to the psychopathology of everyday German life, a psychopathology of everyday repressiveness to which even Freud's discovery succumbed. It is with the values of art that that reading contrived to invest kidnapping and explosives—qualities of fierce, dialectical brilliance which the French reading of Freud displays. But art is a different combustion of the dream.

Art pursues the dream but is not the dream; yet the dream reveals the reality of something terrible distorted by horror, blanketed by ordinary neurosis.[34] Art is the narration of the dream; all of its life is in principle the dream. But as there is no representation in Kafka of a dream that isn't also waking, there is no single action that is dream*like* in his work. Everything, Adorno noted, unlike dream and its prelogical logic is excluded, including "real" dreams themselves.[35]

The difference, now, between the text of the dream in Kafka and the text of the dream in Freud is that Kafka's dream excludes all commentary and deciphering; "the scriptures are unalterable and the comments often enough merely express the commentators' despair."[36] Kafka's script instead calls attention to the act by which it is narrated. There is consciousness *of* dream narration. Kafka develops a fictional language which excludes decipherment even by allusion to the properties of the narrator or to an identification of the dream as dream. There is only the world of the horrible dream distanced in a narrative perspective remarkable for the reticence of its effects. Kafka's superiority is evident in the narrow sector of his work which reveals *that the dream is being narrated.* The fictive consciousness positions itself in the gap between a representation of the content of the dream and a decipherment of the dream: only "the limited circle is pure."[37] What is narrated is accessible in only one way— through the perspective of the narration; its mode of being is a being-towards-narration, which includes its own reflection, flame in a mirror.

Kafka appears to know two things with great clarity: First, the revelation of truth and the swerve from truth are not an affair of intersubjectivity, of "dialogue"; truth is self-authentication, "a great fire . . . in which [everything] perishes and rises up again,"[38] but the swerve is everywhere—"the horror." Second, the condition of registering this truth is writing fiction; this means inscribing within the dream-text, by means of random breaks, the awareness that this text of fire and "flinching" is being narrated.[39]

The repeated point of narrative departure, just outside the dream, does not compose another language except as it communicates the consciousness of a distance. This constructed consciousness is the third term missing from the specular reading of Freud. It is the condition of existence outside the intersubjective relation, a margin which is without life and yet is not painless. "Art for the artist," said Kafka—on Janouch's authority—"is only suffering through which he releases himself for further suffering."[40]

Kafka's last word on the question of cure is, as it ought to be, fictive. "A Country Doctor," which critics have read as an explicit rejection of psychoanalysis, is a literary text par excellence, constituted by two principles: first, consciousness of the narration of fiction (the difference inside narration, the narration of a difference); second, the refusal of a theory of cure—i.e., of intersubjective truth—which would imply the elimination of the constitutive difference of fiction. If we substitute in the formula "Art, for the artist, is only suffering through which he releases himself for further suffering" the words "curing" for "art" and "doctor" for "artist," we could enter the story.

The story thematizes the doctor who cannot cure both his patient and himself. The patient is a wounded boy, "quite blinded by the life within his wound." Kafka, hostile to all forms of superiority, immediately robs the doctor (-narrator) of his vantage point and puts him to bed with the boy, who whispers shrewdly, "Why, you were only blown in here, you didn't come on your own feet. Instead of helping me, you're cramping me on my deathbed. What I'd like best is to scratch your eyes out [your voyeuristic eyes] . . . 'Right,' I said, 'it is a shame. And yet I am a doctor [a narrator]. What am I to do? Believe me, it is not too easy for me either.' "

Here is the form of the cure, or as much of a cure as we're shown. To the patient who reveals "A fine wound is all I brought into the world, that was my sole endowment," the doctor replies: "My young friend, your mistake is: you have not a wide enough view . . . Your wound is not so bad. Done in a tight corner with two strokes of the ax. Many a one proffers his side and can hardly hear the ax in the forest, far less that it is coming nearer to him."

The "cure" of the wound, such as it is, is the *knowledge* of its privilege. "It is enough," wrote Kafka in his *Diaries* "that the arrows fit exactly in the wounds that they have made."[41] The sufferer's privilege is that his wound, properly part of a universe of wounding, has been revealed with eminent clarity.

The patient seems pacified, but a striking change missing from the Muir translation occurs at the level of the signifier. The narration suffers a perturbation and passes abruptly into the past tense, then back into the present tense, a present of eternal wounding: the doctor cannot leave the scene of the wounding/cure. "Slowly, like old men, we crawl through the snowy wastes . . . Never shall I reach home at this rate; my flourishing practice is done for. Naked, exposed to the frost of this most unhappy of ages . . . old man that I am, I wander astray . . . Betrayed! Betrayed! A false alarm (*Fehlläuten*) on the night bell once answered—it cannot be made good, not ever." Essential Kafka. Essential literature?

The doctor has a truthful consciousness of his failure. This consciousness is enabled for Kafka by the fact that he figures at once as the central perspective, the "perspectival hero," of one of his fictions and as the narrator congruent with his narration. A crucial difference is in play in a narrator who addresses in the first person no other person at all, a margin which assures a disparity of the self to itself and hence the permanence of its "wound." Nowhere does the doctor register the belief that his narrative is a response to the fantasized interlocution operated by the silent image of an auditor.

The fact that he does not cure the other or himself is not of course a *result* of his failure to address another. Only as a speaker whose language is for himself can his assertions be taken seriously: they speak of the impossibility of cure except at the cost of a wound; curing wounds the curer.[42]

Behind this speaker are distinctively Kafkan acts of narrative transgression—arbitrary and inconspicuous. There is yet another consciousness in play, a distance, which to maintain is still not a matter of producing such an effect as cure. Cure, because it implies a crossing over, is avenged by the wound assailing the healer. Both cognitive and therapeutic features of the model are joined in the notion that the cost of noting the wound is being wounded; the condition of understanding suffering is unrelieved suffering. The doctor who cannot close a wound thematizes the scriptor who cannot close the distance to his narration, cannot be allowed to forget that he narrates narrating and that his life is the narrating of a dream.

Supposing Kafka were right: what is the affliction which French Freud has suffered in the course of its confident treatment of Freud?

None—if Lacan's phrase can stand for the rest: The French stance, whether toward Baader/Schleyer or Freud, is one of being unharmed by the cure, secure in "freeplay." Not "man" but French Freud has protected itself by flinching in awe of the power of its insight. The turning away, for being sublime, recovers from pain, escapes final wounding, whereas Kafka—uncertain that there is knowledge—knows that if there were, it could be had only at the cost of unspeakable suffering. Genuine thought inflicts the suffering in its object upon the thinker. But wrote Kafka, "I have not experienced the eternal hell of the real writer."[43]

Here we would have to study the phantom text in Kafka— Hölderlin—and proceed to the link, in "When on a Holiday" ("Wie wenn am Feiertage"), between the terms "self-inflicted wound" (*selbstgeschlagene Wunde*) and the struggle, *die Leiden des Stärkeren [mitzuleiden]*—this highest cognitive effort "of suffering the sorrows of the god." For "nothing . . . is more painful than unriddling suffering" (*Und nichts ist schmerzlicher . . . Denn Leiden zu enträtseln*).[44]

Postscript

What is distinctively literary about literature? It foregrounds the act of narration (disrupts it *or* allows its conventions to occur "naturally," is never naive with respect to it). It makes sharp the noncoincidence between *what* is being said, and—with a change of a single letter—that (something) is *being said*.[45]

Freud has been taken as being literary precisely because he seems to assert the omnipresence of a rhetorical or narrative factor in psychic life. His awareness of the rhetorical character of psychic manifestations—of behavior, dreams, neurotic symptoms—is seen as paralleling the consciousness which writers have and inscribe in their fiction.

But is this understanding properly literary? Freud has discovered the *narrated dimension* but not narration, not the "that-it-is-being-said" of what is being said. He is like the first Malte Laurids Brigge, of Rilke's novel, who says of a jewel case: "I opened it up: it was empty. I can say this after so long a time. But then, when I had opened it, I saw only what this emptiness consisted of."[46] Not to distinguish narration from the narrated is finally to deprive the narrated of its specificity; for narrating touches differently the *points de capiton* which "pin or unpin the signifier onto the signified."[47] It is not enough to declare that object relations are like the figures in a text. With what consciousness, across what distance, are they constituted there?

The analyst figure as a *Gradiva*-like text awakens the patient from his sleep of reason but enters his dream at one special place— a point where the manifest content of the dream and the reality of the awakener coincide. The text is all on the side of the analyst's reality, and here where "narration" is thinnest, least in play, here the membrane around the dreamer can be punctured. In awakening the dreamer, the analyst annihilates dreamer and dream, as if they were uniformly constituted. This fictional psychoanalysis does not specify the "that-it-is-being-dreamt" of the dream content—just as it elides the "that-it-is-being-narrated" of the awakener's reality into which the patient's reality flows. The story does not specify the dream equivalent of narration, of the conscious rhetorical factor in fiction.

Freud is inspired in grasping dream, memory, all transcripts of interiority as not unlike fiction—provoking in turn that reading of his work (by a species of mimicry), by which he is read as the undecidable transcript of a dream not unlike fiction and thus as having the character of literature. But he has only to be faced with an actual fictional text in order to want to insert it into the reality of biological, instinctual life, of genetic and reactive schemes. Freud is "pre-*littéraire*," but "pre-" should not denote nearness to instincts that could be reckoned an origin.

His plainness in aesthetic matters is still preferable to a certain French reading of Freud shaped by Lacan's early reaccentuating of the psychoanalytic interview, in which the patient, as he produces a text before the silent analyst, is viewed as a double agent, offering in between imposing absences of questions not himself but the lineaments of his image of that silence (a silence, true, growing ever noisier as Lacan's ellipses are being filled in). It is then only a short step to read Freud as if he too were addressing ourselves, the reader, in order to disarm us, to bribe us with the profit of a *philosophy of reading*. Kafka offers a different account: "Do you call that conversation if the other is silent and, to keep up the appearance of a conversation, you try to substitute for him, and so imitate him, and so parody him, and so parody yourself?"[48]

Shoshana Felman attributes to literature the power to cure psychoanalysis of its delusions of authority despite its captivation by the master-slave dialectic. Its speculum is "irony," a term which in Felman's discussion has very much the force of my term "consciousness of narration," the effect of the random breaks which bring the self-absorbed narrator into court. Felman explains how

> one crucial feature which is constitutive of literature . . . is essentially lacking in psychoanalytical theory, and indeed in theory as such: irony. Since irony precisely consists in dragging authority as such into a scene which it cannot master, of which it is *not aware* and which, for that very reason, is the scene of its own self-destruction, literature, by virtue of its ironic force, fundamentally deconstructs the fantasy of authority in the same way, and for the same reasons, that psychoanalysis deconstructs the authority of the fantasy—its claim . . . to power as the sole window through which we behold and perceive reality. . . Psychoanalysis tells us that the fantasy is a fiction, and that consciousness is itself, in a sense, a fantasy-effect. In the same way, literature tells us that authority is a *language effect*, the product or the creation of its own *rhetorical* power: that authority is the *power of fiction*.[49]

This discussion stresses the power of literary irony to achieve results: such power, like psychoanalysis for Lacan, should indeed strike us with awe. But what is left out of this account is the vulnerability of literary irony to destruction at the hands of its own authority, namely, its irony. Kafka perceives that the cost of exercising a power to cure is being wounded by that power. And indeed the point of Kafka's narrational irony is not that it leaves behind such positive results as that "literature tells us that authority is a *language effect*": what literature "tells" when all the deaths have been counted is that its frame displays the perfect emptiness of consciousness, "the impersonality of consciousness . . . its utter lack of quality of individuating attributes, its 'nature' as a . . . point without substance or consistency," to which one would have to add the variable factor of its intensity.[50]

Here it is interesting to evoke Kafka's distinction with respect to the effects of his fiction: "I can still have passing satisfaction from works like *A Country Doctor*, provided I can still write such things at all. . . . But happiness only if I can raise the world into the pure, the true, and the immutable."[51] What does this mean, "the pure, the true, the immutable"? An Objective Idealist reference does not seem appropriate. Especially toward the end of his life Kafka conceived of such absolutes in terms of quantity and formality, in the spirit of Nietzsche's apothegm: "from a *quale* grows the desire for an increase in quantum" (*WP*, 304). Kafka wrote, for example, of an autobiographical persona: "He does not live for the sake of his personal life; he does not think for the sake of his personal thoughts. It seems to him that he lives and thinks under the compulsion of a family, which, it is true, is itself superabundant in life and thought, but for which he constitutes, in obedience to some law unknown to him, a formal necessity."[52]

The compulsion might be understood as the factor of consciousness, of proportionality pure and simple, capable of a heightening but not of qualification. This law functions for Kafka as an arbiter allowing him, perhaps, to perceive that "the disproportion in the world is mercifully quantitative."[53]

To an extraordinary degree Kafka identifies his self with the impersonal factor of consciousness; he wants the self to come to light as its light. The self is a surplus with respect to its perceptions, a distance whose strict analogy is the gap between the author and the dream narrated in his text. This factor is clearest in the Kafkan instance of the empty narrator, the narrator of *The Castle*, for example, who is detached from his participation in his narrative only for it to be revealed that "he" knows nothing more than the perspectival hero. His superiority is a matter of difference without quality. One narrative perspective glassily envelops another.

The empty narrator, produced by a break in perspective, reflects the author, whose very being is an affair of the consciousness of narrating, of a superiority impossible to fill in with a value. The sole superiority of consciousness is in perceiving itself as empty. What distinction therefore remains to "the pure, the true, the immutable" beyond the perception of the nullity of cure? Like innocent fire, consciousness can grow to any intensity of light, becoming purer, the great fire in which "everything . . . the strangest fancies . . . perish and rise up again."[54] This is the surplus of narrative strength at which Kafka anxiously marvels, "a merciful surplus . . . at a moment when suffering has raked me to the bottom of my being and plainly exhausted all my strength. But then what kind of surplus is it?"[55] What dreams arise around this intensity of consciousness? That Kafka cannot answer this question should not suggest that Freud has had the last word.

Notes

1. "The Hunter Gracchus," in *Selected Stories of Franz Kafka*, trans. Willa and Edwin Muir (New York: Modern Library, 1952), p. 187. Translation modified.

2. *The Diaries of Franz Kafka*, 1914–1923 (New York: Schocken Books, 1948), p. 114.

3. "Wir lagen", Paul Celan, *Lichtzwang* (Frankfurt: Suhrkamp, 1970), p. 13.

4. *New York Times*, October 20, 1977, p. 1.

5. Although this rhetorical habit was not much commented on, Nietzsche wrote " 'Being' as universalization of the concept 'life' (breathing), 'having a soul,' 'willing, effecting,' 'becoming.' The antithesis is: 'not to have a soul,' 'not to become,' 'not to will.' Therefore: 'being' is *not* the antithesis of non-being, appearance, nor even of the dead."

6. Each (deluded) reader finds in its image of the other the solidity of the other, with respect to which each asserts its separate identity. But this impression of solidity is won only at the cost of cutting off reflection on the play of difference within the other. The impression of separate identity each has of himself is a litotes, being obtained by denial of the threatening convergence of the other (in his difference) with what is originally other, and hence productive of difference, in himself: "I am *not* divided, i.e., not-unselfsame." The critique of the litotes or denial then takes the form of showing that it is only the blind metaphor of an original *aversion* from self.

7. Consider the unseemly haste with which Croissant, alleged mediator for terrorists, was extradited to Germany.

8. The pseudoexchange I have described (and to which Glucksmann's *Les maîtres penseurs* should be assimilated) belongs to the unwritten history of specular readings of France/Germany, in which two moments are immediately important: (1) Nietzsche's uneasy admiration for French clarity. In 1885, in a preface for the project of *The Will to Power*, Nietzsche describes this work as "a book for *thinking*, nothing else. . . That it is written in German is untimely, to say the least: I wish I had written it in French so that it might not appear to be a confirmation of the aspirations of the German Reich." A few sentences later, however, he says, "Formerly I wished I had not written my Zarathustra in German." And now? Cited in *WP* xxii–xxiii. (2) The

mood of conservative Germany during the First World War, which assimilated Nietzsche to an attack on French "enlightenment," French "ideas." Thus Thomas Mann writes in *Reflections of a Nonpolitical Man*, "I well remember the laugh which I had to repress when one day Parisian *literati* whom I sounded out on Nietzsche gave me to understand that *au fond* he had been nothing more than a good reader of the French moralists and aphorists." Mann instead recalls Nietzsche's "depth," his allegiance to Germany as the "recalcitrant" factor in European life.

9. In the *Interpretation of Dreams* Freud himself all but explicitly identifies the process of the repression of repression as the fault of Adler's closed system: His "masculine protest," writes Freud, is nothing else than repression unjustifiably sexualized. I shall not be detailing more than a few moments of this reception, which I imagine is now already understood in its basic directions or can be so understood, thanks mainly to the generous mediation of Jeffrey Mehlman. See his edition of *Yale French Studies (French Freud: Structural Studies in Psychoanalysis)* (1972), no. 48, from which the phrase "the repression of the discovery of repression" (p. 7) is taken, and better still his admirable *Structural Study of Autobiography* (Ithaca: Cornell University Press, 1974) and the "Introduction" to his translation of Jean Laplanche's key study, *Life and Death in Psychoanalysis* (Baltimore: Johns Hopkins University Press, 1976).

10. "Deconstruction has been much misrepresented, dismissed as a harmless academic game or denounced as a terrorist weapon." Paul de Man, *Allegories of Reading* (New Haven: Yale University Press, 1979), x. But Anthony Wilden, who generally has a fair sense of the intellectual movement in France, describes a "great number" of thinkers associated with or influenced by Lacan as possessing an "intellectual terrorism . . . not unrelated to Lacan's own" *The Language of the Self* (Baltimore: Johns Hopkins University Press, 1968), p. xiv. John Searle notes, "Michel Foucault once characterized Derrida's prose style to me as 'obscurantisme terroriste' " (*New York Review of Books*, October 27, 1983, p. 77). And Richard Howard, the eminent poet and translator of Barthes and others, registers at least the French rhetorical habit of associating literature and terrorism in his "Note on S/Z": "Only when we know—and it is a knowledge gained by taking pains, by renouncing what Freud calls instinctual gratification—what we are doing when we read, are we free to enjoy what we read. As long as our enjoyment is—or is said to be—instinctive it is not enjoyment, it is terrorism." Roland Barthes, *S/Z* (New York: Hill and Wang, 1974), p. i.

11. The cited phrase is Lacan's, in his "Function of Language in Psychoanalysis" (short title), translated by Anthony Wilden, *The Language of the Self*, pp. 1–87. There the context is madness, and the relevant phrase reads, "In madness, of whatever nature, we must recognize . . . the negative liberty of a Word which has given up trying to make itself understood" (pp. 42–43).

12. Paul de Man, *Blindness and Insight* (New York: Oxford University Press, 1971). p. 18.

13. Mehlman, *A Structural Study of Autobiography*, p. 113.

14. Freud, *The Interpretation of Dreams*, in *The Standard Edition of the Complete Psychological Works*. James Strachey, ed. (London: Hogarth Press, 1958), 5:514.

15. This is to take seriously the proposition "Freud is (or is not) a literary text," which inside the discourse of French Freud is itself of course entirely vertiginous, since the claim that Freud is or is not a literary text arrives in the rear of the avant-garde polemical statement denying the very distinction between literary and nonliterary texts.

16. *Selected Stories*, p. 187.

17. Freud provides an analogue to this situation in his account of how the patient undergoes an auspicious and "permanent alteration of his mental economy" through transference. "[Transference] is used to induce the patient to perform a piece of mental

work—the overcoming of his transference-resistance. . . . The transference is made conscious to the patient by the analyst, and it is resolved by convincing him that in his transference-attitude he is re-experiencing emotional relations which had their origin in his earliest object-attachments" [*Autobiography*, James Strachey, tr. (New York: Norton, 1937), p. 85]. If we transform these sentences by metaphorical substitution, we find that the force linking deviant sentences is illocutionary, is rhetorical: The stammering speaker becomes able to *thread* sentences *through* his own baby talk when he has once repeated the enabling sentence belonging to another (having been "induced to, convinced").

18. Perhaps the courted dissolution of the subject could be traced to a desire to arrive at a vantage point outside the subject, as the alibi of "objectivity."

19. Friedrich Nietzsche, *Basic Writings of Nietzsche* trans. and ed. Walter Kaufmann (New York: Modern Library, 1966), 383 ff.

20. Cited in J. Kamerbeek, "Dilthey Versus Nietzsche," *Studia Philosophica, Jahrbuch der Schweizerischen Philosophischen Gesellschaft* (1950). 10:56.

21. "Such awe" translates *tel effroi,* and indeed the English word mutes more than the French the component of terror in the experience. Lacan, however, approved the translation.

22. Thomas Weiskel, *The Romantic Sublime: Studies in the Structure and Psychology of Transcendence* (Baltimore: Johns Hopkins University Press, 1976), p. 83ff.

23. Harold Bloom, writing on Derrida's use of hyperbole, sees "the more sublime . . . trope of hyperbole" as indeed having "close relationship to the defense of repression." *Map of Misreading* (New York: Oxford University Press, 1975), p. 48.

24. Stuart Schneiderman, *Jacques Lacan: The Death of an Intellectual Hero* (Cambridge: Harvard University Press, 1983), p. 179.

25. Cf. "Refoulement," in Jean Laplanche's and J. P. Pontalis' *Vocabulaire de la Psychanalyse* (Paris: Presses Universitaires de France, 1973), p. 392ff.

26. Some elements in the French case: First, it must have been with some irony or diffidence that Laplanche projected his study of schizophrenia and poetry as *Hölderlin* (not *Kafka*) *et la question du père* (Paris: Presses Universitaires de France, 1961). Second, the recalcitrant figure in the deconstructive program has been Blanchot who, if he did not explicitly declare the extent of his indebtedness to Kafka, testified to it in writing some of the most accurate pages ever written on him. (Deleuze-Guattari's carefree book on Kafka certainly changes nothing in this reckoning.) Finally, there is but one bare word on Kafka (to my knowledge) in Derrida (*Of Grammatology*. Gayatri C. Spivak, tr. [Baltimore: Johns Hopkins University Press, 1976], p. 272), though Derrida has recently delivered a lecture on Kafka's parable "Before the Law," and Foucault writes only one bare word in *The Order of Things* (London: Tavistock, 1970), p. 384.

27. *Complete Psychological Works,* 5:350–51.

28. Kafka wrote to Milena, "I consider the therapeutic part of psychoanalysis to be a hopeless error." *Letters to Milena,* Willy Hass, ed., Tania and James Stern, trs. (New York: Schocken Books, 1953), p. 217.

29. *Dearest Father,* Tania and James Stern, trs. (New York: Schocken Books, 1954), p. 41.

30. *Diaries,* 1910–1913, p. 26.

31. *Diaries,* 1914–1923, p. 212.

32. *Selected Stories,* p. 187.

33. Gustav Janouch, *Conversations with Kafka,* Gotonwry Rees, trans. (New York: New Directions, 1971), p. 56.

34. In the relation of dreams to neurosis as explanatory instruments, Freud, in the *Interpretation of Dreams,* privileges neurosis: "Though my own line of approach to the subject of dreams was determined by my previous work on the psychology of the neuroses, I had not intended to make use of the latter as a basis of reference in the present work. Nevertheless I am constantly being driven to do so, instead of proceeding, as I should have wished, in the contrary direction and using dreams as a means of approach to the psychology of the neuroses" (*Complete Psychological Works,* 5:588).

35. Theodor W. Adorno, "Notes on Kafka," in *Prisms,* trans. Samuel and Shierry Weber, (London: Spearman, 1967), p. 250.

36. *The Trial,* Willa and Edwin Muir, trs. (New York: Modern Library, 1956), pp 272–73.

37. *Diaries,* 1910–1913, p. 300.

38. *Ibid.,* p. 276.

39. Derrida's essay "The Purveyor of Truth," *Yale French Studies* (1975) 52:31–113, which treats Lacan's "Seminar on 'The Purloined Letter' " (in *Yale French Studies* [1971] 48:38–72), also focuses on the deficient treatment in Lacan of the question of narrative. His analysis is linked to a "destruction" of Lacan's familiar absolutization of the intersubjective field, as in Lacan's proposition, "The register of truth . . . is situated strictly speaking at the very foundation of intersubjectivity. It is located there where the subject can grasp nothing but the very subjectivity which constitutes an Other as absolute" (p. 49).

All Kafka's work from 1912 on exists as the project of criticizing, of destroying, this notion. This project originates as the refinement of the narrative form called monopolized perspective (*Einsinnigkeit*), which he scrupulously breaks at points. Derrida writes with great cogency of Lacan's neglect "of the narrator's position, the narrator's involvement in the content of what he seems to be recounting" (p. 100) and of a more "original function" too termed "scription," which guarantees the distinction between "the textual fiction" and narration (p. 52). But how then can Derrida maintain with any force that "the 'form' of the Freudian text . . . belongs no more clearly to the tradition of scientific discourse than to a specific genre of fiction" (p. 38)? The specific genre of the Freudian text does not sufficiently complicate narration so as to bring to light "the invisible but structurally irreducible frame around the narration" that confirms the fiction. Freud does not redouble this frame—as does Kafka, par excellence, on the far edge of the text of the "narrated narrator" by inscrutable disruptions enacting the distinction between scription and narration. Pace Derrida, the distinction between the scientific text and the literary fiction is "guaranteed . . . from the formal point of view" (p. 50), which discovers the textual staging of a distancing consciousness of narration.

40. Janouch, *Conversations,* p. 28.

41. *Diaries,* 1914–1923, p. 206.

42. "Why is it meaningless to ask questions? To complain means to put a question and wait for the answer. But the questions that don't answer themselves at the very moment of their asking are never answered. No distance divides the interrogator from the one who answers him" (*Ibid.,* p. 131).

43. *Briefe,* 1902–1924, Max Brod, ed. (Frankfurt: Schocken Books, 1958), p. 98.

44. Hölderlin, *Sämtliche Werke* (Stuttgart: Kohlhammer, 1961), 4:21. For Kafka (in the words of Benjamin and Scholem) "the absolute-concrete is of course what is purely and simply the unrealizable." This moment figures as the repetition of a moment of Hölderlin's critique of Fichte: Hölderlin perceives that the requirement of con-

sciousness determines that "the absolute Self shall be (as a self) nothing" *Briefwechsel*, 1933–1940, Walter Benjamin and Gershom Scholem (Frankfurt: Suhrkamp, 1980), p. 39; Jean Laplanche, *Hölderlin et la question du père*, p. 37.

45. I could thus agree with Gadamer that whatever "unity" a literary work possesses—"unity and facility and so, too, its own manner of being true"—is given to it by "an enigmatic form of the nondistinction between what is said and how it is said." Hans Georg Gadamer "The Eminent Text and Its Truth," in Paul Hernadi, ed., *The Horizon of Literature*, p. 46. (Lincoln: University of Nebraska Press, 1982), p. 46.

46. *The Notebooks of Malte Laurids Brigge*, M. D. Herter Norton, tr. (New York: Norton, 1964), p. 198.

47. Lacan, cited in Wilden, *The Language of the Self*, p. 273.

48. *Diaries*, 1914–1923, p. 228.

49. Shoshana Felman, "Introduction," *Yale French Studies* (1977), 55/56:8.

50. Fredric Jameson, "Imaginary and Symbolic in Lacan," *Ibid.*, p. 343.

51. *Diaries*, 1914–23, p. 187.

52. *The Great Wall of China*, Willa and Edwin Muir, trs. (New York: Schocken Books, 1970), p. 269.

53. *Dearest Father*, p. 38.

54. *Diaries*, 1910–1913, p. 276.

55. *Diaries*, 1914–23, p. 184.

The Narcissistic Drama and Reader/Text Transaction in Kafka's *Metamorphosis*

J. Brooks Bouson*

Provoked by the text, critic after critic has puzzled over the meaning of Gregor Samsa's transformation. Why is Kafka's character transformed into an insect? readers have long asked. Critical reactions to *The Metamorphosis*, which range from abstract philosophical and linguistic speculations to affective responses, reveal that the fantasies and defenses located in the text have been elicited from a number of its interpreters.[1] The defensive shields of fantasy, black humor, and narrative structure—*The Metamorphosis* is carefully organized around Gregor's repetitive enclosures and escapes—protect against but do not camouflage the horrors of Gregor's insect existence. And yet unconsciously responding to the defensive stratagems of the text or attempting to fend off Gregor's fictional presence, a number of interpreters have likewise veered away from Gregor's situation, focusing attention instead on the sociological, political, philosophical, or religious implications of Kafka's narrative or on its linguistic puzzles

*Adapted from *The Empathic Reader: A Study of the Narcissistic Character and the Drama of the Self* (Amherst: University of Massachusetts Press, 1989). © 1989 by The University of Massachusetts Press.

or structural features. Other critics, reacting affectively to Gregor's plight, have reproduced in their criticism the angry substructures of this text which originated in Kafka's conflict with his family and his feelings of deep self-rejection. Such critics variously accuse Gregor, his family, or his exploitative economic system for his insect transformation. And still other critics have responded to Gregor's need for confirming attention and rescue. Engendering a potent reader-character transaction, *The Metamorphosis* re-presents and reactively defends against the narcissistic needs, anxieties, and vulnerabilities that inform it. Reading *The Metamorphosis* in a new context—that provided by psychoanalyst Heinz Kohut in his pioneering studies in the narcissistic disorder—provides insight not only into the experiential core of Gregor's predicament but also into the critical responses this text has engendered.

Developing through the psychoanalytic process what he came to call the "psychology of the self," Kohut centers his attention on fundamental aspects of human behavior which other accounts of psychological man and woman ignore or minimize: the deep-rooted needs for empathic responsiveness and for a sense of connection with others. "The self," in Kohut's words, "arises in a matrix of empathy" and "strives to live within a modicum of empathic responses in order to maintain itself . . ." ("Remarks," n. 5, 752). The narcissistically defective individual, he explains, suffers from a defect in the self because of traumatic empathic failures on the part of the parents during the early stages of self-development. As a consequence, such an individual lacks the inner resources of healthy narcissism: sustaining self-esteem and inner ideals. Instead, he is dominated by the regressive needs of the "archaic grandiose self" (which perceives itself as omnipotent, the center of attention, and in control of others) and/or the "archaic idealizing self" (which feels empty and powerless unless merged with an all-powerful other). Because the narcissistically defective adult cannot provide himself with sufficient self-approval or with a sense of strength through his own inner resources, he is forever compelled to satisfy these essential needs through external sources: by extracting praise from or exercizing unquestioned dominance over others or by merging with idealized figures. Lacking a "stable cohesive self"—that is, a stable sense of himself as a unitary agent, an initiator of action, and a continuum in time—he suffers from a fundamental weakness and deficiency in the center of his personality. He may harbor feelings of greatness side by side with low self-esteem. He may respond to the frustration of his exhibitionistic impulses with shame and to the failure of his grandiose ambitions with rage. Subject to what Kohut calls "disintegration anxiety"—"dread of the loss" of the self (*Restoration*, 104–5)—he is, like Gregor Samsa, compelled endlessly to enact the same primitive, fixated behavior in his frustrated search for wholeness. As Kohut himself observed, Kafka's *Metamorphosis* provides an "artistic anticipation" of the self-disorder (see *Restoration*, 285–88). What Kafka so poignantly captures in this story, in Kohut's words, is the experience of an individual "who finds himself in nonresponsive surroundings," whose family speaks of him coldly, in the "impersonal third pronoun," so that he becomes a "nonhuman monstrosity, even in his own eyes" ("Psychoanalyst," 718, "Future," 680, *Restoration*, 287). To depersonalize Gregor or turn him into a philosophic or linguistic abstraction, as some interpreters have done, is thus to reenact the narcissistic trauma presented in the text. In the critical conversation surrounding *The Metamorphosis*, as we shall see, we find an unwitting reperformance of key aspects of the text's hidden narcissistic script.

What is so central to the self-drama of Gregor Samsa—the insect-Gregor's desperate need for attention—is also central to the reader's transactions with Kafka's hapless character. Indeed, from the very first sentence of *The Metamorphosis* and throughout the narrative, Kafka focuses the reader's attention on the insect-Gregor. The narrator, located both within and without Gregor's subjectivity, acts as an objective reporter of his plight and as an extension of his consciousness. While essentially confined to Gregor's perspective and drawn into his inner world, the reader is also positioned at a slight remove from him, this partial detachment serving to ward off potential reader anxieties about being enmeshed in his claustrophobic insect's world. Encouraged to experience a wide variety of emotional responses, ranging from disgust and physical revulsion to pity and a desire to see Kafka's antihero rescued, the reader, above all, is compelled to rivet attention on the insect-Gregor. Inscribed in *The Metamorphosis* is Gregor's protracted attempt to procure the notice of others so he can temporarily sustain his defective self.

The root trope of *The Metamorphosis*, Gregor's insect transformation, is a complex, overdetermined psychosymbol. A reification of his self-state, it reflects not only his inner feelings of worthlessness and powerlessness but also his repressed grandiosity, a grandiosity made distorted and grotesque because it has not been responded to empathically. Like the biblical Samson (the name Samsa, as critics have noted, is an allusion both to Samson and Kafka),[2] he is at once enfeebled and imbued with secret, magical power. Both the suddenness of his metamorphosis and its magical, fantastic quality signal the eruption of the archaic grandiose substructure of the self and a surfacing of archaic feelings of omnipotence. Significantly, Gregor awakens as a "monstrous" insect (3) and he uses his "gigantic brown" body (36) to frighten others away. Although one of his initial worries, as he rocks himself out of bed, is that he will make a "loud crash" and thus perhaps cause his family "if not terror, at least anxiety"

(8), unconsciously he wants to provoke just this response from those gathered outside his door. At the very outset of his ordeal, he, while disavowing his need for attention—he claims he wants to be left alone—listens to the discussion about him between the office manager and his parents, intent on not missing "a word of the conversation" (10). Later, when they stop talking, he imagines that they might be leaning against his door and listening to the noises he is making. Moreover, he is "eager" (12) to learn what they will say when they see him. As the office manager complains, Gregor is determined, albeit unconsciously, on exhibiting himself and "flaunting [his] strange whims" (11). Just as Gregor eavesdrops on his family and imagines his family listens in on him, so the reader is situated as an eavesdropper on the Samsa household. *The Metamorphosis* dramatizes, activates, and fulfills the regressive need for eavesdropping.

In the black comedy of his initial confrontation with the office manager and his family, Gregor satisfies his desire for attention and his grandiose wish to exert magical power over others. For when he makes his first appearance as an insect, his father clenches his fist as if to strike, then falters and begins to sob; his mother collapses; the loathed office manager, obeying Gregor's unconscious wish to get rid of him, slowly backs out of the room, then, his right hand outstretched, approaches the staircase "as if nothing less than an unearthly deliverance were awaiting him there" (17), and finally flees. But Gregor's exhibitionistic display is short-lived. His traumatic rejection at the very moment he shows himself points to a central cause of his self-disorder as it repeats and telescopes his experience of early parental rejection and the long series of similar rejections he has suffered throughout his life, these rejections pivotal in the formation of his distorted self-image.

Just as his family turns away from him, so the reader, while encouraged to sympathize with Gregor, is at the same time prompted to shun him as the text insistently focuses attention on his physically repulsive insect's body. And while we are meant, as one critic has observed, to "respond to the plight of the loathly son" in this scene, it is also true that "our compassion and our understanding seem mocked by the opposing image of a man shooing away a bug." In part, this scene reads like some sort of "grotesque joke" (Eggenschwiler, 206). Replicating the text's split perceptions of Gregor— that he is a repulsive bug and a dependent son in need of his family's support—critics are split on Gregor's nature. "When Gregor first appears before his family," writes Mark Spilka, "they are appalled by his condition, and their revulsion gives the full measure of his deformity" (Spilka, 77–78). While some critics claim that Gregor, as a vermin, remains "morally identical with his former self," which is "sweet, timid, and amiable" (Landsberg, 130), others feel that his metamorphosis makes manifest his real parasitic nature (Greenberg, 76) or that he "conceals" his "parasitical nature . . . beneath his solicitude" (Henel, 254; translated by Corngold, 135).

Punished for his self-assertiveness, Gregor is "[p]itilessly" (19) driven back into his room by his father and then made a prisoner. But Gregor's prison is also his refuge. Narcissistically damaged in each of his confrontations with the external world, he retreats to the protective isolation of both his room and his insect's shell. His public display rebuffed, he, from the refuge/prison of his room, attempts to defend his vulnerable self and become the center of his family's attention. Gregor's need for confirming attention is verified by the narrator. When Gregor, just after his metamorphosis, attempts to turn the key of his door, the office manager encourages him, "but," as the narrator comments, "everyone should have cheered him on. . ." Gregor, in the false belief that they are "all following his efforts with suspense" (14), musters the necessary strength to complete his difficult task. Narcissistically defective, he needs external sources of approbation if he is to counteract feelings of helplessness and find the inner determination to act. In serving as an extension of Gregor's consciousness, the narrator makes Gregor the focal point of and dominant over the reader's perceptions and thus acts out, by proxy as it were, Gregor's repressed grandiose needs.

Two preoccupations which initially emerge in Gregor's sequestered, locked-room existence—a craving for food and for the eye glance—are narcissistic metaphors that express his desire for a nurturing, mirroring response. After his transformation, Grete, the only family member he feels close to, becomes his sole source of narcissistic supplies. When Gregor rejects the milk she brings him, he symbolically rejects his sickly, asthmatic mother who faints, that is, becomes nonresponsive, the first time he displays himself—this being a repetition of his early relationship with this emotionally unavailable and depleted woman. When his mother allows Grete to become his caretaker, she disclaims her responsibility for him and, in essence, abandons him. Disavowing his need to be noticed, Gregor determines he "would rather starve" than draw Grete's attention to his hunger. But he also feels "an enormous urge" to "throw himself at his sister's feet, and beg her for something good to eat" (23–24). When Grete first brings him food, he greedily devours the food that appeals to him. But the fact that what he eats is garbage does more than remind us of his repulsive insect state. It also suggests that his needs are not truly being met and thus serves to indict his family. In effect, he says through this behavior, "I know that this is all I'm worth to you. I'm garbage and so I'll eat garbage." Recognizing that his sister finds him repulsive, he hides under the sofa when she is in his room[3] and he fancies that she gives a thankful look when he covers with a sheet the small portion of his insect's body that protrudes from the sofa. In other words, he must efface and sequester himself—disavow his grandiose needs—to win approval and attention. Gregor's sensitivity to eye glances indicates his unmet, primitive need to be mirrored, to be the "gleam in the mother's eye" (see Kohut, *Analysis*, 117–18). While Gregor craves attention, he also is ashamed to have others look at him, his shame a response to his exhibitionistic wishes and his distorted self. Emotionally abandoned by his mother, he finds a mother-surrogate figure in his sister. But tragically when Grete becomes his sole caretaker and thus becomes the center of Gregor's and her parents' attention, she begins to make narcissistic use of him as she asserts her own grandiose needs. Not only does she assume complete dominance over him, jealously guarding her caretaker's rights and flying into a rage when Mrs. Samsa cleans his room, an act that Grete interprets as a threat to her authority, she also begins to lose interest in him. As time passes, she comes to treat him more and more as an encumbering nuisance, an object.

Of perennial fascination to readers of *The Metamorphosis* is Gregor's initial reaction to his transformation. What shocks readers is passively, if not blandly, accepted by Gregor. Instead of reacting with open anxiety, Gregor thinks, at length, about his job and family; he becomes anxious about the passing time and preoccupied with his new bodily sensations and his strange aches and pains. In prolonging the narrative account of Gregor's initial discovery of his transformation, the text acts out what it depicts: Gregor's attempt to avoid confronting his diffuse, preverbal fears. Similarly, readers are shielded from full awareness of the anxieties subtending this scene. Despite this, the text discloses, in other ways, Gregor's sense of body-self estrangement and impending fragmentation: through his initial inability to control the chaotic movements of his insect legs and his later "senseless crawling around" his room (34); through his increasingly disorganized appearance, his growing lethargy and depression; and through his dissolving sense of clock time, an indicator of his loss of a sense of himself as a cohesive continuum in time. Suffering from a crumbling sense of self, he experiences what Kohut describes as the "fragmentation of" and "estrangement from" the mind-body self (*Restoration*, 105). Gregor's metamorphosis gives experiential immediacy not only to what Kohut calls the "devastating emotional event" referred to as a "severe drop in self-esteem" ("Reflections," 503) but, more significantly, to the terrifying experience of the breakup of the self. As Gregor's fragile self falls apart, Kafka, as if unconsciously bent on aiding his vulnerable anti-hero, makes him more and more human in his needs and thus has prompted many readers to respond sympathetically to his character's growing helplessness and need for rescue.

When Gregor makes his second escape from his room, his mother faints and his sister, mirroring Mr. Samsa, responds first with open hostility and then by isolating Gregor, cutting him off from herself and his mother. Similarly, on both this occasion and the first time Gregor shows himself, his mother faints when she sees him, i.e., when he expresses his narcissistic needs and anger, and then he is rebuffed and attacked by his father and subsequently isolated by being locked in his room. Behind the manifest content of these repetitive incidents, which provide a mimetic recapitulation of infantile experiences of parental unavailability, rejection, and narcissistic injury, there lies an intricate cluster of archaic fantasies, fears, and defenses. The fainting mother, for example, suggests a telescoped memory of the nonresponsive mother and the anachronistic fantasy of the depleted mother who is harmed or destroyed through the infant's intense narcissistic neediness and rage. The hostile father and sister, moreover, simultaneously represent a telescoped memory of the angry father, warded-off aspects of the self—Gregor's enraged grandiosity—and a condensed image of the punishing oedipal father and the split-off "bad" mother who causes self-threatening, narcissistic injuries. Intrapsychically, all the authority figures in the novel depict both split-off aspects of Gregor's self and the omnipotent mother-father images. In a series of interlocking, peripheral incidents featuring authority figures, the three boarders assume power over the family only to be sent "hopping" off, insectlike; Gregor imagines telling his remote, godlike boss exactly what he thinks of him and thus making him fall off his desk; and he thinks that the office manager might wake up an insect one day (56, 4, 9–10). This repetitive thwarting of authority figures expresses Gregor's defensive devaluation of, projected rage against, and fantasized depletion or harming of the parental imagoes as well as his abortive attempts to display his own sequestered grandiosity. Narcissistically fixated, Gregor exists in a strange, twilight world of resonating fears and fantasies. When he, in his current situation, reexperiences his primal traumas with his family members, his atrophied self slowly wastes away. Because he lacks a stable, cohesive self, he is deeply threatened by his own narcissistic needs and anger and by any behavior that he perceives as rejecting, neglectful, or hostile.

As Gregor's condition progressively worsens, he briefly succumbs to narcissistic rage, which is expressed as oral greediness. Angered at the "miserable" way he is being treated, he fantasizes taking from the pantry the food that is rightfully his. He wants, in other words, to appropriate the narcissistic sustenance that he feels he is entitled to. But as his sister increasingly neglects him—twice a day she "hurriedly" shoves into his room "any old food" available (43)—he loses his appetite, begins to shun the scraps of food that she gives him, and thus slowly starves to death. When Grete becomes a mirror image of his neglectful, rejecting parents, he refuses the food she gives him just as he, at the outset of his ordeal, refused the mother's milk given him. Through his self-starvation, Gregor makes one last, desperate plea for attention as he masochistically complies with his sister's—and family's—wish to get rid of him. In mute protest, he sits in some particularly dirty corner when Grete comes in, attempting to "reproach" her for the filthiness of his room (43). But to no avail. Latent in Gregor's silent reproach is repressed rage which is later voiced by the middle boarder when he gives notice and considers taking some sort of legal action against the Samsas because of the "disgusting conditions prevailing" in the household and family (50). Instead of openly expressing his anger, Gregor responds in a seemingly accepting but really resentful way to his family's neglect when he observes how difficult it is for his "overworked and exhausted" family to find time to "worry" about him more than is "absolutely necessary" (42). Moreover, despite his mother's outrageous neglect of him, he defensively protects her against his anger through splitting: he keeps intact his conscious image of her as the unavailable (absent) but "good" mother and projects her "badness"—her rejecting, narcissistically injuring behavior—onto others. Hovering on the margins of the written text of *The Metamorphosis* is another more potent drama that is split off and evaded: that of the nonresponsive mother. A central cause of Gregor's blighted existence is his relationship with his absent, emotionally vacant mother.

In stark contrast to their neglect of Gregor, Grete and Mrs. Samsa do find the time to bother about, if not dote on, Mr. Samsa; moreover, the three boarders, who dominate the family, become the center of the Samsas' attention. Gregor watches while the family prepares lavish meals for the three boarders who then stuff themselves with food while he, abandoned, is starving to death. But though ignored by his family, he remains the focus of the reader's attention. Because he seems so much the passive victim, some critics have acted as his advocate and denounced his family members. Such critics, speaking for the mute, submissive insect and articulating his disowned hostility, verbally accuse his oppressors. One critic, for example, who describes "consideration" as Gregor's "basic impulse," condemns Grete for her "self-centered meanness" and Mr. Samsa for his "sheer animal hostility" (Rolleston, 63). Another critic, who claims that the other characters in the story, especially the authority figures, are the "real vermin," comments that the "worst insect among the vermin in the story is . . . the parasitical father" (Spann, 67).

When Gregor hears his sister playing the violin, he makes his final and fatal escape from his room. Although he is a hideous sight with his festering wound and filthy, deteriorating body, he feels no shame as he, in his desperate desire for human contact, advances over the clean living-room floor. At his most physically disgusting in this scene, he is also, to many readers, most touchingly human and thus most salvageable. Compelled because of what he thinks he hears in the music—authentic emotional expression—he wants Grete's eyes to meet his. He craves a confirming, healing gaze. Feeling as if the "way to the unknown nourishment" he longs for is "coming to light" (49), he wants to take Grete into his room and never let her out so long as he lives. His desire to possess Grete exclusively reveals his archaic needs. He wants to extract praise from her (he imagines she will be touched and will admire him when he tells her how he had meant to send her to the conservatory); he wants to dominate her (he disavows this need, imagining that she will stay with him of "her own free will" [49]); and he wants to merge with her power and strength. Not only does his plan miserably fail, he is both subject to the unempathic stares of the three boarders and made aware of how ashamed his family is of him when his father tries to prevent the boarders from viewing him.

At this point, Gregor, disappointed and weak from hunger, is verbally attacked. "I won't pronounce the name of my brother in front of this monster," his sister says to her parents as she pronounces judgment on him. "[A]nd so all I say is: we have to try to get rid of it. We've done everything humanly possible to take care of it and to put up with it; I don't think anyone can blame us in the least" (51). By refusing to recognize him as her brother, Grete invalidates him. Impaired, enfeebled, Gregor crawls back to his room, his "last glance" falling on his impassive mother who is "fast asleep" (53). Again, when he displays himself, his depleted mother becomes non-responsive, he is punished, then locked in his room and, on this final occasion, left to die. Disavowing his anger and disappointment, Gregor, just before he dies, thinks of his family with "deep emotion and love" (54). Gregor's masochistic compliance and profound neediness have induced many readers to take his side and pass judgment on the family for their neglect of him. And the question which is asked when Gregor is drawn to Grete's violin playing—"Was he an animal, that music could move him so?" (49)—has prompted critic after critic to, in effect, rescue Gregor from his insect state by suggesting his newfound awareness of his aesthetic and/or spiritual needs.

When Gregor agrees with his sister's "conviction" that he must "disappear" (54), he expresses, on the family drama level, his feeling that his family is better off without him. This feeling is corroborated by the narrator's description of the family's cold, uncaring response to his death. "[N]ow we can thank God!" (55), Mr. Samsa pronounces when the family gathers around Gregor's emaciated body. "Stop brooding over the past," Mr. Samsa further insists (57). Abruptly, the family members leave off mourning and rejuvenate as they begin to celebrate their liberation from the insect-Gregor, their release from a shameful, secret family burden. In agreeing to "disappear," Gregor also acts out his deep self-rejection and masochistic desire to remedy his situation by effacing himself and thus nullifying his agonizing sense of worthlessness and defectiveness. Moreover, through his death he both punishes himself for his hidden aggression against the family and magically undoes his hidden crime against them. For as an invalid, he has passively exerted power over and devalued family members by obliging them to get jobs and thus assume with their employers the subordinate role he once was forced to play. His death, hence, revitalizes his family. In stark contrast to his sister's transformation— she has "blossomed into a good-looking, shapely girl" (58)—Gregor has been reduced to a thing, an "it." His "flat and dry" carcass (55) reifies his empty, depleted self. It is fitting that the cleaning woman, an embodiment of the neglectful, hostile aspects of the family, disposes of his body. Desperately seeking but never receiving the self-confirming attention, that "matrix of empathy" which Kohut feels the individual needs to form and sustain a cohesive sense of self, Gregor, in the end, is destroyed. His fragile self has been eroded, bit by bit, by the emotionally invalidating responses of his family and by his own sequestered anger. "The deepest horror man can experience," Kohut comments, "is that of feeling that he is exposed to circumstances in which he is no longer regarded as human by others, i.e., in a milieu that does not even respond with faulty or distorted empathy to his presence" ("Reflections," 486–87). In *The Metamorphosis* Kafka conveys, in exacting detail, the horror of such a situation.

Creating a compelling reader-character dyadic relationship, *The Metamorphosis*, which grew out of Kafka's quarrel with his family and with impersonal authority,[4] has incited endless quarreling among the critics. Ignored by his family, Gregor has been the center of a lively critical discussion as reader after reader has been seduced into explaining who is to blame for his condition. Some critics feel that Gregor is responsible. "[T]he final criticism," writes Edwin Honig, "seems not to be leveled against society so much as against Gregor, who sinks into his dilemma because he is unable to find his real self" (67). Franz Kuna, who views Gregor's metamorphosis as symbolic of his submission to the role of "economic man," blames Gregor for "allowing himself . . . to be forced into this subordinate and self-annihilating role" (51–52). Other critics blame the family for his plight. Members of the family frequently have been condemned for their pettiness, their mindless cruelty, their parasitism on the preinsect Gregor, and their failure to love Gregor. Edmund Edel, for example, feels that after the metamorphosis Gregor needs his family's support but they fail "this chance of a humane existence for themselves" (translated and summarized by Corngold, 103). For Douglas Angus "the entire story is one long, varied and agonized appeal for love. . ." (70). Gregor's experience, in Carol Cantrell's view, "emerges as part of a coherent and destructive pattern of family life" (579).

A highly polemicized text, *The Metamorphosis* has provoked critics to make authoritative pronouncements on Gregor's plight—on who or what is to blame for his transformation—as well as on prior interpreters of the text. Stanley Corngold's description of how the "richness and subtlety and fidelity to the text" of a certain critic's commentary makes one "resent the intrusions and dislocations" of other interpreters (74) is not atypical of the irritable tone sometimes found in the criticism this text has engendered. Observing that the many interpretations of *The Metamorphosis* "hardly take account of each other" and "contradict one another in the crassest way," Benno Von Wiese, in an apparent desire to rescue the text from its interpreters, calls for "strict textual interpretation" of Kafka's work (translated and summarized by Corngold, 247–48). Meno Spann's anger against critics who denigrate Gregor is also revealing. Arguing that "the people surrounding the metamorphosed Gregor are the real vermin" (67), Spann denounces those critics who have denounced Gregor and who have, thus, missed the "paradox" which the "skilled reader" understands: namely, that the actual vermin in the story are the " 'normal' people" depicted in the text while Gregor "increasingly becomes a true human being in spite of his monstrous shape" (73).

And still other critics, acting out the needs to both ward off and rescue the hapless Gregor, have responded with interpretations which, as Benno Von Wiese aptly puts it, "liberate Gregor Samsa as rapidly as possible from his repulsive image and instead lend him a mysterious metaphysical status" (319; translated by Corngold, 247). But some of these approaches, in depersonalizing Gregor, also repeat the central narcissistic trauma dramatized in the text. Wilhelm Emrich, for example, finds Gregor's insect state inexplicable. "The beetle is, and remains, something 'alien' that cannot be made to fit into the human ideational world. That alone is its meaning. It is 'The Other,' 'The Incomprehensible,' pure and simple, beyond the reach of any feeling or imagining. . . . It is interpretable only as that which is uninterpretable" (147). In Stanley Corngold's view, Gregor's insect transformation points to the author's "radical aesthetic intention" (9). "Is it too odd an idea," asks Corngold, "to see this family drama as the conflict between ordinary language and a being having the character of an indecipherable word?" (11). Corngold conceives Gregor "as a mutilated metaphor, uprooted from familiar language" (12). He writes, "In organizing itself around a distortion of ordinary language, *The Metamorphosis* projects into its center a sign which absorbs its own significance. . ." (27–28). Is it too odd an idea to suggest that critics like Emrich and Corngold are responding to the reader's transient sharing of Gregor's intrapsychic world, a world that is frighteningly alien, distorted, and empty?

Kafka, in the words of Theodor Adorno, shakes the "contemplative relation between text and reader . . . to its very roots" (246). "A book for Kafka," writes Silvio Vietta, "should act as a blow on the head of the reader" (211). Temporarily implicated in the incognizable insect world depicted in *The Metamorphosis*, the reader palpably experiences Gregor's feelings of dislocation and self-unreality. No wonder some critics take refuge in the safer confines of abstract philosophic or linguistic constructs. That Kafka's narrative may also engender a wish in readers to escape from Gregor's proximity—a wish the closure acts out—is suggested in some observations made by Roy Pascal. Describing the "intense enclosedness of Kafka's stories," Pascal comments: "There is no escape from the spell they weave, scarcely an opportunity for reflexion, contemplation, for a relaxation of tension, until the spell is broken by the death of the narrator's chief medium, the chief character. And at that point the reader looks back in almost uncomprehending horror, cut off from this strange experience as the awakened sleeper is cut off from his nightmare" (57). While it is true that the narrative "completedness" of *The Metamorphosis* "forces" readers, in Pascal's words, to search out "the coherence of this apparent incoherence" (40), the fact that critics seem to feel strangely helpless before this text, which insistently demands and resists interpretation, suggests that the insect-Gregor's feelings of powerlessness may be induced in readers not only as they share Gregor's perceptions but also as they grapple with the resistant preverbal puzzles encoded in the narrative.

Creating in *The Metamorphosis* a character who is real and unreal, replete with meaning and empty of self, Kafka encourages the interpreter to fill in the deficit, the void that exists at the center of the insect-Gregor's self. Critics have long commented on the repetitive nature of Kafka's fiction. The "form" of Kafka's fiction, as one critic puts it, is "circular": the "basic situation" of a given narrative "emerges again and again like a trauma" (Anders, 37). Reading *The Metamorphosis* through the lens of self-psychology, we can gain significant insight into both the source of and our reaction to that central, narcissistic trauma.

Notes

1. For an overview of the critical response to *The Metamorphosis* up to 1972, see Stanley Corngold's critical bibliography—*The Commentators' Despair*—which includes the work of American, English, Spanish, French, German, and Italian critics.

2. The Samson allusion has been noted, for example, by Norman Holland (148–49)

and Jean Jofen (349). In a conversation with Kafka, Gustav Janouch commented that the name Samsa sounded "like a cryptogram for Kafka. Five letters in each word. The S in the word *Samsa* has the same position as the K in the word *Kafka*. The A . . ." To this, Kafka replied: "It is not a cryptogram. Samsa is not merely Kafka, and nothing else" (32).

3. Gregor's hiding under the couch recalls the behavior of one of the infants observed by Margaret Mahler and her collaborators. "[W]hen in distress," writes Mahler, "she would lie flat against the surface of the floor, or on the mattress on the floor, or would squeeze herself into a narrow space; it was as if she wanted to be enclosed (held together) in this way, which would afford her some of the sense of coherence and security that she was missing in the relationship with her mother" (94).

4. Essentially a family story, *The Metamorphosis* reflects, as many critics have noted, aspects of Kafka's life: his submissive relationship to his father, his alienation from his mother, his hidden anger and resentment, his hypochondria, depression, feelings of worthlessness, powerlessness, physical imperfection, loneliness, and isolation. Although most discussions of the autobiographical elements of *The Metamorphosis* focus on Kafka's relationship to his insensitive, domineering father, which is well documented in his autobiographical *Letter to His Father*, Margarete Mitscherlich-Nielsen, in her "Psychoanalytic Notes" on Kafka, offers an interesting speculation on his early relationship with his mother, pointing to a disturbance in the early mother-child relationship. "The early death of his [Kafka's] brothers and his mother's reaction to their loss—probably warding off emotion on the surface but deeply depressed beneath," she writes, "must have had a profound effect on Kafka . . ." (5). Equally suggestive are recent discussions of Kafka's narcissistic relationships with Milena (see Böhme) and Felice (see Bernheimer, 152–61).

Kafka, in the words of biographer Ronald Hayman, used writing to "give him the illusion of inching his way towards his objective of being understood, of bringing the reader to know him as well as he knew himself" (198). In *The Metamorphosis*, Hayman comments, Kafka allegorized "his relationship with the family, building out from his sense of being a disappointment, a burden" (151). That Kafka was thinking of his own family situation when he wrote *The Metamorphosis* is revealed in the few recorded comments he made about the story. After its publication, he remarked to an acquaintance, "What do you have to say about the dreadful things happening in our house?" (Urzidil, 18). In a conversation with Gustav Janouch, he described the story as an "indiscretion." "Is it perhaps delicate and discreet," he asked, "to talk about the bugs in one's own family?" When Janouch described the story as "a terrible dream, a terrible conception," Kafka responded, "The dream reveals the reality, which conception lags behind. That is the horror of life—the terror of art" (Janouch, 32).

Works Cited

Adorno, Theodor. "Notes on Kafka." In *Prisms*, translated by Samuel and Shierry Weber. Cambridge: MIT Press, 1981.

Anders, Gunther. *Franz Kafka*. Translated by A. Steer and A. K. Thorlby. London: Bowes and Bowes, 1960.

Angus, Douglas. "Kafka's *Metamorphosis* and 'The Beauty and the Beast' Tale." *Journal of English and Germanic Philology* 53 (1954): 69–71.

Bernheimer, Charles. *Flaubert and Kafka: Studies in Psychopoetic Structure*. New Haven: Yale University Press, 1982.

Böhme, Hartmut. "Mother Milena: On Kafka's Narcissism." Translated by

John Winkelman. In *The Kafka Debate: New Perspectives for Our Time.* Edited by Angel Flores. New York: Gordian, 1977, 80–99.

Cantrell, Carol. "*The Metamorphosis:* Kafka's Study of a Family." *Modern Fiction Studies* 23 (1977–78): 578–86.

Corngold, Stanley. *The Commentators' Despair: The Interpretation of Kafka's Metamorphosis.* Port Washington: Kennikat Press, 1973.

Edel, Edmund. "Franz Kafka: *Die Verwandlung,* Eine Auslegung." *Wirkendes Wort* 4 (1957–58): 217–26. Translated and summarized by Corngold.

Eggenschwiler, David. "*The Metamorphosis,* Freud, and the Chains of Odysseus." *Modern Language Quarterly* 39 (1978): 363–85. Reprinted in *Modern Critical Views: Franz Kafka.* Edited by Harold Bloom. New York: Chelsea House, 1986.

Emrich, Wilhelm. *Franz Kafka: A Critical Study of His Writings.* Translated by Sheema Zeben Buehne. New York: Frederick Ungar, 1968.

Greenberg, Martin. *The Terror of Art: Kafka and Modern Literature.* New York: Basic Books, 1968.

Hayman, Ronald. *Kafka: A Biography.* New York: Oxford University Press, 1982.

Henel, Ingeborg. "Die Deutbarkeit von Kafkas Werken." *Zeitschrift für deutsche Philologie* 86, no. 2 250–66. Translated and summarized by Corngold, 134–35.

Holland, Norman. "Realism and Unrealism: Kafka's 'Metamorphosis.'" *Modern Fiction Studies* 4 (1958): 143–50.

Honig, Edwin. *Dark Conceit: The Making of Allegory.* Evanston: Northwestern University Press, 1959.

Janouch, Gustav. *Conversations with Kafka.* 2d ed. Translated by Goronwy Rees. New York: New Directions, 1971.

Jofen, Jean. "Metamorphosis." *American Imago* 35 (Winter 1978): 347–56.

Kafka, Franz. *Letter to His Father.* Translated by Ernst Kaiser and Eithne Wilkins. New York: Schocken, 1966.

———. *The Metamorphosis.* Translated and edited by Stanley Corngold. New York: Bantam, 1972.

Kohut, Heinz. *The Analysis of the Self.* New York: International Universities Press, Inc., 1971.

———. "The Future of Psychoanalysis." *Search* 2: 663–84.

———. "The Psychoanalyst in the Community of Scholars." *Search* 2: 685–724.

———. "Reflections." *Advances in Self Psychology.* Edited by Arnold Goldberg. New York: International Universities Press, 1980.

———. "Remarks About the Formation of the Self. *Search* 2: 737–70.

———. *The Restoration of the Self.* New York: International Universities Press, 1977.

———. *The Search for the Self: Selected Writings of Heinz Kohut 1950–1978.* 2 vols. Edited by Paul H. Ornstein. New York: International Universities Press, 1978. Vols. 3 and 4 are forthcoming.

Kuna, Franz. *Franz Kafka: Literature as Corrective Punishment.* Bloomington: Indiana University Press, 1974.

Landsberg, Paul. "'The Metamorphosis.'" Translated by Caroline Muhlenberg. *The Kafka Problem*. Edited by Angel Flores. New York: Octagon, 1963. 122–33.

Mahler, Margaret, Fred Pine, and Anni Bergman. *The Psychological Birth of the Human Infant: Symbiosis and Individuation*. New York: Basic Books, 1975.

Mitscherlich-Nielsen, Margarete. "Psychoanalytic Notes on Franz Kafka." *Psychocultural Review* 3 (1979): 1–23.

Pascal, Roy. *Kafka's Narrators: A Study of His Stories and Sketches*. Cambridge: Cambridge University Press, 1982.

Rolleston, James. *Kafka's Narrative Theater*. University Park: Pennsylvania State University Press, 1974.

Spann, Meno. *Franz Kafka*. Boston: Twayne, 1976.

Spilka, Mark. *Dickens and Kafka: A Mutual Interpretation*. Bloomington: Indiana University Press, 1963.

Urzidil, Johannes. *There Goes Kafka*. Translated by Harold A. Basilius. Detroit: Wayne State University Press, 1968.

Vietta, Silvio. "Franz Kafka, Expressionism, and Reification." *Passion and Rebellion: The Expressionist Heritage*. Edited by Stephen Eric Bronner and Douglas Kellner. New York: Universe, 1983. 201–16.

Von Wiese, Benno. "Franz Kafka: *Die Verwandlung.*" *Die deutsche Novelle von Goethe bis Kafka*. Vol. 2. Düsseldorf: Bagel, 1962. 319–45. Translated and summarized by Corngold. 247–54.

KAFKA AND THE READER

Rich Text/Poor Text:
A Kafkan Confusion

Ruth V. Gross°

1

The major work of the decade in practical criticism is Roland Barthes's
S/Z. The tale Barthes discusses, Balzac's "Sarrasine," is a classic work,
a text with a copious style. The five "codes" of reading he applies
to it—proairetic (action), semic (setting), hermeneutic, referential,
and symbolic—are the "already-given" within and without the text;
in other words, they are the several simultaneous channels through
which Balzac's text passes. Barthes describes the ideal (or writerly)
text (the "triumphant plural") as one without beginnings, one to
which "we gain access . . . by several entrances,"[1] but *S/Z* is a
reading of an "incompletely plural" work, a text "whose plural is
more or less parsimonious" (p. 6). Through what he calls "connotation," Barthes gains entrance into his chosen text by applying the
five codes and reveals "the limited plural" that makes the work
realistic. His method raises fundamental questions for analysts of style:
Is Barthes's method dependent on the copiousness of a "rich" text?
What would a similar method yield when applied to a self-consciously
"poor," or meager, text,[2] such as Kafka's short piece "Eine alltägliche
Verwirrung" 'An Everyday Confusion' (1917)?

Kafka's story is a skeletal text, an X ray or diagram of a fully
"styled" story—for instance, one written by Balzac, Thomas Mann,
or Kafka himself. The story's characteristic feature is a lack of detail:
it is one page long: the protagonists are called A and B; adverbs,
adjectives, and specific verbs are, for the most part, avoided. Although
the codes of reading are as applicable to Kafka's story as they are
to "Sarrasine," they necessarily operate differently. According to
Barthes, a rich, classic text satisfies the reader's demand that all codes
be adequately filled; a meager text, on the contrary, seems to deny
the reader certain codes. Ironically, however, the less copious the
text, the more unlimited the reading. In Barthes's words, "The more

°Reprinted from *PMLA* 95 (March 1980): 168–82.

plural the text, the less it is written before I read it" (p. 10). The skeletal text can be fleshed out by the reader in an indefinite number of ways.

In the poor text, certain codes remain undeveloped and other codes abound. Kafka's text, as already noted, is skeletal. Detail and description are kept to a minimum. Of the five codes designated by Barthes, the proairetic, semic, and symbolic are constituted *within* a text. In "Eine alltägliche Verwirrung," these codes, of course, exist for the reading. For example, when "he [A] goes to H for the preliminary discussion," the proairetic and semic codes operate. The opening line of the story, "Ein alltäglicher Vorfall," as my reading explains, demonstrates the symbolic code at work *(Vorfall* meaning both contextually "occurrence" and symbolically "before the fall"). The two remaining codes, however—the hermeneutic and the referential—are constituted *outside* a text; the hermeneutic code is constituted in the reader's logical faculty, and the referential in the reader's logical faculty (or archive). The proairetic, semic, and symbolic codes, because they are formed within a text, will be as shrunken or skeletal as the text itself. In Kafka's story the textual substance that would give them their flesh is missing. Yet, in such a text—for which a model might be a parable of Jesus or a fable of Aesop's—the hermeneutic and referential codes are not correspondingly emaciated, since they are constituted more by the reader than are the other codes. Realizing this, the reader of "Eine alltägliche Verwirrung" first expects to confront a primarily hermeneutic text, in effect either a mathematical story problem or a moral tale like a parable. But Kafka toys with the reader's hermeneutic anticipations, allowing the hermeneutic code to function in this story in a particularly negative fashion. The discourse suggests nothing or holds nothing in suspense that is disclosed in the end. It tends to mislead rather than to lead to a reading. Indeed, the existing scholarly interpretations of this text are either psychological or moral hermeneutics. Thus, the decoding reader is left to consider an unexpectedly referential tale, since the body of knowledge that the story refers to is "common" *(alltäglich)* knowledge—common sense—proverbial wisdom.

The referential, or cultural, code is the "voice of knowledge" (Barthes's translator, Richard Miller, renders *voix de science* as "voice of science," which is certainly inexact). Based on a body of public knowledge, this code is the language in which the text reaches out to the already-written and the already-thought. Through this code, Kafka's story becomes accessible; because readers know what is signified, they can relate it to the text and to a world outside the text—hence, the referentiality.

The referential code has two voices: the "endoxal" voice and the voice of a single reader. In the *endoxa* reside the commonplace, the topos, the axiom, the proverb. It is the voice of every reader (and of no reader); it represents enthymemic assumptions of informal knowledge, *Wissen* rather than *Wissenschaft*. Sayings belong to everybody; they are, as Barbara Herrnstein Smith has remarked, "a part of the lexicon of a linguistic community,"[3] which may vary for different cultures but not for readers within a single culture. Yet different readers will read a text in different ways, since they will each relate their readings to what they have already read. In this way the referential code is a kind of Rorschach of reading, in which "people create their personal style [of reading] from many different things."[4] It is learned rather than inherited knowledge. *Wissenschaft* rather than *Wissen*. Thus the referential code, the code that mediates text and reality, is always a double code—*my* reality and *their* reality, my "already-read" (which obviously has its own areas of wealth and poverty) and the "always-already spoken" of the proverb (what my proverbial grandmother taught me).

Traditionally, critics approach Kafka's works in one of three ways: biographically (psychologically), theologically, or symbolically.[5] Recently, however, structuralist readings have begun to form another entry to Kafka. Dorrit Cohn has described the Kafka of the structuralists as a figure "more potential than actual,"[6] and certainly the uses of structuralist and poststructuralist attitudes remain to be tested. Barthes himself believes that his codes cannot unlock an "ideal" text since an absolute or "triumphant plural" will not yield to interpretation. Clearly, this is a paradoxical statement, for it declares that reading such a text is impossible. The plurality of Kafka's works is confirmed by ". . . all the special features Kafka critics have so insistently reserved for their subject: unstable and ambiguous narrative voices, reversible and openended actional sequences, enigmas of plot that remain unresolved, flickers of meaning that resist consistent interpretation, contradictory symbolic hints, unstable cultural references" (p. 184). Because an incompletely plural or classic text is satisfyingly balanced among the five codes, it would seem to provide a rich reading, while a meager text, one in which the codes are not in balance, would provide a reading that is in some sense poor. I do not mean to imply, however, that such a reading is small or empty, because in a sense the very balance of a rich text prevents any one of its codes, even the dominant one (and there will always be a dominant one), from consuming, almost malignantly, the body of the text and its potential readings. In "Eine alltägliche Verwirrung," the imbalance caused by one code's overwhelming the rest creates discomfort, but not chaos. The story is as puzzling a laboratory example as one could wish, bloated in one code, withered in the others; yet the narrative may be entered: there is no roadblock.

Following Barthes's model, I have broken the text into units of reading from which we may draw meanings. Each unit functions by itself and in relation to the text as a whole. I have chosen to display the doubleness of the referential code by the two columns of commentary: the left column is endoxal, consisting of German proverbs without which a full reading of the text is impossible and on which the story itself is an oblique commentary; the right column is my individual response, the personal references evoked in a single reader's attempt to read the text.[7]

Although the intense scrutiny involved in this sort of reading and the personal and proverbial responses it promotes would hardly be suitable to any text, even to any other by Kafka, this approach does seem appropriate to "Eine alltägliche Verwirrung" once the referentiality of the story has been identified. My discussion represents a "practical" response to a unique text, rather than a programmatic prospectus for future readings of Kafka. Nevertheless, while this close reading reveals the errors of past interpretations, it is also essentially within that tradition of Kafka criticism which stresses Kafka's use of "ordinary language."

2
Eine alltägliche Verwirrung

Ein alltäglicher Vorfall: sein Ertragen eine alltägliche Verwirrung. A hat mit B aus H ein wichtiges Geschäft abzuschließen. Er geht zur Vorbesprechung nach H, legt den Hin- und Herweg in je zehn Minuten zurück und rühmt sich zu Hause dieser besonderen Schnelligkeit. Am nächsten Tag geht er wieder nach H, diesmal zum endgültigen Geschäftsabschluß. Da dieser voraussichtlich mehrere Stunden erfordern wird, geht A sehr früh morgens fort. Obwohl aber alle Nebenumstände, wenigstens nach A's Meinung, völlig die gleichen sind wie am Vortag, braucht er diesmal zum Weg nach H zehn Stunden. Als er dort ermüdet abends ankommt, sagt man ihm, daß B, ärgerlich wegen A's Ausbleiben, vor einer halben Stunde zu A in sein Dorf gegangen sei und sie sich eigentlich unterwegs hätten treffen müssen. Man rät A zu warten. A aber, in Angst wegen des Geschäftes, macht sich sofort auf und eilt nach Hause. Diesmal legt er den Weg, ohne besonders darauf zu achten, geradezu in einem Augenblick zurück. Zu Hause erfährt er, B sei doch schon gleich früh gekommen—gleich nach dem Weggang A's; ja, er habe A im Haustor getroffen, ihn an das Geschäft erinnert, aber A habe gesagt, er hätte jetzt keine Zeit, er müsse jetzt eilig fort.

Trotz diesem unverständlichen Verhalten A's sei aber B doch hier geblieben, um auf A zu warten. Er habe zwar schon oft gefragt, ob A nicht schon wieder zurück sei, befinde sich aber noch oben in A's Zimmer. Glücklich darüber, B jetzt noch zu sprechen und ihm alles erklären zu können, läuft A die Treppe hinauf. Schon ist er fast oben, da stolpert er, erleidet eine Sehnenzerrung und fast ohnmächtig vor Schmerz, unfähig sogar zu schreien, nur winselnd im Dunkel hört er, wie B—undeutlich ob in großer Ferne oder knapp neben ihm— wütend die Treppe hinunterstampft und endgültig verschwindet.[8]

An Everyday Confusion

An everyday occurrence: the enduring of it an everyday confusion. A has an important business deal to conclude with B from H. He goes to H for the preliminary discussion, gets there and back in ten minutes each way, and at home boasts of this exceptional speed. The next day he goes to H again, this time for the conclusion of the deal. Since this will presumably take several hours, A leaves very early in the morning. But although all accessory conditions, at least in A's opinion, are exactly the same as on the previous day, this time it takes him ten hours to go to H. When he arrives there weary in the evening, he is told that B, angry at A's delay, left one half hour ago for A's village and that they actually would have had to meet on the way. A is advised to wait. But A, anxious about the business deal, starts immediately and hurries home. This time he covers the distance, without particularly noticing it, in only an instant. At home he learns that B came very early, right after A's departure; why, he even met A on the doorstep, reminded him of the deal, but A said he had no time now, that he had to leave quickly. Despite this incomprehensible behavior on A's part, B did remain here to wait for A. To be sure he often asked whether A was not back yet, but was still upstairs in A's room. Happy still to be able to speak to B and explain everything to him, A runs up the stairs. Almost at the top he stumbles there, suffers a pulled tendon and, almost faint with pain, incapable even of screaming, only whimpering in the dark, he hears how B—it is unclear whether at a great distance or very close to him—stomps down the stairs in a rage and finally disappears.

The more indeterminate the origin of the statement, the more plural the text.

ROLAND BARTHES

Der von Max Brod gewählte Titel führt in die Irre, weil er auf einem gravierenden Lesefehler beruht: Die von ihm zur Überschrift erhobenen Worte aus dem ersten Satz des Textes lauten richtig im Manuskript: ". . . ein alltäglicher Heroismus."

HARTMUT BINDER

The title chosen by Max Brod leads astray, because it is based on an aggravated error in reading: the words taken as a title from the first sentence of the text read correctly in the manuscript: ". . . an everyday heroism."

1. *Eine alltägliche Verwirrung* 'An Everyday Confusion.'

The title juxtaposes "everyday" and "confusion," forming an oxymoron or a condensed paradox. Paradox, literally "contrary to opinion," stands as the first figure of the story (and Kafka's "ein alltäglicher Heroismus" is no less oxymoronic), but it is denatured by the "everyday" aspect of the events. The paradoxal form of the title, therefore, is undone by its content (whether confusion or heroism), and a certain conflict is set up between what is "contrary to opinion," the figure of paradox, and the verbal vehicle of opinion, the commonplace or proverb—endoxal knowledge.

The title is a determinate statement about the story. The text was named (misnamed) by Max Brod, because it is usual for published stories to have names or titles. Endoxal statements, however, appear to have no origin. They are the proverbs or sayings that are the commonplaces of language, as Archer Taylor writes in his work *The Proverb*,[9] the most enduring sayings are the most general, the ones that apply to many situations and the ones whose origins are least determinable. This indeterminate voice speaks through the discourse; the commonplace is the "already-there" of language. Its antidote is paradox.

> Wovon Kafka ausgeht, ist nicht mehr ein gemeinsamer Glaube, der Symbole aus sich wachsen ließe; sondern allein die *gemeinsame Sprache*. . . .
>
> GÜNTHER ANDERS
>
> Kafka proceeds not from a common belief that allows symbols to develop from it, but, rather, simply from *common language*. . . .
>
> DIALELUMENON
>   1. ASYNDETON.
>   2. *Conversational style.*
>
> RICHARD A. LANHAM

2. *Ein alltäglicher Vorfall* . . . 'An everyday occurrence. . .'

The dialelumenon is an elliptical rhetorical figure of conversational style. Without giving any indication of who is speaking, the discourse has an everyday tone, using phrases instead of sentences, making authoritative comments without explanations.

The repetition of "everyday," this time with a masculine noun, emphasizes the commonplace, the universality of events. "An everyday occurrence" is an offhanded conversational comment, a suggestion of the anecdotal. The lack of a verb speeds, the dialelumenon and colon abbreviate, and the result is an almost complete parataxis, suggesting shorthand—the conversational commonplace.

The "occurrence" is a *Vorfall*, literally "before the fall." The language prefigures, at this point, the pun that crowns the story. The fall is a linguistic fall, a fall into the materiality of language, as the pun suggests.

Ertrage and entbehre.

Endure and do without.

> With these routinizations, *rules* in some form always come to govern.
>
> MAX WEBER

3. . . . *sein Ertragen eine alltägliche Verwirrung* '. . . the enduring of it an everyday confusion.'

The use of a nominalized verb as the subject of the sentence universalizes the whole incident. Events occur; people endure them routinely. The individual, however, is left out, so that the sentence appears to be an apothegm. The discourse has set up a rule: "The enduring of everyday events is a common confusion." It gets the authority to do so because the enduring of everyday events is routine and, as Weber says, routines produce rules. If this is true, then A follows the first rule of the discourse. He endures, but with great confusion. He trusts the wisdom of the proverb "Ertrage und entbehre," for he endures and wants. By the end of the first sentence, then, the endoxal voice of referentiality has begun its rule making, and the language has already begun to break the rules. Beneath the paradoxical title, an intimate conversational voice utters an apothegmatic, universalized rule, signaling the conflict between story and discourse.

Wer A sagt, muß auch B sagen.

Whoever says A must also say B.

Ein Geschäft begonnen, heißt noch nicht gewonnen.

A business deal begun is not yet won.

> The student of arithmetic who has mastered the
> first four rules of his art and successfully striven
> with money sums and fractions finds himself con-
> fronted by an unbroken expanse of questions known
> as problems. These are short stories of adventure
> and industry with the end omitted, and though
> betraying a strong family resemblance, are not with-
> out a certain element of romance.
>
> STEPHEN LEACOCK

4. A hat mit B aus H ein wichtiges Geschäft abzuschließen 'A has an
important business deal to conclude with B from H.'

Since there are no periods after the letters A, B, and H, they must
be complete names, not initials. A, the first letter of the alphabet, is
a common character of algebraic discourse, but it is not the unknown—X. In the story A is from the world of the everyday, not of
the uncanny and unknown. According to a familiar proverb, whoever
says A must also say B. This proverbial connection is the entire theme
of the story. B is specified as the B from H, as opposed to some
other B. H, clearly not in the same set as A and B, is the place A
must go to see B. The letter H also graphically describes A's journey.
Hat, the first verb of the story, is in the active indicative form of
the present tense; its subject is A. We know that we are in the world
of small business because A is handling the deal himself and it is
important. In this world of personal, noncorporate business, ideas
and values are based not on rational calculation but on rules of
conduct found in proverbs.

The letters conjure the realm of algebraic story problems, where
the proper setup and the necessary information always yield solutions.
The expectation that there is a "right answer" is the principal "snare"
(to use Barthes's term) of the story. Our first attempt to solve the
problem is by arithmetic, and the failure of arithmetic leads us into
psychology and allegory; but the problem is linguistic. In this sense,
Leacock's delightful parody of the story problem is also a commentary
on Kafka criticism.

Der Baum fällt nicht vom ersten Schlag.

The tree is not felled by the first blow.

Rom ward nicht in einem Tag gebaut.

Rome was not built in a day.

Was man auf einem Weg verrichten kann, da soll
man nicht zweimal nachgehen.

Whatever you can accomplish in one trip do not
pursue in two.

> En face "d'alphabet" le mot, il existe "alphabet"
> la chose, et "alphabet" la chose répond diligem-
> ment, sitôt qu' "alphabet" est prononcé.
>
> MICHEL LEIRIS

> Along with the word "alphabet" there exists the
> thing "alphabet," and as soon as "alphabet" is said,
> "alphabet"—the thing—quickly responds.

5. *Er geht zur Vorbesprechung nach H . . .* 'He goes to H for the
preliminary discussion. . .'

The story itself, as opposed to the discourse, begins here. A's going
is the initiating act, but the verb is an empty one that tells us very
little. We do not know, for example, how A goes. Because A makes
the effort to go to B, we infer that the deal is more important to A
than to B. A's behavior is "proper" in that he tries to be "busi-
nesslike," following the proverbial wisdom of commerce.

Leiris' grammatological comment on the "thinghood" of the
alphabet reminds us that H is a solid balanced form, standing on two
feet and unlikely to collapse or roll. H is not only A's goal but the
only identified locus in the tale. The moment of naming characters
and places calls attention to the formal system that makes the naming
possible. Alphabetic names and places point not to things but to the
alphabet.

Zeit ist Geld.

Time is money.

Wie gekommen, so gegangen.

As it comes, so it goes.

Wer langsam geht, kommt auch ans Ziel.

Whoever walks slowly also reaches his goal.

> Whether romance begins with a hero whose birth
> is, as Wordsworth says, a sleep and a forgetting, or
> whether it begins with a sinking from a waking
> world into a dream world, it is logical for it to

> begin its series of adventures with some kind of
> break in consciousness, one which often involves
> actual forgetfulness of the previous state. We may
> call this the *motif of amnesia*. . . The change in
> mind may be brought about by the wrath of god,
> usually at the kind of errors most apt to make gods
> nervous, such as boastfulness.
>
> NORTHROP FRYE

> Such boastings as the Gentiles use,
>   Or lesser breeds without the Law.
>
> RUDYARD KIPLING, "Recessional"

6. . . . *legt den Hin- und Herweg in je zehn Minuten zurück und rühmt sich zu Hause dieser besonderen Schnelligkeit* '. . . gets there and back in ten minutes each way, and at home boasts of this exceptional speed.'

The use of the verbs without repeating the subject speeds up the tempo of the sentence, in keeping with the meaning. An absence of events—the travel time is the only thing of importance to A—makes it sound as if all A did was to go to H and back. A's boasting about this speed is the first indication of his character. The trip to H was out of the ordinary—*besonders*—because of the speed with which A completed it. This trip to H was not *alltäglich;* therefore the first day of the story, related in one sentence, is out of the ordinary, although nothing happens.

What does "ten minutes" mean? It is not a measurement of distance, but it leads us to believe that H is not far from A's village. Distance measured in time is a language commonplace.

The uncommon speed with which A completes his trip initiates his descent into confusion in the story. If there is a break in A's consciousness, it must occur here. He breaks the rules or laws of everyday with his speed, and perhaps he further violates some holy law by his boastfulness. If one wishes to give an allegorical reading to the story, a reading of "sin-and-fall," A's boasting provides an archetypal source of amnesia, of a fall into a hellish dreamworld. Such allegorism is Sokel's approach, although he attributes A's sin to impatience rather than to boasting. But the discourse gives no indication that A has left the "waking world" for a "dreamworld," that logic is *Alltag* and confusion a dream. The allegorical reading always injects another story into the story it is reading.

Man soll nicht den Tag vor dem Abend loben.

Do not praise the day before evening.

> None of this contradicts the pleasure principle; repetition, the reexperiencing of something identical, is clearly in itself a source of pleasure.
>
> SIGMUND FREUD

7. *Am nächsten Tag geht er wieder nach H, diesmal zum endgültigen Geschäftsabschluß* 'The next day he goes to H again, this time for the conclusion of the deal.'

The second action of the story is the repetition of the first; the binary expectation, first day/second day, is imitated in the clause structure. The verb *gehen* is no more explanatory here than it was the first time. A is still functioning in the present active indicative. The assumption that the deal is more important to him than to B is reinforced, since again A has to make the effort. The final settlement is on the second day; therefore it must be a small deal, small business. This fact places the size of the deal in the reader's mind, but not in the actor's mind, since for A the transaction is important. Although A may wish to experience repetition as the pleasure of speed and success, he does not. Instead he experiences the repetition of a trip whose entire focus is on its speed, not on its goal. As the first day made no mention of the *Vorbesprechung* 'preliminary discussion,' it is structurally logical that a repetition would also omit the subject of the trip and emphasize its form.

Erstens kommt es anders, zweitens als man glaubt.

First it happens differently, secondly than one thinks.

Was morgen anders kann sein, das nenne nicht dein.

Do not call yours that which can change tomorrow.

Morgenstunde hat Gold im Munde.

The morning hour has gold in its mouth.

Es ist nicht jede Meinung eine Wahrheit.

Not every opinion is a truth.

> *Différence et répétition*
>
> GILLES DELEUZE

> When you sit with a nice girl for two hours you think it's only a minute. But when you sit on a hot stove for a minute you think it's two hours. That's relativity.
>
> ALBERT EINSTEIN

> . . . Alle Wissenschaft wäre überflüssig, wenn die Erscheinungsform und das Wesen der Dinge unmittelbar zusammenfielen. . .
>
> KARL MARX

> Science would be superfluous if there were no difference between the appearance of things and their essence.

8. Da dieser voraussichtlich mehrere Stunden erfordern wird, geht A sehr früh morgens fort. Obwohl aber alle Nebenumstände, wenigstens nach A's Meinung, völlig die gleichen sind wie am Vortag, braucht er diesmal zum Weg nach H zehn Stunden 'Since this will presumably take several hours, A leaves very early in the morning. But although all accessory conditions, at least in A's opinion, are exactly the same as on the previous day, this time it takes him ten hours to go to H.'

In this unit the narrator becomes more expansive. He now tells us what A thinks and why A leaves very early in the morning: because A presumes the deal will take a long time. The presumption is correct, but not in the way A thinks. Even when he "sees in advance"— *Voraus-sicht*—he cannot know what will happen. A leaves very early to catch his worm and to find gold.

The problem is one of synonymity: repetition and difference. On a mathematical scale, A's second trip differs from his first by a factor of sixty; on a verbal scale, by a factor of one (the substitution of "hours" for "minutes"). Again, spatial distance is measured in time. How far is H from A's village? The answer is ten minutes *and* ten hours. What are the "accessory conditions"? We do not even know what the major ones are.

For the third time the verb *gehen* describes the action. We still do not know how A goes, but the unit brings with it an expansion of language. Within the context of the story and compared with previous sentences, this passage is rich in hypotactic terms that explain: *da, obwohl aber, diesmal.* A complex construction appears three times, clearly indicating hypotactic thought. Parataxis fails because of the increasing complexity of the story.

It is in this unit that reason, too, fails. A would like to repeat the success of the previous day, and although the circumstances appear to be the same, the trip takes him sixty times as long. We search for A's break in consciousness, so that we may apply Frye's "motif of amnesia"; thus, A either must have forgotten how he got to H on the previous day or must be mistaken in thinking that all the circumstances are the same. We want to blame A for getting himself (and us) into this predicament, but the discourse provides us with no grounds. A has descended from order into chaos, but not from consciousness to subconsciousness, or from the waking world to a dreamworld. Given the chaotic situation, A must now deal rationally or proverbially for the best possible results.

Wenn die Tante Räder *hätte*, wär sie ein Omnibus.

If my aunt had wheels, she would be a bus.

> This time is out of joint.
>
> *Hamlet I.v*

> "Contrariwise," continued Tweedledee, "if it was so, it might be; and if it were so, it would be: but as it isn't, it ain't. That's logic."
>
> LEWIS CARROLL

9. *Als er dort ermüdet abends ankommt sagt man ihm, daß B, ärgerlich wegen A's Ausbleiben, vor einer halben Stunde zu A in sein Dorf gegangen sei und sie sich eigentlich unterwegs hätten treffen müssen* 'When he arrives there weary in the evening, he is told that B, angry at A's delay, left one half hour ago for A's village and that they actually would have had to meet on the way.'

There is a change of tense and mode within the sentence. A is still in the present indicative, but B "left." This most "everyday" relationship of grammar emerges into the story: A and B are working in two different tenses and two different time frames. A question occurs. Who is *"man"*? Who says that B left? The world is filled with nameless, faceless people who know what is going on, who live according to the wisdom of proverbs. The endoxal voice has arrived at a logical conclusion: A and B would have had to meet. Like Tweedledee, the voice needs the subjunctive mode to explain logic, because logic, like the subjunctive, is based on "if, then" propositions. In German the word for the subjunctive is *Konjunktiv*, a joining together, and it is impossible except in the subjunctive to join together what remains "out of joint." The syntax of the sentence becomes more complicated, requiring a modal in the perfect tense of the subjunctive, as the complexity of the story increases.

A and B must get together for the event to take place, but "the time is out of joint." Assuming that A and B exist in the same universe of time and space, B left H nine and a half hours after A started out for H. An implied shift from narrator to "endoxal speaker," to the voice of common sense, adds to the confusion. When the endoxal voice tells A that A and B "hätten sich treffen müssen," the implication is that even that which must happen does not. Suddenly there are two levels of the puzzle—A's puzzlement and the reader's.

Habe Rat vor der Tat.

Be advised before acting.

Wem nicht zu raten ist, dem ist auch nicht zu helfen.

Whoever cannot be advised cannot be helped either.

Guter Rat ist Goldes Wert.

Good advice is worth gold.

> For we are saved by hope: but hope that is seen is not hope: for what a man seeth, why doth he yet hope for?
> But if we hope for that we see not, *then* do we with patience wait for *it*.
> ROMANS viii.24–25

10. Man rät A zu warten 'A is advised to wait.'

Who tells A to wait, and why? When A is given this advice, he hears the voice of his own ideology—of petty bourgeois patience; it is in effect *his own voice*. But he does not heed the advice to wait. He is disturbed by his experience; for him proverbiality is collapsing. Yet the voice of proverbiality continues, even praising its own advice.

Wer warten kann, kommt auch noch an.

Whoever can wait also gets there.

Wer in Geschäften die Fußwege nicht findet, der läuft sich bald den Atem ab.

Whoever cannot find the paths in business runs himself out of breath.

Angst macht auch den Alten laufen.

Fear makes even the old man run.

> If to do were as easy as to know what were good to do, chapels had been churches, and poor men's cottages princes' palaces.
> *Merchant of Venice I.ii*

11. A aber, in Angst wegen des Geschäftes, macht sich sofort auf und eilt nach Hause. 'But A, anxious about the business deal, starts immediately and hurries home.'

The alliterative a's in the first phrase of the unit, "A aber, in Angst," point only to B's absence. As Leiris suggests, the alphabet appears as things replicating, here, A's inability to find B. A is anxious about the deal. His small-business mentality is emphasized again and again. A is functioning according to a proverb in which he believes—time is money—but he is violating the endoxal voice of patient waiting. The paths of proverbiality having divided, A is "always-already" lost and (proverbially) "out of breath."

Wer warten läßt, zählt nach Sekunden; wer warten
muß, nach Stunden.

Whoever keeps one waiting counts by seconds;
whoever must wait, by hours.

> An instant of time, without duration, is an imaginative logical construction.
> ALFRED NORTH WHITEHEAD

> Werd' ich zum Augenblicke sagen;
>   Verweile doch! Du bist so schön!
>   *Faust* I, 1699–1700

> If to the moment I should say:
>   Abide you are so fair—
>   *trans.* WALTER KAUFMANN

> Ha, welch ein Augenblick!
>   *Fidelio* I

> Ah, what a moment!

12. Diesmal legt er den Weg, ohne besonders darauf zu achten, geradezu in einem Augenblick zurück 'This time he covers the distance, without particularly noticing it, in only an instant.'

With duration, time and space suddenly disappear, the time and space that have dragged on A all day. A does not notice, because there is nothing to notice; A exists, but time and space do not. The same distance has now taken ten minutes, ten hours, and a moment.

Die Zuschauer sehen mehr als die Spieler.

The spectators see more than the players.

> . . . it can be so maddening to argue with someone who utters proverbs in reply to one's carefully thought out proposals or empirically verified observations. . . It is like waging battle with an adversary who is both immovable and immortal.
>
> BARBARA HERRNSTEIN SMITH

13. *Zu Hause erfährt er, B sei doch schon gleich früh gekommen— gleich nach dem Weggang A's* . . . 'At home he learns that B came very early, right after A's departure. . .'

Again the question arises, who is informing A? Whoever it is repeats the earlier verbal structure—B in the past tense, A in the present. The endoxal voice keeps A and B in different time streams.

A mystery presents itself: B came early. If B arrived shortly after A's departure in the morning, how could he have left H only a half hour before A arrived there? Is time moving in reverse? Or are A and B moving in mirror images of time? This mystery is a crisis for both A and the reader, but not for the discourse. A is perturbed, the reader is perturbed, but not the story; the narration, after all, is about an "everyday" confusion.

It appears that A and B have different conceptions of *früh* 'early.' In unit 8 we discover that A left "very early," but it must not have been early enough, for in unit 9 B is angry because of A's delay, and in this unit we find out that A was considered late before he left, because B came just after A's departure. "Early" is a relational word, thus a word that can cause confusion. One word, two definitions—again language separates A and B.

Eile mit Weile.

Hurry leisurely.

> It takes two to speak the truth—one to speak, and another to hear.
>
> HENRY DAVID THOREAU

> In keiner Sprache kann man sich so schwer verständigen wie in der Sprache.
>
> KARL KRAUS

> In no language is it as difficult to communicate as in language.

14. . . . ja, er habe A im Haustor getroffen, ihn an das Geschäft erinnert, aber A habe gesagt, er hätte jetzt keine Zeit, er müsse jetzt eilig fort . . . why, he even met A on the doorstep, reminded him of the deal, but A said he had no time now, that he had to leave quickly.'

A hears only the accusing voice of commonplace wisdom, which is always ready to explain any failure, since one is always in violation of some proverb. The "ja" interjects a conversational tone, the same tone as established in the first sentence by the rhetorical dialelumenon. The endoxal voice is surprised that A is so confused.

The unit introduces the second crisis—a spatial one: A and B had met on A's doorstep. A is told that the event occurred and that he took no notice. B supposedly reminded A of the deal, but A, being in a hurry to see B, had no time to see him. To A, the means again seem to be more important than the end. According to the endoxal voice, A and B have conversed, but A paid no attention. The paratactic sentence structure indicates the breakdown of explanation. A's explanation for his haste seems ironic—"Er hätte jetzt keine Zeit"—since A never has any time for B: he is in a different time stream (tense). Here we learn of the one face-to-face meeting of A and B in space, but linguistically the meeting is in the subjunctive of indirect discourse, not in indicative time.

Warten ist nicht schenken.

Waiting is not giving.

Es irrt der Mensch, solang er strebt.

Faust I.317

Man errs as long as he will strive.

trans. WALTER KAUFMANN

15. Trotz diesem unverständlichen Verhalten A's sei aber B doch hier geblieben, um auf A zu warten. Er habe zwar schon oft gefragt, ob A nicht schon wieder zurück sei, befinde sich aber noch oben in A's Zimmer 'Despite this incomprehensible behavior on A's part, B did remain here to wait for A. To be sure he often asked whether A was not back yet, but was still upstairs in A's room.'

The endoxal voice is everywhere—*hier* and in H. A's behavior is termed "incomprehensible," but it is unclear whether to B or to the endoxal voice or to the discourse. B, following other proverbial rules than A does, has decided to wait. In the course of this unit, B moves out of the past into the present subjunctive (though this change cannot be grammatically reflected in the English translation). B is now not only in A's time but also in A's space—his room, which is as bare of description as A. Another promise is set up with the upstairs/downstairs structure. Since B is still upstairs, the event—the actual encounter of A and B in the present, not in the present subjunctive or the past—cannot be far off. If spatial and temporal rules were intact, A and B would now be in the same building, soon to meet. The interventions of language that have kept them apart would soon be overcome.

Besser spät als nie.

Better late than never.

Die Erklärung ist dunkler als der Text.

The explanation is darker than the text.

> Explaining metaphysics to the nation—
> I wish he would explain his explanation.
> BYRON, *Don Juan*, "Dedication" ii

16. *Glücklich darüber, B jetzt noch zu sprechen und ihm alles erklären zu können* . . . 'Happy still to be able to speak to B and explain everything to him. . . .'

The story is almost ended, and we see another sign of emotion in A—happiness. His confusion, however, manifests itself in his belief that he can "explain everything." His happiness is premature, as was his satisfaction about completing the business deal. Even if A were to meet B, could A explain everything? Since language has invaded the story from the discourse, the story cannot be explained, only repeated. Any other language would provide another story. Explanation is always a translation, "another story," and A is incapable of retelling the story because, as the proverb says, "Die Zuschauer sehen mehr als die Spieler" 'The discourse sees more than the story.'

Fast bringt nichts ins Haus.

Almost brings nothing into the house.

Dem Stolpern folgt leicht das Fallen.

Stumbling is easily followed by the fall.

> Mit seiner Hauptbedeutung bezeichnet *Sehne* heute
> die Bänder die Muskeln und Knochen verbinden.
> So gilt die Sehne als Sitz der Körperkraft. . . .
> *Trübners Deutsches Wörterbuch*

> In its primary meaning *tendon* today signifies the
> bands connecting muscles and bones; therefore the
> tendon is the seat of bodily strength.

> . . . Ich will Euch von nun an noch eifriger dienen,
> will meine dürren Sehnen in Eurem Dienst . . .
> abarbeiten.
> SCHILLER, *Die Räuber* iv.ii

> I will serve you from now on more diligently than
> ever; I will work off my withered tendons in your
> service . . .

17. . . . *läuft A die Treppe hinauf. Schon ist er fast oben, da stolpert er, erleidet eine Sehnenzerrung* . . . '. . . A runs up the stairs. Almost at the top he stumbles there, suffers a pulled tendon. . . .'

The expectation of the meeting builds. Anticipation is set up in the sentence structure, starting with *schon* and using *fast*. A stumbles and, in addition to all his other troubles, "suffers a pulled tendon." This is the most specific detail in an undetailed story. We are told the exact nature of A's injury, not just that he hurt his foot. According to the *Worterbüch* definition, the tendon is considered the seat of bodily strength, and it has been used as such throughout German literature. The *Sehnenzerrung* is both "a pulled tendon" and "the pull of longing." All day, A has longed to see B; the result of his longing is this *Sehnenzerrung*. The word generates many images— *Zerrbild* 'caricature,' *Verzerrung* 'distortion,' and *Sehnen zehrung* 'consumption by longing.' This pun ironically complements, in fact creates, the content of the pun on *Vorfall* in the first line of the story. The allegorical reading that attributes A's confusion to some figurative "fall," from either boastfulness or impatience, fails to recognize that the story to this point is *Vorfall*. The fall is both a literal one and— the precise destruction of literality—a pun. The definition also remarks that the tendon connects, or joins, muscles and bones. Here, ironically, that which joins prevents A from connecting with B.

Wer keine Treppe steigen kann, wird nie hochkom-
men.

Whoever cannot climb stairs will never get up high.

> The way up is the way down.
>
> HERACLITUS, *Fragments*

> Die dir zugemessene Zeit ist so kurz, daß du, wenn
> du eine Sekunde verlierst, schon dein ganzes Leben
> verloren hast, denn es ist nicht länger, es ist immer
> nur so lang, wie die Zeit, die du verlierst. Hast du
> also einen Weg begonnen, setze ihn fort, unter allen
> Umständen, du kannst nur gewinnen, du läufst keine
> Gefahr, vielleicht wirst du am Ende abstürzen, hät-
> test du aber schon nach den ersten Schritten dich
> zurückgewendet und wärest die Treppe hinunter-
> gelaufen, wärst du gleich am Anfang abgestürzt und
> nicht vielleicht, sondern ganz gewiß. . . . Solange
> du nicht zu steigen aufhörst, hören die Stufen nicht
> auf, unter deinen steigenden Füßen wachsen sie
> aufwärts.
>
> KAFKA

> The time allotted to you is so short that if you lose
> one second you have already lost your whole life,
> for it is no longer, it is always just as long as the
> time you lost. So if you have started out on a walk,
> continue it whatever happens; you can only gain,
> you run no risks, in the end you may fall over a
> precipice perhaps, but had you turned back after
> the first steps and run downstairs you would have
> fallen at once—and not perhaps, but for cer-
> tain. . . . As long as you don't stop climbing, the
> stairs won't end, under your climbing feet they will
> go on growing upwards.
>
> *trans.* TANIA STERN AND JAMES STERN

18. . . . *und fast ohnmächtig vor Schmerz, unfähig sogar zu schreien,
nur winselnd im Dunkel hört er, wie B—undeutlich ob in großer Ferne
oder knapp neben ihm—wütend die Treppe hinunterstampft . . . '* . . .
and, almost faint with pain, incapable even of screaming, only whimpering in the dark, he hears how B—it is unclear whether at a great
distance or very close to him—stomps down the stairs in a rage. . .'

The unit provides a summary of A's impotence—"fast ohnmächtig,"
"unfähig," "winselnd im Dunkel"—all bad qualities for business. A
is in the dark about the whole matter, both literally and figuratively.
Spatial laws are still not in synch. The confusion about the distance

between A and B may be due either to A's pain or to the different zones of movement the two figures may be in. After all, how wide can a staircase be? We do know, however, that although A and B have reached the same temporality, the present indicative, they are still moving in opposition to each other—A runs upstairs/B stomps downstairs, A is almost faint/B is in a violent rage, A is listening and unable to communicate/B is noisy.

Contrary to Heraclitus' dictum, the way up is not the way down. If any doubt remained that A was lost from the start, it would vanish in this unit. The ideas about lost time and uncompleted actions that Kafka expressed in "Fürsprecher" apply to "Eine alltägliche Verwirrung" as well. With A's fall, his climbing ceases and his possibilities end, but if the narrator of "Fürsprecher" is correct, A was lost as soon as he "lost a second," in other words, when he failed to get to H on time. Yet, it is impossible to "lose time." One can only lose something that exists in space. To "lose time" is simply a cliché, another language commonplace that exists in a discourse. Thus, from the start, A was lost in the same sense that time is lost, lost in the figurality of language. When language as system or as object emerges in the discourse, communication disappears. A's muteness stands (in the symbolic code, to be sure) for his real condition throughout the story.

On the staircase, A cannot communicate. He has no language, language being the connector between mind and world. The staircase should connect A to B, but it fails, as language fails. In a sense, the pun is a staircase, connecting the sound and the sense of language. Thus the staircase, the tendon, the pun—all liminalities—prevent A and B from meeting at the critical moment.

Wer in Geschäften Maß hält, bleibt auf den Beinen,
wenn ein anderer fällt.

Whoever maintains moderation in business stays on
his feet while another falls.

Les mots ne sont pas des étiquettes collées à des choses qui existent en tant que telles indépendamment d'eux. Quand on écrit, on ne fait que cela; l'importance de ce geste est telle, qu'il ne laisse place à aucune autre expérience. En même temps, si j'écris, j'écris de quelque chose, même si ce quelque chose est l'écriture. Pour que l'écriture soit possible, elle doit partir de la mort de ce dont elle parle; mais cette mort la rend elle-même impossible, car il n'y a plus quoi écrire. La littérature ne peut

devenir possible que pour autant qu'elle se rend
impossible. Ou bien ce qu'on dit est là présent,
mais alors il n'y a pas place pour la littérature; ou
bien on fait place à la littérature, mais alors il n'y
a plus rien à dire.

TZVETAN TODOROV

Word are not labels pasted to things that exist as
such independently of them. When we write, we
do merely that—the importance of the gesture is
such that it leaves room for no other experience.
At the same time, if I write, I write about something,
even if this something is writing. For writing to be
possible, it must be born out of the death of what
it speaks about; but this death makes writing itself
impossible, for there is no longer anything to write.
Literature can become possible only insofar as it
makes itself possible. Either what we say is actually
here, in which case there is no room for literature;
or else there is room for literature, in which case
there is no longer anything to say.

trans. RICHARD HOWARD

19. . . . und endgültig verschwindet '. . . and finally disappears.'

The second use of *endgültig* ends the story: in unit 7 the word
referred to the final settlement of the deal; unit 19 *is* the final
settlement. A's fears have come true. The business deal has failed.
The terminating action of the story is B's disappearance, down the
drain, into space, never to be seen again. B's disappearance is a
purely literary sign, the signal in the discourse that the story is over,
the "off switch." Language, which has prevented the meeting of A
and B in the story, now forbids it forever, arrogantly asserting its
dominion over the future (of which there will be none for A and B).
Todorov's paradox is the paradox of "Eine alltägliche Verwirrung":
words create a world, the world creates the words; the two cannot
become one and cannot exist separately; yet they exist. Whoever says
A must say B; yet whoever says A cannot say B. This is the paradox
maintained by the discourse.

3

Any reading of "Eine alltägliche Verwirrung" that stops at the
level of the story must remain confused itself, and thus unable to
penetrate the story's confusion. A key to the story is that *language*
is an important character *in* it. The world of time and space is taken
over by the discourse and is overwhelmed. The speed of time is

changed in the discourse (from breezy parataxis to belabored hy-
potaxis), while similar tricks occur in the story. The *spatial* demands
of A and B, to find each other in a common place, are undermined,
mimicked, and parodied by the consistent suggestion of German
commonplaces, whose futility embodies the great metapun of the
story, that A and B can find no commonplace, *Gemeinplatz.* Kafka
separates his characters by language (A in present, B in past) or joins
them teasingly in the *Konjunktiv* (used in German for *indirect* discourse). At their only moment of true meeting (in the present indicative), on the staircase, a pun prevents their success. Since the
pun is the great "confusion" of language, the "staircase" between
the materiality (sound) of language and its sense, the pun creates a
verbal as well as a physical liminality in which a meeting is impossible.
Again the discourse dominates the story and embodies the metapun
of the impossible commonplace.

The text spills over with references to German commonplaces.
From the first mention of A, it is clear that the text will present the
reader with a B. Why? Because, as every German-speaking reader
knows, "Wer A sagt, muss auch B sagen." No other combination of
characters would satisfy this proverbial necessity; thus, once B "has
been said," the reader assumes the text's domination by the commonplace and the referential code, and the consistently proverbial
undertone of the rest of the story upholds this dominance. The theme
of the story, however, denies the discourse that makes it possible.

From the beginning of the story, it is clear that the scope of the
tale is the world of small business,[10] a world that is half rationalized
and half personalized, as opposed to the fully rationalized world of
big business. In the former world, there remains a debt to endoxal
knowledge rather than to fully rationalized calculation, and an important part of this endoxal knowledge is the proverb, or saying, a
half-rationalized, half-personalized commentary on a given situation,
"the adherence to the middle way," as Archer Taylor has pointed
out (p. 168). The proverb seems to contain the weight of human
experience in the form of a commonplace; it resides in the language
at that level. Kafka, whose despair of the metaphor and of literary
language often caused him "to conquer the treacherous nature of
language . . . through word play,"[11] has created a one-page wordplay
with "Eine alltägliche Verwirrung," and it is precisely a play on
Kafkan language—*gemeine Sprache.*

In her article "A Common Confusion," Elizabeth Trahan states,
"Three times in the course of our story do A and B come together
in time and space, and still they are unable to meet" (p. 275). Trahan
fails to see that the language of this story makes it impossible for A
and B to come together. A and B have no common place within or
without the text. On the first day, the text gives no indication that

A ever saw B; only the speed of his trip bears mentioning. On the second day of the story, A "is told" of his meeting with B on the doorstep; accordingly, this meeting takes place in the text in the subjunctive mood, the *Konjunktiv,* which should *join* A and B, but does not. Why? Because at the precise moment of their meeting, A himself remarks that *he has no time.* Throughout the story, A and B are in different temporalities. Without a common time, they cannot arrive at a common place. Only at the end, after A has suffered his injury, are A and B in the same temporality—the present indicative—but they are on a staircase, the common passage between up and down, of ascent and descent. The staircase structures the phenomenology of separation between A and B. It also parallels the original journey to B. On both the staircase and the road to H, a meeting between A and B would be possible; yet it does not occur. As A sits on the staircase whimpering, B stomps down and disappears. At the moment when a meeting is possible, A has no language, no power to communicate. There is no "linguistic community" for A and B, so that even at the exact moment of the same time and the same space on the staircase the lack of a common language maintains the A/B structure. To meet, to talk, to communicate, A and B need a common time, a common place, and a commonplace, one of which is always absent at the crucial moments in the story. Yet the simple transformation that will change A/B into A-B, their simple meeting, proves impossible as soon as language captures the story. The barest element of language, the *lexical* element, becomes an issue as soon as the characters are named; the nominations A and B are our first clues to the presence, the materiality, of language in the text. This presence extends through all the linguistic elements. *Grammar* parts A and B in time, while *syntax* alters the pace of temporality. The *semantic* texture, though proverbial and potentially reassuring *(alltäglich),* leads to its own destruction in the metapun. In other words, just as the story is dominated by a single code, the referential, that code is in turn dominated by its language. Just as the story proves hermeneutically impossible, so the referential code proves itself impossible, even though it constitutes my reading of the story. Whoever says A cannot also say B. Only language remains undefeated.

This referential reading of "Eine alltägliche Verwirrung" *seems* to avoid plurality by offering a discourse dominated by one code. Yet this very referential reading indicates only the delusion of referential readings, opening an abyss into which the story itself falls. As Barbara Johnson has pointed out, a text's (deconstructive) difference is what differentiates it not from other texts but from itself. "It is a difference *within.* Far from constituting the text's unique identity, it is that which subverts the very idea of identity, infinitely deferring the possibility of adding up the sum of a text's parts or meanings and reaching a totalized, integrated whole."[12] The deconstructive punning in Kafka's tale functions like castration in Balzac's "Sarrasine." It is the difference that obliterates difference. In a tale full of commonplaces, there is no common place.

I have designated "Eine alltägliche Verwirrung" a poor text; its style is meager and undercoded as opposed to that of a rich, copious, fully coded text. The skeletal story frustrates hermeneutics while it draws attention to the code on which it relies. In this way, the text seems to be a running commentary on that code. The text is also a critical commentary on its own style, in that a poor text is one in which a single code dominates and even consumes the body of the text. This is precisely what causes A's catastrophe and the commonplace confusion. In a sense, then, A's "life (and psychology)," or the system of signs by which A functions, is a poor text, one that Kafka criticizes, perhaps even satirizes, in his own poor text.

Notes

1. Barthes, S/Z, trans. by Richard Miller (New York: Hill and Wang, 1974), p. 5.

2. In using the terms "rich" (or "copious") and "poor" (or "meager"), I refer to a fullness or paucity of stylistic detail, *not* to pluralities in or of meaning.

3. Smith, "On the Margins of Discourse." *Critical Inquiry*, 1 (1974), 793.

4. Norman N. Holland, *Poems in Persons* (New York: Norton, 1973), pp. 159–60.

5. In *Franz Kafka: Tragik und Ironie* (Munich: Langen-Müller, 1964), Walter Sokel structures a theory of tragedy in Kafka on the basis of a rich and stimulating exegesis of "Eine alltägliche Verwirrung." Interpreting the story psychologically, Sokel sees the horrible confusion to be a result of A's sin of omission, that is, his failure to recognize B on his doorstep. In Sokel's view A's haste causes his own unhappiness. Drawing on Kafka's aphorisms, Sokel demonstrates Kafka's feelings about impatience *(Ungeduld)* and provides a strong argument for reading "Eine alltägliche Verwirrung" as an expressionistically alienating representation of thoughts Kafka had stated clearly in the aphorisms. Elizabeth Trahan, in her article " 'A Common Confusion': A Basic Approach to Franz Kafka's World" *(German Quarterly*, 36 [1963] 269–78), considers the story as an "entrance" into "Kafka's world." But by using a translation of the text and retelling the plot of the story, she fails to see the important element of Kafka's language and thus understands the story as dealing primarily with "man's relationship to man." (Meno Spann, in his *Franz Kafka* [Boston: Twayne, 1976], points again and again to the mistakes critics have made when relying on translations of Kafka's works—an "unadvisable procedure" [p. 60]—instead of dealing with the German.) As Stanley Corngold has distinguished the "metamorphosed metaphor" from Sokel's "extended metaphor" and removed "Die Verwandlung" from an expressionist tradition *(The Commentators' Despair* [Port Washington, N.Y.: Kennikat, 1973]), I distinguish between traditional interpretations of "Eine alltägliche Verwirrung" as the "hero's psychological *Selbsttäuschung*" of despair and a reading of the text as a system of linguistic commonplaces and grammatical dimensions. The latter approach incorporates the important tradition in Kafka studies of Günther Anders, a tradition that stresses Kafka's inspiration

in "ordinary language," while avoiding psychological speculations about the "characters" or about Kafka himself.

6. Cohn, "Trends in Literary Criticism: Some Structuralist Approaches to Kafka,"
German Quarterly, 51 (1978), 183.

7. All the proverbs cited in the left column of Part II can be found in Karl
Friedrich Wilhelm Wander's *Deutsches Sprichwörter Lexikon*, 5 vols. (1867; rpt. Aalen:
Scientia Verlag, 1963), or in Jerzy Gluski's *Proverbs* (New York: Elsevier Publishing
Co., 1971). All the translations are my own, and I have tried to make them as literal
as possible. Although there are often comparable proverbs in English, the images and
metaphors of the German sayings are important to the argument.

    The sources for the quotations in the right column of Part II are as follows
(unless otherwise indicated, the translations are my own): Barthes, "The Dissolve of
Voices," *S/Z*, p. 40. Binder. *Kafka Kommentar zu sämtlichen Erzählungen* (Munich:
Winkler Verlag, 1977), p. 236. Anders, *Kafka pro und contra* (Munich: C. H. Beck
Verlag, 1967), p. 40. Lanham, *A Handlist of Rhetorical Terms* (Los Angeles: Univ. of
California Press, 1969), p. 33. Weber, *From Max Weber: Essays in Sociology*, ed. and
trans. H. H. Gerth and C. W. Mills (New York: Oxford Univ. Press, 1946), p. 297.
Leacock, "A, B, and C—the Human Element in Mathematics," *Literary Lapses* (London:
John Lane, 1950), p. 82. Leiris, "Alphabet," *La Règle du Jeu I, Biffures* (Paris: Gallimard,
1948), p. 39. Frye, *The Secular Scripture* (Cambridge: Harvard Univ. Press, 1976), p.
102. Freud, *Beyond the Pleasure Principle*, std. ed., trans. James Strachey (London:
Hogarth Press, 1964), p. 36. Deleuze, *Différence et répétition* (Paris: Presses Universitaires, 1968). Einstein, quoted in obituary article, *New York Times*, 19 April 1955,
p. 27. Marx, *Das Kapital*. III (Zurich: Ring Verlag, 1934), Pt. II, Bk. III, 870. Carroll,
"Tweedledum and Tweedledee," *Through the Looking Glass* (New York: Macmillan,
1899), p. 68. Whitehead, *Science and the Modern World* (New York: Macmillan, 1929),
p. 95. Smith, "On the Margins of Discourse," *Critical Inquiry*, I (1974), 795. Thoreau,
"Wednesday," *A Week on the Concord and Merrimack Rivers* (New York: Scribners,
1921), p. 197. Kraus, *Auswahl aus dem Werk*, ed. Heinrich Fischer (Munich: Kösel
Verlag, 1957), p. 339. *Trübners Deutsches Wörterbuch*, ed. Walther Mitzka (Berlin:
Walter de Gruyter Verlag, 1955), VI, 307. Kafka, "Fürsprecher," *Gesammelte Schriften*
(Prague: Heinrich Mercy Sohn, 1936), p. 139. Stern and Stern, trans., "Advocates,"
Franz Kafka: The Complete Stories, ed. Nahum N. Glatzer (New York: Schocken, 1946),
p. 451. Todorov, *Introduction à la littérature fantastique* (Paris: Editions du Seuil,
1970), pp. 183–84. Howard, trans., *The Fantastic* (Ithaca: Cornell Univ. Press, 1975),
p. 175.

8. Kafka, *Gesammelte Schriften*, ed. Max Brod, 2nd ed. (New York: Schocken
Books, 1946), v, 122–23. The translation that follows is my own.

9. Taylor, *The Proverb* (Cambridge: Harvard Univ. Press, 1931), p. 168.

10. Corngold relates Kafka's attributing the "unreadable ending" of "Die Verwandlung" to a business trip Kafka had to take just as he was nearing the end of the
story (p. 1).

11. Heinz Politzer, "Franz Kafka's Language." *Modern Fiction Studies*, 8 (Spring
1962), 20.

12. Johnson, "The Critical Difference," *Diacritics*, 8 (June 1978), 3.

The Reader on Trial: Or, Is Reading Necessarily an Injudicious Act?

Jonathan Baldo*

Trying the reader in at least two senses of the word, *The Trial* parades a series of reflections of the reader and the act of reading. Only gradually does the novel allow us to realize the extent to which we are implicated in Joseph K.'s case, not simply as juror (if we are a casual reader) or judge (if we aspire or pretend to the rigors of criticism), but also as fellow defendant. It is the reader's judgment that Kafka brings to judgment in *The Trial*. Used to serving as judge, the reader is, like Joseph K., being tried by what he or she usually claims to be sitting in judgment of. I believe Kafka intended the reader, like Joseph K., to be just as slow in coming to understand the charges brought against him or her. The novel questions whether it is possible to be other than injudicious as a reader. One might regard the novel as a send-up of reader-response theory, a welcome and necessary development in the history of twentieth-century criticism, but a development that generally rests on a vulnerable notion of the subject and misplaced confidence in the possibility of judgment conceived as an act that unites or harmonizes cognition and performance.[1] I hope to indicate one possible direction for reader-response criticism by placing it in the company of a text that puts the reader and our very notions of reading on trial.

The Author as Warden of the Captive Reader

Like Joseph K., we are arrested at the beginning of the work of fiction. Like K.'s, ours is a peculiar form of arrest because we are free to leave as we please the house of fiction, the site of our detainment. (From the moment of our arrest, we are "parolees," we readers who have chosen to languish in the midst of so many *paroles*.) Joseph K. cherishes his (possibly illusory) freedom toward the beginning of his tenure as an accused man. "But he was still free," the narrator avers shortly after the arrest,[2] mirroring the circumstances of the reader, who after merely a few pages is somewhere between freedom and captivity. Later the dream of "living completely outside the jurisdiction of the Court" may return more frequently (266) for both Joseph K. and the captive reader, but it seems increasingly implausible in both cases.

*This essay was written specifically for this volume and is published here for the first time by permission of the author.

In the cathedral, K. again experiences the exhilaration of that precarious moment when he is poised between freedom and arrest. Having been addressed directly by a priest who turns out to be a prison chaplain, he muses, "For the moment he was still free, he could continue on his way and vanish through one of the small, dark, wooden doors that faced him at no great distance. It would simply indicate that he had not understood the call, or that he had understood it and did not care" (262). This moment of "arrest," like the apparently more literal one at the beginning of the novel, coincides with the beginning of a story, the priest's parable of the doorkeeper. A narrative, of course, is one of the most effective instruments for arresting the reader, whose captivation by Kafka is enacted here by the auditor Joseph K.: "But if he were to turn round he would be caught, for that would amount to an admission that he had understood it very well, that he really was the person addressed, and that he was ready to obey" (262). K.'s hesitation is surely a ploy familiar to any reader of fiction, who may nonchalantly pretend that the work is *not* addressed to him or her, just as Joseph K. wonders if he should pretend that he has not been correctly identified by the priest's call.

Joseph K.'s arrest leads to a single-minded absorption in the trial to the detriment of all business matters and practical affairs. Like the absorption of the accused man in his case, our arrest leading to submersion in the work of fiction may temporarily eclipse the world of practical affairs, especially when that work, like Kafka's *The Trial*, deliberately avoids the panoramic scope and ambitions to totality of the traditional novel. Because *The Trial* often seems as narrow and constricting in its vision as the long passageways that abound in the novel, it afflicts us with the kind of amnesia or forgetfulness that repeatedly visits Joseph K. The novel practices brilliantly the very inducement of forgetfulness that K. concluded must be an important weapon in the lawyer's arsenal. Upon watching the humiliating entreaties of the lawyer Huld by the tradesman Block, K. concludes that "the lawyer's methods . . . amounted to this: that the client finally forgot the whole world and lived only in hope of toiling along this false path until the end of his case should come in sight" (242). Joseph K. resorts to the apparently evasive thought that remembering the world in all its sweep and scope will buy him a reprieve, relief from a trying concentration on his case. Similarly ambivalent about our arrest (for certainly fascination is a form of arrest) by this concentrated work of fiction, we readers of Kafka are likely to tease ourselves with the beguiling dream of emerging, through a similar act of remembering what his novel has forgotten or suppressed, from the jurisdiction of *The Trial*.

From Power to Paranoia: An Allegory of Reading

The Trial judges reading a literary text to be a bizarre contest for power, the reader alternately asserting the ultimate power of adjudication of a dispassionate judge and the paranoiac fears of utter powerlessness like those of Joseph K. The relation between reader and text, *The Trial* suggests, is always out of balance.

That the reader should try to lay claim to ultimate power over the "disposition" of the text, in the legal, rhetorical, and ordinary senses of that word, should not surprise us. (*Dispositio* is a rhetorical term designating the arrangement of arguments; it is the second of the five traditional parts of rhetoric.) Toward the beginning of *Le Père Goriot*, Balzac voices the novelist's inherent mistrust of the reader, whom he implicitly compares unfavorably to the more engaged (and presumably powerless and less judgmental) spectator of drama. "The chariot of civilization, like the chariot of Juggernaut," Balzac hyperbolically asserts (in his prose style resembling the heart-crushing chariot of Juggernaut), "is scarcely halted by a heart less easily crushed than the others in its path. It soon breaks this hindrance to its wheel and continues its triumphant course. And you will show the same insensibility, as you hold this book in your white hand, lying back in a softly cushioned armchair, and saying to yourself, 'Perhaps this one is amusing.' "[3] Unlike the spectator in a theatre, the reader of fiction holds absolute power over the disposition of the text. The disposition of the text also lies in the reader's hands in another sense: the pressures that an interpretive or second-level discourse brings to bear on a text are certainly great enough to change its disposition entirely—to alter it from tragedy to farce, for example. Unless, of course, the text itself forestalls any judgment we try to make about its disposition. K. himself doesn't know the disposition of his own case in this sense: "If this was a comedy he would insist on playing it to the end" (8). Similarly, the reader's power over the disposition of the text is limited when, as is the case with *The Trial*, the reader cannot identify the apparent disposition of the text—either the temperament of the work or the proper arrangement of its chapters, which has long been contested by scholars.

In a certain sense the work of literature is the most vulnerable of discourses. Of course, it is highly susceptible to adjudication by the reader, unlike ordinary and more practical forms of discourse— that is, those with the more limited aim of transmitting information— which we do not generally approach in the manner of a judge. In addition, the literary text, like Joseph K. and any target of litigation, stands in need of representation. In moments of self-confidence and frustration with his lawyer, Joseph K. vows he will represent himself before the Court, even as others try to convince him of the folly and futility of doing so. His decision seems an allegory of the literary work in the modernist period, whose hermeticism amounts to an assertion of independence from the court of public opinion and a claim to be able to serve as its own representative. But it is the modernist work that, precisely because of its avowed self-sufficiency, stands most in need of representation by counsel or critic. Like Joseph K., the modernist work slides easily from arrogance to neediness.

The role of the reader is always double and, arguably, triple. For convenience we might call the reader in his or her more active role a "critic" and reserve "reader" to designate the more passive aspect of the act of reading fiction, in which judgments of the truth or falsity of what we are reading are suspended. Dividing still further, the critic—the reader in his or her sterner aspect—doubles as lawyer or counsel (undertaking the work of representation or interpretation) and judge (fulfilling the tasks of evaluating and of passing sentence on other critics). *The Trial* shows that there is little or no continuity among these three roles. Reading fiction, the allegory of *The Trial* suggests, is a schizophrenic activity in which we may too easily careen from fantasies of power to paranoia and back again.

Deleuze and Guattari, enacting the more imposing of the three roles, adopt the juridical terminology of the novel in passing stern judgment on those critics who set too much store by the order in which Max Brod arranged (or "disposed") the chapters: ". . .The texts in *The Trial* should be used only with great care. The primary problem has involved misjudging the relative importance of these texts and making unwarranted assumptions about their placement in the novel, as is especially evident in the ways that Max Brod arranged things to support his thesis of negative theology."[4] Such confident adoption of the vocabulary or "juris-diction" of the novel is reminiscent of Joseph K. in his more unselfcritical and injudicious moments. For the novel paradoxically implies that the judicial vocabulary and habits of thought are perhaps the least judicious of those available to us. One of the primary objections that Deleuze and Guattari raise has to do with the undue importance that is usually attached to the penultimate chapter (in Brod's arrangement or disposition), "In the Cathedral." Certainly it was injudicious of them not to mention that in casting that chapter as a key witness, Brod, who it is true has been followed by most subsequent critics in this regard, was himself following Joseph K. Remarks K. to the priest in the cathedral, "I have more trust in you than in any of the others" (267).

The vocabulary of the Court, which in the brief passage I have cited insinuates itself into the discourse of two of the more astute critics of Kafka, also invades the discourse of the narrator and of Joseph K. K. is thereby admitted to the bar and seated on the bench without realizing it. Shortly after his arrest, he is already posing as judge, speaking of "the justice or injustice" of the behavior of the warders and the Inspector (19). A few pages later, his confidence in his own judgment presumably shaken, K. seeks the supplementary "judgment of a sensible woman," Frau Grubach (27). Characters in the novel continually prejudge one another and their actions, whether in a benevolent way (Frau Grubach's presumption that K. must be innocent, even though she knows nothing of the charges) or a sinister one. (K. is quick to judge the warders, whom he characterizes as "coarse" and as "degenerate ruffians" [54]; Block, whom he dismisses as a "petty tradesman" [213]; and his uncle, who is "visibly prejudiced" against Leni [125]. There is almost no one in *The Trial* who is not prejudged by someone else. There are countless judges and numerous courts in *The Trial*, including the court of public opinion, which threatens to censor, K. believes, Fräulein Bürstner's behavior with him (37). The haste with which K. frequently acts is another form his injudiciousness takes. He rushes to the first interrogation "without taking the time to think or co-ordinate the plans which he had drawn up during the week" (42), and he later perceives his rushing off to Titorelli as similarly rash. K. jumps to many conclusions about the Court, which is therefore the victim of many prejudgments itself, about others, and about the doorkeeper in the priest's parable. Of the latter the priest says, "Many aver that the story confers no right on anyone to pass judgment on the doorkeeper" (276), suggesting that it is no longer a unitary author but something like the Court's bewilderingly complex structures of authority to which we must apply and mandarin procedures of authorization that we as interpreters must follow. He decides that the lawyer's claim that "all proceedings were still in their early stages" was "obviously well calculated to lull the accused and keep him in a helpless state" (157). The strength of his convictions, measured by words such as *obviously* and *inevitable* ("the conclusion was inevitable that the case must be withdrawn from Dr. Huld as soon as possible" [159]), itself indicates a judgmental and injudicious mind. In fact, K. may be on trial for precisely his tendency to try others, his proneness to usurp the position of judge and the indiscretions he is guilty of committing in that role. But to assume that we can avoid such prejudgments and purge our own discourse of judicial indiscretions of the kind K. repeatedly commits is to forget that any apparently neutral description, as well as the simplest cognitive act, is already shot through and through with judgments.

The novel demonstrates that it is not possible to live "outside the jurisdiction of the Court" because juridical diction is everywhere. In everyday speech, there are countless trials going on and judgments being passed down. The hasty judgments characters pass on one another reflect one propensity of the reader of fiction, who like

Joseph K. is used to forming a judgment about a character on very short acquaintance. And among the countless judgments we are called upon to make in the course of reading and interpreting anything as complex as a work of fiction, a multitude of them are bound to be prejudgments, or rash judgments, in the manner of Joseph K.'s.

Just as the reader has a more passive role to perform than the roles of solicitor and judge, so does the literary text sometimes appear to us to be like the powerful and mysterious Court of Kafka's novel. Kafka's novel reminds us of the ancient and close association between literature and the law.[5] The dark side of the resounding sentence with which Shelley closes his *Defence of Poetry*, "Poets are the unacknowledged legislators of the World,"[6] is explored in *The Trial*, which is a parable of the text not as a legislative body but as a court. And it is a court of a peculiar kind, in many ways disarmingly like the court of Kafka's fiction.

The structures of authority presiding over a literary work are no less elusive, no less difficult to arrange a confrontation with, than those that inform Kafka's bizarre parables about authority. The Court that has summoned Joseph K. to appear before it at some endlessly deferred date may be among other things a grotesque caricature of the fictional text. A literary text might be defined as one that defers a direct confrontation with the elusive and invisible structures of authority that preside over it. More practical and everyday forms of discourse, in contrast, do not hide their juridical apparatus in the secret attics of outlying suburbs—even though on closer examination those lower courts of practical discourse may turn out to be kangaroo courts. A literary text, unlike more ordinary forms of discourse, never tacitly says, "By the authority vested in me. . . ." Rather, it leaves the sources of its claims to authority behind, concealed in, and beyond the stifling attics from which literature proverbially is disseminated— those same attics in which, according to *The Trial*, that ominous "other" system of justice that dogs Joseph K. has its offices.

We are now used to the defense that literature is a form of discourse that puts all claims to authority into question, that it is language interrogating, and perhaps relinquishing, its own claims to authority, which usually (outside of literature) go unexamined. Joseph K.'s hope of living outside the jurisdiction of the mysterious Court altogether, then, might be fulfilled in the very medium of literature with which the reader of *The Trial* is engaged. That is an all-too-optimistic view, it seems to me, that overlooks the enormous pres-tige—and authority—that we have granted to the author since the romantic period and our modern tendency to revere literature as if it were a Supreme Court. The forms of criticism that locate the authorizing structures of literature not in the author but in some extraliterary domain—economic structures, class conflict, the family romance investigated by Freud, the history of ideas—do not bypass but merely displace questions of authority in the study of literature. To bypass or supersede them is no more plausible than K.'s dream of living beyond the jurisdiction of the Court. "What authority could they represent?" K. muses about the men who arrest him (7). A few pages later he poses the question openly to Franz, Willem, and the Inspector: "What authority is conducting these proceedings?" (16). These are questions that are just as apt to be posed by the reader to the literary text, and their answers will be as elusive as those Joseph K. seeks.

The prevailing twentieth-century view that the author is not powerful enough to "authorize" the literary text seems affirmed by Kafka's parable of the Court in two ways. First, its principal character—an author-surrogate, as critics have noted time and again,[7] in addition to a reader-surrogate—cannot, in spite of urgings by other characters to do so, serve as his own source of authority or the legitimating agency for his own judgments.[8] Second, the novel constantly defers that author-surrogate's quest for a confrontation with the higher or supreme authorities. Only the lower ones seem to work in the attics in which authors, in the tradition of nineteenth- and twentieth-century bohemianism, habitually dwell. The author is at best a minor official of the Court.

In addition, our contemporary view is that traveling to what seems to be extraliterary terrain entails crossing neither a border nor the boundaries of fiction, since that terrain is arbitrarily constructed, or constructed like a language (e.g., Lacan's unconscious); Kafka's intimation that everything and everyone belongs to the Court seems to anticipate this view, which presides over our critical thought today. Everything belongs to the Court, or to use a more contemporary formula, "There is nothing outside the text."[9] If we take the infinite extension of the Court's apparatus as an allegory of language, then it is a view of language that, against the mainstream of modernism, refuses to acknowledge a decisive break between literary and practical uses of language and refuses, above all, to regard literature simply as the most scrupulous and liberal form of discourse, one that consistently challenges and questions (without, however, reenacting) those claims to authority made by practical forms of discourse. In addition, if discourse is coextensive with the Court's apparatus in *The Trial*, then all language is engaged in a quest for an always endlessly deferred confrontation with the higher authorities that would validate our claims to speak with authority. Hence, neither we readers nor Joseph K. can simply ignore or relinquish our respective trials. Every reader, writer, and interlocutor is a Joseph K.

From a certain perspective literature is the most tentative of discourses, forsaking the assertive element, the prerogative to assert propositions with truth claims, that is natural to nonliterary discourses. Yet literature often impresses us as more *impositional* than other discourses for precisely the same reason. It is a discourse that is arguably immune from, or at least resistant to, procedures of veri- fication and falsification—that is, ordinary courtroom procedures of calling witnesses and presenting evidence. Literature, then, may be the most arbitrary of juridical apparatuses, like the Court in *The Trial* that doesn't bother to confront the accused with a specific charge.

Furthermore, the reader of literature, like Joseph K., has an ambivalent attitude toward the authority that both pursues and eludes him. Although we sometimes like to resist the enchantments of a discourse that disables our powers to falsify it or show it to be false (and therefore our powers of resistance), we often want literature, and by extension language in general, to carry more authority and weight than they are capable of bearing. Literature may represent not that form of discourse that foregoes customary claims to authority, but rather the promise of a more authoritative discourse. Sometimes literature succeeds in persuading us that it possesses such authority. To invoke the parable of Kafka's other great unfinished novel, lit- erature makes us feel that we are in the shadow of a great castle, whose incomparably wise authorities residing in the most distant chambers are nearly impossible to confront directly. And like Kafka's castle and court, literature always grants us the *illusion* of freedom, the reassuring sense that we are free to go (simply by closing or finishing the book) at any time. Yet like Kafka's protagonists, we are strangely attracted to those imposing structures of *auctoritas*, of au- thorship and authority, because if we simply depart their looming presence it guarantees us nothing but reduction to silence (life without *parole*) or sacrifice of the hope of finding a meaning for our lives.

Literature, then, is an adjudicative pursuit, which never makes clear who is authorized to do the adjudicating, the reader, author, text, or structures beyond the text; it is a pursuit like Joseph K.'s, it never becomes clear who is pursuing, and who pursued. There is nothing that is more like Joseph K.'s pursuit of and by the Court than the pursuit of reading. The suspense we experience when we read is in large part our suspense between power and paranoia. As a parable of the act of reading, *The Trial* shows that an asymmetry or imbalance of power is truly native to it.

Surprise and Prejudice

We all know, and most of us deplore, people who in life thrive on complications and who instinctively manufacture them when they don't already exist. However sensible we think we are in life, all of us become irrational people when we read narrative fiction, although, as the criticism of the first half of this century stressed, literature makes a pitch toward the law-and-order side of our personalities (eager for the order, even of the simulated or dissimulated kind that eludes us in life). Literature also makes an appeal to the side of us that thrives on entanglements, and there may be good reasons for the irrational behavior that all readers exhibit. Not unexpectedly, without complications there can be no surprise. Joseph K. has made a habit of resisting surprise. His life at the bank—the antitype of traditional narrative—proceeds with mechanical regularity. Asked by the Inspector immediately following his arrest if he has been surprised by the morning's events, he responds, "Certainly, I am surprised, but I am by no means very much surprised" (15). Asked for a clarification, K. proceeds, "I mean that I am very much surprised, of course, but when one has lived for thirty years in this world and had to fight one's way through it, as I have had to do, one becomes hardened to surprises and doesn't take them too seriously" (15–16). It is as though this fictive court, or perhaps court of fiction, is trying K. for his resistance to surprise. Perhaps it is fiction that is trying through a kind of shock therapy to reawaken in Joseph K. the capacity for surprise and thereby certify him as a reader. Even his own body helps conspire to release him from the bonds of regularity and predictability. Emerging from the stifling air of the law offices, his body experiences a sudden burst of energy and buoyancy, and "he became almost afraid of his own reaction. His usually sound constitution had never provided him with such surprises before" (90).

In his attitude toward surprise, Joseph K., who I have been arguing is above all a figure for the reader, appears more like anti-reader, since readers usually anticipate with pleasure the ample surprises in store for them. But shortly after the arena of his personal life has been complicated by the arrest, Joseph K., seemingly in spite of himself, expresses the sentiments of the reader of *The Trial* and indeed of any reader of fiction with respect to surprise: "In the Bank, for instance, I am always prepared, nothing of that kind could possibly happen to me there, I have my own attendant, the general telephone and the office telephone stand before me on my desk, people keep coming in to see me, clients and clerks, and above all, my mind is always on my work and so kept on the alert, it would be an actual pleasure to me if a situation like that cropped up in the Bank" (26–27). At the first interrogation, however, K. misjudges the audience's relative estimation of order and disorder, assuming as he does that the spectators in the gallery (and by extension the readers of Kafka's narrative) share his aversion to surprise and complication. When the proceedings are interrupted by the shrieks of the washerwoman, "whom K. had recognized as a potential cause for disturbance from the moment of her entrance," "K.'s first impulse was to rush across the room, he naturally imagined that everybody would be anxious to have order restored and the offending couple at least ejected from the meeting, but the first rows of the audience remained quite impassive, no one stirred and no one would let them through" (58–59). The audience at the proceedings seems to be a reflection of all of us readers who remain impassively seated while scenes of crisis and disorder erupt before us, not in the least outwardly perturbed by the disruptions, in part because we fully anticipated them. They were, in fact, half the reason we came.

Surprise bears an especially intimate relation with prejudice or prejudgment, which I have argued is a particularly common and injudicious form of law that nearly everyone practices in *The Trial.* When we are surprised, our prejudgments or expectations are proven wrong. So one might say that surprise and prejudice are antithetical and mutually exclusive values. We might judge surprise—the reader of literature's habitual delight in surprise—to be a sign of our (relative) immunity to prejudice except that one who makes no prejudgments or has no prejudices and no preconceived notions of what will be the case cannot be surprised. The reading of narrative, which has built into it a pleasure in being surprised, may then be necessarily founded on a bedrock of prejudgment. Although it is tempting to look down upon K. for his tendency to prejudge persons and events and to make hasty judgments, it is almost certain, and by this point certainly no surprise, that Kafka is therein showing the reader his or her own reflection.

Joubert's Paradise of Memory

Narration of a novelistic sort, telling the story of one's life, at one point strikes K. as a far more satisfactory mode of defense than representation by a lawyer. He contemplates writing a defense that he would subsequently hand over to the Court: "In this defense he would give a short account of his life, and when he came to an event of any importance explain for what reasons he had acted as he did, intimate whether he approved or condemned his way of action in retrospect, and adduce grounds for the condemnation or approval" (142). A written defense startlingly combines the roles of defendant, witness, lawyer, and judge. A narrative prejudges the case in at least two ways: most obviously, by voicing either approval or condemnation of the actions it recounts, but also, because this would be a short and therefore highly selective account of his life, by making judgments as to which events should be included and which events are "of any importance." A little later, K. will imagine a different kind of narrative, one that is not in the least selective and that will eliminate the role of judge, now limiting himself to the roles of accused, witness, and counsel: "to meet an unknown accusation, not to mention other possible charges arising out of it, the whole of one's life would have to be recalled to mind, down to the smallest actions and accidents, clearly formulated and examined from every angle" (161). This second, nonselective form of narrative strikes K. as the dreariest, not to mention most hopeless and interminable, task imaginable. "And besides how dreary such a task would be! It would do well enough, perhaps, as an occupation for one's second childhood in years of retirement, when the long days needed filling up. But now, when K. should be devoting his mind entirely to work, when every hour was hurried and crowded—for he was still in full career and rapidly becoming a rival even to the Assistant Manager—when his evenings and nights were all too short for the pleasures of a bachelor's life, this was the time when he must sit down to such a task!" (161).

Besides containing several barbed asides to the reader (whose implicit leisure looks bad in comparison with the hurried pace and crowded schedule of the ambitious Joseph K.'s life), this passage also expresses a weariness toward and misgivings about the very ambitions of the genre of the novel. In contrast, a notebook entry by Joseph Joubert, written toward the beginning of what might be characterized as the era of the novel (1798), might serve well—as well as Proust's *A la recherche du temps perdu*—as an explanation and justification of the novelistic project.

> *This life: the cradle of our existence*—What do they matter then— sickness, time, old age, death—which are merely the various degrees of a metamorphosis that perhaps only begins here on earth. Alas! these clarities escape us! and this is one of the insurmountable fatalities of our present lot. I would like to be able to remember, however, in that far-distant future, all the fugitive moments of my present life which by then will have been in the eternal past for such a long time. The ones who will be happiest are those who will not have a single moment from their lives that cannot be represented directly and with pleasure in memory—There as here our memories (which will be sharp) will make up the better part of what is good and bad in us. This very moment that I am speaking to you, this moment in which I am saying this, will be repeated forever. Man lets time get lost, but there are no lost moments.[10]

Paradise is imagined as a perfect memory that is able to gather all previously fugitive moments so that none will be lost. The first part of the entry, imagining that earthly "sickness, time, old age, and death" are merely the beginning stages of an extended process of metamorphosis that continues after death, reveals a narrative pleasure in continual development or change. The last part of the quotation reveals why such perpetual motion is not threatening to the narrative sensibility. The perpetual motion machine that every narrative aspires to be affords an obvious pleasure in the continual variety produced by change. But it seems that narrative can afford to buy such pleasure only because it reverses, even as it recounts, the effects of change. Narrating is a form of remembering or repetition that undoes the "various degrees of a" protracted metamorphosis.

Joubert's is a remarkable revision of the Christian myth because it regards the afterlife as one in which time and change will continue (presumably to ensure the production of new material for the memory, that master storyteller, to work on), but in which all such change is reversible through memory, a form of repetition that undoes the sequentiality of events. It also apparently foregoes the Christian element of judgment, the *sorting out* of "what is good and bad in us," an element that K.'s hypothetical second narrative cannot forego precisely because it cannot forego the element of interpretation (events must be "examined from every angle"), a necessary supplement to the recounting of events that always entails the handing down of judgments. Kafka's novel shows all interpretation to be a variation on the law, and every interpreter a judge. Every moment of a life, therefore, is not merely "fugitive," as in Joubert's account, but a fugitive from justice, from the complicated (and probably injudicious) system of justice that every interpretive method entails. Memory does not serve in *The Trial* as it does in Joubert's notebook entry as the superintending and powerful agent that can undo all change and swim easily against the current of history. In Kafka's account, memory is demoted to a minor official of the court, hemmed in by an elaborate juridico-interpretive apparatus that regards the retrieval of fugitive moments as a mere secretarial task.

K.'s reflection on the dreariness of a nonselective narrative of his own life seems an ironic echo of Joubert's fantasy, an echo from an age that has lost confidence in the reconstitutive powers of narrative. In addition, Joseph K.'s narrative is after a recuperation of a different kind, not of events vividly recounted and repossessed, but of their meaning. The most telling difference between the two passages is the importance that the Kafka passage grants to the need for interpretation. K. must not only "clearly formulate" "the smallest actions and incidents" but also examine them "from every angle." Joubert, in contrast, implies that the distinct representation of past incidents will suffice. These two plans for recuperating the past appear in Joseph K.'s account to be mutually exclusive or antithetical. The clarity and distinctness of the narrative, which for Joubert is the very point or aim of remembering and the source of its redemptive power, may be undone by the need to submit stories to interpretation, "to survey all the conclusions arising from the story" (277). The stress on the necessity of interpretation in *The Trial* projects doubts about the real clarity of the apparently uninterpreted story, doubts about the presentational power of narrative on which Joubert's fantasy of memory as an instrument of redemption is based. Like that of Kafka's parables and paradoxes, the clarity of *The Trial* is misleading and beguiling. Otherwise the narrative would not need the pressure of an interpretive act to persuade it to yield up a meaning. Furthermore, the promise of greater clarity held out by the act of interpretation proves as illusory as the original story's clarity. When K. tries to interpret the parable of the doorkeeper with the prison chaplain, "the simple story" loses "its clear outline," causing K. to want "to put it out of his mind" (277).

Needless to say, the prospectus by Kafka raises questions of judiciousness that Joubert's does not. Surveying events from every possible point of view as the priest recommends seems so hopeless a prospect that a judicious reading may be the greatest fiction of all, as improbable a story as the termination of Joseph K.'s trial.

Cases and Casements

I should like the window to open onto the Lake of Geneva—and there I'd sit and read all day like the picture of somebody reading.
—JOHN KEATS, *letter to Fanny Keats*[11]

In his essay "The Open Window and the Storm-Tossed Boat," art historian Lorenz Eitner identifies the pure window view, or view through a single open window, as a romantic invention. The window in romantic painting (most memorably the works of Caspar David Friedrich) is usually expressive of longing and acts as a threshold between ordinary experience and an intensified or more imaginative state of awareness.[12] It is also an instance of one of the governing metaphors of romantic literature, the spatial metaphor of inside/ outside. It is a metaphor by which the romantics characterized not only the relation between self and world but also those between text and world (the text being conceived for the first time as an organism with its own "inner" defining criteria and organization) and reader and text. Among the major English romantic poets, the window is favored most heavily by Keats (who employs it in "Ode to Psyche," "Ode to a Nightingale," and "Eve of St. Agnes," among other texts), and it is a dominant image in Emily Brontë's *Wuthering Heights*.

It would be possible to show that many modern painters and authors adopt what is primarily a romantic image, that of the window, to discredit many of the distinctions that windows in romantic painting and literature express and support. In the first part of *To the Light-house*, "The Window," Woolf's development of the image of the window points toward the erosion in modern fiction of the difference between ordinary consciousness and the heightened state of awareness the romantics called imagination and toward the questioning of romantic conceptions of the self and of consciousness based on metaphorical distinctions between inside and outside. Except to the children James and Cam, the window that is so pervasive a presence throughout the first section of *To the Lighthouse* fails to suggest the anticipated distinctions between the near, familiar, and quotidian on the one hand and the distant, strange, and exotic on the other, between perception and imagination.

Woolf's modernist variations on a romantic motif resemble those of Matisse, who in his paintings of open windows subverts our expectation that the window will act as a threshold between two spaces or worlds by eliminating distance and moving the view outside the window into the same plane as the objects in his interiors. During a radio interview in 1942, Matisse was asked, "Where does the charm of your paintings of open windows come from?" The painter responded, "Probably from the fact that for me the space is one unity from the horizon right to the interior of my work room, and that the boat which is going past exists in the same space as the familiar objects around me; and the wall with the window does not create two different worlds."[13]

In romantic painting, the window frame within the composition functions as a second-order frame: It suggests a second discontinuity (duplicating that between beholder and painting) of the beholder from the world beyond the window that is itself beyond the world enclosed by the picture frame. Those discontinuities posited by windows in romantic painting are reassuring, helping to establish differences (e.g., between the quotidian and the strange, between perception and imagination, or between a representation and a world to which it makes reference) that ultimately ensure their mediation. Such mediation cannot take place when the differences themselves are blurred, as in certain poems by Keats that feature images of the window and in *The Trial*.

In romantic painting the pictured window frame imitates the function of the picture frame, thereby providing us with a means of "reading" the picture frame; in most modern paintings that have views through windows, this duplication of the frame within the composition serves to undo rather than to reinforce the function of the frame. Windows in most modern paintings point to the frame's failure to suggest the transparency of the surface of the canvas, the fiction on which western painting since the Renaissance has been founded.[14] Not that modern painting divests itself of the illusions conjured by windows in romantic painting. Even though windows in modern painting signal a rejection of the distinctions fixed or stabilized by romantic windows, the aim of windows in romantic and modern painting seems to me substantially the same. In both cases the window is instrumental in the pursuit of an elusive self-reflexiveness, one that will guarantee to the modern painter no less than the romantic one a transparency of the work to itself. The window is an attempt on the part of the painting or text to account for itself; it is a bid for self-possession based on self-reference and self-description. In romantic painting the locus of the self-reflexive act summoned by the window is the beholder, whose surrogate usually stands or sits by the window represented in the composition. (Alternately, one might postulate that the romantic figure by the window stands for both author and beholder and thereby helps to accomplish an identification similar to that between author and reader fostered by most romantic poetry.) Far fewer modern paintings featuring windows, including those of Matisse, place a surrogate beholder by the window, and so in modern painting it is perhaps the painting that must be designated as the site of the self-reflexiveness mirrored by the window. One of the first (and only) things we learn about most rooms and passageways in Kafka's novel is whether or not they have windows and how many windows they contain. Taken together, the various windows in *The Trial* mark a rejection of the hope that the literary text's self-reflexiveness—its attempt to include a description of and thereby to account for its own procedures—will issue in a transparency of the text to itself.

Kafka's windows, like Woolf's, dirty or obscure most of the differences established by windows in romantic painting. In both *To the Lighthouse* and *The Trial*, windows are suggestive of the constantly readjusted act of framing that all writing and reading entail (hence the constant shifting of narrators in much modern fiction), and so in modern literature they help put into question the difference between the acts of writing and reading, between the so-called creative and interpretive acts. They are an emblem of certain distinctions that the text will interrogate, even put on trial; for example, the distinction between interiority (the reader's; the text's; Joseph K.'s) and exteriority—that founding fiction of so much of our thought—and the fiction on which the very notion of literariness depends.

Windows also suggest the framing or interpretation of that framing as a frameup, like the one that opens the novel: "Someone must have traduced Joseph K., for without having done anything wrong he was arrested one fine morning" (3). That "someone," whoever else it may be, is in a sense none other than the novelist, who has slandered K. simply by choosing to write a novel about his arrest and trial and who has framed his fiction (at one end) with the account of K.'s arrest. The novelist's framing of Joseph K. will continue throughout the fiction; the particular glimpses he gives us of K. and the ways in which he chooses to frame those episodes will help (pre)determine our responses to them. In *The Trial* the window suggests the framing that every interpretive act accomplishes (again, including so-called descriptions among interpretive acts) and the frameup that every such act entails. And the reader, like the author, cannot refrain from framing K., so we will inevitably come to resemble the criminal more than an impartial judge.

Just as the implicit trope of the surface of the canvas as a window frame in Renaissance painting supports the newly discovered art of perspective, windows in *The Trial* are closely affiliated with shifting perspective and point of view. In *The Trial* the figure of the window that constantly dogs our reading reminds us of K.'s difficulty gaining a perspective or retaining his sense of perspective, a difficulty that the reader shares as well. The act of framing is necessary to put things in perspective. But if every choice of frame is to some extent arbitrary, then every framing, every such grasping at intelligibility, may produce a framing in another sense, the slanderous sort with which the novel begins. Interpretation and slander, interpretation and prejudgment—these, I submit, are codefendants in Kafka's *Trial*.

Windows in *The Trial* are associated with both reading and storytelling and are one of many devices in the novel that tend to erase the boundary between those two activities. K. gazes out of the window in his uncle's car, for instance, while relating his story. On entering Frau Grubach's living room on the morning of his arrest, K. discovers "a man who was sitting at the open window reading a book, from which he now glanced up" (5). He snaps at K., "You should have stayed in your room! Didn't Franz tell you that?" (5). The reader's mind, which has no doubt by this time wandered out of the room in which he or she reads, is brought up short. Could the author be chiding us for reading *The Trial* and thereby leaving our rooms, the rooms in which we read, and forgetting our affairs? K. will be charged with the latter offense more than once. "I can at least give you a piece of advice," the Inspector says to K. "Think less about us and of what is going to happen to you, think more about yourself instead" (17). The remark is bound to make the reader feel like one of the guilty, or at least one of the accused.

Through the windows in *The Trial* we may catch a glimpse of narration in two of its aspects. They are associated with shifts in point of view, or (judicious) attempts to see or put things in perspective as well as (injudicious) claims to omniscience such as when K. prides himself on having far better working quarters than those of the "pauperized" law courts, for he "had a large room in the Bank with a waiting-room attached to it and could watch the busy life of the city through his enormous plate-glass window" (75). Windows suggesting more judicious claims to knowledge include the window by which K. stands after the manufacturer's aborted interview with him and at which he recovers his composure (165–66). Needing "to view the position as clearly as the moment allowed," K. decides to open the window, which he does with great difficulty, but through the great window comes only "a blend of fog and smoke" (168). Imagining the two creatures across the way gazing at him through their window apparently helps K. suddenly achieve an uncharacteristic flexibility in his point of view. "K. was surprised, at least he was surprised considering the warders' point of view, that they had sent him to his room and left him alone there, where he had abundant opportunities to take his life. Though at the same time he also asked himself, looking at it from his own point of view, what possible ground he could have to do so" (12).

Upon being informed of his arrest by the two warders, "K. felt he must sit down, but now he saw that there was no seat in the whole room except the chair beside the window," recently vacated by the warder Willem, the reader at the open window (6). K. neither advances toward that chair nor considers sitting down in it, perhaps because he is afraid to challenge the authority of his warders; or perhaps it is because that chair, recently vacated, is reserved for you or me, the reader. K. himself cannot successfully become the reader of his own life, which would be asserted tacitly by claiming that seat at the open window. Whether we can claim that seat is another matter. Perhaps it does not matter, as the window begins to take on more sinister associations with frameups, with the reader's countless injudicious acts rather than with an impartial perspective or a broad, panoramic vision.

The reader at the window in Kafka's novel differs markedly from the one conjured by Keats in my epigraph: "I should like the window to open onto the Lake of Geneva—and there I'd sit and read all day like the picture of somebody reading." For Keats, imagining himself "the picture of somebody reading" by a window fascinates because it unites in a single reversible image the world, the text, and the reader-critic. As is characteristic of Keats's references to windows, it is not clear through which side of the window we are gazing. In fact, we seem to be on both sides simultaneously—gazing with the reader out of the window and at the reader from the other side of the window that frames him, domesticates him, and allows him to possess himself in the act of reading. The apparent effect of the image is to cast a net around the act of reading or interpretation, countering its dispersive and dilatory effects, as the unexpected ending to the sentence—"like the picture of somebody reading"—suddenly situates us on the other side of the window frame. The reader becomes a picture, framed by a window, to which the picture frame has implicitly compared itself from the Renaissance to early modernism. In Keats's image the tenor and vehicle of this founding metaphor of illusionistic painting are reversed. The window frame poses as a picture frame, rather than the other way around, and that figural picture frame in turn is a figure for the window frame. This reversibility of picture frame and window frame in Keats's imagining of the window promises to mediate a series of oppositions generally based (especially since the romantic period) on the spatial metaphor inside/outside: reader and text, text and world, self and world, all the former terms marking a privileged interiority. These very distinctions are put on trial in Kafka's novel. What windows in *The Trial* might mock, finally, is the transparency and judiciousness of the very distinction between reader and text, a distinction on which *both* the modernist and romantic notions of the work of art, as they are framed in the Titorelli chapter, rest their cases, as I shall try to demonstrate momentarily. *The Trial* denies both the reader's claim to occupy a space ulterior to the text and the text's related claim to autonomy (that is, to being fully constituted prior to the act of reading) or to occupation of a privileged and separate space of representation (set apart from everyday utilitarian discourses). It is the attempt to keep one's distance in the act of reading that is mirrored in Joseph K.'s futile attempts to persuade himself that he has nothing to do with the Court that seems to pursue and envelop him.

The reader's illusion that he or she occupies a space ulterior to the text is reflected in all those acts of voyeurism in *The Trial*, including the girls peering through the cracks of Titorelli's door and the "pair of eyes" that appears "at the peephole in the lawyer's door" (208). Looking out his window on the first page of the novel, peering through that ancient figure for artful framing of the kind that produces meaning or instills order, Joseph K. finds his gaze met by the reader; that is, "the old lady opposite, who seemed to be peering at him with a curiosity unusual even for her" (3–4) and who is arguably the first of many figures of the reader in Kafka's novel. A couple of pages later, both K. and the old woman have shifted rooms and perspective. K. now sees her from the livingroom window, while she, "with truly senile inquisitiveness had moved along to the window exactly opposite, in order to go on seeing all that could be seen" (5). Before the chapter ends, she is joined first by "an even older man" (11), then by a tall "man with a shirt open at the neck and a reddish, pointed beard, which he kept pinching and twisting with his fingers" (15). Scolded by K., who shouts across to them, "Go away," "they did not remove themselves altogether, but seemed to be waiting for the chance to return to the window again unobserved" (18). Reflections of the voyeuristic reader, this trio resembles several other characters who will become troubled when the omnipotence and detachment of their gaze are challenged by the gaze of another. When K. notices the elderly Chief Clerk of the Court sitting in a dark corner of Huld's sickroom, the Clerk is "obviously displeased to have his presence made known" and makes gestures that probably signify that "he only wanted to be transported again to the darkness where his presence might be forgotten. But that privilege could no longer be his" (130). It is a privilege often taken for granted by the reader of fiction, but Kafka has long since withdrawn it from his reader. Functioning this time as author-surrogate, Joseph K. deprives another reader-surrogate, the Chief Clerk of the Court, of the privilege of not being seen or of not having his gaze returned, just as Franz Kafka has done for the reader on so many occasions.

We readers are, according to the novel, potentially deceitful and treacherous, like the red-haired man, as well as senilely inquisitive like the elderly woman. "His very hair is of the dissembling color"— that is, red like Judas Iscariot's—says that master dissembler Rosalind of the man she is enraptured by in *As You Like It*. The red-haired man gazing from the window opposite into Joseph K.'s apartment is analogous in certain ways to author and reader—both capable of a Judaslike betrayal like the anonymous (and therefore representative) one to which the opening sentence of the novel refers. The powerful author is always free to frame whomever he or she pleases; rather than amassing evidence, as in a trial, the author plants it and manipulates it, as in a frameup. And the presumedly deceitful and treacherous red-haired man is also a surrogate-reader, who is always figuratively undercover when he or she reads.

Only once in the novel are windows associated with reciprocity and community. In the suburb where the first interrogation is to take place, the "high gray tenements" of Juliusstrasse inhabited by poor people, windows become much more benign than they were in the preceding chapter on K.'s arrest, where they become associated with the extremes of power and powerlessness (as an instance of the latter, K. becomes a "spectacle" for the trio opposite his window). In Juliusstrasse, windows become an equalizing force: "This being Sunday morning, most of the windows were occupied, men in shirtsleeves were leaning there smoking or holding small children cautiously and tenderly on the window-ledges. Other windows were piled high with bedding, above which the disheveled head of a woman would appear for a moment. People were shouting to one another across the street" (43). In a courtyard, "a line was stretched between two windows, where washing was already being hung up to dry" (44). As readers, we too are figuratively seated at a window, gazing—pruriently, voyeuristically, or perhaps in the more casual and apparently humane manner of the people of Juliusstrasse—through the frame of Kafka's novel. The reciprocal exchange of glances back and forth across the windows of Juliusstrasse and the symbolic line stretched between two windows represent a suspension of the activity of interpreting or framing so often allegorized by windows in *The Trial*. It is a choice that is never open to the reader. That suspension of framing or reading metaphorized by the people in the windows of Juliusstrasse takes two forms: the listlessness and inactivity of some (tantamount to a suspension of interpretation) and the "shouts" of others, presumably an intensification of language that bypasses the need for interpretation and short-circuits the complicated semiotic relays, motions, remands, judgments, and counterjudgments entailed by the most innocent uses of language. The figurative windows through which readers and texts exchange glances are more like the windows of K.'s experience, fostering inequalities, asymmetries, and imbalances of power rather than parity.

The founding metaphor of the picture frame as a window is behind the multiple references to frames and windows in Titorelli's room. Titorelli's window can't be opened. It's "hermetically sealed" (194), suggesting perhaps that art is claustrophobic and does not allow us the panoramic and sweeping perspective on the world. The new critical and prevailing modernist conception of the work of art as a "well-wrought urn" may easily be interpreted to imply a kind of windowless claustrophobia.

Titorelli's apartment is also the scene of Kafka's framing of a second and equally assailable view of the work of art. The romantic myth of an immediate perception that manages to do without an acculturated or artful or interpretive element is caricatured by Titorelli's pile of unframed heathscapes ("Wild Nature") underneath the painter's bed (203). Their lack of frames simulates an immediacy that bypasses the need of framing (of the sort accomplished by windows or picture frames) to produce intelligibility or meaning. The fallaciousness of this claim that art can do without frames is driven home by K.'s discovery that each painting is an exact replica of the others. "Here's the companion picture," announces Titorelli. The narrator informs us, "It might be intended as a companion picture, but there was not the slightest difference that one could see between it and the other, here were the two trees, here the grass, and there the sunset" (204). When K. decides to humor the painter and agrees to purchase both the original picture and its "companion," Titorelli brings out a third: "But it was not merely another study," the narrator informs us, "it was simply the same wild heathscape again" (204). To abjure framing produces not a giddy immediacy, a wild naturalness, or an "originality" owing to a return to origins ("Wild Nature") but rather a slavish repetition of the same (unframed) scene, an inability to see the same scene from different perspectives, that is, "framed" in different ways.

The Trial distances itself from both the romantic and the modern conceptions of the work of art, neither of which stresses the process of reading as framing. For the New Criticism, the work of art—self-defining, self-constituted, and in some sense "hermetically sealed,"—frames itself. Much of the romantic tradition held that the work of art might be approached only through an act of identification, an ecstatic union with the author or work of art, that abolishes all frames and barriers. Although the modernist conception of the work of art, unlike the romantic one, might stress the need for evaluative judgments, the judicial proceeding it imagines is of a far less complex kind than the one that engulfs Joseph K., for it is one that neglects to place the reader on trial. Generally blind to the implications of its own activity, New Criticism reserved the adjudicative responsibilities and prerogatives for the critic-priest, who in his or her role as mediator of sacred texts is reflected by the prison chaplain "in the cathedral."

Windows and doors are perhaps the two most frequent images in *The Trial*.[15] Doors are associated with structures and relations of authority, windows with cognition. That cognition and judgment are divided between these two often closely associated images suggests the gulf between them, the difficulty of authorizing or legitimizing our acts of cognition, the difficulty of joining knowledge and performance in an authoritative judgment. On the other hand, the close affiliation of these two sets of images, which are constant companions throughout the novel, like the interchangeable pairs of minor characters that keep appearing in Kafka's fiction (two warders, two executioners), suggests another related difficulty. The difficulty is not of uniting them, but of even distinguishing between them (a distinction prior to and necessary for the staging of their ultimate reconciliation). Pure acts of cognition that don't already pass judgments and that are not always already performative are perhaps nowhere to be found. Windows have a way of becoming like doors in *The Trial*—forbidding and almost always associated with relationships of power.

My remarks, no doubt, have been all too cursory. Surely it is a form of critical injudiciousness to shirk the scholarly responsibility of displaying a commanding array of footnotes, our equivalent of calling witnesses to the stand, or to pretend that I have done any sort of justice—even the woolly frontier variety—to Kafka's text, avoiding as I have close interrogation (or cross-examination) of most of its episodes. To appeal to the reader on the grounds that my methods have been heuristic or to submit that this is an opening statement rather than a closing one or to plead that this has been no more than a lawyer's brief for use in conducting my case and not the trial itself wouldn't exonerate me. I could only applaud the judicious spirit of those readers who might be moved to declare a misTrial, make a motion for a reTrial, or appeal to a higher court.

Lest the reader try to negotiate an out-of-court settlement for damages sustained, let me elaborate. Far from trivializing or circumscribing the reader's part, *The Trial* bestows on the reader a sense of election that used to befall epic or tragic heroes and their poets. As the lone auditor in the cathedral, Joseph K. and/or the narrator (as so often in the novel, the distinction of voices is impossible) wonders, "But was there really going to be a sermon? Could K. represent the congregation all by himself?" (261). Every interpretive reading (and certainly in the case of *The Trial* there is no other kind) becomes by the light of Kafka's cathedral an act of heroism that is also criminal, an unwarranted assertion that one can represent the congregation of all readers by oneself. Such an assumption may be the most injudicious a reader can make, and certain brands of reader-response criticism—most notably that of Stanley Fish—have left themselves open to the charge. It is an assumption that K. makes implicitly several times before the chapter "In the Cathedral," where it suddenly takes the explicit form of a dream of representational power, a dream shared by author and reader. In writing a novel, the author claims the power to represent (in the aesthetic sense of the term) the totality of the world; in reading a novel, we implicitly lay claim to the power to represent (in the political sense of the term) the world as well—that is, the set of all possible readers.

One of the more injudicious assumptions that Joseph K. makes throughout the novel (most of us probably make it whenever we read) is that what strikes us as platitude must be either trivial or false, that is, it cannot be persuasive for another reader in other circumstances. Witnessing the humiliating interview between Block and his lawyer, "K. had the feeling that he was listening to a well-rehearsed dialogue which had often been repeated and would be often repeated and only for Block would never lose its novelty" (241). Block seems to be that obtuse reader who has an infinite tolerance for repetition and for whom nothing ever becomes platitude. Musing on the future of his own case should he retain the services of the lawyer Huld, K. reflects, "The same old exhortations would begin again, the same references to the progress of the petition, to the more gracious mood of this or that official, while not forgetting the enormous difficulties that stood in the way—in short, the same stale platitudes would be brought out again either to delude him with vague false hopes or to torment him with equally vague menaces" (235). In assuming with absolute confidence that he knows how to distinguish platitude from nonplatitude, K. is both a hubristic reader who assumes that he can represent the entire congregation and a particularly inept reader-response critic who thinks he knows and practices a form of reading that is not context-bound and context-limited.

We should, however, be cautious of assuming too hastily that we are more judicious in our habits—and theories—of reading than Joseph K. was, that we can avoid his mistakes in judgment. "You have not enough respect for the written word and you are altering the story," says the priest to K. in the course of their interpretations of the parable of the doorkeeper (270). To interpret with absolute respect for the written word, without "altering the story," may be the only judicious form of reading, but it also goes against the nature of reading, which necessarily entails a measure of troping or turning or alteration.

As one of the most probing examinations of the relation of the reader to the literary text, *The Trial* seems to me a corrective for the more naive forms of reader-response criticism, those that trumpet the return of the reader, that formerly disenfranchised member of the literary community, to prominence or even a position of dominance. The more judicious forms of reader-response criticism grant the reader and the experience of reading a privileged position only to show that reading is as vexed an activity as writing. Much of what goes by the name of "reader-response criticism" makes what Roland Barthes in an early piece christened "The Death of the Author"[16] seem far from a somber and funereal affair but rather a cause for rejoicing on the part of his or her presumptive heir, the reader. Most of Derrida's work, for instance, gives a different impression, suggesting it is unwise for the reader even to wish to be mentioned in the author's will, given the rigors of the labors to which he or she will hereafter be condemned.

Above all, *The Trial* shows that questions of authority or *auctoritas* are not displaced by "the death of the author." In fact, Joseph K.'s functioning as both an author-surrogate and a figure of the reader suggests that the novel regards writing and reading to be sometimes indistinguishable activities, the author sharing the adjudicative responsibilities usually regarded as the province of the reader (filing countersuits, placing the reader on trial) and the reader, like Joseph K., alternately searching for and claiming to possess the authority we generally attribute to authors. So much is suggested by Franz Kafka's having divided and dispersed his name between at least two characters: Franz, one of Joseph K.'s two warders in the opening chapter, and Joseph K. That the author should cast himself in the parts of both the accused man and his warder reinforces our impression from the episode in the cathedral, where the priest similarly doubles as story-teller and interpreter. The author is more than simply the warder of the captive reader: He too is a reader on trial.

Notes

1. For a brilliant discussion of the concept of judgment in just these terms, see Barbara Johnson, *The Critical Difference* (Baltimore: Johns Hopkins University Press, 1980), 79–109.

2. Franz Kafka, *Der Prozess* [The Trial], trans. Willa and Edwin Muir, rev. E. M. Butler (New York: Random House, 1964), 8. All citations in text are from this edition.

3. Balzac, *Old Goriot*, trans. Marion Ayton Crawford (Harmondsworth: Penguin Books, 1951), 28. The contrast between narrative fiction and drama is developed throughout the text by a class of drama metaphors.

4. Gilles Deleuze and Félix Guattari, *Kafka: Toward a Minor Literature*, trans. Dana Polan, Theory and History of Literature, vol. 30 (Minneapolis: University of Minnesota Press, 1986), 44.

5. See, for instance, Kathy Eden, *Poetic and Legal Fiction in the Aristotelian Tradition* (Princeton: Princeton University Press, 1986). The commentary on literature's relationship to the law is vast, especially in the area of medieval literature. Exceptional among recent work is R. Howard Bloch, *Medieval French Literature and Law* (Berkeley: University of California Press, 1977).

6. Donald Reiman and Sharon B. Powers, eds, *Shelley's Poetry and Prose* (New York: W. W. Norton, 1977), 508.

7. The fact that Fräulein Bürstner, for instance, has the same initials as Kafka's friend Felice Bauer has been noted repeatedly in the voluminous criticism on the novel that is biographical in nature. The less obvious identification of Joseph K. with the reader has been made by Todd Kontje, "The Reader as Joseph K.," *Germanic Review* 54, no. 2 (1979): 62–66. Kontje focuses primarily on the flux of the narrator's voice between the extremes of omniscience and *erlebte Rede* and on the frustrations and confusions of both reader and Joseph K. as they try to make sense of the trial.

8. For instance: " 'Pay no heed to anyone,' said the lawyer, 'and do what seems right to yourself' " (240).

9. Jacques Derrida, *Of Grammatology*, trans. Gayatri Chakravorty Spivak (Baltimore: Johns Hopkins University Press, 1976), 158.

10. *The Notebooks of Joseph Joubert*, ed. and trans. Paul Auster (San Francisco: North Point Press, 1983), 42.

11. *The Letters of John Keats, 1814–1821*, vol. 2, ed. Hyder Edward Rollins (Cambridge, Mass.: Harvard University Press, 1958), 46.

12. Lorenz Eitner, "The Open Window and the Storm-Tossed Boat: An Essay in the Iconography of Romanticism," *The Art Bulletin* 37 (1955): 281–90. See also Jean Clay, *Romanticism*, trans. Daniel Wheeler and Craig Owen (Secaucus, N.J.: Chartwell Books, 1981), 25f. and 66–67; Hugh Honour, *Romanticism* (New York: Harper and Row, 1979), 107f.

13. Jack D. Flam, *Matisse on Art* (London: Phaidon Press, 1973), 93. See also Pierre Schneider, *Matisse*, trans. Michael Taylor and Bridget Strevens Romer (New York: Rizzoli, 1984), 442–55.

14. See the Renaissance treatise by Leon Battista Alberti, *On Painting*, trans. John R. Spencer (New Haven: Yale University Press, 1966).

15. Pierre Schneider, *Matisse*, notes the companionship of windows and doors in Matisse's paintings as well as Matisse's tendency to favor the hybrid French window, both a window and a door. It would be tempting, though probably injudicious, to try

to extend my suggestion about windows and doors in Kafka to the work of a modern painter. Unfortunately, doors do not seem to have the same association for Matisse as they do for Kafka. Matisse refers to the "mystery" of the partly opened door, but doors for him do not appear to be associated with power and authority of the kinds that Kafka's doors open onto.

16. Roland Barthes, *Critical Essays*, trans. Richard Howard (Evanston: Northwestern University Press, 1972).

"I'm the King of the Castle": Franz Kafka and the Well-Tempered Reader

Deirdre Vincent*

Despite recent claims to the contrary,[1] the literary critic continues to encounter a serious problem as soon as he sets out to address himself to the task of interpreting Kafka's work. The problem is this: how can he avoid engaging in a process of instant falsification if, in seeking merely to sum up the narrative, he inevitably finds himself acting as interpreter? Was Joseph K. really arrested that morning in his bedroom, for example? Any answer to this question is an instant interpretation of the novel as a whole, just as any refusal or failure to answer the question is similarly an act of interpretation. But such a question refuses to go away, and similar questions lie at the heart of every work that Kafka ever wrote. Did Georg Bendemann really have a friend in Petersburg, for example ("The Judgment")? Or was Gregor Samsa really turned into a large insect overnight ("The Metamorphosis")? However naive or sophisticated the response to these questions may be, the fact remains that they must be answered somehow, and any answer the reader-interpreter may give essentially determines his whole understanding and interpretation of the work in hand.

Though it is now well over fifteen years since the literary-critical fraternity began seriously to register the fact of Kafka's "uninterpretability,"[2] the constant tide of secondary material on his works has continued to swell rather than to abate. Kafka's writings have by now been exposed to far more than those "three armies of interpreters" to whom Susan Sontag referred some time ago, meaning Marxist, Freudian and Christian critics.[3] The newer audience-oriented criticism has added to these armies many more: other rhetoricist critics also interested in ideology and message; semioticians and structuralists eager to highlight and expose certain codes and conventions

*Reprinted from *Modern Language Studies* vol. 17, no. 4 (1987) by permission of *Modern Language Studies*, the journal of the Northeast Modern Language Association.

underlying both writing and reading; phenomenologists who see in
the convergence of text and reader the ground for a desired and
desirable recovery of meaning; subjectivist critics who do not flinch
before the notion of reading as an act of mere personal self-replication;
Rezeptionsästhetiker who explore alleged divergence and convergence
between a work and its various publics throughout time; hermeneu-
ticists both 'positive' and 'negative' who respectively believe and
disbelieve the premise that the task of the interpreter is to examine
a given text for its ultimate statement of broad (universal?) validity.[4]
To all of these approaches Kafka's texts have by now been exposed
and yet the enigmatic quality remains intact, the questions remain,
augmented in their importance by the weight of the interpretive
material that continues to accumulate around them. Each work has
at its core the same difficulty, whether it be a lengthy novel or a
tale of a few lines only; it is a difficulty which stems from the fact
that a huge gap exists between narrative and narratee,[5] between the
internal and external happenings of the text. As Iser, among others,
has shown,[6] it is in the nature of the reading act that the existence
of such a gap activates the reader's creativity, stimulating him to
provide his own 'missing' bridges as he strives for a sense of clarity
and synthesis in his dealings with the narrative. That the resulting
bridges are legion in response to Kafka's texts is clear; that they must
be so is perhaps not yet quite as clear as it should be. Taking *The
Castle* as an example, I hope to offer some insight both into the
inevitability of Kafka's enigmatic quality for the critical reader and
also into the inevitability of the endless variety of critical responses
which his writing provokes. I would also like to suggest that Kafka
may perhaps have known all along that we must respond to him as
variously as we do, united though we may be in praise of his work.
We, his critics and interpreters, are treated by him through his
writings in much the same way as the Hunger-Artist treats those
guards who watch him very closely all through the night and are
rewarded in the morning with a sumptuous breakfast for which he
gleefully, even gloatingly, pays the bill.[7] But this will all become
rather clearer as we consider some of the central issues of *The Castle*.

The first question to ask, and one that has not yet been sufficiently
explored, is surely: how does this text manage to force its readers
into a seemingly endless quest for understanding of what seems, on
the face of it, an amazingly dull novel? After all, what is the story?
A young man, using various means, strives to gain access to a village
castle, the (supposed) seat of his (supposed) employer, but repeatedly
fails to do so. Such is in essence the "action" of Kafka's novel.
However, such a summary is clearly inadequate since it suggests a
wholly static narrative, whereas we are strangely aware that this is
somehow a dynamic novel, apparently lacking in progression and

thematic excitement but in reality full of inner movement and tension. It is precisely this movement and tension of which the reader becomes aware and into which he is progressively drawn that must be examined if we are to discover just how and why the text succeeds so well in sustaining his interest in such an ostensibly uninteresting tale.

But exactly where do the movement and tension spring from, if not from the minimal action of the novel itself? Primarily from ourselves, of course, from our relationship with Kafka's material as we read and attempt to digest it, for this material forces upon us the perception of a realm sensed vaguely at intervals by many of us but thoroughly explored by few; it is the realm that exists between the empirical and ideational, between experience and expectation— a disturbing realm in which, metaphorically, the meaning of the traffic lights keeps changing, so that one can never be sure whether green means GO or STOP. Just such a realm is central to all of Kafka's work—the Law in *The Trial*, the Castle in *The Castle*, the concept of the physician in "A Country Doctor," the father in "The Judgment," the officer and the machine in "In the Penal Colony," etc. What these texts do is to lure us into an earnest search for underlying principles of consistency and rationality in a world whose chief characteristics seem to be arbitrariness and illogicality. Apparently bounded by and subject to the physical laws of time and space, and seeming to acknowledge the familiar dictates of cause and effect, this world in Kafka's work nevertheless appears to manifest its own laws, at times reinforcing yet at others wholly defying the rational thought-processes of the reader.

The Castle operates quite openly with three distinct modes of thought, only two of which are made constantly explicit, with the third throwing each of these into relief. The first mode is exemplified by the minor characters, the second by K., and the third by narrator and reader alike. The narrator, however, reveals only occasionally his seemingly objective hold on everyday reality, whereas the reader constantly clings to it in his attempt to make sense of the story as a whole—structurally, semiotically, phenomenologically, semantically, or however he will. I hope to be able to illustrate clearly that neither K.'s thinking nor that of the villagers is fundamentally acceptable to the reader and that the clash of these two modes of thought creates the basis from which he proceeds towards his own particular interpretation, which itself so often tends to be a piece of "littérature engagée" in view of the fact that it is impossible for Kafka's critical reader to remain an impartial observer-consumer. The narrative imposes on him, rather, the role of someone obliged to yield ground repeatedly or to relinquish the act of reading. "Normal" expectations and values are progressively assaulted by implication in the continued reading act, and the result is often an attempt to regain lost ground

by the reader who offers one of the various 'comfortable' interpretations of Kafka's work, e.g., as the record of an earnest theologian
seeking his God, or as the outpourings of a clever neurotic whose
symptoms may be clearly documented.[8] The list of such approaches
is a long one, for at all costs Kafka's readers keep wanting to do to
him what Georg Bendemann of "The Judgment" wants to do to his
father—that is, put him to bed and tuck him in.[9] The fact that we
cannot do so is his triumph over us as writer over critic, his guarantee
of our continuing absorption in him, as we attempt to avoid death
by drowning in the sea of incomprehensibility he has created for us.

But how does *The Castle*, like Kafka's other texts, manage to put
us on the defensive in this way? Adorno is right to talk of the force
with which Kafka's every sentence demands interpretation,[10] but
exactly how and why is this so? To begin with, each protagonist
cleverly embodies values endorsed by society at large, thereby establishing a sense of fellow-feeling in the reader who is gratified by
the seeming coincidence of his own "horizon of expectation" and
that of the central character. In this particular novel, for example,
the reader-interpreter is easily lured into accepting K. as 'his man
in the village' since K., in the goals he establishes early on, seems
quite simply to represent a recognizable Mr. Everyman to whom
approval may readily be granted. All that he wants, it seems, is the
opportunity to work for an employer whose demands he understands
and to whose presence he has access, plus the opportunity to marry
and to settle down. However, as the novel progresses, things change
slowly and imperceptibly for the reader, so that by the end he finds
himself in retrospect having unwittingly endorsed a multitude of
values and beliefs very much at odds with those he once believed
himself to share with K. For, strange though it may seem, the logical
abstractions of *The Castle* would ultimately be as follows:

1. Authoritarian bureaucracy has a salutary dictatorial stranglehold on the
   lives of all.[11]
2. Striving for justice is vain.[12]
3. Moral principles are degenerate.[13]
4. The possibility of human communication is an illusory falsehood.[14]
5. The principle of causality is unfounded.
6. The laws of time and space are highly questionable.

Note, however, the qualitative difference for the reader between
points 1–3 and 4–6. The last three involve the overturning of principles which secure not only his self-image as a reader but also his
capacity to order and cope mentally with the world around him.

Precisely these are the principles that are questioned again and again by and through every Kafka text. A closer look at *The Castle* will serve to illustrate my meaning, though what I have to say is not limited to this one work alone. In *The Castle* the physical world itself is both capable and incapable of objective verification. At times it appears to have an undeniable, verifiable existence, while at others it appears to derive its identity solely from the character and personality of its inhabitants. It seemingly exists at one moment within given boundaries of time and space and at the next within infinity, which presupposes the existence of no such boundaries. Both village and castle are ready examples of this; each reaches into the other without any apparent physical link between the two. Take, for example, the physical entity which is the castle—that castle which is the seat of authority for all, apparently accessible to all but K., yet which does not possess the constant, identifiable properties of a castle. If we consider the description of the castle in the course of the novel, we see that it begins as an edifice that satisfies K.'s expectations: "On the whole this distant prospect of the Castle satisfied K.'s expectations."[15] As K. approaches, however, the appearance of the castle changes, and so too the descriptive tone: ". . . if K. had not known that it was a castle he might have taken it for a little town" (11). Even closer, the description changes to "only a wretched-looking town, a huddle of village houses" (11–12), and finally the castle is relegated in disgust to the position of "so-called castle" (12), though efforts to reach it are never abandoned. Despite the descriptive emotionalism which seems to surround the presentation of the castle and thus to blur its image for the reader, however, it nevertheless appears to have an undeniable physical existence, even though for K. it may be only in the form of a collection of dilapidated houses. But what of this existence? Apparently no road leads to the castle: ". . . it [the street] only made toward it, and then as if deliberately, turned aside, and though it did not lead away from the Castle, it led no nearer to it either" (14). Thus no physical access seems possible. How then do the various castle officials reach the village? How do they return to the castle? When K. is first awakened at the inn and told: "whoever lives here or passes the night here does so, in a manner of speaking, in the Castle itself" (4), perhaps he is being told a lot more than he, and we, as readers of his tale, first suppose. What if both he and we have already arrived at the goal we have set for ourselves? What if the act of reading this text were itself the already achieved goal? What if the act of refusing to stop reading-interpreting were the manifestation of a "neurosis" akin to that which is so often attributed to K. himself? These questions have to be asked because of the evident analogy which can be drawn between K.'s relationship to the castle and that of the reader to the novel. K.

embarks on his attempt to penetrate successfully into the heart of the castle just as the reader embarks on his attempt to establish his own understanding of the novel. Both K. and the reader approach their respective tasks armed with experiences and expectations which they believe to be helpful in achieving their ends, but both are ultimately mistaken. Both fail, yet neither admits to failure. Rather, K.'s demonstrably futile attempts to establish meaningful links with the castle continue into an infinity guaranteed by the fragmentary nature of the novel, while the reader continues in a similar way to produce a steady flow of interpretive material whose ever-elusive goal remains a "satisfactory" penetration of the tale in one way or another.

In addition to the observed lack of convincing physical accessibility in space there is the castle's curious lack of continuous physical existence in time. It seems to have the self-governing capacity to appear and disappear at will: "The Castle above them, which K. had hoped to reach that very day, was already beginning to grow dark and retreated again into the distance" (21). Is this merely a reflection of K.'s fluctuating sense of purpose? Is the castle a physical entity at all? If it is, then why does it not fulfill the minimum requirements for a physical existence, such as having a definable place in space or time? If it is not, then why does it have such an apparently irrefutable presence?

In the proposition "I see it, therefore it is" lies a causal connection supplied by the mind, but what if this connection is eliminated? What if the senses are deemed an unreliable foundation for knowing? In that case every physical existence outside one's own becomes unknowable and one's own existence is only secured by virtue of the thinking self. This is a part of what we absorb from *The Castle*, but it is not merely some odd form of substantiated Cartesianism that we find in Kafka's writings, for the thinking self is presented as equally questionable. Indeed, it is precisely this questionableness which is particularly significant in any examination of the reader's awareness of the disquieting dynamism of Kafka's work.

Each of the three types of thinking self referred to earlier—the minor characters, K., and the reader—has an important contribution to make to the understanding of why we refuse to give up on the task of coming to terms with Kafka's writings but prefer instead, in response to the disturbance they create, to seek out varieties of more or less satisfactory interpretations in personal terms, whatever those interpretations may be or however impersonally they may be presented.

In the minor characters there is a complete harmony between expectation and experience. They seem to represent a settled community without serious friction and with the appearance of some continuing function. However, their identity and function depend to such an extent on the identification of what they expect with what they experience that the one constantly becomes the other. The minor characters have in fact no expectations at all other than that which happens to or around them. Alien in this both to K. and in a lesser degree to the reader (for whom they are "obviously" less important), they manage to ensnare both into the expectation of encountering so-called rational behaviour. What makes them successful is the way in which they present themselves or are presented. In their depiction or self-revelation much weight is given to trivial inessentials while the more weighty essentials are ignored; thus a great deal of extraordinary information is passed without anything reliable ever being said. If we look at the way in which Sortini is characterized, for example—that official who has such an impact on the life of Amalia and her whole family—then we see that emphasis is laid only on one facial feature while nothing of his real function or power is revealed:

> It was on the third of July at a celebration given by the Fire Brigade; the Castle too had contributed to it and provided a new fire-engine. Sortini, who was supposed to have some hand in directing the affairs of the Fire Brigade, but perhaps he was only deputizing for someone else—the officials mostly hide behind one another like that, and so it's difficult to discover what any official is actually responsible for— Sortini took part in the ceremony of handing over the fire-engine. There were of course many other people from the Castle, officials and attendants, and true to his character, Sortini kept well in the background. He's a small, frail, reflective-looking gentleman, and one thing about him struck all the people who noticed him at all, the way his forehead was furrowed; all the furrows—and there were plenty of them, though he's certainly not more than forty— were spread fanwise over his forehead, running toward the root of his nose, I've never seen anything like it. Well then, we had that celebration. (244)

Here we have a splendid example of the so-called "ambiguous" or "dialogical" text characterized by Christine Brooke-Rose as one that "*seems* to overdetermine one code . . . and even to overencode the reader, but in fact the overdetermination functions, paradoxically, as underdetermination. . . ."[16] In other words, information is passed to the reader in excess of that quantity necessary to meet purely informational need (= overdetermination), while that same reader is deprived of information necessary for explaining what he already knows as the narrative line (= underdetermination). The resulting text, as in the excerpt given, is a mechanism for *dis*information while ostensibly operating as one whose chief purpose is to inform.

Another of the many examples of how detail is used to confuse rather than elucidate can be seen in Olga's reflection on her brother's activities in the castle and his access to the highest official:

> He's allowed into an office, but it doesn't seem to be even an office, rather an anteroom of the office, perhaps not even that, perhaps a room where all are kept who may not be in the real offices. He speaks to Klamm, but is it Klamm? Isn't it rather someone who's a little like Klamm? A secretary perhaps, at the most, who resembles Klamm a little and takes pains to increase the resemblance and poses a little in Klamm's sleepy, dreamy style. That side of his nature is the easiest to imitate, there are many who try it, though they have sense enough not to attempt anything more. And a man like Klamm, who is so much sought after and so rarely seen, is apt to take different shapes in people's imagination. (237)

Here the two *facts* we are given—that Barnabas is permitted to enter an official's office and that he actually speaks to Klamm—are rendered so totally questionable by all subsequent reflections that eventually it seems likely, if not certain, that neither of them is valid or reliable.

But reliability itself has a time component, in that it stems from an expectation that what was, *is*, and will be, and just this expectation on the part of K. and the reader is constantly denied fulfilment by the minor characters, for whom nothing is ever exactly the same as it was a moment ago. These people never adhere to any consistent rational thought patterns, which is their ultimate weapon against all "outsiders." Their words can hold meaning fleetingly but cannot offer the material with which to form reliable concepts of the relationship between one circumstance and another, with the result that the reader who attempts to take hold of the inconceivable finds that he must either ignore much of the information he has been given or he must simply admit to being at least partially baffled. Such an admission, however, could be equated for the critical reader with K.'s relinquishing the attempt to devise strategies by which to gain access to the castle. It seems less than surprising that such admissions remain few and far between.

Such recurring questions as "Is Momus really Klamm?" or "Is this man whom others call Klamm really Klamm?" reveal the shifting sands of the novel as presented by the minor characters. Part of Gardena's contribution to K.'s understanding of Klamm illustrates this point quite clearly: ". . . the fact that he called her name didn't mean necessarily what one might think, he simply mentioned the name Frieda—who can tell what he was thinking of? And that Frieda naturally came to him at once was her affair, and that she was admitted without let or hindrance was an act of grace on Klamm's part, but that he deliberately summoned her is more than one can maintain" (64). The causal connection between Klamm's shouting "Frieda" and his wish to summon Frieda before him has been completely suspended, leaving K. with more information on Klamm but with *less* knowledge of him than before. This type of information is passed repeatedly and it is just such an equation of more=less which predominates in the treatment of all people and events by the villagers. Everyone and everything is dealt with in such a way as to make K. and the reader believe that they are encountering explicable, recognizable entities, only to discover a short time later that these are in fact problematical enigmas. In this way K. is involved in a process of progressively getting nowhere, while the reader is both involved in the same process and, superficially at least, increasingly distant from it.

K. is of course the mediator between village and reader, the medium through which the reader sympathetically experiences the village and castle. The reader believes himself at first to be standing on secure ground, shoulder to shoulder, as it were, with K., through whom he becomes acquainted with the village and the castle, but that sense of security is progressively undermined as time goes on.[17] Initially the reader seems to share certain values and mental attitudes with K.; both seek, for example, to absorb and synthesize rationally each new experience as it comes along, unlike the villagers, who ignore all recognizably rational thought-processes. Both newcomers aware of their unfamiliarity with their specific surroundings when the novel begins, both K. and the reader are forced to interact with this strange world where expectations derived from life up to now prove to be ultimately inappropriate. K. is bent, it seems, on utilizing his own existing expectations in order to dominate his new situation.[18] Similarly his readers. The expectations of both derive from an implicit faith in logic of one kind or another, from the belief that it is possible to work out consequences, given the basic facts, and K.'s whole concern is to establish a line of approach consistent with the supposed facts he is given. The reader, for his part, "enters" the novel in exactly the same way that K. enters the village, with a set of mental experiences and expectations which he believes will enable him to cope with whatever he may encounter there, unaware, just as K. is, that he may from the very beginning be locked *in* while assuming he has been locked *out*. The word "Schloß" is surely not accidentally ambiguous. Is it surprising, then, that the reader feels a certain rational solidarity with the protagonist in the early stages of the story? This same solidarity is established at the outset in all of Kafka's works and determines a major part of the reading-process that follows.[19] Although the reader's sense of mental kinship with the protagonist swiftly begins to break down, the way in which the increasingly alien K. is kept within the reader's sphere of sympathy and conceptual reach is extraordinarily subtle. In the early part of *The Castle*, for example, just at those points where K.'s apparent lack of logic threatens to separate him from the critical reader's sense of fellow-feeling and understanding, he suddenly displays the same momentary alienation from his situation that the reader is experiencing in regard to him. One example is the point at which K. makes the acquaintance of his "assistants" for the first time:

> Not until he was up with the landlord, who greeted him humbly, did he notice two men, one on either side of the doorway. He took the lantern from his host's hand and turned the light on them; it was the men he had already met, who were called Arthur and Jeremiah. They now saluted him. That reminded him of his soldiering days, happy days for him, and he laughed. "Who are you?" he asked, looking from one to the other; "Your assistants," they answered. "It's your assistants," corroborated the landlord in a low voice. "What?" said K.; "are you my old assistants, whom I told to follow me and whom I am expecting?" They answered in the affirmative. "That's good," observed K. after a short pause; "I'm glad you've come. Well," he said after another pause, "you've come very late; you're very slack." "It was a long way to come," said one of them. "A long way?" repeated K.; "but I met you just now coming from the Castle." "Yes," said they without further explanation. "Where is the apparatus?" asked K. "We haven't any," said they. "The apparatus I gave you?" said K. "We haven't any," they reiterated. "Oh, you are fine fellows!" said K.; "do you know anything about surveying?" "No," said they. "But if you are my old assistants you must know something about it," said K. They made no reply. "Well, come in," said K., pushing them before him into the house. (23–24)

If we examine the passage closely we see that there are several excellent reasons within a short space of time which would militate against K.'s accepting these two men as his assistants. However, his eventual acceptance of them stems from his dogged refusal to accept all their statements about themselves and seems therefore likely to indicate an ulterior motive on his part. In the first instance these men are apparently quite unknown to K., yet when they assert their identity as his assistants and gain support from a third party, he merely repeats his opening "Who are you?" in a qualified and lengthened form. In fact, what he now asks has changed from the original objective question to: "Are you the people I was expecting?"—a subjective question which only he could answer. A simple affirmative is enough to make K. display at least a pretence of accepting them as who they say they are: " 'That's good,' observed K. after a short pause; 'I'm glad you've come.' " And here we have an example of the type of authorial subtlety involved in sustaining K.'s credibility: It is not what K. says at this point, but rather, what he does *not* say in that most important pause that seems to reveal his awareness of

the complexities of the situation. It is a pause which K. shares with
the reader, and because of it the increasing limitations of K.'s credibility seem to be suspended, at least temporarily. Obviously still
caught up in the oddness of these strangers' assertions, K. pauses
once more, then goes on to remark that if they are indeed his
assistants, they certainly took their time in joining him. Again the
pause is effective, as from the reader's point of view it lends to K.
the impression of rational reflection. Can it be that this encounter is
the enactment of a double bluff which K. hopes to win by appearing
to be taken in by these two men? The possibility is heightened as it
becomes clear that K. has done more than pause to reflect on the
strangeness of the situation; he has in fact asserted himself as their
employer through his reproach about their late arrival, so it appears
that he has either been convinced of their identity, odd though this
may be, or he has decided to accept it temporarily for his own ends.
The remainder of the passage is equally inconclusive, yet the reader
tends to give K. the benefit of the doubt as it seems he may have
devised a hidden strategy in order to turn this extraordinary incident
to his advantage.

As the novel progresses, the rational solidarity established in the
beginning between reader and protagonist increasingly focuses the
reader's attention on the breach between K.'s experiences and the
expectations he derives from them; the reader, however, moves on
to the point where he is ready to accept, as K. never does, the
necessity for revising and altering one's expectations in the world of
the castle. Ultimately he comes to realize that K.'s dogged adherence
in this wholly irrational environment to the logical sequence "If A
is true, then B must follow" removes him from the sphere of logical
understanding. Just as the minor characters constantly function in
terms that are at variance with "acceptably" rational thought-processes, K. himself seems to adhere so remorselessly to such processes
that he too places himself beyond the rational reach of the reader
whose sympathy and understanding he once enjoyed. What comes
into being to replace the initial solidarity between the reader and K.
is a double-sided doggedness of purpose in which neither side is
willing to relinquish his hold on his own particular brand of logic.
The reader of course offers no threat to K., circumscribed as the
latter is by the confines of his story, but what of the reverse? K.'s
unwavering adherence to a system of personal logic rests after all on
set patterns of conclusion-drawing which we all share, regardless of
our specific literary-critical allegiance. It seems that K.'s conspicuous
lack of success somehow makes *us* waver—an uncomfortable state of
mind, but one which we dispose of by ensuring that efforts are
redoubled to "explain" the plight of K. in a wide variety of concep-
tually secured ways. And herein lies one of the major achievements

of Kafka's narratives in general: the substance of the works does not exist chiefly within the substance of their respective narrative lines but springs rather from the process initiated by means of any and every narrative line through which the values and expectations of the reader are assaulted—values and expectations set up and reinforced by what he reads initially and accepts as his framework.

Each Kafka text engages the reader in a process of establishing certain expectations that are subsequently confounded—e.g., Josef K. is arrested; arrest takes on a completely new and different meaning for the reader in the course of the novel; Georg Bendemann writes to inform a close friend of his engagement, goes to tell his father and is condemned to death; Gregor Samsa wakes up as an insect, becomes ever more insect, yet his mental characteristics remain those of a human being, etc. In each case the reader establishes an understanding of the "givens" only to realize subsequently that he has somehow imperfectly understood them—a process which goes on throughout each work in defiance of the reader's attempts to derive consistent meaning from the information at his disposal. And should the reader deny the search for primary meaning, dwelling instead on the ever-present multiple possibilities of meaning, then there too he is faced with a problem, namely the problem of what to do with the central claim to consistent understanding made by the minimal framework of each piece of writing. What these works do, *The Castle* included, is to present through the behaviour of the protagonists a hidden *reductio ad absurdum* of the whole process of rational conclusion-drawing necessary both to living and to the act of reading. This seems to me to be the fundamental "law of the book" in all of Kafka's work, by which the reader's own system of values is short-circuited during the reading process.[20]

Taking *The Castle* as an example once more, it becomes clear how normative patterns of thought are implicitly undermined, even parodied. K. starts out with certain aspirations, expectations and concepts that are essentially familiar to the reader and endorsed by him, as we have seen. His subsequent detailed planning based on such concepts contains much that is distinctly odd, however. For example, he has a vision of authority as something orderly, logical and decisive, and this he never abandons, despite overwhelming evidence to the contrary. As well as having a clear concept of the castle authorities, K. also has a clear-cut and seemingly detailed idea of how best to proceed with his undertaking. He plans to work his way into the village community and by this means to gain access to the castle:

> Only as a worker in the village, removed as far as possible from the sphere of the Castle, could he hope to achieve anything in the

> Castle itself; the village folk, who were now so suspicious of him, would begin to talk to him once he was their fellow citizen, if not exactly their friend; and if he were to become indistinguishable from Gerstäcker or Lasemann—and that must happen as soon as possible, everything depended on that—then all kinds of paths would be thrown open to him, which would remain not only forever closed to him but quite invisible were he to depend merely on the favor of the gentlemen in the Castle. (32)

It is important to note here the many illogicalities which go to make up K.'s master-plan. He believes that great physical and psychological distance from the castle authorities is a prerequisite for his achieving anything there; he is confident that the suspicious and seemingly inhospitable villagers will warm to him once he is part of their community, yet such confidence must be regarded as misplaced, given his experiences up to now; he places his whole faith in obliterating all traces of his own distinct identity as quickly as possible in order to achieve his aim of penetrating the castle. This last strategy is of course particularly odd, given that he has now been officially acknowledged by the castle as the Land-Surveyor. In logically objective terms it would seem that the most futile thing he might seek to do would be to make himself "indistinguishable from Gerstäcker or Lasemann."

And yet such strange ideas are those he continues to live by, despite repeatedly unpromising results. He never comes to the point of questioning his evidently highly questionable principle of indirect approach; rather, he simply substitutes other individuals for the faceless villagers—Frieda, whom he believes to be influential because of her former relationship with Klamm, and Barnabas, who as a castle messenger can supposedly penetrate to the heart of officialdom as he himself can not. Gardena, Olga, Amalia and Pepi are also of interest to him for similar reasons. The fact is, K. is so intent on controlling the events of his life through set mental strategies that he fails to recognize what seem to be the positive possibilities inherent in his situation, such as the three unexpectedly momentous opportunities he fails to utilize when he turns his back on the interviews with Momus, Erlanger and Bürgel. Each of these failures is due to K.'s own overriding concept of how progress may best be made: with Momus K. decides the whole situation has come about as the result of a mere whim and as such can have no useful consequences; with Erlanger he decides that co-operative meekness is the best ploy and therefore he does not disturb him; with Bürgel he wishes only to sleep, having just witnessed the collapse of this own master-plan through Frieda.[21]

What the reader eventually comes to see, despite the fact that his critical energies are dissipated and disarmed repeatedly by the weight of ultimately "irrelevant" detail offered by the text, is that K.'s resolute adherence to concepts or expectations derived from a set of supposedly logical sequences, however odd this adherence may be in terms of detail, is a completely inappropriate response to the situation in which he finds himself. K. continually accepts premises and, having accepted these, he then draws a conclusion in order to build a winning strategy, only to find that he has wrongly understood the premises *or* that they have changed. This is the chief characteristic of K.'s thought and behaviour throughout the novel, and the fact that his conclusions turn out to be invariably inappropriate, his strategies irrelevant and futile, simply ensures that the whole process of fruitless cerebration is maintained *ad infinitum.*

But as we have seen, the reader is caught up with the novel in exactly the same way in which K. is caught up with his own situation. In his desire to understand, he is drawn into a situation wholly analogous to, though slightly different from that of K. Having embarked on reading the novel with an initial willingness to accept the antics of its characters, the reader ends up having formed a negative image of K., who in turn has created a dilemma for him, namely how to understand K. who is attempting in his way to understand both village and castle. Whereas K. himself seems able to overlook with amazing equanimity the great gap between what he seeks and what he finds, or to devise some instant strategy which he believes will overcome it, the reader cannot fully accept either of these alternative responses. Why not? Can it be that he not only formulates the plight of K. but that he even creates it? What if K. is simply another man like the "man from the country" in "Before the Law," for whom that one barrier has been erected? What if the village and castle were simply put there for K.? What if merely being there and not getting in were his whole happiness? As he himself says at the point where Frieda suggests that they emigrate: " 'What could have enticed me to this desolate country except the wish to stay here?' " (180). Clearly he wants to stay. Take this wish together with the early assertion to K. when he first arrives that whoever lives or passes the night there does so more or less in the castle itself, and the whole issue of K.'s "failure" is thrown completely open. Doesn't he himself in his question to Frieda implicitly assert the achievement of a goal rather than the misery of failure? And yet the reader feels that it would be little short of lunacy to declare K. a non-failure, let alone either happy or successful. Does he reject such a conclusion simply because he is too aware of the author's own life, or is he merely unable to accept the seemingly irrational without attempting either to trivialize it into abeyance by categorizing it as a masterly illustration of life's absurdity, or to transform it through highly complex intellectual exercises into something resembling its opposite, thereby reassuring himself of control over the text? Do Kafka's readers, sensing that this author's works somehow lay siege to rational thought at every level, press to devise their own strategies for penetrating its meaning and import just as K. presses to devise strategies for penetrating the realm of the castle?

To the critical reader who tries to bring together the substance of what has been said in this novel it seems as if there are three closed systems of thought with which he must contend in the act of reading: his own, that of K. and that of village and castle. The last of these adheres to no rationally discoverable principle other than a lack of rational principle, which is alien to the reader, while K. in an equally alien manner relentlessly pursues strategies meant to outwit and dominate a seemingly inappropriate construct he has made of his situation and of the society around him. Eventually it becomes apparent that these three modes of thought are in significant ways forever separate and distinct, one from the other. Just as the castle road does not lead K. to the castle, the novel does not provide the reader with any real access either to K. or to the village-cum-castle. It may, like the road, lead close, "but then it turns away as if intentionally, and if it doesn't exactly lead further away, it certainly doesn't lead any closer either" (my translation, p. 15).

This same gap exists in all of Kafka's texts to a greater or lesser degree. The question is: can the gap be bridged? Does a mode of thought exist which would help the reader make the transition from self to K. to village/castle? How does one, be one either reader or protagonist, take that non-physical, non-rational, Kierkegaardian leap into the realm of the castle, which simultaneously represents both one's present prison and one's idealized projection of the achievement of freedom? Isn't the fact that K. seems to come closest to the castle at those times when he is least concerned to do so an implicit indictment of the futility of rational thought-processes in general? This may well have been Kafka's own conviction, though his addiction to writing might seem to indicate the opposite. It is a tribute to the author's artistry that he causes such a fascinating yet disturbing question to be raised. In equating the level of artistic value in a literary work with the degree of change of expectational horizon it forces on the reader, Jauß seems to have put his finger very firmly on the pulse of the Kafka text, though not specifically intending to do so.[22] Despite all reader-resistance to change of this kind (and what else explains the ready labelling of K. and Josef K. as victims or failures, for example?), the very awareness of the need to resist the text lies at the root of the fascination and disturbance which the reader senses in his encounter with Kafka.

What unites us, his readers, in our diversity of interpretive approaches and findings seems ultimately to be nothing other than the desire to fill in and thus render harmless the potential abyss that his texts represent. If this is so—and it seems likely—then our interpretations simply afford us a means of creating other texts that in a variety of ways reassert a claim to validity and efficacy for the human ratio, texts that ultimately (and paradoxically) go some way towards cancelling out Kafka's own.[23] That Kafka stimulates and provokes our multifarious responses to his work is without doubt his major achievement, the continuing proof as his standing as King of the Castle. What our standing as readers may be vis-à-vis his whole oeuvre is a question to which no very comfortable answer can be found.

Notes

1. Cf. the introduction to *Franz Kafka: Themen und Probleme*, ed. Claude David (Göttingen, 1980). David claims that scholars have now developed a new-found certainty with regard to the interpretation of Kafka's intentions and have emerged at last from that state of bewilderment which formerly characterized their response to his work. The doubtful nature of such claims can be clearly seen, however, from the reviews and discussions to be found in the Kafka issue of *Monatshefte*, LXXIII, 1 (Spring, 1981), and from the continuing surge of secondary material on the author and his works.

2. Cf. Susan Sontag, *Against Interpretation*, (New York, 1969); Theodor Adorno, "Notes on Kafka," in *Prisms*, trans. S. and S. Weber, (London, 1967), pp. 245-72.

3. Sontag, p. 18.

4. Cf. Peter Beicken, "Typologie der Kafka Forschung," in *Kafka-Handbuch*, ed. Hartmut Binder, vol. 2, (Stuttgart, 1979), pp. 787-824. See also Richard Sheppard, "Das Schloß," in *ibid.*, pp. 445-70. According to Hartmut Müller, a recent count shows that there have been approximately 1,500 pieces of secondary literature written on Kafka in the last ten years: see *Franz Kafka Leben-Werk-Wirkung*, (Düsseldorf, 1985), p. 7.

5. The term "narratee," first introduced by Gérard Genette and Gerald Prince, means much the same as the inscribed reader, that is, the reader involved in and absorbed by the text for the duration of the act of reading.

6. Cf. "Indeterminancy and the Reader's Response in Prose Fiction," in *Aspects of Narrative*, ed. J. Hillis Miller, (New York, 1971), pp. 1-46; see in particular pp. 32ff.

7. Cf. Franz Kafka, "A Hunger Artist," in *The Complete Stories*, ed. Nahum N. Glatzer, (New York: Schocken Books, 1983), p. 269.

8. See Peter Beicken, *Franz Kafka, eine kritische Einführung in die Forschung*, (Frankfurt/Main, 1974), in particular pp. 175-225. That the old desire to see a theological message in Kafka's works lives on is illustrated, for example, by Claude David's reprinted 1980 article, "Zwischen Dorf und Schloß, Kafkas Schloß-Roman als theologische Fabel," in *Ordnung des Kunstwerks*, (Göttingen, 1983), pp. 215-32.

9. Cf. "The Judgment," in *The Complete Stories*, p. 84.

10. Adorno, p. 246.

11. Cf. the seemingly harmonious life of the villagers and their continuing endorsement of the castle; also K.'s unremitting desire to gain access to this castle.

12. Cf. K.'s experiences at the hands of the castle authorities and their village representatives such as the *Dorfvorsteher*, the assistants, etc.

13. Cf. the fate of Amalia and her family.

14. Points 4–6 are exemplified by the remainder of this article.

15. Franz Kafka, *The Castle*, trans. Willa and Edwin Muir, (New York: Alfred A. Knopf, 1956), p. 11. Subsequent citations given in parentheses in the text are taken from this work.

16. "The Readerhood of Man," in *The Reader in the Text*, ed. Susan R. Suleiman and Inge Crosman, (Princeton: Princeton University Press, 1980) 135.

17. Cf. Wayne Booth, *The Rhetoric of Fiction*, (Chicago, 1961), p. 240. Booth characterizes texts which cause such a process to take place as "infinitely unstable." I think this is a perceptive term for all of Kafka's writings and one that lends weight to the argument I develop about reader-response to Kafka's texts below.

18. This changes only in terms of detail in the course of the novel as K. attempts to alter his expectations to fit the experiences he has in the village. In the beginning his behaviour, which is meant to please others and thus help him succeed, is based on ideas he has absorbed from the life he has led up to now. Notice, for example, how he responds first to being wakened and challenged by tidying his hair (p. 6), how he expects his entourage to testify to the rightness of his behaviour (p. 7), how he claims the right to a good salary because of his supposed dependants (p. 11), how he believes that peaceful negotiation is the best solution to any dispute (p. 11) and thinks it best not to say anything that might prove unwelcome to others (pp. 16–17). In this connection I would like to draw attention to the "He" aphorisms, contained in *Description of a Struggle and The Great Wall of China*, trans. Willa and Edwin Muir, (London: Secker and Warburg, 1960), p. 299:

> He has two antagonists: The first pushes him from behind, from his birth. The second blocks the road in front of him. He struggles with both. Actually the first supports him in his struggle with the second, for the first wants to push him forward; and in the same way the second supports him in his struggle with the first; for the second of course is trying to force him back. But it is only theoretically so. For it is not only the two protagonists who are there, but he himself as well, and who really knows his intentions? However that may be, he has a dream that sometime . . . he will spring out of the fighting line and be promoted on account of his experience of such warfare, as judge over his struggling antagonists.

It seems to me that the two opponents referred to might well be interpreted as the subject's mental construct of past and future.

19. Other examples of such initial reader-protagonist solidarity abound throughout Kafka's work. Cf. the opening of *The Trial*. Notice how the injustice of the arrest is emphasized twice in the course of this introductory sentence: "Somebody must have been *telling lies about* Josef K., for *without having done anything wrong* he was arrested." Cf. also the opening paragraphs of "The Metamorphosis," in which Gregor's rational reactions offer a reassuring familiarity to the reader confronted with the extraordinary fact of his metamorphosis: e.g., 1) "Where am I?" 2) "I'll go back to sleep." 3) "What a wretchedly exhausting job I've got! To hell with it!" 4) "A man needs his sleep." 5) "If it weren't for my parents I'd tell my boss what to do with his rotten job." 6) "Better get up, I'm late." Similarly, the strange material of the story of the Hunger-Artist is rendered immediately palatable to the reader by virtue of the journalistic tone of the opening: "The interest in hunger-artists has greatly declined in recent years." Here the reading public is offered an excuse at once for not knowing about hunger-artists at the present time, but in such a way as to imply a mere change in

276 Critical Essays on Franz Kafka

public taste rather than any inherent lessening of the value of such creatures. In this way the reader is both reassured that his ignorance is understandable and challenged to read on by the hidden assertion that hunger-artists were once of great interest. Other stories establish a similar link between the reader and what he is reading, a link which acts as a kind of fish-hook with the reader as fish.

20. The term "law of the book" is Jacques Leenhardt's as used here. Though Leenhardt uses other texts entirely in his research aimed at establishing a sociology of reading, it is interesting to see how fully Kafka's texts bear out Leenhardt's conclusions. Based on responses from a thousand readers in two different countries, he very effectively documents the idea that the reader can be turned away from his own system of values during the act of reading. Once the influence of the reading material fades, the reader's old values are re-established. See "Toward a Sociology of Reading?" in *The Reader in the Text*, esp. pp. 220–21. I would maintain that much Kafka criticism has more to do with the restoration of the reader's values subsequent to the act of reading than with truly registering exactly what is taking place in and through the text. See note 23.

21. See *The Castle*, pp. 145–52; 31–-17; 332–52.

22. "Literary History as a Challenge to Literary Theory," in *New Literary History*, 2, (1970), p. 15.

23. My claim is clearly if unwittingly substantiated, for example, by Richard Sheppard's wide-ranging and good review of the secondary literature on *Das Schloß*. (See note 4.) Under the heading "Problemfelder" he presents seven categories through which to deal with a hundred or more critical responses to the novel, but each of these categories merely highlights the degree to which all questions addressed by the critics arise from their subjective awareness of the existence of rational lacunae in the text. Category 1, for example, bears the heading: "Is K. a Land-Surveyor?"; category 2: "What Is K.'s Goal?"; 3: "Is K. a Hero or an Exploiter?"; 4: "Does K. Develop?"; 5: "Frieda"; 6: "Amalia"; 7: "The Castle Authority." Each category contains and/or implies dozens of further questions which patently arise from the critics' desire to provide rational answers to questions which need not be questions at all in terms of the text. In category 7, for example, ("The Castle Authority") we find consideration given by many critics to questions such as: "Are they humans or gods?" and "Are they a subjective projection of K.'s or an objective power of themselves?" While questions like these may have an undoubted subjective validity for us as critics as we go through the process of restoring our own world-view, any claim to an objective validity in terms of either the questions or the answers would appear somewhat dubious.

INDEX